# Psychology and Environmental Change

# Psychology and Environmental Change

Raymond S. Nickerson

*Tufts University*

LEA

LAWRENCE ERLBAUM ASSOCIATES, PUBLISHERS

2003 Mahwah, New Jersey London

Correspondence regarding this manuscript should be addressed to Raymond S. Nickerson, 5 Gleason Road, Bedford, MA 01730 or r.nickerson@tufts.edu.



Lawrence Erlbaum Associates, Inc., Publishers
10 Industrial Avenue
Mahwah, NJ 07430

Cover design by Kathryn Houghtaling Lacey

**Library of Congress Cataloging-in-Publication Data**

Nickerson, Raymond S.
Psychology and environmental change /
Raymond S. Nickerson
p. cm.
Includes bibliographical references and index.
ISBN 0-8058-4096-6 (cloth : alk. paper)
ISBN 0-8058-4097-4 (pbk. : alk. paper)
1. Environmental Psychology I. Title

BF353 .N53 2002
155.9'1—dc21 2002024585
CIP

Books published by Lawrence Erlbaum Associates are printed on acid-free paper, and their bindings are chosen for strength and durability.

Printed in the United States of America
10 9 8 7 6 5 4 3 2 1

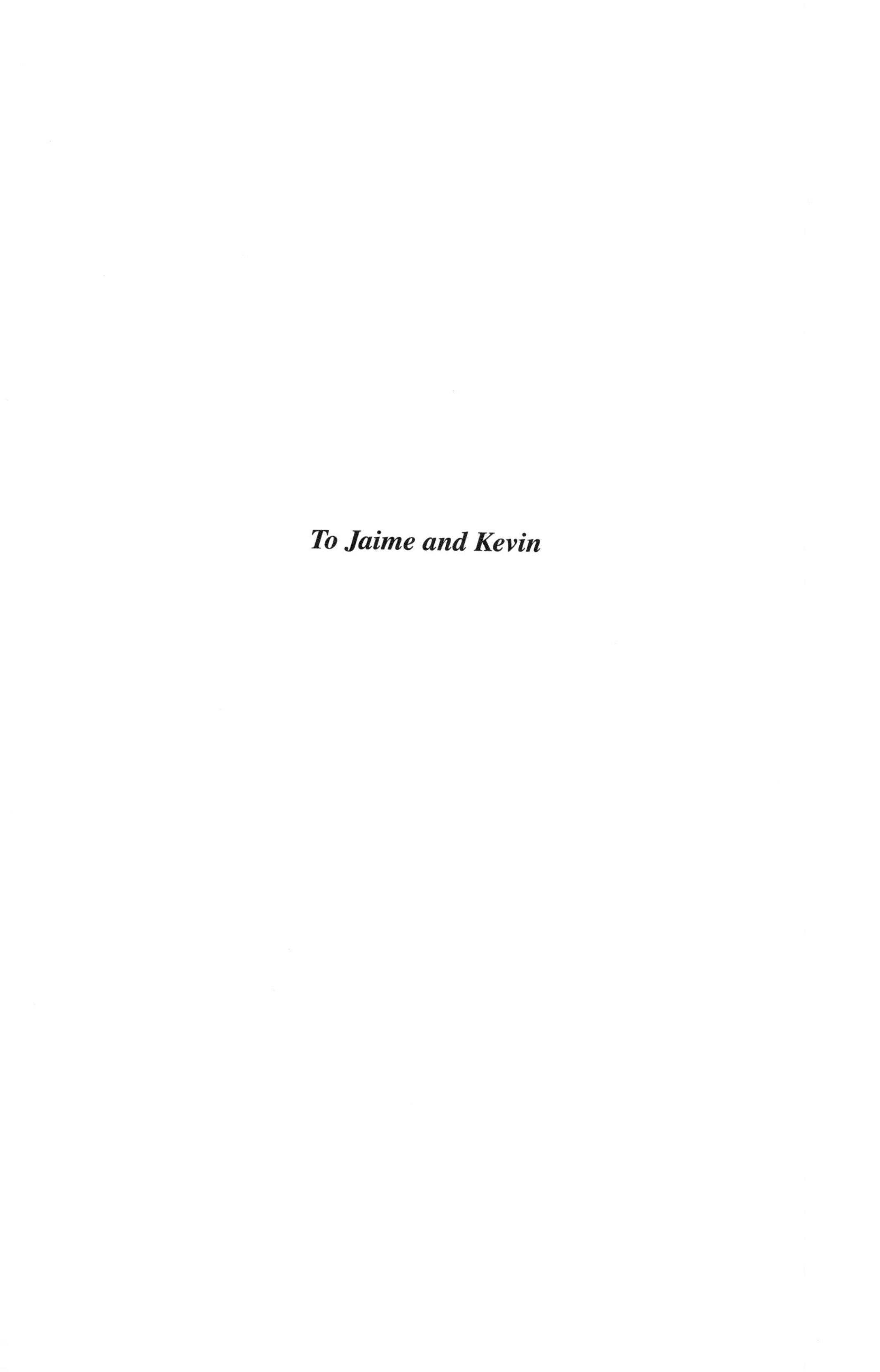

*To Jaime and Kevin*

# Contents

# Preface

## Psychology and Environmental Change

Raymond S. Nickerson

The writing of this book was motivated by the belief that psychology has much to contribute to solving the problem of detrimental environmental change but that what the field has to offer has been realized only to a small degree to date. Some of the opportunities for psychological research that is relevant to the problem have been pursued, but much more could be done if the problem were higher on the priority list for the psychological research community as a whole. My hope was to stimulate greater interest among research psychologists in the area. Although my research has not focused on environmental psychology, I ventured into the area because I believe that the question of adverse environmental change is an exceptionally important one for anyone who is concerned about the kind of future we are helping to shape.

Undoubtedly everyone who has become concerned about the problem of environmental change has a different story to tell, but I suspect that for many people there has simply been a slowly growing awareness of various aspects of the problem and a deepening conviction that it is real and serious. At least that is the case for me. I began to think more than casually about it and about what psychology might have to contribute toward improving the situation sometime in the late 1980s. Between then and now, I have written or spoken a bit on the subject in a few book chapters and talks at meetings.

This book differs from the earlier attempts to address the topic in scope. It discusses various ways in which the quality of the natural environment is threatened or demonstrably in decline, considers how human behavior contributes to the problem, reviews psychological research that has been done on the subject, and notes opportunities for future work. I make no claim of exhaustiveness in the coverage of the literature, but I believe the reader should get a representative sample of the relevant psychological research that has been conducted to date—which includes work on the assessment of attitudes regarding the natural environment, on how to increase participation in energy or materials conservation, recycling, and other environmentally beneficial programs, and on how to make technology more environmentally friendly.

My fondest hope is that some readers will be prompted to give more thought to the problem of environmental change than they otherwise might have and that, as a consequence, they will generate ideas for future research projects that could have beneficial environmental impact. Opportunities for relevant research exist, I believe, in many areas, but they need to be spelled out. Topics considered explicitly here include consumer behavior, risk assessment and communication, cost-benefit and tradeoff analyses, and game theory (competition, cooperation, negotiation and policymaking).

The environment is, at least in some quarters, an emotionally charged topic. Discussions of environmental issues often take the form of polarized debate, with extremists on both sides contributing little but oversimplified analyses and sloganeering. Psychology should be able to facilitate the development of a better understanding of what is a complex multifaceted problem, and to help identify ways in which individuals and organizations can work effectively toward its solution. The intended purpose of this book is to contribute to that end.

Baruch Fischhoff (Carnegie Mellon University), Neville Moray (University of Surrey), and Gene Myers (Western Washington University) all read a draft of the manuscript in its entirety and made numerous helpful suggestions for improvement, for which I am grateful. My lovely granddaughter, Amara Nickerson, did a superb job of checking citations against the reference list and identifying problems, of which there were many, that needed fixing—and she corrected my grammar in a few spots as well. As always, I am especially grateful to my wife, Doris, for her constant love and her support in this endeavor as in all others.

CHAPTER

# 1

# Introduction

The problem of environmental change—especially environmental change that results directly from human behavior—is among the more serious problems we face as individuals, as a nation, and as a species. At least I believe that to be the case, which is my reason for writing this book. I believe further that there are many significant opportunities and challenges for work by applied psychologists in this problem area. What I hope to do here is stimulate thinking on the topic of detrimental environmental change and especially on the question of how research psychologists could help address the problem—to add my voice to those of others (e.g., Gardner & Stern, 1996; Geller, Winett, & Everett, 1982; Howard, 2000; R. Olson, 1995; Oskamp, 2000; Stern, 2000) who have expressed their belief that psychology has something to contribute to the cause of environmental protection. Because environmental psychology is an established field of psychological research, it seems appropriate to begin by saying how the focus of this book relates to that field.

## ENVIRONMENTAL PSYCHOLOGY

Environmental psychology has been recognized as a field of psychological research since the late 1960s (Altman, 1975; Craik, 1970, 1973; Heimstra & McFarling, 1974; Proshansky, Ittelson, & Rivlin, 1976; Stokols, 1977, 1978). Environmental ergonomics is also becoming recognized as a subfield within ergonomics or human-factors research (Mekjavik, Banister, & Morrison, 1988). Russell and Ward (1982) defined *environmental psychology* as "that branch of psychology concerned with providing a systematic account of the relationship between person and environment" (p. 652). As Stokols (1978) pointed out, the boundaries of the area are not easily delimited because "the study of human behavior in relation to the environment, broadly speaking, would seem to encompass all areas of psychology" (p. 254).

For the most part, the focus of work has been on the question of how people perceive and react to their immediate surroundings; this is seen in the subtitle of Proshansky, Ittelson, and Rivlin's (1976) edited volume; *Environmental Psychology: People and Their Physical Settings*. It is also seen too in a comment in the first *Annual Review of Psychology* chapter on Environmental Psychology:

> The novel value of man-environment studies for such professionals as architects, environmental planners, and natural resources managers lies in its systematic analysis of the human behavior that occurs in and responds to the environmental settings they plan, design, and manage. For psychologists, its distinctive attraction is just the opposite, namely, its serious attention to the environmental contexts of human behavior. (Craik, 1973, p. 404)

*Environment* is broadly defined to include not only physical spaces of all sorts, but sociocultural contexts, neighborhoods, institutions, and organizations—essentially any context in which people can find themselves. Sometimes the term *proxemics* is used to connote the relationship between behavior and the physical space in which it occurs (Hall, 1966; Watson, 1972). Stokols (1978) identified the central concern of proxemics as "the manner in which people use space as a means of regulating social interaction" (p. 270), and suggested that it subsumes work on privacy, personal space, territoriality, and crowding. Russel and Ward (1982) argued that interest in these topics has been heightened by concern about the ever-increasing world population, which threatens to make space an increasingly limited resource.

Much attention has been given to the built environment—homes, offices, hospitals, schools—and to the effects of environmental stressors—extreme temperatures, humidity, oxygen deprivation, crowding, noise, air pollution, industrial mishaps—on human performance and well-being (Baum, Fleming, & Davidson, 1983; Baum & Singer, 1982; Baum, Singer, & Baum, 1982; Cox, Paulus, McCain, & Karlovac, 1982; Craik, 1973; Evans & Cohen, 1987; Kasl, White, Will, & Marcuse, 1982; Monat & Lazarus, 1977; Poulton, 1970; Saegert, Mackintosh, & West, 1975; Welford, 1974; Wohwill, 1970). In comparison, relatively little attention has been given by psychologists to the question of how human behavior affects the natural environment and what can be done to protect the environment against behavioral causes of detrimental change. Only 4 of the 43 chapters in the Proshansky, Ittelson, and Rivlin (1976) volume are focused explicitly on the natural environment. The lengthy index contains the entries *air pollution*, *water quality*, and *pollution*, but does not mention *global warming*, *acid rain*, *ozone*, *waste*, *biodiversity*, or *habitat*.

The emphasis of environmental psychology on the built environment is pointed out in the opening statements of Holahan's (1986) review of the field:

> Environmental psychology studies the interrelationship between the physical environment and human behavior and experience. It emerged in the later half of the 1960s as a problem-focused discipline, responding to practical questions posed by architects and planners about real-world design decisions. (p. 381)

This emphasis is borne out by the remainder of the review, which contains no mention of the problem of the deterioration of the natural environment.

As of this writing, environmental psychology has been covered explicitly six times in the *Annual Review of Psychology*. The first review was published in 1973 by Craik. Subsequent reviews were done by Stokols (1978), Russell and Ward (1982), Holahan (1986), Saegert and Winkel (1990), and Sundstrom, Bell, Busby, and Asmus (1996). In all of these reviews, environmental psychology has the broad connotation indicated by the prior quote from Holahan and the emphasis throughout is on the built environment. Some attention is given, especially in the later chapters to the natural environment, but the emphasis remains on the environment's effect on human behavior and experience as opposed to human behavior's effect on the environment and the question of what might be done to mitigate or reverse its negative impact.

Topics prominent in the environmental psychology literature include spatial perception, orientation, and representation (Holding, 1992, 1994; O'Keefe & Nagel, 1978); way-finding (navigation through built or natural environments, development of environmental negotiation skills; Canter, 1983b; Gopal, Klatzky, & Smith, 1989; Heft & Wohlwill, 1987; Hirtle & Hudson, 1991; O'Neill, 1991); cognitive maps (Downs & Stea, 1977; Gärling, 1989; Gärling, Book, & Lindberg, 1984; Kitchin, 1994; Kuipers, 1982); personal space, privacy, and territoriality (Altman, 1970, 1977, 1979; Edney, 1974; Evans & Howard, 1973; Hayduk, 1978; Sommer, 1969; Taylor, Gottfredson, & Brower, 1980); accident prevention and child safety (Gärling & Gärling, 1990); environmental assessment (Canter, 1983a); affective effects of environment (Russell & Pratt, 1980; Russell & Snodgrass, 1987), effects of environmental stressors such as noise (Cohen & Spacapan, 1984), heat (Anderson, 1989; Anderson & DeNeve, 1992), and residential or household crowding (Baum & Gatchel, 1981; Evans, Palsane, Lepore, & Martin, 1989; Heft, 1985; Rohe, 1982; Saegert, 1981) on behavior, mood, and cognition (Aldwin & Stokols, 1988; Evans & Cohen, 1987); the design of offices, classrooms, and other interior spaces (Marans & Spreckelmeyer, 1982; Sundstrom, Herbert, &

Brown, 1982); environmental effects on health and well-being (Evans, Kliewer, & Martin, 1991; Hedge, 1989; Winkel & Holahan, 1985); environmental affordances or deterrents of antisocial and criminal behavior (Perkins, Wandersman, Rich, & Taylor, 1993; Sampson & Groves, 1989; Shaw & Gifford, 1994; Taylor, 1987); and changes in environmental needs with age (Carp, 1987; Lawton, 1985a, 1985b). The list could easily be extended.

The study of geographically or architecturally delimited places—shopping malls, school rooms, subway stations, kitchens, hospitals, sports arenas, nature parks, beaches, prisons—as physical settings of human behavior has been a focus of many investigators (Ajdukovic, 1990; Barker & Associates, 1978; Bronfenbrenner, 1979; Craik, 1970; Stokols & Shumaker, 1981; Wicker, 1979; Wong, Sommer, & Cook, 1992). What characteristics of places or settings should be used to categorize them and distinguish one from another is one question of interest. How the characteristics of places influence human behavior and how behavior helps shape, change, and impose functional and symbolic meaning on the places in which it occurs are others (Moore, 1979; Rapoport, 1982).

Russell and Ward (1982), who considered the place-specificity of behavior to be the "fundamental fact of environmental psychology" (p. 652), pointed out that one is in many places at any given time, all of which can have implications for behavior.

> The environment is seen to be more than a single stimulus; it is a complex of immediate and distant places, psychologically arranged into a hierarchy such that each place is part of a larger place and can be subdivided into smaller places.... One hierarchy, for example, would be nation, region, town, neighborhood, home, dining room, and each person's place at the dining room table.... various relationships may exist between person and environment, and the type of relationship may vary with the level in the hierarchy being studied. The relationship between a person and the room he or she is in probably cannot be described in the same terms as the relationship between a person and the community he or she lives in. (p. 654)

Underlying much of the work in this general area is the assumption that an understanding of behavior is impossible apart from an understanding of the environmental context in which that behavior occurs. This assumption is reflected in the use by some investigators of the term *ecological psychology* to represent their interests (Barker, 1960, 1968; Bronfenbrenner, 1977, 1979; Catalano, 1979; Rogers-Warren & Warren, 1977). In ecological psychology, the basic unit of analysis is the behavior setting, and the focus is on how behavior is influenced by the specific context (sporting event, classroom, restaurant) in which it takes place (Stokols, 1978). Stokols and Shumaker (1981) attributed the emergence of this interest during the late 1960s to doubts among psychologists about the adequacy of stimulus–response models to account for the complexity of behavior as it occurs in nonlaboratory settings. "In light of these concerns, many psychologists shifted their theoretical focus from the micro to the molar environment in the hope of identifying the contextual moderators of environment-behavior relationships" (p. 444). *Environment* is taken to include sociocultural as well as physical contexts. *Ecopsychology* has been coined to denote a related emerging interest in the implications for mental health of the way human beings connect with their surroundings (Roszak, 1993; Roszak, Gomes, & Kanner, 1995).

Stokols (1990) distinguished three views of people–environment relations that can be seen in the history of environmental psychology. Initially, there was the minimalist view, according to which one's environment was assumed not to exert much influence on one's behavior, health, or well-being. As long as this view prevailed, little attention was given to the environment by psychologists. As a consequence, in part, of the writings of such environmentalists as Carson (1962), Ehrlich (1968), and Hardin (1968), Stokols suggested, psychologists became aware of the possible importance of the environment to human health and behavior, and the minimalist view began to give way to instrumental and spiritual views.

The instrumental view sees the environment as a tool—"a means for achieving behavioral and economic goals." The emphasis is on material features of the environment and environmental quality—seen primarily in such objective indicators as behavior, comfort, and health. The spiritual view sees the environment as "a context in which human values can be cultivated." The emphasis is on symbolic and affective features of the environment and environmental quality—seen not only in terms of comfort, health, and behavioral effects, but also in the richness of its psychological and sociocultural meaning. Central also to much of the work in this field is the idea of people in transactional relationships with their environments (Altman, 1975; Baum, Singer, & Baum, 1982; Evans & Cohen, 1987; Ittelson, 1989; Reser & Scherl, 1988; Stokols, 1978; Stokols & Shumaker, 1981).

Although replacement of the minimalist view by instrumental and spiritual views stimulated research aimed at providing a better understanding of people–environment relations, most of this work has focused on the question of how people—their health, productivity, mood—are affected by the environments, especially the built environments, in which they live, work, and play. Much attention has been given to the question of how to design environments that are more congruent with—better able to meet the needs and objectives of—their occupants (Michelson, 1976; Stokols, 1979). The idea that the establishment and maintenance of healthful environments should be a societal objective is a prevalent one (Cohen, Evans, Stokols, & Krantz, 1986; Stokols, 1992). More has been learned about the environment's effects on behavior and health than about the relationship between environmental design and spiritual enrichment, but the symbolic and affective aspects of people's surroundings are receiving increasing attention (Csikszentmihalyi & Rochberg-Halton, 1981; Franck, 1987).

In short, environmental psychology has evolved as a highly applied field, concerned with understanding how people relate to their environments and with improving various environments from the point of view of the people who live and work in them or who use them for recreational purposes. A good representation of the field's major interests may be found in the two-volume *Handbook of Environmental Psychology*, the two-volume *Advances in Environment, Behavior and Design*, the six-volume *Advances in Environmental Psychology*, the six *Annual Review* articles on the subject, textbooks (Bell, Fisher, Baum, & Greene, 1990; Heimstra & McFarling, 1974), and several edited collections of papers (Harvey, 1981; Kaplan & Kaplan, 1978; Proshansky, Ittelson, & Rivlin, 1976; Stokols, 1977; Stokols & Altman, 1987; Stokols & Shumaker, 1981; Zube & Moore, 1987, 1989).

The primary focus of the field, to date, has been on how the characteristics of the environment, and especially the built environment, affect human beings. In his 1978 *Annual Review of Psychology* chapter, Stokols noted that "until recently, environmental psychologists had given very little attention to the consequences of human activity in the environment (e.g., litter, pollution, resource scarcities" (p. 268), and that "relative to other areas of the field, research on human response to the natural environment has been sparse" (p. 276). Stokols was able to point to some studies that appeared to signal a growing interest in these topics. Between then and now, many studies of how people's behavior affects the natural environment and what might be done to make the effects of human behavior more environmentally benign have been done, but the emphasis of environmental psychology has remained on the effects of environmental variables on human behavior and well-being. In making this observation, I do not mean to question the value of that work; I see the focus as deserving of all the attention it is getting and more; I only mean to point out that it continues to be the case that work dealing directly with the relationship between human behavior and the quality of the natural environment—which is the focus of this book—constitutes a small fraction of all the work that is being done under the broad umbrella of *environmental psychology*.

## BEHAVIOR AS A CAUSE OF ENVIRONMENTAL CHANGE

Although research on the question of what can be done to address the problem of detrimental environmental change has not been the primary focus of environmental psychology, psychological work has been published that relates directly or indirectly to this question. The assessment of attitudes regarding the natural environment, attempts to determine how to increase participation in energy conservation or recycling programs, and efforts to identify causes of environmentally destructive industrial accidents are obvious cases in point. One of the purposes of this book is to review this work, not exhaustively, but extensively.

Some psychologists tried very hard to bring psychology to the problem of detrimental environmental change in the 1970s. Studies focused on various means of effecting change in environmentally consequential behavior, including (a) conservation of energy through judicious use of household appliances, hot water, lighting, air conditioning, and heating systems; (b) participation in recycling programs; (c) reduction of water usage; and (d) decrease in littering. These efforts, which have been reviewed in several articles and books (Cone & Hayes, 1980; Cook & Berrenberg, 1981; Geller, 1986; Geller, Winett, & Everett, 1982; Katzev & Johnson, 1987; Tuso & Geller, 1976), did not generate the enthusiasm within the larger research community that the seriousness of environmental change might have led one to expect. Moreover, funding for this type of research was not plentiful, and the work on behavior change for environmental benefit fell off considerably during the 1980s (Dwyer, Leeming, Cobern, Porter, & Jackson, 1993; Geller, 1990). Work continued through the 1990s, but at a modest pace.

This work is much closer to the focus of this book than most of the work that has been done under the umbrella of *environmental psychology*, broadly defined. Much of it has been reviewed by Stern (1992a) in an *Annual Review* chapter entitled "Psychological Dimensions of Global Environmental Change." It has also been covered in a text by Gardner and Stern (1996) entitled *Environmental Problems and Human Behavior*. Edited volumes that reflect many interests in common with this book include Altman and Wohlwill (1983), Stern, Young, and Druckman (1992), Hammond, and Coppock (1990), Chechile and Carlisle (1991), and Wolbrast (1991).

Stern's (1992a) *Annual Review* chapter

> examines the contributions that psychological research has made and might make to understanding the human behavior that has these [specified detrimental environmental] effects and to understanding—and possibly changing—the ways humans respond in the face of potential environmental disaster. (p. 270)

Stern focused on problems that have global implications.

> Environmental effects are called 'global' when their impacts cannot be localized. This attribute differentiates global change from the more familiar localized environmental problems, such as waste disposal, pollution of rivers and local airsheds, or loss of wilderness areas to agricultural or industrial development. (p. 270)

He pointed out, however, that human activities can have worldwide impact either by altering systems (oceans and atmosphere) that flow throughout the earth or through localized changes, the cumulative effects of which can become global in extent.

Stern (1992a) described the role of social and behavioral science in a global-change research agenda as improving understanding

> of how human systems produce the proximate causes, how changes in human systems might change the rate at which people alter the environment, how people perceive changes in the global environment, how people respond to the anticipation of global environmental change and are affected by experienced change, and how changes in human systems might make people less susceptible to the effects of global environmental change. (p. 272)

Stern identified and discussed three areas of psychological research that pertain to environmental change: "the study of environmental attitudes; the analysis of individual actions that, in aggregate, have a high impact on important global changes; and the study of individual effects on collective action, including organizational resource consumption and policies that set the context for resource use" (p. 279). The most important research needs for psychology, he suggested,

> include improved analysis of the determinants of global change-producing behavior and of changes in such behavior, analysis of the barriers to adoption of technologies and practices to mitigate global change, identification of cost-effective interventions by government and other actors, and improved analysis of the bases for individual support for change in environmental policy. (p. 295)

Gardner and Stern (1996) stated as their goal in their book: "to survey the most important theoretical and empirical contributions that psychology and the allied behavioral and social sciences can make to the understanding and solution of environmental problems" (p. 5). As does this book, that one begins with a discussion of various aspects of environmental change and the role of human behavior in contributing to them. It frames the problems as tragedies of the commons, after Hardin (1968), and reviews work that has been done on several approaches to dealing with the commons dilemma in its various environmental manifestations. Gardner and Stern identified and discussed human behavioral predispositions that function as either barriers or aids to the solution of environmental problems, giving special emphasis to the ways in which people perceive and react to environmental hazards. The final major section of the book deals with the question of what behavioral science has to offer by way of helping to solve some of the problems of detrimental environmental change.

Within the subdisciplines of psychology that focus on the design of equipment, jobs, and person–machine systems, as well as the interaction of people with machines—engineering psychology, human factors, ergonomics—very little attention has been paid to the problem of environmental change and the question of what to do about it. A major exception to this broad claim is the work done on human error that is often involved in industrial accidents, many of which have detrimental environmental effects (Rasmussen & Batstone, 1989; Reason, 1990; Senders & Moray, 1991). Opportunities for engineering psychology to have an impact on the problem of detrimental environmental change more generally have been discussed in a few recent publications (Moray, 1993, 1994; Nickerson, 1992; 1999; Nickerson & Moray, 1995; Vicente, 1998).

## CHALLENGES FOR APPLIED PSYCHOLOGY

I believe there are many opportunities for psychological research relating to the problem of environmental change. Without discounting the importance of those attempts that have been made to apply psychology to this problem area, I want to argue that the attention that has been given to it—either by the field of psychology as a whole or its subdisciplines that would seem to have the greatest relevance, including that of environmental psychology—has not been commensurate with what the problem deserves. This is not the fault, of course, of those who have made concerted efforts to bring psychology to bear on it.

Psychologists are not likely to solve the problem of detrimental environmental change, but they can make important contributions to this effort. Inasmuch as many aspects of the problem are the consequences of human behavior, a primary approach to their solution or amelioration must be efforts to modify that behavior. Psychology should be uniquely well positioned to contribute to an understanding of environmentally detrimental behavior and to its modification when that is what is required. Inasmuch as behavior is influenced by knowledge, beliefs, attitudes, values, and desires, efforts to change behavior in ways that would benefit the environment will have to take cognitive and affective variables into account.

Beyond the objectives of understanding behavioral causes of environmental change and finding ways to modify environmentally destructive behavior to make it more environmentally beneficial or benign, there are other opportunities for psychological research to contribute to the general goal of managing environmental change. Some of these fall within the mainstream interests of engineering psychologists and human factors specialists because they have to do with equipment design and the interaction of people with machines; they relate not so much to the goal of modifying behavior through persuasion and attitude change, but to that of designing equipment and products that effectively meet users' needs without doing so at the expense of environmental damage.

Technology is an enabler of change and magnifies the effects of human decisions and actions manyfold. Yet presumably technology has been developed to serve human needs and desires; the challenge is to find ways to have it do that without destroying the environment—and thereby subverting its purpose—in the process. The question of how to make technology and its uses more environmentally friendly deserves attention from many perspectives, those of applied psychology and human factors researchers not least among them. Many aspects of environmental change are global in extent, and effectively addressing them will require communication and cooperation among disparate corporate and governmental organizations and agencies. Much remains to be learned about how communication and negotiation can be improved in the interest of facilitating collaboration on the common goal of protecting the environment. I hope this book makes a convincing argument that psychological research has much to offer on these topics, among others that also have implications for addressing the problem of detrimental environmental change.

## PLAN OF THE BOOK

In the chapters that follow, I review work that strikes me as relevant to the problem of environmental change. I note some of the ways in which the problem provides challenges and opportunities for further psychological and human factors research. In some cases, studies that have already been done point the way to the identification of further research opportunities. In other cases, little, if anything, in the way of psychological research relating to the problems has yet been done.

Chapter 2 reviews evidence that a bona fide problem exists, and it discusses several of its major aspects. Chapter 3 focuses on ways in which human behavior contributes to the problem. Subsequent chapters review representative relevant psychological work that has been done and identify other opportunities for environment-relevant psychological research. Chapter 4 deals with the assessment and change of attitudes, and Chapter 5 looks at studies of change of behavior. Chapters 6 through 8 focus on ways in which psychological research might contribute to the objective of making technology and its products more environmentally benign. Chapter 9 focuses on consumption, Chapter 10 on risk assessment and communication, and Chapter 11 on cost-benefit and trade-off analyses. Chapter 12 deals with competition, cooperation, negotiation, and policymaking. Chapter 13 touches briefly on several other subjects that relate to the objective of protecting the environment, and Chapter 14 contains some concluding observations.

In addition to reporting environmentally relevant psychological research that has already been done, throughout the book I have tried to identify researchable questions that are pressing from an environmental point of view. Here I know I am skating on thin ice. What I have to offer are personal opinions. Some of the suggestions for research build on previous research on the role of human behavior in environmental change or on the question of how to modify that behavior; others have not been addressed by any research of which I am aware. I offer my thoughts about the importance of various research objectives with a keen awareness of how easy it is to be wrong about what will turn out to be important, and in the hope that expressing them will motivate discussion and debate, which will increase the attention that environmental problems receive from psychological researchers. I believe that if, and probably only if, the research community gets sufficiently interested in this problem area to engage in extended discussion and debate about what might be done, feasible and promising possibilities will be identified.

One can argue that the most likely way for psychologists to have an impact of environmental problems is via the knowledge of human psychology (behavior, motivation, decision making, etc.) acquired through basic research. Indeed this may be the case. I strongly suspect, however, that if the results of basic research are to have an impact on environmental matters, their relevance must be articulated. If psychologists do not do this, who will? Moreover, establishing the effectiveness of applying the findings of basic research to environmental problems may, in many cases, require additional research designed for that purpose.

CHAPTER

2

# The Problem

Is there a problem? Is the prospect of environmental change—and in particular change resulting from human activities—that would make the planet significantly less hospitable to human or other life as we know it a genuine threat? Is there a real basis for concern?

There are many who would answer "no" to these questions. Ray and Guzzo (1994) provided an extensive list of pointers to writers who take this position, either with respect to environmental change in general or to specific alleged environmental threats. If there really is no problem, why, one must ask, is there such widespread concern especially among scientists who should have a relatively good understanding of the variables and processes involved? One, somewhat cynical, answer to this question that has been proposed is that many of those who are warning that the sky is falling have a vested interest in promoting this belief (Greve & Smith, 1992; Michaels, 1992; Taubes, 1993). Widespread public concern about the possibility of disastrous environmental change ensures the availability of public funds to support the research that the scientists who are fueling this concern conduct; it legitimizes the establishment of public policies that may serve political objectives other than the ostensible one of protecting the environment, and it can provide business opportunities of a variety of sorts.

This book is motivated by the belief that the threat of detrimental environmental change of significant magnitude is real. I believe that the situation is extremely complex and not well understood, and that a major objective must be to understand it better. Given all the uncertainties, the possibilities exist of reacting too aggressively and of not reacting aggressively enough. However, if many of the projections are even approximately right, failing to act at all is not a rational option. I find it easier to believe that the problem is real than that all the scientists who are sounding the alarm (e.g., Intergovernmental Panel on Climate Change, 2001; Kates et al., 2001; Kendall et al., 1996) are misguided or arousing concern only to ensure funding of their research. In my view, the rational course is to do the best we can to identify the choices we have and to anticipate their consequences, realizing the limitations of our understanding and being willing to change direction when evidence indicates the wisdom of doing so. As Stern (1992a) put it: "Humanity is conducting a grand experiment on its natural environment, and cannot afford to fail. We have only one earth on which to experiment" (p. 271).

The problem of environmental change has many aspects, each of which is a significant challenge by itself. Moreover, the individual aspects interact in complex ways. In view of the importance of the interactions, discussing the problem in piecemeal fashion runs the risk of oversimplification, but it is not clear that there is any reasonable alternative to doing so. What follows is a limited description of several aspects of the problem. I have discussed some of them also elsewhere (Nickerson, 1992, 1999).

## GLOBAL WARMING

The average temperature at the surface of the earth is determined by the combined effects of several variables, or "forcing factors," and is believed to have varied over a considerable range during the earth's history (Budyko, Ronovn, & Yanshin, 1987; Burner & Lasaga, 1989). At the present time, it is about 16 degrees Celsius (60 degrees Fahrenheit). In their current concentrations, carbon dioxide ($CO_2$) and other gases, including methane ($NH_4$), nitrous oxide ($N_2O$), and chlorofluorocarbons (CFCs), keep the average temperature approximately 33 degrees Celsius (about 60 degrees Fahrenheit) higher than it would be without them. These gases tend to trap outgoing radiation of certain wavelengths in the infrared region of the spectrum, some of which is emitted by the earth and some of which is reflected solar energy. The phenomenon has become known as the *greenhouse effect.*

The idea of a greenhouse effect was noted early in the 19th century by the French mathematician, Jean Baptiste Joseph Fourier (1827), who is best known to posterity for his discovery that any complex waveform can be decomposed into a linear combination of sine waves. The amount of warming attributed to the greenhouse effect over the past is clearly beneficial; if all the greenhouse gases in the atmosphere were suddenly to disappear and the mean temperature became

33 degrees Celsius less than it currently is, the planet would be covered with ice and a considerably less hospitable place on which to live. The concern is that the concentration of gases is increasing and the amount of warming they cause is also on the rise. The fact that an increase in atmospheric $CO_2$ in the atmosphere could cause a rise in global temperature was pointed out over a century ago by the Swedish chemist, Svante Arrhenius, and the American geologist, Thomas Chamberlin (Revelle, 1982).

Concern that the concentration of $CO_2$ and other greenhouse gases was indeed on the increase began to be expressed in the middle of the 20th century (Callendar, 1938, 1949; Revelle & Suess, 1957). Revelle and Suess characterized the burning of fossil fuels and the consequential release of carbon dioxide into the atmosphere as a global experiment with the system that has been responsible for the relative stability of the earth's climate. Increased global warming, with attendant severe environmental and economic consequences, is now widely recognized as a possibility deserving serious attention (Bolin & Doos, 1986; Dickinson & Cicerone, 1986; Houghton, Jenkins, & Ephraums, 1990; Houghton & Woodwell, 1989; Kellogg & Schware, 1981; Kerr, 1990, 1996, 2001a; Manabe & Wetherald, 1980; National Academy of Sciences, 1983; Oppenheimer & Boyle, 1990; Ramanathan, 1988; Rosenberg, Easterling, Crosson, & Darmstadter, 1989).

The greenhouse effect is complex and involves many interacting variables; an increase in atmospheric $CO_2$ causes increased warming at the earth's surface, for example, despite that it causes cooling in the stratosphere (Mahlman, 1997). An understanding of the problem is complicated further by the fact that the gases associated with warming as well as with some of the other atmospheric concerns (acid rain, smog, stratospheric ozone loss) together make up less than 0.1% of the atmosphere. The effects of the trace gases appear to be disproportionately large relative to their concentrations (Ramanathan, Cicerone, Singh, & Kiehl, 1985). Because the concentrations are so small, emissions from human activities can have proportionately large effects on them (Graedel & Crutzen, 1989).

Although most of the attention has focused on possible changes in average global temperature, the possibility of different amounts of warming at different latitudes, with the greatest amounts at the polar regions, has been noted (Hileman, 1999). Changes in the amplitude of the annual temperature cycle and in the timing of seasonal variations are also a matter of concern (Thomson, 1995), as is the possibility of an increased frequency of short-term extreme weather patterns that could be caused by general warming. For example, a warming of a few degrees of surface sea temperature could increase the severity of the strongest hurricanes, and a rise of sea level of a few feet could multiply the destructiveness of the most severe floods.

Determining the history of changes in average global temperature is not easy. Today surface air temperatures are taken regularly for purposes of weather tracking and prediction, but this has been true more or less worldwide for only a little over 100 years. Estimates of average surface temperatures before the late 1880s must make use of less direct methods; they rely on incomplete records that go back only about 300 years and are based on measurement techniques of less than perfect reliability and accuracy. Even if one could begin with reliably accurate data, the question of whether the earth has warmed over the past century, and if so by how much, would probably be controversial; long-term trends are difficult to tease out of the considerable short-term fluctuations, such as those caused by major volcanic eruptions like that of Mt. Pinatubo in June 1991 (Minnis et al., 1993).

These difficulties notwithstanding, a widely accepted view is that the average temperature has increased by about one-half degree Celsius over the past 100 years. On the basis of painstaking analysis of as many records as they could find of temperature measurements taken around the world during the last 300 years, Jones and colleagues arrived at this estimate (Jones & Wigley, 1990; Jones, Wigley, & Wright, 1986). Records of glacier retreats combined with models of the sensitivity of glaciers to climate changes have yielded an estimate of somewhat more than one-half degree Celsius warming over the past century (Oerlemans, 1994). Measurements using borehole techniques—changes in surface temperature propagate into the earth's crust, leaving a record of changes that have occurred over time—have yielded estimates of approximately the same amount occurring over the same period (Deming, 1995; Harris & Chapman, 1997; Pollack, Huang, & Shen, 1998). Borehole data also indicate that the increase over the last five centuries has been about 1 degree Celsius, and that the 20th century was the warmest of the five (Pollack, Huang, & Shen, 1998). Tree-ring analyses give a generally similar picture (Briffa & Osborn, 1999; Mann et al., 1998). Indications of a decrease in sea-ice cover in the northern hemisphere over the past few decades are consistent with the assumption of a warming trend (Johannessen, Shalina, & Miles, 2000; Vinnikov et al., 2000). Interestingly, average annual minimal temperatures have increased at about twice the rate of average annual maximal temperatures, which means that the spread between minimal and maximal temperatures has been decreasing; the ecological implications of this phenomenon are largely unknown (Alward, Detling, & Milchunas, 1999).

Estimates of the relative contributions of the major greenhouse gases (other than water vapor) to global temperature and their human-activity origins are shown in Table 2.1. Carbon dioxide, which probably accounts for more than 60% of the problem (Intergovernmental Panel on Climate Change, 1996), comes primarily from industrial power use, heating and cooling of

TABLE 2.1

Greenhouse Gases Resulting From Human Activity and Their Estimated Relative Contributions to Greenhouse Warming

| *Activity* | *Main GH gas* | *Percent* |
|---|---|---|
| Fossil fuel use | $CO_2$ | 46 |
| CFC use | CFCs | 25 |
| Biomass burn | $CO_2$ | 15 |
| Paddy rice | $CH_4$ | 3 |
| Cattle | $CH_4$ | 3 |
| Nitrogen fertilizer | $N_2O$ | 2 |
| Landfills | $CH_4$ | 1 |
| Other | Other | 5 |

*Note.* Adapted from Stern, Young, and Druckman (1992, Table 3-5; data originally from Shine et al., 1990).

buildings, burning of automotive fuel, and burning of biomass. Chlorofluorocarbons come from gases used for refrigeration, aerosol sprays, and various industrial purposes.

The most direct evidence of changes in the concentration of greenhouse gases in the atmosphere over the preindustrial past comes from gases trapped in polar ice; analyses of samples from this record indicate that the current levels of $CH_4$, $CO_2$, and $N_2O$ are higher than at any other time during the last 200,000 years (Raynaud et al, 1993). The increase appears to have been quite regular over the past 250 years; Antarctic ice-core samples show an increase from about 280 parts per million (ppm) in 1750 to almost 290 ppm in 1850 to about 310 ppm in 1950 (Friedli, Lötscher, Oeschger, Siegenthaler, & Stauffer, 1986; Neftel, Moor, Oeschger, & Stauffer, 1985). The accuracy of the estimates based on ice-core data has been challenged on the grounds that the estimation technique assumes that the air trapped in the ice pockets is the same today as it was when first trapped and that this assumption is questionable (Powell, 1994).

The longest continuous record of directly measured atmospheric $CO_2$ concentration, obtained at the Mauna Loa Observatory in Hawaii beginning in 1958, shows the concentration increasing from about 315 ppm in 1958 to about 350 ppm in 1986 (Keeling, 1986). As of 1997, the figure stood at 362 ppm (Vitousek, Mooney, Lubchenco, & Melillo, 1997). Immediately following the Third Conference of Parties to the Framework Convention on Climate Change, held in

Kyoto, Japan, past president of the Intergovernmental Panel on Climate Change, Bert Bolin (1998), estimated that even if the goals for future emission controls were met, the concentration of $CO_2$ would rise to around 382 ppm by 2010.

In the aggregate, the figures suggest that not only has the concentration of $CO_2$ in the atmosphere been increasing, but that the rate of accumulation has been increasing: The amount added during the latter half of the 20th century was greater than that added during the preceding century, which in turn was about twice as great as the amount added in the century preceding that. As of 1990, about 80% of the greenhouse gases were being produced by the industrialized nations, which contain about one third of the world's population (Fulkerson, Judkins, & Sanghvi, 1990), but that picture has been changing rapidly, and the $CO_2$ emissions from developing countries are expected to exceed those from industrialized countries soon (Fulkerson et al., 1989). Some of the other greenhouse gases, including methane and chlorofluorocarbons, which exist in the atmosphere in smaller concentrations than does $CO_2$, are believed to have increased by larger percentages. Ice-core samples show the current concentration of methane to be 2.5 times as great as at any other time during the past 160,000 years (Barnola, Raynaud, Korotkevich, & Lorius, 1987).

Although the present trend is expected to continue well into the 21st century, forecasts of future $CO_2$ emissions vary by as much as a factor of three, depending on assumptions about population, economic growth, and other relevant variables (Sundquist, 1993). Projections are tenuous too because the concentration of $CO_2$ and some of the other greenhouse gases, including carbon monoxide, actually declined from 1991 to 1993 for as-yet unexplained reasons, although the eruption of Mt. Pinatubo is believed by some to have been a major contributing factor (Kerr, 1994c; Novelli, Masarie, Tans, & Lang, 1994). Schneider (1989a) pointed out that, although greenhouse gases other than $CO_2$ are emitted in much smaller quantities, they could have an even greater effect in the aggregate because they are better at absorbing infrared radiation (e.g., methane has nearly 30 times the heat-trapping capacity of $CO_2$), but the future emissions of these gases are hard to predict.

The overall situation is also complicated by other unknowns. There is the possibility, for example, that increased warming due to the accumulation of greenhouse gases could be partially offset by cooling resulting from greater atmospheric concentrations of particulates, or aerosols, especially sulfates emitted from the burning of fossil fuels, which reflect sunlight back into space (Charlson & Wigley, 1994; Karl, Knight, Kukla, & Gavin, 1995; Schwartz & Andreae, 1996). Charlson and Wigley even suggested that, because climate changes due to carbon dioxide concentrations would continue for decades, whereas reductions in sulfur dioxide emissions would quickly decrease the cooling effect of sulfate aerosols, a reduction in the burning of fossil fuels could actually accelerate warming, in the short term, especially over industrial areas of the world. There is also the possibility of an acceleration of warming as a consequence of positive feedback processes triggered by increases in the concentration of greenhouse gases in the atmosphere (Schneider, 1989a). Chemical reactions between aerosols and gas molecules are not fully understood, and a current challenge to atmospheric chemistry is to validate empirically the assumptions regarding them that are used in models of atmosphere mixing (Andreae & Crutzen, 1997). More generally, there is need for a fuller understanding of what determines when the earth's climate will remain in one of its relatively stable phases and what will make it change from one such phase to another (Taylor, 1999).

The increasing concentration of greenhouse gases in the atmosphere has been of concern primarily because of its implications for global warming, but it is not warming, per se, but the anticipated, or possible, consequences of warming that are worrisome. Changes in climate and weather patterns could have implications for water resources, arability of land, maintainability of habitat, and other environmental factors—both in ways that can be anticipated and probably in others not yet determined (Bazzaz & Fajer, 1992). The health implications of an expansion of the tropics are a matter of concern (Stone, 1995). So are the consequences for heavily-populated low-lying areas of a significant rise in sea level from the possible melting of ice sheets currently resting on land (Dahl-Jensen, 2000; Meier, 1984; Peltier & Tushingham, 1989; Schneider, 1997). In the United States, New Orleans and the surrounding area is already under serious threat from the sea under hurricane conditions (Fischetti, 2001); even a small rise in average sea level would magnify that threat.

How much of an increase in temperature is likely to be realized over the next few decades is the subject of continuing debate (White, 1990), and predictions are inherently uncertain at best (Musser, 2001; Schneider, 1994). Global climate models (or general circulation models) that are used to predict future changes consistently predict increases, but of different amounts, most of which fall between 1 and 6 degrees Celsius over the next century (Mitchell, 1989; Schneider, 1989b). Oppenheimer and Boyle (1990) claimed that enough greenhouse gases could accumulate in the atmosphere to heat the earth by more than 8 degrees in 75 years; they caution that all such predictions are highly uncertain, but they also make a case for believing that a 3-degree rise is almost inevitable as a consequence of the extent to which greenhouse gases have already accumulated, even if the concentrations were stabilized at their current levels. According to some projections, $CO_2$ emissions must be stabilized considerably below their current levels during the next century to avoid problematic temperature change (Azar & Rodhe, 1997).

Climate is a complex system in the technical sense of the word (Rind, 1999), and climate modeling is a developing science, the findings of which remain controversial. Even users of the models warn of the limited reliability of forecasts based on them (Schneider, 1989a). Confidence in model predictions is tempered by uncertainties about the roles that could be played in long-term climate change by the oceans (Kumar, Leetmaa, & Ji, 1994; Lubin, 1994), clouds (Baker, 1997; Cess et al., 1995; Ramanathan et al., 1995, 1989), polar ice caps (Kerr, 1994b; La Brecque, 1989; Post et al., 1990; Schneider, 1989b; Sundquist, 1993; Zwally, 1989) and solar activity (Haigh, 1996; Robock, 1996). Another major unknown that is beginning to receive more attention than in the past is how vegetation changes resulting from climate change may function as causal agents in further change; only recently have efforts been made to begin to factor such effects into the models used for predicting climate trends (Baskin, 1993). Mahlman (1997) presented a summary of model projections organized in terms of the degree of certitude afforded them; that atmospheric greenhouse gases are increasing because of human activities, and that changes in greenhouse gas concentrations affect climate are classified, in this summary, as virtually certain facts.

The oceans play a significant role in climate change, although one that is still not well understood because they store most of the carbon that participates in the carbon cycle (Post et al., 1990). Modeling data support the importance of sea surface temperature and coupled variations in the hydrologic cycle as major determinants of atmospheric warming (Graham, 1995; Joos, Plattner, Stocker, Marchal, & Schmittner, 1999). Measurements of world ocean temperatures at a variety of depths have shown a general warming over the last half of the 20th century at least as great as that suggested by atmospheric measurements, and investigators have attributed the warming, at least in part, to the increase of anthropogenic gases in the atmosphere (Barnett, Pierce, & Schnur, 2001; Levitus, Antonov, Boyer, & Stephens, 2000; Levitus et al., 2001).

Clouds cover a sizable portion of the earth's surface at any given time; I have seen estimates ranging from 50% to 75%. They help cool the earth by shading it from the sun, but they also contribute to warming by blocking the escape of radiation of infrared wavelength from the earth's surface. How these two effects trade off against each other is not known precisely—although the aggregate effect at the present appears to be cooling (Baker, 1997)—nor is it certain whether an increase in surface temperature would produce more clouds as a result of increased water evaporation, or fewer clouds as a result of the lower relative humidity of the warmer air. There seems to be general agreement among atmospheric scientists that small changes in cloud cover could conceivably have a large influence on the greenhouse effect, one way or the other. Some have estimated that the greenhouse effect of clouds could be larger than that resulting from a hundredfold increase in the $CO_2$ concentration of the atmosphere (Ramanathan et al., 1989).

A major reason for large differences in the predictions of climatologists regarding changes in the earth's temperature over the next several decades is the result of different assumptions about these matters (Schneider, 1989b; Seitz, Jastrow, & Nierenberg, 1989). The tenability of some of the assumptions become clearer with a better understanding of the microphysical processes involving the ice and water particles, which range in diameter from under a micron to over several millimeters, are found in clouds, and determine their reflective (albedo) and absorptive properties (Baker, 1997). These cloud properties are believed to be affected by various emissions, especially sulfate aerosols, but precisely what the effects and their long-range climatic implications are is not yet well established (Jones, Roberts, & Singo, 1994; Penner, Dickinson, & O'Neill, 1992).

Some scientists believe the concern about global warming has been overstated and the risk of significant change is small—or that we will be able to adapt readily to any increase that is likely to occur. Debate on the topic has been spirited (Ellsaesser, 1991; Jastrow, 1990; Lindzen, 1990; Nierenberg, 1990; Roberts, 1989, 1991a; Seitz, Jastrow, & Nierenberg, 1989; Singer, 2001; White, 1990). Critics of the theory of global warming stress the uncertainties that surround it, many of which are noted previously, and sometimes they point out that as recently as the 1970s a more likely scenario to some was a global cooling that would usher in a new ice age (Ponte, 1976; Ray & Guzzo, 1994). However, the majority opinion appears to be that the problem of global warming is real; and that by the middle of the 21st century, the increase in mean temperature could be enough to cause significant problems and dislocations resulting from effects of temperature on such variables as global and regional weather patterns, sea level, and land productivity (International Panel on Climate Change, 1990, 1996, 2001; Kellogg & Schware, 1981; Kerr, 1992a; 1995a, 1995b; National Research Council, 1977b; Royal Society and Royal Academy of Engineering, 1999). Possible deleterious effects on health, such as those that could come from increases in the ranges of tropical mosquitoes and other carriers of tropical diseases, are also of concern (Stone, 1995), although precisely how a general warming would affect world health is uncertain (National Research Council, 2001).

The earth is believed to have been subject to significant temperature changes from natural causes over its entire history, but there appears to be no analogue in the paleoclimatological record to the kind of climate change-forcing mechanism associated with present-day human activity (Crowley & North, 1991). Studies of climate variations during the recent past have led to the conclusion that the magnitude of increase in temperature during the 20th century was greater than at any other comparable period during the last 1,000 years (Bradley, 2000; Crowley, 2000). Atmospheric $CO_2$ levels are now higher than at any time in recorded history (Petit et al., 1999). As Sundquist (1993) put it, "It is difficult to imagine any natural process that could release $CO_2$ to the atmosphere as rapidly as have human activities" (p. 935).

If a warming trend is in process, it is likely to be several decades before the evidence is sufficiently strong to be considered indisputable (Karl, Heim, & Quayle, 1991; Schneider, Gleick, & Mearns, 1990). Claims and counterclaims based on short-term data are to be expected from believers and unbelievers before the issue is settled (Kerr, 1995a). The question of whether, or the extent to which, human activities are responsible for any warming trend that may exist is also unlikely to be answered with a high degree of certainty for several years (Kerr, 1997). In the meantime, in its 1996 report, the Intergovernmental Panel on Climate Change (IPCC; 1996) concluded that the evidence, on balance, "suggests a discernible human influence on climate" (p. 5). Such an influence was not identified in the first IPCC (1990) report; the change has been attributed to improvements in climate models, the application of more advanced analytic techniques, a shift of focus from 100-year trends to shorter-term (30 year) trends, and accelerated warming in recent decades (Hasselmann, 1997). The IPCC has recently restated its conclusion that human activity is affecting climate, but it has also noted that the future of greenhouse warming remains difficult to predict because of numerous uncertainties involved (Kerr, 2000, 2001a).

In the face of the many uncertainties, what should be done? Ray and Guzzo (1994) argued that, given the differences of opinion among experts, the conclusion must be that no one really knows whether a global warming problem exists, and "when no one knows, it is best to withhold judgment and avoid precipitous action" (p. 14). However, a major concern among those who believe the problem is real is the possibility that, because of the operation of positive feedback mechanisms, detrimental effects could be irreversible by the time the evidence as to whether there is a serious problem is conclusive (Dowlatabadi & Morgan, 1993). Oppenheimer and Boyle (1990) argued that the problem of greenhouse warming is characterized by two menacing features that distinguish it from other environmental issues: irreversibility and the time lag between emissions and effects. The problem is exacerbated, these writers suggested, because these characteristics "have the vicious consequence of increasing the need for an urgent response while at the same time making it politically difficult to implement one" (p. 77).

Some see in such considerations an argument for the adoption of "no-regrets" or "tie-in" policies designed to inhibit runaway global warming, but that would have other beneficial effects even if it turned out that the warming scare was unfounded (Schneider, 1989a, 1989b, 1990). An example of such a policy would be one aimed at developing acceptable alternatives to fossil fuels because our dependence on these fuels is problematic in several respects, and decreasing that dependence would be beneficial independently of the warming threat. An immediate effect of significantly decreasing emissions from the burning of fossil fuels would be a reduction in air pollution, which now is a major cause of respiratory and other health problems worldwide (Cifuentes, Borja-Aburto, Gouveia, Thurston, & Davis, 2001). Another example would be improvement in the efficiency of energy use.

Both of these possibilities figure prominently in the plans of signatories to the United Nations Framework Convention on Climate Change, the treaty that resulted from the United Nations' "Earth Summit" in Rio de Janeiro in 1992, which required signatory countries to develop policies aimed at returning industrial emissions of greenhouse gases to 1990 levels by the end of the century (United Nations, 1992). At a meeting in Berlin to review progress in April 1995, signatory countries concluded that the commitments made at the Rio conference were inadequate to meet the goal of stabilizing greenhouse emissions, and they agreed to work toward new and longer range targets (Koenig, 1995). How fast progress is made toward a better understanding of the determinants of climate change, both natural and anthropogenic, will largely depend on the success of efforts to ensure and facilitate international collaboration in the systematic collection of atmospheric data on a global basis (Zillman, 1997).

Other actions consistent with no-regrets or tie-in policies would be development of better modeling and monitoring capabilities so as to reduce the degree of uncertainty about the problem, phaseout of chlorofluorocarbon production, reforestation and forest preservation, and research on stress- and disease-resistant crops (White, 1990). Development of contingency plans for accelerating the rate of reducing the emissions of greenhouse gases, should further research reveal the problem of global climate change to be more severe than is currently recognized, should also be part of the general approach to the problem of climate change (Holdren, 1990).

## ACID RAIN

The term *acid rain* is used generically to refer to a variety of acidic compounds that accumulate in the atmosphere and fall to Earth in one or another form of precipitation. The most common of these compounds are sulfuric and nitric acids, which are formed when sulfur dioxide and nitrogen oxides, emitted by the burning of fossil fuels in industrial processes and road vehicles, combine with water vapor. Techniques exist for decreasing the amount of acid-forming emissions into the atmosphere and have had a significant impact where they have been applied (Fulkerson, Judkins, & Sanghvi, 1990), but they are not used universally. Even if they were, it is not clear that these, by themselves, would constitute an adequate solution to the long-range problem.

That rain can be acidic has been known at least since the early part of the 18th century (Hales, 1738), and concern was expressed about some of the undesirable effects of acid precipitation in the middle of the 19th century (Smith, 1852, 1872). However, the problem has been given significant attention only since the middle of the 20th century, when evidences of the increasing magnitude of the problem and the seriousness of its effects began to accumulate through studies in Scandanavia (Barrett & Brodin, 1955), Great Britain (Parker, 1955) and the United States (Houghton, 1955).

The detrimental effects of acid rain include the acidification of lakes and streams—in some cases, to the point of lethality to many forms of marine life—destruction of trees, and corrosion of buildings and artifacts, including historical and cultural treasures (Alvo, 1986; Drablös & Tollan, 1980; Likens, Bormann, & Johnson, 1972; Mohnen, 1988; Nriagu, 1978; Schindler, 1988; Schwartz, 1989). Although lakes and streams can become acidified by causes other than acid rain, such as acidic runoff from mine tailings and production of acids by organisms, acid deposition from precipitation appears to be the most detrimental factor in those areas where it is prevalent (Baker, Herlihy, Kaufmann, & Eilers, 1991).

The problem has been severe in the northeastern United States, eastern Canada, and in parts of Europe, especially those countries that make heavy use of coal as a source of industrial power (Cogbill & Likens, 1974; Likens, Wright, Galloway, & Butler, 1979). It is compounded by the fact that the effects are often realized in areas other than, and some distance from, those where the emissions originate. A research objective is the development of better methods to identify the sources of emissions that determine the acid depositions in any given area and predict the distribution of emissions from any given source.

Relative to most other environmental problems, the seriousness of acid rain appears to have been substantially reduced, especially in the eastern United States and Canada, as a result of effective countermeasures taken over the last two decades. In particular, the emission of sulfur dioxide into the atmosphere has been reduced by about half in the United States since 1985, and the reduction was accomplished for a fraction of the originally estimated cost of making it (Kerr, 1998). This unanticipated success has been attributed, in large part, to the flexibility given to industry to meet government-established emission targets in ways of its own devising. The reductions in sulfur emissions that were realized resulted from a combination of factors: effective scrubbers proving to be less expensive than anticipated, switching from more to less sulfur-rich fuels, and use of an emissions-trading system that permitted businesses to treat pollution rights as a commodity that could be bought, sold, or saved for future use. The possibility of generalizing the emissions-trading program so as to make it applicable to other greenhouse gases and on a global level is being considered, but whether it can be effectively scaled up in that fashion is the subject of debate (Kaiser, 1998). Moreover, how sanguine we should be about the success of the program to reduce the effects of acid rain is still not entirely clear (Krajick, 2001).

## AIR POLLUTION AND URBAN SMOG

Air pollution is not a new problem, nor is it only recently recognized to be a problem. Concern about coal smoke in the city motivated the appointment of a commission to study its effects in 13th-century London (Oppenheimer & Boyle, 1990). The Industrial Revolution and the rise of industrial cities helped make the problem the global one that, like the problems of atmospheric warming and acid rain, it is today. Although the problem is not new, knowledge of the details of air pollutants has increased dramatically in recent years; 189 chemicals are identified as hazardous air pollutants in the U.S. Clean Air Act Amendments of 1990 (Kelly, Mukund, Spicer, & Pollack, 1994).

Although it can have complicated effects on natural processes such as the suppression of precipitation (Rosenfeld, 2000), air pollution is of concern primarily because of its implications for health. The adverse health effects of air pollution, especially in the form of sulfur and nitrogen oxides and lead, are well documented (Lave & Seskin, 1977; National Research Council, 1977c, 1978a, 1978b, 1980; Shriner, Richmond, & Lindberg, 1980). The relatively high concentrations of atmospheric pollutants like carbon monoxide in the blood of people living in industrialized societies is believed to be attributable to—in addition to cigarette smoking—emissions from motor vehicles, industrial processes, and home heating and cooking facilities (Goldsmith & Landow, 1968). It has been estimated that, as of 1987, the United States was spending $16 billion annually on health care costs associated with air pollution, and that it incurs $40 billion of costs in decreased worker productivity and about $7 billion as a consequence of damage to buildings, monuments, and other materials (Mitchell, 1987). The annual economic value of avoiding the health effects of tropospheric ozone and airborne particulate matter was estimated, as of 1992, to be about $10 billion in the South Coast Air Basin of California alone (Hall et al., 1992).

Evidence suggests that, in addition to having an impact on physical health, poor air quality can also produce detrimental effects on psychological stability (Strahilevitz, Strahilevitz, & Miller, 1979). There has been some speculation that some motor vehicle accidents may be due, at least partially, to impaired driver performance resulting from driver exposure to air pollutants such as carbon monoxide (Ury, 1968).

Air quality standards in the United States are high compared with those of many industrialized countries, and considerable progress has been made in recent years to reduce concentrations of several of the major pollutants, including lead, sulfur dioxide, nitrogen dioxide, and particulates. Greatly reduced levels of lead in the blood of U.S. children have been attributed to the elimination of lead from gasoline production (Thomas & Spiro, 1994). Ozone and carbon monoxide continue to be serious problems, however; perhaps a third or more of the U.S. population lives in areas that do not meet government standards with respect to one or the other, or both, of these pollutants (Environmental Protection Agency, 1992; Gray & Alson, 1989; National Research Council, 1991; Office of Technology Assessment, 1988; Suhrbier & Deakin, 1988).

Efforts to decrease ozone concentrations in the troposphere have been directed primarily at the reduction of emissions of volatile organic compounds (VOCs) and oxides of nitrogen, which react under certain atmospheric conditions to produce ozone (Finlayson-Pitts & Pitts, 1997; National Research Council, 1991; Stone, 1992). Government regulations aimed at reducing tropospheric ozone have been somewhat effective, but less so than intended and anticipated. One problem seems to have been underestimation of the amount of critical emissions. Emission estimates are based in part on measurements and in part on models of how emission sources (e.g., traffic) are distributed in space and time, so estimates can only be as good as the models are accurate (Seinfeld, 1989). More generally, the problem of determining the contribution of vehicle emissions to air pollution and the effectiveness of various possible methods for decreasing it are not well understood (Calvert, Heywood, Sawyer, & Seinfeld, 1993). Decreasing ozone by controlling VOC emissions is complicated because relative reactivity—ozone-forming potential—can differ by more than an order of magnitude from one compound to another, and such differences have not been reflected in emission regulations (Russell et al., 1995).

Another problem relating to tropospheric ozone management is uncertainty regarding what constitutes a harmful level of concentration. On the basis of medical and epidemiological data showing that prolonged exposure to moderately high concentrations can have deleterious health effects, the Environmental Protection Agency (EPA) has proposed a new and more stringent National Ambient Air Quality Standard. Many of the rural areas that are in compliance with the existing standard would be out of compliance with the new one (Chameides, Saylor, & Cowling, 1997).

The situation is much worse in many areas of the world than it is in the United States. Eastern Europe and parts of the former Soviet Union have severe air pollution problems largely because of uncontrolled use of high-sulfur fuels in heavy industry (Chandler, Makarov, & Dadi, 1990). One estimate has more than 70 million people there being exposed to at least five times the official pollution limits (Wirl, 1991). According to another estimate, 88 Soviet cities with a combined population of 42 million people had toxic air pollution levels 10 times the "maximum permissible" as of 1989 (Chandler, Makarov, & Dadi, 1990). The environmental implications of the recent political upheavals in this part of the world are unclear (Khabibullov, 1991).

Most of the concern about air quality has been focused on the problem of industrial and automotive emissions and their effects on outdoor air in and around urban areas. Less attention has been paid to other sources of air pollution and to the problem of indoor air quality. The problem is not negligible. There is evidence to suggest that people are likely to have their greatest contact with toxic substances in homes, offices, or automobiles (Ott & Roberts, 1998; Wallace, 1995). The main sources of indoor air pollution, according to Ott and Roberts, include, in addition to cigarette smoke, "moth repellents, pesticides, solvents, deodorizers, cleansers, dry-cleaned clothes, dusty carpets, paint, particle board, adhesives, and fumes from cooking and heating" (p. 91). The toxic substances in these products include polycyclic aromatic hydrocarbons (compounds produced by incomplete combustion), carbon monoxide (also formed from incomplete combustion), paradichlorobenzene (found in moth repellents, toilet disinfectants, and deodorizers), and chloroform (formed from heated water that has been chlorinated). In much of the world, especially in developing countries, indoor air is often polluted by injurious smoke from fuels traditionally used for cooking and water heating (Holdren, 1990). The effect of tobacco smoke on nonsmokers in buildings has been an increasing concern in the United States (Eriksen, LeMaistre, & Newell, 1988; Fielding & Phenow, 1988), and some attention is being given to the problem of poor air quality in office buildings more generally (Mendell & Smith, 1990).

Apparently air quality can be poor without people being keenly aware of it. People who live in areas of high pollution are considerably less likely to acknowledge air pollution as a problem if indirectly queried about it, by being asked, for example, to list the five most serious problems in their community, than if asked about the presence of air pollution explicitly (Creer, Gray, & Treshow, 1970; Rankin, 1969). The relative insensitivity to this problem may be due in part to the fact that some major pollutants (e.g., carbon monoxide) are odorless and colorless, so their presence is not perceptible directly. Accommodation may also help account for it; people who live continuously in polluted areas may come to view the prevailing situation as normal (Evans, Jacobs, & Frager, 1982a, 1982b).

The problem of air pollution is closely linked with that of soil and water contamination because air pollutants fall to the ground as particulate matter or as solutes in precipitation. Many of the chemicals used for industrial and agricultural purposes (e.g., polychlorinated biphenyls [PCBs] and pesticides) are transported by the atmosphere to areas far removed from where they were used and can have a variety of effects, some long-lasting and cumulative, on soil and groundwater supplies. PCBs are artificial, stable compounds used in the manufacture of a variety of consumer products. Because of their chemical stability, they accumulate over time—among other places, in the food chain. Their effect on animal and human health is a matter of debate and has stimulated considerable political controversy (Stix, 1998).

## STRATOSPHERIC OZONE DEPLETION

The problem of ozone depletion in the upper atmosphere, or stratosphere, is distinct from the problem of ozone concentration in the lower atmosphere, or troposphere. The 20-kilometer thick (but extremely diffuse) blanket of ozone that envelops the globe in the stratosphere and helps protect it from ultraviolet radiation appears to have been getting significantly thinner, especially, but not exclusively, over Antarctica (Farman, 1987; Farman, Gardiner, & Shanklin, 1985; Proffitt, Fahey, Kelly, & Tuck, 1989; Stolarski, 1988; Watson, Prather, & Kurylo, 1988).

No hole comparable to that detected over Antarctica has yet occurred over the Arctic, but a downward trend in ozone concentration has been observed in latitudes above 30° North (Brune et al., 1991), and researchers anticipate that continued increases in greenhouse gases could cause a greater depletion of Arctic ozone (Santee et al., 1995). Significant reduction in total stratospheric ozone has been observed in all seasons at middle and high latitudes in both the Northern and Southern hemispheres (Stolarski et al., 1992). Getting a clear picture of the situation is complicated by the fact that atmospheric ozone is subject to natural year-to-year fluctuations and by events such as the volcanic eruption of Mount Pinatubo, which can produce aerosols that persist in the stratosphere for years (Gleason et al., 1993). Reliable long-term trend indications require the integration of measurements over two or three decades (Marshall Institute, 1991).

The possibility that the thinning of ozone in the stratosphere is at least partially due to an increase in the concentration of chlorofluorocarbons (CFCs) was first pointed out in a widely cited paper by Molina and Rowland (1974; see also Rowland & Molina, 1975). CFCs are now generally considered to be the primary agents of stratospheric depletion (Kerr, 1988), although lesser effects are believed to be due to emissions from high-altitude aircraft (Harrison, 1970; Johnston, 1971) and even airborne particles from nitrogenous fertilizers (Crutzen, 1970). Some observers have claimed that thinning over Antarctica had occurred as early as the 1950s, before CFCs had been emitted in significant amounts (Ray & Guzzo, 1994; Rigaud & Leroy, 1990), but the basis of this claim has been contested (Newman, 1994). Ultraviolet radiation decomposes CFCs and the chlorine atoms thus freed catalyze the conversion of ozone, $O_3$, to molecular oxygen, $O_2$, which does not have the same ability to absorb ultraviolet rays as does $O_3$. Chlorine atoms normally constitute only about one ppb of the atmosphere, but small amounts of chlorine are able to decompose large amounts of ozone—a single chlorine atom destroys approximately 100,000 molecules of ozone (Rowland, 1989)—so any increase in the concentration is considered problematic.

Stratospheric bromine is also a concern because, although its concentration in the stratosphere is considerably lower than that of chlorine, it is more efficient than chlorine in destroying ozone (World Meteorological Organization, 1992, 1995). It too is emitted as a by-product of industrial processes, such as the production and use of halons and methyl bromide.

Critics of the idea that stratospheric ozone depletion is a serious problem have argued that the amount of chlorine released to the atmosphere from CFCs is minuscule compared with that emitted from seawater, erupting volcanoes, and other natural sources (Ray & Guzzo, 1994). The research community is far from unanimity on the issue (Crutzen, Grooß, Brühl, Müller, & Russell, 1995), but the prevailing opinion appears to be one of serious concern. Some scientists believe that the problem could be more severe and worsening at a greater rate than was generally believed likely only a short time ago (Kerr, 1991, 1992b, 1994a). The results from major ozone-measuring efforts, presented in several reports in *Science* (27 August, 1993), provide little comfort on the issue.

Although the effects of whatever ozone loss has occurred are not yet clear and there is a range of opinions among scientists as to what the results of investigations will eventually reveal, an increase in ultraviolet (UV) radiation reaching the earth's surface is believed by many to be likely to have a variety of detrimental consequences. There is some evidence that the total amount of UV radiation reaching the earth's surface has not increased in recent years (Penkett, 1989). However, readings taken hourly over a 4-year period in Toronto suggest that UV radiation reaching the earth in the spectral region most absorbed by ozone (around 300 nanometers) has been increasing at the rate of about 35% per year in winter and 7% per year in summer (Kerr & McElroy, 1993). Perhaps the most widely publicized concern is the increased risk of skin cancer from direct exposure to UV light; cataracts are also believed to be caused by such exposure (Leaf, 1989). There is some evidence of an effect on Antarctic marine ecosystems because of a significant reduction in the production of phytoplankton in the Antarctic during periods of ozone reduction (Smith et al., 1992).

Hydrofluorocarbons (HFCs) have been proposed as one feasible substitute for CFCs. Results from analytical modeling studies indicate that the potential that HFCs that contain a $CF_3$ group have for depleting stratospheric ozone is relatively small (Ravishankara et al., 1994). Use of CFC-based aerosols was banned in the United States as of the late 1970s, and their use began to decline a few years before the regulations went into effect (Moomaw & Kildow, 1991). Signatories of a 1987 international agreement, known as the Montreal Protocol, agreed to discontinue use of CFCs by 1996. As of the mid to late 1990s, evidence was being obtained that the agreement was having some beneficial effect and some scientists were reporting that the concentration of atmospheric chlorine from industrial sources had peaked and appeared to be on the decline (French, 1994; Kerr, 1996; Montzka et al., 1996). Concerns remain about the possible effects of noncompliance by some signatories to the Protocol and the use of CFCs by developing countries (Gibbs, 1995). Also, because of the complicated interactions of the variables involved, even with great success in decreasing the emissions of CFCs into the atmosphere, the return of ozone to its preindustrial levels in the stratosphere may not occur until late in the 21st century (Waibel et al., 1999).

## WATER CONTAMINATION AND DEPLETION

For many people today in certain regions of the world, insufficient fresh water is a serious and growing problem; Myers (1997) put the number of water-short people at 550 million and suggested that it could grow to 3 billion by 2025. The problem becomes most obvious during periods of drought, when water supplies that are marginally adequate under normal conditions become insufficient to sustain a regional population and necessitate major dislocations and emergency interventions. Contamination is a serious problem in some areas, as is lack of easy access in many others; water piped to one's home is the exception to the rule in much of the developing world (Postel, 1985). According to another estimate, a billion of the world's population lack access to safe water, 1.8 billion do not have adequate sanitation facilities, and over 3 million people die of waterborne and sanitation-related diseases every year (Doyle, 1997).

In recent years, the question of the long-term adequacy of the fresh water supply has become a matter of concern in parts of the world, including areas in the United States—especially the southwest (Doyle, 2001)—that had viewed water as a boundless resource in the past. Projecting the effects on global water resources of a rapidly increasing world population, coupled with those of anticipated climate change, is an inexact science, but investigators acknowledge reasons for concern (Vörösmarty, Green, Salisbury, & Lammers, 2000).

About 70% of the total use of water worldwide goes to agriculture and roughly a quarter goes to industry; residential and other municipal uses account for less than 10% (Postel, 1985). In the United States, agriculture uses almost seven times as much water as do all the nation's city water systems combined (Udall, 1986). Much of the increase in agricultural productivity has been attributed to a greatly increased worldwide use of irrigation during the last few decades (Crossen & Rosenberg, 1989). About 40% of the food grown worldwide uses irrigation (Serageldin, 1995). Some of the water used is returned to the hydrologic system, but not all of it is. In some major agricultural regions, the annual withdrawal of groundwater exceeds the natural recharge rate by large amounts, and this fact would appear to spell trouble for a number of states in the relatively near-term future. Severe water scarcity has been called the biggest threat to future food production (Postel, 2001).

The protection of U.S. groundwater from contamination is a major national concern (Office of Technology Assessment, 1984). The Safe Drinking Water Act of 1974 (PL93-523) requires the Environmental Protection Agency (EPA) to promulgate national standards for drinking water and regulations for enforcing them, and it directs the EPA administrator to arrange for the study of adverse effects on health attributable to contaminants in drinking water. What is known about various types of contaminants (microorganisms, particulate matter, inorganic and organic solutes, and radionuclides) and their effects on human health was reviewed in a report of the National Research Council (1977a), the first in a series of NRC reports relating to the U.S. freshwater supply.

Groundwater becomes contaminated in many ways: agricultural runoff containing pesticides and fertilizers, dumping of sewage into rivers, from salt used for deicing of highways—according to the Salt Institute (1980), the use of salt on the highways increased by a factor of more than 12 between 1950 and 1980—chemical emissions into the atmosphere that return to the earth in precipitation, improperly disposed-of hazardous wastes, and from leachate from municipal dumps (Epstein, Brown, & Pope, 1982; Hibbard, 1986; Smith, Alexander, & Wolman, 1987; Weddle & Garland, 1974). Happily, the concentration of lead in water is believed to have declined significantly in recent years due largely to decreased use of leaded gasoline.

Most of the efforts to clean up the nation's waterways have focused on controlling *point sources* of pollution, as distinct from *nonpoint sources*, such as urban and agricultural runoff. The effects of nonpoint sources on water quality are more difficult to determine than those of point sources, but they are assumed to be substantial.

## DEFORESTATION

The fraction of the earth's surface that is forest land is decreasing at what some observers consider an alarming rate (Bryant, Nielsen, & Tangley, 1997; Myers, 1980, 1989; World Bank, 1998); Oppenheimer and Boyle (1990) estimated that, as of 1990, as much as half of the world's tropical forests may have been destroyed since mid-century. Some of the shrinkage is caused by appropriation of forest land for agriculture or for industrial, commercial, or residential development. Myers (1995) claimed that over half of all tropical deforestation is due to slash-and-burn agriculture. Some of it is the result of the harvesting of timber, which frequently is done in ways that make the land less conducive to forest growth or that delay reforestation (Repetto, 1990). The forces that lead to deforestation are expected to get stronger as the population of the world, and especially that of developing countries, continues to increase (Brown, 1991; Keyfitz, 1989).

The annual rate at which tropical forests are being lost worldwide has been estimated to be 142,000 square kilometers by the Friends of the Earth and between 160,000 and 200,000 square kilometers by the World Resources Institute. Terborgh (1992), who cited these estimates, pointed out that extrapolating even the lower one would show the more than 7 million square kilometers of tropical forests that remained as of 1990 disappearing completely by 2045, and this assumes no increase in the rate of destruction. According to Shukla, Nobre, and Sellers (1990), continuation of the current rate of deforestation in the Amazon region of South America could mean loss of most of these forests within 50 to 100 years. Other regions in South America are also suffering forest loss, in some cases to the cultivation of coca and poppies to support the international drug trade (Goodman, 1993). Data suggesting that the rate of forest clearing in this area is decreasing have been reported from time to time; whether this marks the beginning of a continuing trend remains to be seen. Unfortunately, data indicate that the annual rate of deforestation in South America, as bad as it is at 0.6%, is being surpassed in some parts of the world, such as Central America (1.5%) and Southeast Asia (1.6%) (Aldous, 1993).

Deforestation has implications that extend beyond the immediate areas in which the loss occurs because of the role that forests play in maintaining the earth's carbon cycle (Phillips et al., 1998; Reddy & Goldemberg, 1990; Wofsy, 2001), the habitat they provide for a large percentage of the earth's biota (Wilson, 1989), and a variety of other valuable services they provide (Costanza et al., 1997). Inasmuch as trees and other vegetation remove $CO_2$ from the atmosphere and return oxygen, any significant reduction in the amount of the earth's surface that is covered with forests will contribute to a greater concentration of

$CO_2$ in the air. Trees use from 10 to 20 times as much carbon per unit area as is used by pastureland or land growing crops (Revelle, 1982). Deforestation that results from the need of underdeveloped countries to export timber for income can have the doubly unfortunate effect of not only contributing to the world-wide accumulation of $CO_2$ in the atmosphere, but also of depleting the country's natural assets.

Some evidence has been obtained that turnover rates—rates at which trees die and new flora are recruited into an area—in mature tropical forests have increased substantially during the latter half of the 20th century. A stepped-up turnover rate is expected to increase the prevalence of climbing plants, gap-dependent species, and species that would benefit from increased atmospheric $CO_2$. A secondary effect could be to move a primary forest in the direction of becoming a net carbon source instead of a sink, thus contributing to further accumulating of $CO_2$ in the atmosphere (Phillips & Gentry, 1994). Turnover acceleration is also expected to lead to decreased biological diversity because of its effect on species' habitat (Pimm & Sugden, 1994).

## DESERTIFICATION

Desertification refers to the transformation of once-arable land into land on which crops will no longer grow. It can happen as a consequence of soil erosion, salinization from irrigation, or other processes, including overgrazing or improper crop management (Pillsbury, 1981; Schlesinger et al., 1990). Trimble (1999; see also Glanz, 1999) presented data suggesting that, at least in some areas, the problem may not be as severe as many estimates indicate. More data are needed to provide a clear picture of what is happening with the earth's topsoil. However, many earth scientists appear to believe that the problem of soil degradation is a serious one.

Crossen and Rosenberg (1989) defined *desertification* broadly to include several forms of soil degradation. "Among the most important forms are erosion by wind and water and the consequent loss of soil productivity; degradation of rangelands in the arid, semiarid and subhumid regions; and waterlogging and salinization of irrigated lands" (p. 128). They claimed that about 60% of the agricultural land outside humid regions of the world is believed to be experiencing desertification to some degree, although they cautioned that the accuracy of attempts to quantify the problem of desertification is uncertain because definitions of terms vary, and in most areas of the world accurate estimates of degradative processes are not available. Daily (1995) gave 43 as the percent of the earth's terrestrial vegetated surface that has diminished because of recent impacts of land use.

Pimentel et al. (1995) estimated that, during the last 40 years, almost one third of the world's arable land has been lost to erosion alone; they also estimated the annual costs of soil erosion to be about $44 billion in the United States and about $400 billion worldwide. Erosion is a natural process, but it is especially severe when steeply sloping land is used for agriculture, as it increasingly is because of a growing population's food demands (Lal & Stewart, 1990).

According to the National Research Council's Panel on the Improvement of Tropical and Subtropical Rangelands (1990), about 40% of the earth's land surface is rangeland and about 80% of that is degraded to some extent. Brown (1991) claimed that the fodder needs of the livestock in nearly all Third World countries now exceed the sustainable yield of the countries' foraging resources. This is worrisome because overgrazing diminishes the productive capacity of the land, thus ensuring increasing disparity between supply and demand, even assuming no increase in demand.

Agriculture, at least in the more developed countries of the world, is an impressive success story. Thanks to the mechanization of farming, the development of high-yield crop species, and the use of effective fertilizers and pesticides, it has been possible for a small fraction of the populations of these countries to raise enough food for everyone and even to have problematically large surpluses. The per-hectare yield of grain more than doubled between 1950 and 1984, and during most of this time the area under cultivation steadily increased, as did the use of irrigation (Brown, 1991). Even in undeveloped countries that have suffered food shortages, the most difficult problems have been those associated with the distribution of food rather than its availability.

There is some concern among earth scientists that the production of enough food to meet the world's needs may become much more difficult in the future than it has been in the past because of the loss of arable land to desertification, ability of pests to evolve pesticide-resistant strains, and increasing concern about the long-term health risks associated with the use of pesticides and fertilizers (Moffat, 1992). The scarcity of water for irrigation in some parts of the world is seen as problematic, as is the experiencing of diminishing returns from the increased use of fertilizers. The agricultural implications of desertification are summarized graphically by Brown (1991): "Each year, the world's farmers are trying to feed 88 million more people, but with 24 billion fewer tons of topsoil than the year before" (p. 165). There is also concern that the problem of food production might be exacerbated by any significant increase in global temperature. The question of how to increase agricultural productivity without further damaging soil, water, and natural ecosystems will get increasing attention.

Interest has been growing for some time in sustainable agriculture, which attempts to ensure the long-term productivity of the soil and is also sensitive to other environmental problems such as groundwater contamination, energy costs, and risks to health and wildlife habitats (Lal & Stewart, 1990; Reganold,

Papendick, & Parr, 1990). Sustainable agriculture is contrasted with conventional agriculture, which makes heavy use of chemical fertilizers and pesticides without sufficient regard to their long-term effects on soil quality and other environmental variables.

Sustainable agriculture makes use of many aspects of modern technology, but attempts to do so in ways that take the possibility of undesirable secondary effects into account. Some observers believe that it may be possible for farms that grow a variety of crops with little use of chemicals to be as productive as farms using more conventional techniques, and perhaps even more profitable because of lower input costs, especially if the indirect costs associated with environmental degradation and health effects are taken into account (National Research Council, 1989a; Reganold, Papendick, & Parr, 1990).

## WETLAND LOSS

Wetlands are lost, as wetlands, when they are drained or filled in to provide space for highways, shopping centers, residential lots, and so on. Until fairly recently, wetlands were viewed as wastelands, and their reclamation for useful purposes was encouraged by the government. One estimate of the effect of such reclamation activities on the wetlands of the contiguous 48 states of the United States is that over half of them have already been lost (Wallace, 1985). In some places (e.g., coastal southern California), estimated losses are much greater. According to Steinhart (1990), the remaining U.S. wetlands are being lost to farms, shopping centers, highway corridors, airport runways, marinas, industrial parks, and housing tracks at a rate of 300,000 to 500,000 acres a year.

Perhaps the most visible problem involving wetlands in the United States is that of the Florida Everglades. About half their original size, the Everglades have become the focus of a major restoration effort, the success of which is anything but assured. According to Holloway (1994), when the restoration effort began in the 1980s, "only one fifth of the water that used to reach the ecosystem at the turn of the century was getting there, often at the wrong times. Only 5 percent of the wading birds that used to nest in the wetlands were still doing so" (p. 100). The threat to the Everglades has come largely from demands for land for agriculture and urban development and from measures taken for flood control.

The importance of wetlands as a wildlife habitat and the critical role they play in the total ecosystem is now more widely recognized. The government has established a no-net-loss policy, according to which wetlands reclaimed for development must be offset by the creation of an equal amount of new wetlands or the restoration of that amount of previously reclaimed land to wetland status. Implementation of the policy has proved to be problematic, however. Debates have often centered on how wet a parcel must be to qualify as wetland for compliance purposes. Creating new wetlands that are the same in all critical respects as those that have been lost to development has proved to be exceedingly hard to do (Malakoff, 1998; Roberts, 1993).

## DECREASING BIODIVERSITY

Species come and go. The vast majority of those that have existed at one time or another are now extinct (Jablonski, 1991). However, except for the possibility of a few catastrophic prehistoric events that could have caused major extinctions, it is generally believed that, until fairly recently, species changed gradually over periods of time measured in millions of years. Raup (1988) estimated the natural (not catastrophe-related) extinction rate to be about $10^{-7}$ species per species per year. The number of species that currently exist on Earth is not known. Only about 1.4 million have been given scientific names (Wilson & Peter, 1988), but estimates (not undisputed [Mann, 1991]) of the total that may exist go as high as between 10 and 100 million (Ehrlich & Wilson, 1991). Applying Raup's formula to this range of estimates gives between 1 and 10 per year as the natural rate of species extinction at the present time.

Although some scientists argue that the data are too sparse to permit firm conclusions on the matter (Mann, 1991), others are claiming that, because of human activities that have implications for wildlife habitats, species are now disappearing at an unusually rapid, and perhaps accelerating, rate (Kohm, 1991; Lawton & May, 1995; Reid & Miller, 1989; Soule, 1991). Wilson (1989) estimated that the loss due to the clearing of large sections of the rain forests is between 4,000 and 6,000 species a year. Ehrlich and Wilson (1991) argued that a much higher rate is not out of the question. Some scientists believe that 99% of all animal species can be found in the tropics (Robinson, 1991). Nevertheless, Mares (1992) pointed out that it is a mistake to focus exclusively on the disappearance of the rain forests as a cause of decreasing biodiversity because, in the case of mammals, the drylands are more species-rich than they are. Pimm, Russell, Gittleman, and Brooks (1995) suggested that species are currently disappearing at 100 times the natural background rate. According to a report from a task force of the National Science Board (1989), from ¼ to ½ of the earth's species could become extinct within 30 years if current trends continue. (See Reid & Miller [1989] for a discussion of several extinction-rate estimates and Pimm, Russel, Gittleman, and Brooks, [1995] for specifics regarding the complexities involved in predicting future extinction rates.)

The implications of decreasing biodiversity are also a matter of debate; not all ecologists see species loss as a serious problem (Baskin, 1994; Grime, 1997). "How many people lose sleep because it is no longer possible to see a live Dinosaur?" (Beckerman, 1994, p. 194). Yet given the permanence of extinction, lack of concern about unnecessary loss seems an unwise reaction to uncertainty on this point. Jablonski (1991) made the thought-provoking point that rare geographically restricted species are likely to be more vulnerable to environmental perturbations, like the habitat alteration and fragmentation caused by human activity, than are more widely distributed and adapted species. Consequently, such activity may be expected to produce "a biota increasingly enriched in widespread, weedy species—rats, ragweed, and cockroaches—relative to the larger numbers of species that are more vulnerable and potentially more useful to humans as food, medicines, and genetic resources" (p. 755).

Forest and wetland loss can have effects far beyond the immediate areas in which they occur. Evidence of this is seen, for example, in changes in the populations and patterns of behavior of migratory species. Birds that winter in the tropics and summer in temperate zones can be affected by changes in either. Destruction of tropical forests and loss of wetland habitat in Alaska have both been seen as the cause of shrinkage in migratory bird populations (Askins, 1995; Conner, 1988; Lipske, 1990). Data collected in Rock Creek Park in Washington, D.C. showed a decline between 1940 and 1970 of almost 90% in long-distance migrating birds. Estimates based on radar-detection facilities of the numbers of migratory birds passing over the Louisiana coast decreased by 50% between the mid-1960s and the late 1980s (Terborgh, 1992). Another hypothesized contributor to the declining population of some species that nest in forests is their vulnerability to predators and parasitic birds, like cowbirds, when they nest in small forest patches rather than in large entirely forested areas (Robinson, Thompson, Donovan, Whitehead, & Faaborg, 1995).

The U.S. Congress showed concern about the problem of species extinction in its enactment in 1973 of the Endangered Species Act. Some species that were close to extinction, including the American bald eagle and the whooping crane, have been making encouraging comebacks as a result of explicit efforts to preserve them. Preservation of biodiversity in the national forests is one objective of the National Forest Management Act of 1976. However, as of the early 1990s, the U.S. government's list of endangered or threatened domestic plants or animals contained 650 species, and it seems the list would be much longer if the agencies responsible for it had the resources to do what has to be done to determine how many of the more than 3,000 species on a waiting list as of 1992 should be added to it (Gibbons, 1992). However, many in Congress feel that enforcement of the act has been too aggressive and the sentiment for weakening of federal regulations has been strong.

Concern about decreasing biodiversity can be justified on ethical, aesthetic, or economic grounds. An economic consequence of the extinction of populations or species is the loss of some of the free services that ecosystems provide (Ehrlich, 1987). A specific loss that concerns some biologists is that of the countless natural antibiotics, insecticides, and fungicides—some discovered, many not—that have been developed by the multitudinous life forms that exist in the tropics (Robinson, 1991).

Realization of the importance of plants as sources of medicinal substances has increased greatly in recent years, as has the discovery and use of plant-based drugs, among the best known examples of which are aspirin and digitalis. According to Cox and Balick (1994), flowering plants and ferns have yielded about 120 commercially sold drugs and account annually for about 25% of all prescriptions issued in North America. Inasmuch as only a tiny fraction of the world's flora has yet been studied for possible medicinal value, the elimination of species represents the loss of resources of unknown, but possibly great, medical worth.

Although there is considerable agreement among naturalists that biodiversity is declining and that human activity is a major causal factor, natural ecosystems are so complex and interact in so many ways that what would constitute appropriate corrective action is not always clear.

Well-intentioned efforts aimed at conservation and species preservation can have detrimental effects on the systems they are intended to protect (Livingston, 1981). Moreover, steps to protect species often conflict, in appearance or fact, with other interests, especially involving the use of land for agricultural, industrial, or residential purposes. This problem is complicated by the difficulty of distinguishing between real and apparent conflicts and by the tendency of extremists on both sides of the issue to make unwarranted claims.

On the brighter side, there appears to be a growing interest in restoration ecology as a discipline and some examples of successful restoration or rehabilitation projects (Dobson, Bradshaw, & Baker, 1997; Wali, 1992). Controlled experimentation, small and large scale, is becoming increasingly used as a means to gain a better understanding of ecological systems and the effects of various interventions on them, although the usefulness of the results to date is a matter of debate (Carpenter, Chisholm, Krebs, Schindler, & Wright, 1995; Roush, 1995). Community-based natural resource management programs intended to conserve species while helping human communities meet their own needs are being tried in several wildlife-rich nations in Africa (Getz et al., 1999). However, finding arrangements that satisfy the goals of both conservation and local development is proving to be difficult (Inamdar, de Jode, Lindsay, & Cobb, 1999).

## WASTE

Waste is a double-edged problem. Wastefulness in production and consumption means inefficient use of resources. Given that many of the resources involved are in limited supply, this is an inefficiency that probably cannot be tolerated for the long term. Waste matter, whether in the form of useless by-products of the production of valued goods or services or in that of residues of once-useful products, represents a disposal problem.

Waste is a global problem—indeed it is even beginning to be recognized as a serious problem in space (Johnson, 1998)—but is most severe in developed countries. It is a problem of staggering proportions in the United States and Canada. According to one analysis, the U.S. economy extracts more than 10 tons of mass (excluding atmospheric oxygen and fresh water) per person per year from the environment, only about 6% of which ends up in durable goods, the other 94% being converted into waste residuals almost immediately (Ayers, 1989). These residuals are relatively invisible to the average consumer and do not show up in most estimates of per capita amounts of solid or municipal waste generation, which focus on the kind of visible waste that finds its way to community incinerators, dumps, and landfills. North Americans produce much more waste, on a per capita basis, than do our closest rivals in this regard (Herman, Ardekani, & Ausubel, 1989; Tchobanoglous, Theisen, & Eliassen, 1977). Bureau of the Census (1990, Table 355) figures show the solid waste generated per person per day increased by about 32% between 1960 and 1985.

According to EPA estimates, Americans were generating about 180 million tons of (visible) municipal solid waste per year as of 1988 (Hoffman, 1992). This is almost 1500 pounds per person per year, or about 4 pounds (1.8 kilograms) per person per day. Estimates from other sources vary, but they are all high: The World Resources Institute (1992) gave 1,900 pounds per person per year or about 5.2 lbs (2.4 kgs) per person per day; Hirschhorn and Oldenburg (1991) gave 6.6 lbs (3 kgs) per day. Estimates for Canada are similar (Statistics Canada, 1993). More than 20 years ago, Tchobanoglous, Theisen, and Eliassen (1977) gave an estimate of 3,600 pounds as the annual per capita amount of waste (solid and liquid combined) produced by Americans, which was about 4.5 times as much as was produced by the Japanese, who rated second on the waste production scale. Morse (1991) gave nearly two tons per person per year as the rate of solid waste production in California and claims that about 90% of this finds its way to solid landfills. According to Melosi (1981), since 1920, the amount of solid waste generated by Americans has grown about five times as rapidly as the population.

Again according to EPA estimates, about 40% of the municipal solid waste produced by Americans is paper. We lead the world in the consumption of paper and use about half again as much, per capita, as West Germany—our nearest rival in this regard (Bureau of the Census, 1990). It would be interesting to know how much of this paper is used to store (temporarily) and transmit information that, at least in principle, could be stored and transmitted electronically.

The problem represented by the sheer bulk of waste products is compounded by the fact that some materials, such as nonbiodegradable plastics, tire rubber, and toxic chemicals, pose special difficulties for disposal (Kiefer, 1974; Powell, 1990; Westerman, 1975). Automobile and truck tires are problematic both because of the difficulty of disposal and the quantity involved. Worn-out tires do not make good landfill, and they cannot be easily incinerated without contributing to air pollution. It is important that cost-effective ways to recycle them be found.

## TOXIC AND RADIOACTIVE WASTE

Toxic and radioactive waste are even more problematic than conventional waste for obvious reasons (Cohen, 1984; Davis & Lester, 1988; Lave & Upton, 1987). Toxic waste is generated by a variety of industrial processes; some also comes from solvents and chemicals used in the home. Chlorinated solvents widely used to remove oil from clothes or machinery are among the most common contaminants of ground water at toxic waste sites (National Research Council, 1994). According to one EPA estimate, there are about 30,000 toxic chemical waste disposal sites in the United States, and the number is increasing (Upton, Kneip, & Toniolo, 1989).

The U.S. government has recognized the problem and enacted legislation—most notably, the Comprehensive Environmental Response, Compensation, and Liability Act of 1980 (as reauthorized and amended in 1986)—to address it. Generally known as Superfund, the legislation mandates the cleanup of problem sites. Cleanup is expensive, however, and progress has been slow; only a small fraction of the sites included on a National Priority List compiled by the EPA have been completely cleaned up. Moreover, the full extent of the problem of toxic waste is not known. Gute (1991) gave 67,000 as the approximate number of chemicals in use in the U.S. commercial market, on only about 30% of which any human health effects data exist, and for only about 2% of which the data that exist suffice to quantify human health effects.

The problem of toxic waste disposal is especially severe in parts of Eastern Europe. Since the unification of Germany, for example, it has been estimated that there are at least tens of thousands of potentially toxic dump sites in largely unidentified locations in the old eastern zone (Cezeaux, 1991).

A major contributor to the problem of toxic waste that has attracted some attention in recent years is medicine. According to Hershkowitz (1990), there are about 6,000 substandard medical-waste incinerators at hospitals in the United States emitting toxins—including dioxin, heavy metals, and acid gases—into the air often in populous areas.

Mercury, which is found in thermometers, thermostats, barometers, flourescent lights, and gauges of various sorts, as well as in dental amalgam used for tooth fillings, represents a health hazard as waste because it is transformed by bacteria into methylmercury, a neurotoxin, that can accumulate in the food chain and contaminate fish consumed by humans. Mercury can enter the atmosphere by the burning of fossil fuels or the incineration of municipal or medical waste, and it finds its way to water when it falls during precipitation.

High-level nuclear waste (waste with a high concentration of radioactive elements with a relatively long half-life) exists in the United States both as spent nuclear reactor fuel rods and as the acid in which fuel rods have been dissolved in the production of plutonium. As of 1998, the amount of spent fuel stored at U.S. nuclear power plants exceeded 30,000 metric tons and was growing by more than 2,000 metric tons per year. Projections had the total amount of such waste reaching 75 metric tons by 2020 (Hollister & Nadis, 1998).

Most of the spent fuel (still highly radioactive) is stored in cooling ponds near the reactors that produced it, but such storage is intended to be temporary. Finding long-term repositories for this material remains a problem about which controversy continues. Radioactive liquid waste is stored in steel tanks at the Hanford Military Reservation in the state of Washington and at the Savannah River plant in South Carolina. Significant amounts of radioactive material are believed to have been released to the ground, water, and air (Shulman, 1989). The cost of cleanup of radioactive leakage from U.S. military weapons facilities has been projected to be about $130 billion over the next few decades (National Academy of Sciences, 1989). The question of how and where to store high-level radioactive waste for the long term promises to be a matter of intense debate for some time to come (Hollister & Nadis, 1998; Whipple, 1996).

Low-level radioactive waste disposal also constitutes a major unsolved problem. Much of this waste comes from the use of radioactive materials in medicine and in biotechnological research and development. Experts disagree on what represents safe storage of such waste and about the nature and magnitude of risks associated with specific proposals (Cohen, 1994). A *Science* editorial by Philip Abelson (1995a) regarding a specific proposed repository for low-level radioactive waste, a sample of the letters it evoked (Althuis, 1995; Budin, 1995; Grossman, 1995; Warf, 1995; Wilshire, 1995), and Abelson's (1995b) rejoinder illustrate the point.

Radioactive waste disposal is bound to become increasingly problematic in the near future because about 50 nuclear power plants in the Western world are, or soon will be, ready for decommissioning and dismantling—about 12 U.S.

reactors were ready for retirement as of 1989 (Shulman, 1989). The problems of selecting long-term storage sites and transporting radioactive waste to them have proved controversial among the general public. In view of the lack of agreement among experts on how best to manage radioactive waste, it is perhaps not surprising that the public has shown considerable distrust of the efforts of government and industry in this regard (Binney, Mason, Martsolf, & Detweiler, 1996; Greenberg, Lowrie, Krueckeberg, Mayer, & Simon, 1997; Slovic, 1993) and has persisted with nearly uniformly negative attitudes toward nuclear waste that are influenced very little by opinions of those technical experts who argue that safe disposal is feasible with current storage techniques (Slovic, Flynn, & Layman, 1991). Safety is a major concern, but not the only one; the prospect of siting a hazardous waste facility in one's community can also evoke strong resistance because of the actual or anticipated effect on property values or the quality or status of the community (Greenberg & Schneider, 1994, 1996; Greenberg, Schneider, & Choi, 1994).

Efforts to deal with the problem of hazardous waste have been of three types: (a) cleanup or remediation of existing hazardous waste repository sites, (b) reduction of the amount of hazardous waste produced, and (c) identification of new and safer ways of disposing of or managing hazardous waste (Portney, 1991b). The cost, complexity, and uncertain effectiveness of cleanup operations make the case for the importance of both reducing the amount of hazardous waste produced and finding more effective ways of disposing of or managing what is produced.

## CONTAMINATION FROM INDUSTRIAL ACCIDENTS

In addition to the immediate costs they incur in terms of injury, death, and property loss, industrial accidents sometimes have environmental consequences that last a long time. Major accidents like the nuclear-reactor incidents at Three Mile Island and Chernobyl, the chemical plant emissions in Bophal, and the oil spill from the *Exxon Valdez* make news headlines and get a great deal of attention as they should. What may have greater long-term implications for the environment, however, are the cumulative effects of the countless industrial accidents resulting in spills and emissions that individually do not get media attention or that may not even be detected or reported.

The implications of industrial accidents for safety and health have received a great deal of attention. Accidents that are responsible for large numbers of fatalities or serious physical injuries, or that result in readily identified illnesses over a period of time, are likely to get much notice. There is growing evidence that the occurrence of industrial accidents of certain types, and perhaps even the threat of their occurrence, can have detrimental psychological and psychophysiological effects on people who live close to where they have occurred or might occur (Baum & Fleming, 1993; Hatch, Wallenstein, Beyea, Nieves, & Susser, 1991; Wandersman & Hallman, 1993), and that such effects can last for several years if not become chronic (Baum, 1990; Baum, Gatchel, & Schaeffer, 1983; Gatchel, Schaeffer, & Baum, 1985). Industrial (human-made) disasters are believed by some investigators to be more stress-inducing than comparable natural disasters (Baum, 1987; Baum, Fleming, & Davidson, 1983) perhaps because they are seen to be avoidable in principle. Therefore, their occurrence represents a loss of control in situations where control was possible.

Human error is known to be a primary cause of industrial accidents. Essentially, every major incident that has been investigated has revealed one or more critical points at which preventable mistakes occurred. In addition to problems stemming from poor training, inadequate documentation, inappropriate operating procedures, and ineffective management policies, errors are often traceable to poorly designed person–machine interfaces (Reason, 1990; Senders & Moray, 1991).

## NATURAL DISASTERS

Natural disasters—earthquakes, floods, hurricanes—have always occurred and undoubtedly always will. There are several reasons for mentioning them in a discussion of psychology and the environment. Our knowledge of such events and our growing ability to predict, at least statistically, the occurrence of some of them have implications for behavior. For example, the knowledge that a particular area is highly likely to experience severe earthquakes within a given time span has implications for the kinds of structures that should be allowed in that area and for the kinds of preparations that should be made to deal with such events when they occur.

Conversely, human behavior has implications for the consequences of natural disasters that do occur. Careful planning that takes the probabilities of predictable natural disasters into account can lessen their effects; planning that ignores those probabilities has the potential to magnify their effects manyfold. The Yucca Mountain site being prepared as a repository for spent reactor fuel is located between two prominent earthquake faults. This has contributed to the controversy stimulated by this selection (Shulman, 1989).

Despite a much greater ability to predict, statistically, when and where certain types of natural disasters are likely to occur than we had in the past, we have not yet learned how to make effective use of this ability. There is need for much improvement in methods of preparing for such events, for limiting and controlling their damage, and for providing assistance to their victims when they occur.

## INTERDEPENDENCE OF ASPECTS

The problem of environmental change is complex not only because it has many aspects, but because those aspects are interrelated in many ways. The problems of global warming, deforestation, and desertification are interconnected in complicated cause–effect ways by virtue of the role of vegetation in the carbon cycle. The decline in biodiversity is, in part, a direct consequence of deforestation, the loss of wetlands, and, possibly, of stratospheric ozone thinning. Waste and its disposal have implications for air pollution and water contamination. Water depletion and contamination are causal factors in desertification, and so on. Moomaw and Kildow (1991) argued that many of the recent catastrophic failures of a systemic nature that have had significant environmental consequences—Three Mile Island, Chernobyl, the mercury poisoning of Minamata Bay—"represent incremental breakdowns over long periods of time that went unnoticed until they reached thresholds that triggered massive dislocations as they became visible" (p. 269), and that what the systems involved have in common is complexity that precludes an understanding of them in operation.

There are interactions also stemming from the fact that technological approaches to some problems can have inadvertent deleterious effects on other problems. The deleterious effects may remain invisible for a considerable time (Levine, 1991), in part, because they may occur through a chain of cause–effect relationships and, in part, because they are unanticipated. The use of solar energy to pump water from underground aquifers, for example, has the unquestioned advantage of being cleaner from an environmental point of view than is the use of fossil-fueled pumping facilities. However, if the solar energy proves to be less expensive as well, the effect could be to increase the drain on already stressed aquifers, as some of those in the southwestern United States, and to increase the probability of depletion (Ehrenfeld, 1981).

The interactions appear even more complex as we attempt to look to the future because changes with respect to any given aspect may affect or be affected by changes in others. For example, because water resources are the net result of evaporation and precipitation processes, they are likely to be greatly affected by any significant change in climate. More generally, projecting the ramifications of continuing environmental change is exceedingly difficult and most predictions must be considered tenuous; we should try to understand the possibilities, but must be prepared for the unexpected as well.

In addition to the fact that the variables involved in environmental change interact in many ways, the picture is complicated too by the time scale on which many environmental changes take place and the sometimes long delays between the time when the behavior that causes some change occurs and the time when evidence of the change becomes clear. As Gardner and Stern (1996) pointed out, even once a cause–effect relationship between human behavior and an environmental change is recognized, it is likely to be some time before any remedial action is taken (it may not be entirely clear what action is required; even if that becomes clear, mobilizing the action is likely to take additional time), and more time—perhaps a long period—may have to pass before the effects of the action that was intended to be remedial can be determined with much precision.

## URGENCY OF THE PROBLEM

Some scientists question the seriousness of one or another aspect of the problem of detrimental environmental change—global warming, for example—or argue that the bleakness of the situation has been overstated. No doubt excessive claims have been made, sometimes sincerely because they are believed to be true, and sometimes perhaps for self-serving reasons. However, the prevailing attitude among the majority of scientists who have studied the problem from one or another vantage point seems to be that the problem is not only real, but more significant than many of those that get much more attention from policymakers, scientific investigators, and society in general. Some 1,600 scientists have jointly issued a statement of intense concern (Union of Concerned Scientists, 1993). Concern also seems to be growing among the general public, not only in the United States, but throughout the world (Bloom, 1995).

The problem is not new, nor is it only recently recognized. There are many evidences in the literature, some of them quite old, of concern about certain aspects of it. Writing in 1556, George Agricola summarized some of the arguments that opponents of mining made in his day as follows:

> Shafts in search of ore render fields sterile; therefore there was once in Italy a law that none should dig down in the earth for ore, and thus destroy fruitful fields and plantations of wine and fruit. Woods and groves were felled, since unlimited amounts of wood are needed for buildings and for tools as well as for smelting. By this felling of woods and groves, many birds and other animals are exterminated, many of which serve as fine and pleasant food. The ores, they allege, have to be washed, and this washing poisons brooks and rivers and thereby either drives the fish away or kills them. Since therefore the inhabitants of the surrounding countryside, owing to the desolation of the fields and of the woods, the groves, the brooks, and the rivers suffer great embarrassment as to how they can obtain the necessities for their livelihood, and since on account of the lack of wood, the cost of building their houses is raised it is clear to all eyes that driving the shafts causes more harm than any use obtained from the ores obtained by mining. (Klemm, 1964, p. 147)

Here are concerns about water pollution, deforestation, habitat destruction, and resource depletion that predate large-scale industrialization and fossil fuel consumption. Agricola goes on, it must be said, to make a case for mining despite such concerns expressed by its opponents.

One characteristic that marks the current-day problem of detrimental environmental change is its global extent. Although there are local and regional manifestations of specific environmental troubles—aquifer depletion in California, unbreathable air in parts of eastern Europe, stratospheric ozone loss over Antarctica, the acidification of lakes and streams in eastern Canada and the northeastern United States—the potential for all of these problems exists everywhere. Given that they derive, to a large degree, from activities associated with industrialization and technological advancement, they are likely to become increasingly evident in developing countries as those countries industrialize and engage more and more in technologically based activities like those of the West. Even when specific environmental difficulties are confined to particular regions, secondary effects of these difficulties can have much greater scope; in the era of the global village, the effects of regional problems can travel far and rapidly in a variety of ways. Finally, some aspects of environmental change are intrinsically global; the possibility of atmospheric warming with its attendant climatic changes is the most obvious case in point.

Another characteristic of the problem is the rapidly increasing rate of change in the variables that are likely to have environmental impact. In 1989, MacNeill described the situation this way: "Since 1900, the number of people inhabiting the earth has multiplied more than three times. The world economy has expanded 20 times. The consumption of fossil fuels has grown by a factor of 30, and industrial production has increased by a factor of 50; four fifths of that increase has occurred since 1950" (p. 153). Although its implications for the future are not well understood, there can be little doubt that this rate of growth—to say nothing of the acceleration in the rate of growth—is not sustainable indefinitely. There is room for disagreement on how long it can be sustained, but who can question the impossibility of it continuing indefinitely?

According to the findings of the Earth Transformed Project, an international collaborative effort to document global and regional environmental change, in 7 of 13 dimensions of change considered, "half of all the change during the past 10,000 years happened within our lifetimes" (Kates, 1994, p. 117). The 13 dimensions referred to were: "terrestrial vertebrate diversity, deforested area, soil area loss, sulfur releases, lead releases, carbon tetrachloride releases, marine mammal populations, water withdrawals, floral diversity, carbon releases, nitrogen releases, phosphorus releases and sediment flows" (p. 116).

The problem of environmental change gains urgency from the prospects of some of its more serious aspects getting worse and increasingly difficult to counteract over time. Again, global warming is perhaps the most obvious example of a problem that will be exceedingly difficult to correct if it gets out of hand. The disposal of radioactive waste has also received much attention because it has implications for many years to come. Other problems have the potential to linger for unacceptably long times even after some serious attempt is made to do something about them.

A large ecosystem may be able to absorb a great deal of pollution over the years because of its size. Yet if the effects cumulate exponentially with a long time constant, they may become noticeable only when the rate of change exceeds some threshold, and because the growth is exponential, the point of noticeability may not be far from that at which the situation becomes critical. Delays in dealing with such problems will ensure both amplification of the magnitude of effects and their extension in time; beyond some point of deterioration or depletion, full recovery may not be possible over periods that are meaningful for human planning. In short, failure to address the problem of environmental change effectively now could have disastrous long-term consequences. As difficult as preventing or slowing some types of environmental changes may be, reversing them after they have occurred will be much more difficult and, in some instances, perhaps not possible at all.

CHAPTER

# 3

# Behavior as a Cause of Environmental Change

The foregoing discussion of several aspects of the problem of environmental change is incomplete and fragmentary, but perhaps it suffices to establish the seriousness of the problem. To a substantial degree, the types of detrimental environmental change that are being observed now and those that are anticipated in the future have their causal roots in human behavior.

The ability to affect the global environment in a major way is one that we, as a species, have only relatively recently acquired. When the human population was considerably smaller and technology much less powerful, environmentally detrimental behavior could have local effects, but it was unlikely to cause lasting global damage. The situation is sufficiently different that some scientists have concluded that human behavior has become the primary agent for future global change. Vitousek, Mooney, Lubchenco, and Melillo (1997) reviewed the role of human behavior in transforming from one third to one half of the earth's total land surface, increasing the carbon dioxide in the atmosphere by some 30% since the beginning of the Industrial Revolution, and materially affecting the earth's major ecosystems in a variety of other ways. We live, they concluded, on a human-dominated planet. "The rates, scales, kinds, and combinations of changes occurring now are fundamentally different from those at any other time in history; we are changing Earth more rapidly than we are understanding it" (p. 498).

Gell-Mann (1994) argued that the evolution of human culture is rapidly becoming a more powerful change agent than biological evolution.

> Our effect on the biosphere is so profound and our ability to transform life (not just by ancient and slow procedures like dog breeding but by modern methods like genetic engineering) will soon be so great that the future of life on Earth really does depend in large part on crucial choices made by our species. Barring some spectacular renunciation of technology (very difficult to accomplish in view of the enormous human population we are already committed to sustaining), or the self-destruction of most of the human race—followed by the reversion of the rest to barbarism—it looks as if the role of natural biological evolution in the foreseeable future will be secondary, for better or for worse, to the role of human culture and *its* evolution. (p. 246)

As a species, we interact with the environment in many ways. To survive, we must effect changes; merely to provide ourselves with the nutrients needed to sustain life requires that we decompose some compounds and synthesize others. To have any type of civilization, we must transform some matter into energy and change a certain amount of matter from one form to another. Yet an assumption that underlies this book, and one that I believe most scientists who are concerned about detrimental environmental change make, is that the types of demands that humankind *must* make on the environment are not such as to pose a threat to long-term stability, given a global population not greatly larger than it currently is. (Many would not make the same assumption for a population a lot larger than the present one.) At the present time, the problem seems to be that we are making demands on the environment that are greater than they need to be and are degrading it unnecessarily. At least here the focus is on what is presumed to be *avoidable* detrimental environmental change, one might say change effected by environmental abuse, as distinct from that that might result from judicious environmental use.

An exhaustive list of the things we do that damage the environment and the environmentally beneficial activities that we leave undone would be a long one. I mention a few of the items that would appear on such a list. Other accounts of how human behavior affects the environment, or aspects of it, may be found in Geller, Winett, and Everett (1982), Fischhoff and Furby, (1983), Sjöberg (1989), Turner et al. (1991), Gore (1992), Meadows, Meadows, and Randers (1992), Stern (1992a), Stern, Young, and Druckman (1992), Gardner and Stern (1996), Wackernagel and Rees (1996), and Oskamp (2000).

Individuals act, but so do corporations, communities, and nations. Gardner and Stern (1996) argued that more pollution is caused by organizational than individual behavior. In this chapter, a sharp distinction is not made between individual and organizational behavior; most of the behaviors discussed are engaged in by individuals and organizational entities alike—individuals use energy, for example, as do industries, towns, and countries—and this use can be more or less efficient at all levels. It is obvious that making the behavior of a large organizational entity more environmentally friendly does more good than changing the behavior of a small organizational entity or an individual by a comparable amount, but the behavior of organizations is the consequence of the influence of the individuals who make them up. In the final analysis, it is what individuals do—directly or indirectly through the organizations they comprise or control—that matters.

## INEFFICIENT USE OF ENERGY

Since the beginning of the 20th century, the world population has increased by a factor of about 3.5; during the same period, worldwide energy consumption has increased by a factor of about 15. In other words, there are 3.5 times as many people in the world today as there were in 1900, and each one, on average, is consuming about four times as much energy (Gibbons, Blair, & Gwin, 1989). In view of such numbers, it is not surprising that energy is one of the three major components—along with agriculture and manufacturing—of the growth and globalization of human activity that have had the greatest impact on the environment (Clark, 1989). Anticipated population and economic growth in the near-term future provides the basis for an expectation of continued exponential growth of energy demands (National Research Council, 1979). If historical trends continue unabated, the current level of worldwide energy use could quadruple by the middle of the 21st century, although, according to Starr, Searl, and Alpert (1992), concerted efforts to conserve energy and develop and use energy-efficient systems could reduce this expectation by about one half.

Consumption is much greater, of course, in developed than in developing countries. About one fifth to one fourth of the world's population consumes about 70% of the commercially available energy; so it is not surprising that about three quarters of the world's greenhouse gases are generated by about 20% of the world's population (Oppenheimer & Boyle, 1990). The per capita rate of energy consumption in the United States is a little more than 5 times as great as the world average and over 10 times as great as it is in the Third World (Sassin, 1980; United Nations, 1991). However, the energy demands of Third World countries are increasing rapidly and are expected to grow much faster than those of developed countries in the future. Recently, commercial energy consumption has been increasing at the rate of about 4% per year in less developed countries, which is about four times the rate of increase in industrialized parts of the world (Goldemberg, 1995).

According to the U.S. Department of Energy (1989), as of 1986, the use of energy in the United States was distributed over four major sectors as follows: industrial, 35%; transportation, 28%; residential, 21%; and commercial 16%. Conservation efforts between 1972 and 1986, spurred by the increases in oil prices by the OPEC producers in the early 1970s, were more successful in the industrial and residential sectors than in commerce and transportation; together the industrial and residential sectors accounted for about 74% of the conservation that was achieved. Despite this fact, fewer than one quarter of U.S. households that might have done so claimed tax credits for conservation expenditures (Hirst, Clinton, Geller, & Kroner, 1986). This suggests that the amount of conservation realized was small relative to what could possibly have been achieved.

More generally, the efficiency of energy usage has increased substantially throughout the industrialized world since the early 1970s crisis (Gibbons, Blair, & Gwin, 1989; Hamilton, 1990), but the efficiency increases that have been realized do not come close to what is theoretically realizable (Ross & Williams, 1981; U.S. Department of Energy, 1988). According to some estimates, the United States uses nearly twice as much energy per unit of production as does either Japan or Western Europe (International Energy Agency, 1987). Much greater savings could be realized in the future by the greater use of energy-efficient lighting—in the United States, about one fourth of the electric energy produced is used for lighting purposes (Fickett, Gellings, & Lovins, 1990)—and by the use of control systems to match energy production to short-term fluctuations in need. Greater fuel economies for private automobiles are technically feasible at modest cost over the next few years; however, the availability of low-cost fuel provides a disincentive to realizing them, and there is the possibility that gains effected by more fuel-efficient cars would be offset by more driving as a consequence of the lower per-mile driving cost (DeCicco & Ross, 1994).

The efficiency with which energy is used has significant environmental implications, but this is only part of the story. Assuming that we manage to use energy much more efficiently in the future than we have in the past, the total worldwide demand for energy is likely to continue to increase, and it probably cannot do so indefinitely without serious environmental effects—independently of any risk of depleting limited natural resources. Atmospheric and oceanic heating, with attendant climatological changes, are among the possibilities already noted. Increased energy use seems likely to mean increased production and consumption, more land development, more waste generation, and so on. In other words, greatly increasing the use of energy seems likely to amplify other troublesome environmental effects, most of which require energy to produce.

## OVERRELIANCE ON FOSSIL FUELS

The major sources of energy have changed dramatically during the last century or so. Wood was the dominant source before the 20th century. In industrialized countries, wood gave way to coal, which in many places eventually gave way to oil. Estimates of what percentage of the world's total energy expenditure comes from the burning of fossil fuels vary somewhat, but are in agreement that it is high. Davis (1990) gave 78%; Gibbons, Blair, and Gwin (1989) gave 88%. McKibben (1990) said simply, "Over the last century a human life has become a machine for burning petroleum" (p. 144). Oppenheimer and Boyle (1990) estimated that today oil accounts for about 38% of the energy used worldwide, coal accounts for about 30% and natural gas for about 20%. Gibbons, Blair, and Gwin (1989) pointed out that the amount of fossil fuel expended worldwide in a single year took nature about 1 million years to produce.

Generally speaking, energy generated by the use of renewable resources such as the sun and wind, is preferred to energy generated by the consumption of nonrenewable resources—both because the resources are renewable and because the environmental effects are typically more benign. The means that are used to generate electrical energy have been dictated primarily by economic considerations, but environmentalists are likely to feel that those considerations fail to give appropriate weight to the long-term costs of environmental effects. The figures given in the preceding paragraph vary, of course, from country to country, but in most cases renewable resources account for a small percentage of total use. In addition to environmental issues, the fact that nonrenewable resources are in limited supply is also a matter of concern. Although precisely how much recoverable oil is contained in the world's reserves is not known with any precision, some specialists believe that the demand for oil will begin to be greater than production in the relatively near future (Anderson, 1998; Campbell & Laherrère, 1998; Deffeyes, 2001).

The consumption of fossil fuels and the high-temperature smelting of metallic ores are the major sources of atmospheric pollution (National Research Council, 1981). The burning of fossil fuels is a major source of the atmospheric carbon dioxide believed to be contributing to increased greenhouse warming (Schneider, 1989b). It, in conjunction with other human activities, is believed to be responsible for about 90% of all the sulfur, the major ingredient in the production of acid rain, that is emitted into the atmosphere (Likens, Wright, Galloway, & Butler, 1979). It contributes to the dispersal of such toxic metals as mercury, lead, zinc, and cadmium (Bertine & Goldberg, 1971; National Research Council, 1980).

According to a National Research Council (1981) estimate, the total consumption of fossil fuel energy has increased by about 5% per year, on average, since 1900. This means that the consumption has doubled approximately every 15 years, which represents a 100-fold increase over the course of the century. There is little evidence that the demands for fossil-fuel energy are likely to decrease in the near future; rather, the expectation is that they will grow at a rapid rate. Since the 1992 Earth Summit in Rio de Janeiro, at which the participating nations agreed to attempt to stabilize greenhouse gas emissions, the use of fossil fuels globally has continued to increase (Herzog, Eliasson, & Kaarstad, 2000).

## OVERRELIANCE ON INEFFICIENT TRANSPORTATION

U.S. citizens rely on private transportation—personally owned automobiles—more than do the citizens of any other country. The population of cars in the United States was about 140 million in 1988—about one car for every 1.75 persons (Bureau of the Census, 1990). This compares with a world average of about one car for every 10 people; the 140 million cars in the United States represent about 28% of all the cars in the world (Compton & Gjostein, 1986). In the former Soviet Union, the ratio of cars to people was about 1 to 20; in China, it was about 1 to 1,000.

About one fourth of all energy used in the United States is used for transportation (Transportation Research Board, 1988). According to Bleviss and Walzer (1990), about half of the world's oil consumption is used to fuel road vehicles. Before the use of leaded gasoline was curtailed, the automobile was believed to account for about 60% of the air pollution in the United States (Dorf, 1974). Even after the banning of leaded gasoline, the introduction of catalytic converters, and the development of more energy-efficient engines, about 20% of the carbon dioxide emissions to the atmosphere in the United States comes from the burning of fuel used for personal transportation (Office of Technology Assessment, 1991).

Worldwide, the population of cars is increasing faster than the population of people; one prediction has the total number quadrupling between the late 1980s and 2025 (Keyfitz, 1989). In view of the fact that automobiles are major consumers of fossil fuels, major emitters of atmospheric pollutants, major sources of urban congestion and noise, and a major contributor to accidental deaths, the anticipated rate of growth in their numbers and utilization over the next few decades is sobering.

## INEFFICIENT USE OF WATER

Greatly increased use of irrigation—the amount of irrigated land worldwide tripled between 1950 and 1985 (Postel, 1985)—in conjunction with the use of fertilizers, pesticides and herbicides, and genetically altered crops, has been largely responsible for farmers' ability to meet the ever-increasing food demands of a rapidly growing population. According to World Bank figures, the spread of irrigation accounted for half or more of the increase in agricultural output of developing countries from 1960 to 1980 (Crossen & Rosenberg, 1989). Expansion of water usage at anything like the recent rate cannot continue indefinitely, however; in some areas, supplies are already being strained.

As it is currently practiced in many places, irrigation is highly inefficient because only a small percentage of the water used actually gets to the roots of the growing plants (La Rivière, 1989). Moreover, unless irrigation is properly controlled, not only can it deplete the aquifer from which the water is drawn, but it can degrade the quality of the soil for future use by causing the build up of salt. That irrigation can have detrimental long-term effects on soil is not a new problem; the demise of several ancient civilizations has been attributed to the salinization of their once arable lands as a consequence of irrigation (Pillsbury, 1981).

Although agriculture accounts for more water worldwide than do all other uses combined, the other uses are not incidental, and inefficiencies deserve attention in both industry and the home. Efforts to encourage water conservation in home use have resulted in the occasional publication of estimates of how much can be saved in a typical household as a consequence of various actions—fixing leaky faucets, installing water-conserving shower heads and toilets, adopting water-conserving methods of showering, tooth brushing, dishwashing, and so on. Little is known regarding the extent to which recommended practices are being adopted, however, and how much impact their adoption is having. Many communities impose restrictions on water use for such purposes as lawn and garden watering and car washing; such restrictions are often motivated by concern about abnormally low water supplies and a desire to avoid the realization of emergency levels.

## BURNING OF TROPICAL FORESTS

Data collected on space flights by NASA indicate that, contrary to the prevailing belief that most of the carbon dioxide in the atmosphere comes from the burning of fossil fuels, a probably equal amount comes from the burning of tropical rainforests and savannas (Newell, Reichle, & Seiler, 1989). The burning of fossil fuels is believed to be the major source of atmospheric carbon dioxide in the Northern Hemisphere while the burning of biomass is seen as the major source of it in the Southern Hemisphere. Gases other than carbon dioxide that are emitted into the atmosphere in significant quantities by the burning of biomass in the tropics include carbon monoxide, several hydrocarbons, especially methane, and a variety of other compounds (Crutzen & Andreae, 1990).

The slashing and burning of tropical forests for agricultural purposes account for about 70% of the loss of forest lands in Central America, where about

55% of the forest land has already disappeared. The remaining 30% of the loss is attributed about evenly to timber extraction and cattle ranching (Robinson, 1991). In other parts of the world, the use of wood for domestic fuel is a major factor in forest depletion. According to Robinson, one and one-half billion people worldwide get more than 90% of their energy from fuelwood.

## PRACTICE OF NONSUSTAINABLE AGRICULTURE

Agriculture in the United States and some other industrialized countries has been an unparalleled success story from some points of view. The productivity of the average U.S. farm worker has steadily increased as the fraction of the working population required to produce more than enough food for the entire nation has steadily decreased from about 70% during the middle of the 19th century to less than 3% today. One hundred and seventy years ago, the average farm worker produced enough food and fiber for about four people. Today, one farmer can provide enough for almost 20 times that many; the number of person hours needed to produce 100 pounds of cotton in the United States went from about 42 in 1945 to about .07 in 1975 (Rasmussen, 1982).

Unfortunately, the same technological developments—the use of fertilizers and pesticides, irrigation, and application of scientifically gained knowledge about crop rotation, irrigation, breeding, and hybridization—have had unanticipated environmental costs. Moreover, those costs have escalated to the point of global concern as the total amount of cultivated land worldwide has increased dramatically during the last couple of centuries in keeping with the increase in the world population (Matson, Parton, Power, & Swift, 1997). If the population doubles during the 21st century, as some projections suggest it will, the agricultural challenge will be, as Crosson and Rosenberg (1989) put it, "not only to provide food for the 10 billion people who will probably be living a century from now but also to achieve that level of production with less environmental damage than is apparent today" (p. 132).

In Crosson and Rosenberg's view, this means reducing the environmental burden of pesticides and fertilizers, reducing the demand for irrigation water, and improving crop production per unit of land use. These writers argue that more difficult than the development of new technologies and management practices for accomplishing these goals will be creation of the policies and institutions that will induce farmers to adopt them. They surmise that the most successful approaches will involve the merging of individual and societal interests rather than the enforcing of one type of interest over the other. Others have claimed that even a 50% increase in world population will ensure that the demand for food will be the major driver of environmental change during the 21st century, and that the discovery and implementation of mechanisms and policies for keeping the impact within acceptable bounds is a major challenge (Tilman et al., 2001).

Unsustainable agricultural practices are those that cannot be continued indefinitely because they make the land less and less suitable for farming purposes. Whether sustainable practices are seen as cost-effective may depend on how much long-term and off-farm effects (e.g., soil erosion, groundwater contamination from pesticide and fertilizer runoff, and destruction of wildlife habitat) are taken into account (Holmes, 1993).

It is assumed that what developing countries need is an infusion of agricultural technology from the industrialized world so they can become agriculturally self-sufficient in the same way. This assumption is being challenged, and more thought is being given to alternative approaches to agriculture that will permit developing countries to meet their food needs in cost-effective, but sustainable, ways (Bray, 1994).

## NONSUSTAINABLE HARVESTING OF FORESTS AND FOREST PRODUCTS

The worldwide demand for wood and wood products has kept pace with the increasing world population. The demand comes from developed and undeveloped countries alike, but the supply has come, more and more, from parts of the world (e.g., West Africa and Southeast Asia) where old-growth forests have represented an opportunity to generate much-needed cash. The rush to meet the demand for wood and wood products has led, in several tropical countries, to a boom-and-bust pattern of forest harvesting and exportation, in which initially high earnings give way to forest depletion and economic decline (Repetto & Gillis, 1988; Vincent, 1992).

In some parts of the world, especially in densely populated areas not heavily industrialized, the demand for firewood greatly exceeds the sustainable supply. As of 1982, India, for example, had an estimated fuelwood demand of 133 million tons, whereas its forest land could sustain an annual harvest of only 39 million tons (Brown, 1991). Overcutting is one response to this problem. Similar situations prevail in many parts of Africa. Despite considerable attention to the problem and several international initiatives to conserve forest lands, somewhat less than .02% of the world's tropical forests were being managed for sustainability as of 1998 (Bowles, Rice, Mittermeier, & de Fonseca, 1998). Moreover, how best to manage forest resources is a matter of continuing debate (Chazdon, 1998).

*Sustainable forestry*, in its broadest sense, refers to the preservation not only of trees and vegetation, but also of forest animals. Several countries have been adopting policies aimed at encouraging the sustainable harvesting and use of forest products, including wildlife. The problem of ensuring the preservation of viable populations of many species, especially of larger animals that are hunted for consumption or sale as food, is complicated by the greatly increased ease of access to forest interiors as a consequence of road networks developed to service the logging industry (Robinson, Redford, & Bennett, 1999).

## OVERUTILIZATION OF OTHER NATURAL RESOURCES

More nonfuel mineral resources have been consumed worldwide during the half century since the end of World War II than during all preceding human history (Wellmer & Kursten, 1992). Whether this should be considered overutilization can be debated because estimates of remaining reserves are crude and have tended to increase along with consumption (Hodges, 1995). However, it seems clear that a rapidly accelerating rate of consumption cannot continue indefinitely, although projected population growth and the industrialization of developing countries suggest that it is expected to do so.

The nonsustainable harvesting of forests and forest products is symptomatic of the more general problem of treating many natural resources as if the supply were unlimited and thereby risking depletion. Some natural resources, like fossil fuels, exist in finite, albeit unknown, quantity and do not replenish themselves on a time scale relevant to near-future generations. Others renew themselves at least under favorable conditions. Resources of the latter type presumably can be used indefinitely, provided the level of ongoing use is not so high as to disturb the renewal process.

A prime example of a renewable source of food is fish. Until fairly recently, this source was viewed as essentially inexhaustible; the worldwide catch was constrained only by the size of the global fishing fleet. We now know that the supply is exhaustible, and that some species currently are in danger of being fished to extinction (McGinn, 1998). In addition to overfishing, pollution, especially of coastal areas, contributes to dwindling populations of many species of fish. Roughly half of the species in American and European waters for which assessments have been made have been classified as overutilized. Although sustainable harvesting of fish and other marine resources is seen to be an attainable goal from a technological point of view, achieving it will require the resolution of nontrivial political issues (Rosenberg, Fogarty, Sissenwine, Beddington, & Shepherd, 1993).

MacNeill (1989) noted that most developing countries as well as parts of many industrialized countries have resource-based economies, which is to say economies are based on their stocks of environmental resources, and that the poorer countries have been depleting this capital over the recent past. The obstacles to sustainable economic development, MacNeill argued, are primarily social, institutional, and political. Many of the agricultural practices most destructive of the environment are direct consequences of governmental policies that provide incentives for such practices (e.g., clearing of forests, planting of marginal lands, excessive use of fertilizers and pesticides, and of water in inefficient irrigation systems).

## DESTRUCTION OF HABITAT

Wildlife habitat is destroyed whenever forests are cleared or wetlands reclaimed for agricultural, industrial, or residential use. Few people would argue that all forests and wetlands should be preserved in their pristine states, which would be tantamount to taking the position that any use of land for agricultural, industrial, or residential purposes is bad. Yet indiscriminate clearing or reclamation can have long-term detrimental effects that may outweigh the benefits even if only the welfare of our own species is taken into account. With respect to other species, the loss of habitat can mean, in some cases, a greatly increased probability of extinction.

## USE OF CHLOROFLUOROCARBONS (CFCs)

The increased concentration of CFCs in the stratosphere is believed to be a direct consequence of the wide use of CFC products. This is an interesting case of a problem growing out of what was believed to be a solution to an earlier concern. When invented by Thomas Midgley in 1931, CFCs (nontoxic, nonflammable, and noncorrosive) seemed an ideal solution to the nasty environmental and safety problems associated with the toxic, flammable, corrosive chemicals such as ammonia and sulfur dioxide that were then being used in home refrigerators. They were quickly adopted for that purpose (Glas, 1989); in time they were also used as aerosol propellants, foam-blowing agents, and solvents. No one suspected that their emission to the atmosphere could have the negative effects they are now believed to have.

There seems to be fairly general agreement among governments that CFC emissions must be reduced—witness the "Montreal Protocol," an international agreement that called for a 50% reduction in the production of CFCs by the end of the 20th Century (United Nations Environment Program, 1987) and the European Economic Community's 1989 announcement of its intention to ban *all* uses of CFCs by the end of the century (Dickson & Marshall, 1989), but effecting an adequate reduction without causing major economic and standard-of-living problems has been seen as a major challenge. As of 1989, the installed equipment in the United States that is dependent on CFC products was estimated, to be worth more than $135 billion (Glas, 1989).

Although the use of CFCs as aerosol propellants has declined markedly over the past two decades, some other uses have not. In general, however, the effort to cut back production and use of CFCs globally seems to be having an effect. According to one study, worldwide consumption of CFCs, after maintaining a plateau from the early 1970s through the early 1980s, grew from roughly 875 million kilograms around 1983 to about 1.3 billion kilograms in 1988, and then dropped to about 510 million kilograms by 1990 (French, 1994). Another study concluded that tropospheric chlorine attributed to anthropogenic halogens peaked in 1994 and began declining slightly thereafter (Montzka et al., 1996).

## UNNECESSARY RELEASE OF TOXIC MATERIALS

Toxic materials are released to the soil, water, or air by many industrial processes. Until quite recently, information regarding who was releasing what was not readily available to the general public or even, in many cases, to policymakers. This situation was changed by the Emergency Planning and Community Right-To-Know Act of 1986, which requires that the Environmental Protection Agency prepare annually a Toxic Release Inventory that reports the amount of toxic material released by each manufacturing facility. This information is available to the general public and can be accessed in paper or electronic form (U.S. Environmental Protection Agency, 1989). The Act appears to have motivated considerable activity by private industry (Baram, Dillon, & Ruffle, 1990).

I have already mentioned the extensive use of pesticides and herbicices in agriculture as a major source of toxins that can accumulate in the soil. Seepage of chemicals from materials discarded in landfill dumps is another source of ground toxins. The use of cyanide to stun tropical fish, thus making them easier to catch to service a world market, has been the cause of the destruction of coral reefs in the Phillipines, Indonesia, and other parts of Southeast Asia (Simpson, 2001).

## BUSINESS DECISIONS

Although the private business sector has been associated with environmental problems primarily in connection with by-products and waste from production processes and with unintentional releases to the environment, it makes many decisions that can have positive or negative environmental effects (Rappaport & Dillon, 1991). Decisions that have environmental implications include those regarding what products the company will offer, the materials it will use in the manufacturing process, the technology that will be used to produce its products, the company location, and others. Even the accounting methods it will use can be environmentally relevant: "use of methods that discount future environmental liability or that require rapid payback to show profitability will prevent a company from investing in process changes that reduce waste at the source" (p. 242). Rappaport and Dillon argued that, "the key change required of industry to support sustainable development and improve environmental management is a shift from short- to long-term planning horizons" (p. 261).

## UNNECESSARY WASTE GENERATION

Waste is unavoidable in any society, but how much is generated depends on attitudes and behavior of producers and consumers alike. There seems to be little question that we are generating much more waste than is necessary or than is in our best long-term interest. Ours is a throw-away society. We manufacture countless products intended to be used once and then discarded: paper and plastic eating utensils, paper towels, disposable diapers, unrefillable pens, and so on. I do not mean to argue that such products have no legitimate uses, but I do suggest that, as a society, we make far greater use of disposable products than we probably would if we were more sensitive to the long-term implications of this practice and less influenced by the momentary convenience.

Most of the consumer goods we buy come packaged in one way or another. About 75% of all glass and about 50% of all paper is used for packaging purposes (Wahl & Allison, 1975). Some items are packaged that need not be; many are overpackaged, which is to say that much more material is used for the packaging than is necessary.

Unnecessary or excessive packaging presumably serves a variety of purposes, such as inhibition of shop-lifting (by making items larger and more difficult to conceal in pockets), advertising (making items more conspicuous), and consumer convenience (individually wrapped cheese slices, single-serving packages of cereal). Whether the advantages that this wasteful use of resources represent are worth their costs, to the consumer and to society as a whole, is questionable. We need a better understanding of the various purposes that product packaging serves and the exploration of resource-efficient ways of realizing those purposes.

## IMPROPER WASTE DISPOSAL

The improper disposal of waste material has received considerable attention from the media in recent years. Stories that make the news tend to be those that involve incidents of illegal dumping of toxic wastes by one or another industrial or military establishment. There have been many of them, including several that have led to class-action suits against the alleged polluters. The pollution of waterways by the discharge of raw or inadequately treated sewage and waste products from industrial processes has also been a focus of concern. Perhaps because of the media attention that this problem has received, toxic waste disposal appears to be among the more prominent environmental concerns of the American public (Kohut & Shriver, 1989).

Improper disposal of industrial wastes can be seen as one way of charging part of the real cost of the products we use today to future generations. Peterson (1991) put it this way: "The dumping of hazardous wastes over past decades permitted the selling in the marketplace of better things for better living at lower costs. But now it appears that it will take fifty years and hundreds of billions of dollars, charged to future production and future taxpayers, to clean up the inherited mess" (p. 192).

The U.S. military has been criticized by the media for its long history of contributing to environmental degradation in a variety of ways and without, until recently, even the same degree of accountability as private industry. According to Renner (1991), it is responsible for more pollution than the top five international corporations combined. Pointing to thousands of acres containing abandoned unexploded ordnance; polychlorinated biphenyls, benzene, trichloroethylene, and other toxic chemicals; spilled oil and other fuels; and lead and other heavy metals, *Time* magazine referred to the military as the nation's Number 1 polluter (Van Voorst, 1992). (By one estimate, 30% of the bombs dropped on the Ho Chi Minh Trail in eastern Laos during the Vietnam War failed to explode [Lovering, 2001].) The cost of cleanup is impossible to estimate with any confidence, but analysts agree that it will be very high. Recently, the EPA issued an order to the military to find and remove unexploded ordnance from the Massachusetts Military Reservation on Cape Cod; an initial, but tentative, estimate of the cost of this one operation was $320 million (Williams, 2000).

Less dramatic, but no less problematic, are the difficulties associated with the disposal of household trash. Until fairly recently, the conventional way to dispose of almost all types of trash was to deposit it at the community dump, usually located at the edge of town, where it was either used as landfill or burned. We now know that this relatively uncontrolled method of disposal has many environmental liabilities, including the possibility of long-term seepage of toxic materials into underground water reservoirs and the problems that burning entails. The use of community dumps is becoming much more tightly managed than it was in the past, and certain materials that once were acceptable for disposal are no longer so. These include automobile tires, used motor oil, oil-based paints, and household solvents and other chemicals. As a consequence of effective recycling, composting, incineration, and salvage, the accumulation of solid waste could be drastically reduced, possibly by as much as 90%, according to one estimate (Daniels, 1992).

Littering, a manifestation of improper waste disposal, is prevalent in many local areas, and that began to receive national attention in the United States as a result of the Keep-America-Beautiful campaign in the late 1960s and early 1970s (Keep America Beautiful, Inc., 1968, 1970). This problem does not pose the threat to irreversible change that many of the other problems considered in this book pose, but it is an irritant to many people and especially frustrating because it seems to reflect a "the-world-is-my-personal-waste-basket" attitude on the part of the people who litter.

Although changes have been made in the waste-disposal policies and procedures of many communities in recent years, including in some cases, the closing of dumps altogether, the question of how to dispose of community wastes in environmentally benign ways cannot be considered answered in any final sense. There remains a need for the development of better approaches than those that now exist and also for a better understanding of how to ensure the compliance of individual residents with the policies and approaches adopted in the interest of environmental preservation.

## EXCESSIVE CONSUMPTION

Consumer buying is generally seen as a positive thing from an economic point of view. When consumers buy goods and services, the production of those goods and services provides jobs and livelihoods to people and the economy is robust; when consumers fail to buy, job opportunities decrease and the economy suffers. The greater the consumer demand, the healthier the economy will be—or at least that is the prevailing assumption.

This view is being challenged as an oversimplified representation of the facts. What it overlooks are the potentially enormous long-term costs of overconsumption. These costs are largely unaccounted for, indeed unrecognized, and are sometimes exacted through environmental devastation. Sadly, according to some observers, even forgetting its unaccounted-for long-term costs, overconsumption does not satisfy the social, psychological, and spiritual needs to which the promotion of unconstrained consumerism often appeals.

The rapidity of the growth of consumerism over the last few decades has been phenomenal. "Measured in constant dollars, the world's peoples have consumed as many goods and services since 1950 as all previous generations put together. Since 1940, Americans alone have used up as large a share of the earth's mineral resources as did everyone before them combined" (Durning, 1992, p. 38). These are impressive and thought-provoking claims.

The problem of overconsumption is exacerbated by the enormous disparities among the various parts of the world with respect to the demand for energy and material goods. According to Durning (1992), the industrialized countries, which contain about one fourth of the world's population, account for over 80% of the world's consumption of chemicals, paper, aluminum, iron, and steel. Daly (1993) asked the obvious question: "What will happen if the entire population of the earth consumes resources at the rate of high-wage countries?" (p. 54). Perhaps the question should not be "if," but "when"; China's rate of economic growth alone—a doubling of GNP between 1980 and 1990 (Oppenheimer & Boyle, 1990)—suggests the time may not be as far in the future as one might have thought.

This question is simply ignored by many economists, Daly claimed. But the push to bring the consumption of three quarters of the world more into line with that of the industrialized countries is strong. Many in the business community see the underdeveloped world as emerging markets for their products and are working hard to accelerate that emergence. We who live in the industrialized world, and enjoy the superabundance of consumer goods, are in no position to criticize those who live in the underdeveloped world for wanting to do so too. What is really unsettling, however, is the thought that by the middle of the 21st century there could be twice as many of us, all wanting ever more.

Daly (1993) argued that we need to make "the elementary distinction between growth (a quantitative increase in size resulting from the accretion or assimilation of materials) and development (the qualitative evolution to a fuller, better or different state)" (p. 57). This could be a difficult distinction for many to accept. Growth has been equated with progress in Western economic thought for a long time. An expanding consumer base—not just a growing population, but a growing population with increasing purchasing power—has been seen as the engine that drives the economy and keeps it robust. "An economy that is steady in scale" but is able "to develop a greater capacity to satisfy human wants"—Daly's description of what is needed—is likely to prove to be a hard sell. As Schumacher (1973) put it, "There are poor societies which have too little; but where is the rich society that says: 'Halt! We have enough?' There is none" (p. 25).

I do not mean to suggest that the problem of overconsumption is a simple one and that the solution to it is obvious if only we had the will to effect it. Some changes in prevailing beliefs regarding the importance of a superabundance of material goods as the *sine qua non* of the good life would undoubtedly be useful, but not necessarily a complete solution. Myers (1997) argued that consumption, as such, is not the problem, but the overconsumption of unrecyclable resources—the use of resources that are limited and not easily recycled as if they were inexhaustible: "A key question is whether consumption uses resources or uses them up" (p. 54). Vincent and Panayotou (1997) also argued that the main problem is not overall level of consumption, but consumption unguided by environmental concerns: "The root cause of environmental degradation is not the level of consumption, but rather market and policy failures that cause consumers and producers to ignore the full social costs of their decisions.... Attention should focus on changing consumption and production patterns, not on capping consumption levels" (p. 56).

The distinction between consumption of limited nonrenewable resources and plentiful or easily renewed resources is undoubtedly an important one from an environmental point of view, and decreasing consumption of the former clearly deserves more effort than decreasing consumption of the latter. However, as long as consumerism retains the *summum bonum* status that it now seems to enjoy in developed countries, it is doubtful whether this distinction will have much practical effect. The assumptions underlying the promotion of life styles that depend on unrestrained consumerism as the best, or only, way to personal and national happiness deserve closer scrutiny than they usually get (Elgin, 1993).

To this point, the emphasis in my examples of behavioral contributions to environmental change has been on *sins of commission*, things we do that have, or can have, detrimental environmental effects. There are also *sins of omission*, or, if one prefers, problems of neglect. They involve failures of purpose, failures of motivation or resolve, and failures of execution. In some cases, something is being done, but not enough, so the problem is to increase the extent and effectiveness of an existing effort. In other cases, essentially nothing is being done.

## FAILURE TO CONSIDER LONG-TERM AND INDIRECT COSTS AND BENEFITS

Much of the human behavior that has significant environmental implications is motivated by financial or economic factors. However, the costs and benefits that are considered, tend to be short term only. Moreover, they tend to be only those that are to be borne or realized directly by the individuals (companies, industries, countries) involved. The prices of timber on the international market, for example, reflect the immediate commercial value of wood, and are not much influenced by the long-term value of forests as sources of benefits, such as the provision of biological habitat, absorption of carbon dioxide from the atmosphere, or growth of harvestable nontimber forest products.

Quantifying costs and benefits is difficult in some environmental contexts. How the value of the benefits derived from the preservation of a tropical forest compare with the income that can be realized from logging and agricultural use of the land may depend, for example, on the perspective—local, national, or global—from which the assessment is made. A continuing challenge is that of finding ways to compensate nations or regions for taking actions for global benefit at local expense (Kremen et al., 2000).

The almost exclusive focus of private enterprise on short-term goals is common knowledge. Businesses appear not to be unique in this regard, however. In general, neither currently incurred costs that must be paid by future generations nor the possibility of establishing benefits that would accrue to them are given much weight in decisions that determine here-and-now behavior, and this pertains not only to businesses but to individuals and governments. To make the point in slightly different terms, we appear to be willing to purchase present comforts and conveniences at great cost so long as the bill is to be paid in future generations' coin.

## FAILURE TO MAINTAIN AND REPAIR

I am not aware of reliable figures that would give a clear indication of what percentage of the potential use we get, on the average, from the various products and consumer goods we buy and use, but I suspect that if such figures were available they would show that we typically do not realize anything close to what is possible. My suspicion is that we tend to "wear things out" and discard them without getting from them what they have the potential to deliver.

In other words, according to this conjecture, we do not do a good job of maintaining vehicles, appliances, electromechanical equipment, or even simple household and personal items with a view to keeping them in serviceable condition for a long time. Often, our tendency is to give inadequate attention to maintenance and to discard and replace items that are still serviceable or at least have the potential to be put into serviceable condition.

I am not arguing that it is necessarily wrong to wish to replace an old but still serviceable item with a new one, but I do mean to suggest that a concern for environmental preservation should motivate us to maintain equipment in such a way as to prolong its useful life and attempt to see that it gets to another user, rather than to the dump, if we elect to replace it while it is still serviceable.

Failure to maintain can have an adverse effect on the environment not only by way of wasteful use of resources, but in other ways as well. In the United States, urban carbon monoxide comes primarily from motor vehicle emissions; such emissions are also major contributors of ground-level ozone and the hydrocarbons and oxides of nitrogen from which urban smog is formed. As a consequence of the institution of emission control policies and regulations, late model vehicles emit less, on the average, than older models. However, measurements of on-road vehicle emissions have shown that differences due to different states of maintenance for vehicles of a given age are greater than differences attributable to the average effect of vehicle age (Beaton, Bishop, Zhang, Ashbaugh, Lawson, & Stedman, 1995).

## FAILURE TO RECYCLE

Many communities have established recycling facilities and programs. Provisions vary from recycling centers, to which people can bring specified materials for disposal, to curbside pickup of recyclable trash on a regularly scheduled basis (Milner, 1989). Some curbside pickup programs require the recyclable trash to be separated before pickup into several categories (e.g., paper, glass, metals, plastics), others permit all types to be commingled, and some require intermediate degrees of separation. The community in which I live requires a two-way separation into paper and containers (glass, metals, plastics). There is at least suggestive evidence that curbside recyclable trash pickup programs that allow commingling of the various types of recyclable material attract more participants than programs that require separation; some such programs have been considered successful if falling short of their full potential (Gamba & Oskamp, 1994; Oskamp, 1995).

More generally, however, although it is too early to tell how successful specific programs will be in the long run, community recycling efforts appear to have been only marginally successful so far. This is despite the fact that most people, when asked, express support for the idea of recycling (Belsie, 1990; DeYoung, 1989). The disparity between what people say and what they do with respect to recycling has led some investigators to think of recycling as altruistic behavior: When it comes to altruism, most of us are apparently more likely to approve of it than to practice it (Hopper & Nielsen, 1991). Early studies indicate that efforts to get people to voluntarily recycle paper (Couch, Garber, & Karpus, 1978–1979; Geller, Chaffee, & Ingram, 1975) or plastics (Powell, 1990) have been less than spectacularly successful.

Only about 20% of the paper, plastic, glass, and metal goods made in the United States are made from recycled materials, although roughly 50% could be and at considerably less expenditure of energy than is required to make the same goods from new raw materials (Ross & Steinmeyer, 1990). Some metals represent an exception to this generalization because, in these cases, recycled material accounts for more than half of the total production (Makar, 1993). Apparently this is because recovering certain metals from scrap requires less energy and, therefore, is less costly than extracting them from ore.

Most studies of recycling have focused on the behavior of individuals or families; by comparison, relatively little attention has been given to date to recycling by businesses, which produce about half the country's solid waste (Oskamp et al., 1994). Multiapartment dwellings pose special problems for recycling that have barely begun to be addressed (Yuhas & Hyde, 1991).

## FAILURE TO DESIGN FOR MAINTAINABILITY, REPAIRABILITY, RECYCLABILITY, AND DISPOSABILITY

*Planned obsolescence* is an interesting concept. The idea is that of designing products so they will become obsolete relatively quickly, thus ensuring a market for successor products. Whether products are sometimes actually designed in accordance with this idea, I do not know. What does seem fairly clear is that during the design process, too little emphasis is placed on such considerations as maintainability, repairability, recyclability, and disposability, especially the latter two. This is a serious neglect for industries whose products are known to have a short life expectancy. The computer industry is a case in point. Technology has been advancing so rapidly in this field that computers become outmoded almost as soon as they are purchased, and there appears to be little demand for used machines. According to a recent *Scientific American* news item, the result is that an estimated 20.6 million PCs fell into disuse in 1998, only about 11% of which were recycled (Pescovitz, 2000). According to the same item, as many as 150 million PC carcasses, with their leachable lead, mercury, and chromium components, could be in U.S. landfills by 2005.

Little consideration is given to such questions as: Are there other uses that might be found for a product when it is no longer usable for its primary intended purpose? How can the design be improved from the point of view of maximizing recyclability of a product or its components? What kinds of problems will unrecyclable parts of the product cause when they are ready for disposal?

## FAILURE TO LIMIT POPULATION GROWTH

Much of the behavior believed to be responsible for many aspects of detrimental environmental change today is not particularly new. Evidence of abusive land use goes back at least to the ancient Greeks (Runnels, 1995). What is different is that there are many more of us today; with the help of technology, we have multiplied manyfold the environmental damage that each of us can inflict.

A simple model of how population combines with two other variables to determine the impact of human behavior on the global environment has been proposed by Ehrlich and Holdren (1971; Ehrlich & Ehrlich, 1991). According to this model, environment impact is determined by the multiplicative interaction of three variables—a population's size, the average affluence of its members, and the environmental effect of the technologies (per unit of affluence) on which that affluence rests. In other words, each of these variables can be thought as an amplifier of the effects of the other two. More affluent people tend to have a greater impact on the environment than less affluent people, and the more of them there are the greater the impact in the aggregate. Technology can either magnify or decrease the (detrimental) effects of behavior, depending, for example, on the extent to which it is designed to be environmentally friendly. Oskamp (2000) pointed out that decreasing average affluence is unlikely to be as attractive an alternative for environmental protection as limiting population growth and finding more effective ways of exploiting technology to the environment's benefit.

The population of a species—human or other—can exceed the carrying capacity of the area it inhabits—the size of the population the area can support indefinitely—only for a limited time because the continuing excessive demand makes the area less and less habitable. Resources needed to sustain life become depleted beyond the level at which they can replenish themselves—the seed corn is eaten—and a reduction in population is forced by circumstances. Such a reduction sometime takes the form of a crash, which brings the population far below the area's original carrying capacity. How many people the earth can support indefinitely—the earth's human carrying capacity—has been the subject of debate for a long time. Estimates have varied over an astonishingly wide range, from as low as fewer than 3 billion to as high as 1 trillion (Cohen, 1995). Cohen's analysis of a large set of such estimates that are in the literature, beginning with one of 13.4 billion by Leeuwenhoek in the 18th century, suggests that from about 8 billion to about 12 billion might be considered as close to a consensus range as one is likely to be able to identify.

Uncertainty about the earth's carrying capacity notwithstanding, there can be no doubt that many scientists consider the increasing population to be the single greatest threat to the future quality of the environment (Brown, 1991; Brown & Kane, 1994; Cousteau, 1991; Ehrlich, 1991; Hodges, 1995; Keyfitz, 1989; Petereson, 1991). This is not the same as claiming that bringing population growth under control now would automatically make everything else all right; but it is to say that if population is not brought under control, little else that is done will matter much for very long.

It is sobering indeed to reflect that the world's population today is more than six times as large as it was 200 years ago (according to U.N. figures, it had not yet reached 1 billion by 1800), and that at the most recent doubling (from 3 billion–6 billion only took about 40 years. Nevertheless, it must be pointed out that not all scientists are convinced that there is necessarily a population explosion problem, or at least it is the case that not all scientists believe the population will continue spontaneously to grow exponentially until the growth is stopped by a disastrous corrective process. Deevey (1960; Kates, 1994) believes that we are currently partway through the third of three major surges in world population in human history. Each surge is assumed to have been caused by a technological advance that increased the carrying capacity of the earth, the first by the emergence of tool making, the second by the spread of agriculture, and the third by industrialization. This analysis supports the expectation that the rate of population increase will fall off and that the population will more or less stabilize, as it has following the earlier surges, when the current surge runs out of steam—perhaps during the next century.

This view gets some support from statistics showing a recent decline in population growth in certain parts of the world, especially in the developed countries (Bongaarts, 1998; United Nations, 1998). However, although the rate of increase has declined somewhat after hitting a high in the 1960s, sustaining the current rate will produce a doubling during the 21st century. According to the World Resources Institute (1992), the high was more than 2.5% per years; Horiuchi (1992) gave 2.06% per year as the high; these two sources are close with their estimates of the rate as of the early 1990s, however, at somewhere around 1.7%.

Howard (2000) pointed out that despite the fact that the growth rate declined regularly over the three decades from 1960 to 1990, the annual increments in world population increased during each of those decades: "Records for increases in world population continue to be broken year after year, with little respect for this trend reversing in the foreseeable future" (p. 150). In its projections issued in 1998, the Population Division of the United Nations projected the world population in 2050 to be between 7.3 and 10.7 billion, with 8.9 billion as the most likely count (Potts, 2000). The 1997 *Statistical Abstract of the United States* (U.S. Bureau of the Census, 1997) shows the expected growth rate decreasing steadily to around 0.6% in 2040. This yields an expected world population of about 9.3 billion in 2050—an increase of about 64% over the population in 1995.

The growth is expected to come mainly in the developing world—especially Africa, Asia, and Latin America (Bongaarts, 1998; Potts, 2000)—which is projected to at least double by mid-century, whereas the developed world is expected to have about the same population in 2050 as it does now. The projections are sensitive, of course, to fractional changes in the fertility rate (United Nations, 1996, 1998). According to Bolin (1998), the population is expected to be at about 7 billion by 2010, and at that time about 80% of it will be living in developing countries. Recently, the population has been growing about five times as fast in developing regions of the world as in developed ones (United Nations, 1994). In less developed countries, the growth in population is being accompanied by a rapid increase in urbanization. Keyfitz (1989) pointed out the although only about 17% of the population in these countries was urban in 1950, over 50% of it is expected to be by 2000.

One example of a region that has especially high population growth is sub-Saharan Africa. The relatively high fertility of this region is attributed to socioreligious factors, such as the association of child bearing with virtue and barrenness with evil, the expectation of fathers to receive more from their children than they spend on them, a form of land tenure that gives large families a greater share of land, and a belief that the deceased maintain contact with the living and a consequently deeply rooted fear of dying without descendants (Caldwell & Caldwell, 1990). Caldwell & Caldwell anticipated a decline in fertility as a consequence of a confluence of factors that will moderate some of these effects, but probably not until the population of this area has reached 2.5 billion by the late 21st century. My purpose in mentioning this situation is not to pass judgment on the belief system that motivates the high birth rate in this part of the world, but simply to illustrate that the reasons for continuing population expansion are complex and differ in different areas. Research could provide a better understanding of the relative importance of the various reasons—lack of information regarding birth control, cultural mores, economic considerations—that people have large families.

Deevey's theory of population growth, if correct, is not necessarily a justification for complacency regarding the present situation and the prospects of even doubling of the current population, which would be consistent with the surge model. As already noted, there are differences of opinion as to the ability of a population of double the current one to feed itself; some believe that mass starvation is inevitable with a population this size, others think food should not pose a serious problem (Bongaarts, 1994a). The future availability of adequate fresh water is as uncertain as the future availability of sufficient food. According to Postel (2001), "Over the next quarter of a century the number of people living in water stressed countries will climb from 500 million to three billion" (p. 51). In light of the evidence that a population of the present size is able to have a considerable detrimental impact on the environment, one can hardly be sanguine about what a further doubling will mean.

The concept of carrying capacity is sometimes given a context-specific connotation. In the context of natural recreation areas, for example, the concept has been defined as

> the number of a particular type of users, having specified "packages" of experience preferences (e.g., for solitude, tranquility, etc., or for affiliation, exhilaration, etc.), that an area can accommodate under given biophysical and cultural resource conditions and specified management inputs, including location and types of trails, information programs, and other types of actions that regulate use. (Driver & Brown, 1983, p. 323)

It should be clear that the carrying capacity of an area may be exceeded for one set of experiences before it is exceeded for another. For example, the carrying capacity of a hiking and camping area will be exceeded from the point of view of people who seek quiet and solitude before it will be considered exceeded by those who prefer lots of company in their wilderness experiences (Lime & Stankey, 1971; Stankey, 1973).

Some economists see close connections among population, poverty, and environmental stress, with each of these factors influencing and being influenced by the other two (Kiessling & Landberg, 1994). Commenting on the fact that fetching water in Rajasthan, India, occupies several hours a day for every household, Dasgupta (1995) described the interdependence this way:

> As resources become increasingly sparse and distant, additional hands become more valuable for such daily tasks, creating a demand for families to have more

> children. The burgeoning population puts more pressure on the environment, spurring a need for even more offspring in a cycle of increasing poverty, population and environmental change. (p. 41)

In other words, there appears to be a positive feedback mechanism in effect.

> As the community resources are depleted, more hands are needed to gather fuel and water for daily use. More children are then produced, further damaging the local environment and in turn providing the household with an incentive to enlarge. When this happens, fertility and environmental degradation reinforce each other in an escalating spiral. (p. 44)

Developments that are believed to have the potential to slow population growth, especially in those parts of the world where population tends to grow the fastest, include greater educational opportunities and literacy for women and increased opportunities for them for gainful employment.

The fact that gains in environmental protection can be offset by increasing demands from population growth is illustrated by trends in carbon dioxide emissions over the last 150 years. According to Kates (1994), the amount of carbon used per unit of production has been decreasing steadily by about 1.3% per year since the mid-19th century as a consequence of the use of less carbon-rich fuels and more efficient production techniques. Despite these beneficial changes, however, carbon dioxide emissions to the atmosphere have increased by about 1.7% per year over the same period because of economic growth, which is spurred, in large part, by the steadily growing population.

It is estimated that the current population of a little over 6 billion people emitted a little over 6 billion tons of $CO_2$ to the atmosphere per year—roughly 1 ton per person per year. If current consumption patterns continue, a doubling of the population would mean a doubling of the emissions. This is food for thought, especially in view of Kauppi's (1995) claim that avoidance of danger requires that greenhouse gas concentrations would have to be stabilized at between 1 and 2 billion tons per year—something close to preindustrial levels.

One thing is certain, the rate of population growth will eventually have to fall to zero, if not go negative. No one knows for sure what the carrying capacity of the earth is, but whatever it is any positive nonzero growth rate ensues that it will be exceeded in time. Even an annual growth rate of 1% produces a doubling every 70 years The question is not whether the population will stop increasing, but when and in what fashion.

Population psychology is a recognized subfield of psychology and offers opportunities for work on this problem of unquestioned importance (Fawcett, 1970, 1973; Newman & Thompson, 1976; Thompson & Newman, 1976). Much of the work in the field focuses on the practices of contraception and birth control and is aimed at understanding the variables that determine people's attitudes and behavior in this regard. The need to understand methods of population growth control in terms of both probable effectiveness and acceptability among a populace is critical. The problem is a delicate one on which to do research because of the deep feeling people have—often based on religious convictions or traditional mores, which may differ considerably from culture to culture. Determining what works is likely to be considerably easier than determining what is acceptable, but an understanding of the latter is essential if knowledge of the former is to be useful.

The list of ways in which human behavior contributes to detrimental environmental change could easily be extended, but it is time to turn to the question of what psychological research may have to contribute toward solutions to the problem or specific aspects of it.

CHAPTER

# 4

# Attitude Assessment and Change

Given that human behavior is the cause, directly or indirectly, of most of the detrimental environmental change that is the focus of this book, a major challenge is to find ways to induce behavioral change to make it more environmentally friendly. Behavior in this context includes that of individuals and groups, and the groups of interest range from social, political, and corporate entities to neighborhoods, towns, and nations. The challenge is especially keen for psychology, the science that deals most directly with behavior and behavior change. Meeting the challenge is unlikely to be easy. As Ruckelshaus (1989) put it, speaking only of the problem of controlling greenhouse warming: "It means trying to get a substantial proportion of the world's people to change their behavior in order to (possibly) avert threats that will otherwise (probably) affect a world most of them will not be alive to see" (p. 166).

It is generally assumed that *attitudes*—here given a sufficiently broad connotation to include *beliefs* and *values*—are major determinants of behavior, which is to say that people typically, although not always, behave in a way that is consistent with their attitudes. It is not surprising to find, for example, that attitudes regarding personal responsibility and capability to effect change are somewhat predictive of environmentally relevant behavior (Fleishman, 1988; Hueber & Lipsey, 1981; Webster, 1975; Weigel & Newman, 1976). This being the case, it makes sense to attempt to change behavior by changing attitudes. There is also the view that attitude change can be an effect, as well as a cause, of behavior change. So attention has also been given to the possibility of effecting behavior change directly, without attempting to modify attitudes first; that idea is the subject of chapter 5.

## ATTITUDE ASSESSMENT

Researchers have shown considerable interest in the questions of what attitudes people hold toward environmental issues, what factors determine those attitudes, and how attitudes relate to their holders' behavior. Several questionnaire instruments have been developed for assessing people's attitudes toward environmental issues. These include the Environmental Response Inventory (McKechnie, 1974), the New Environmental Paradigm Scale (Dunlap & Van Liere, 1978), the Environmental Concern Scale (Weigel & Weigel, 1978), and the Environmental Appraisal Inventory (Schmidt & Gifford, 1989), among others. The last-mentioned instrument focuses on 24 environmental hazards that can be classified with respect to three factors: origin of hazard (nature–technology), range of influence (global–local), and length of impact (long–short). This inventory was also intended to provide a basis for assessing perceived threat to self, perceived threat to the environment, and perceived degree to which the threat could be controlled.

Fridgen (1994) expanded the Environmental Appraisal Inventory by adding four hazards to the 24 already in the instrument. The resulting 28-item list is as follows: (1) water pollution; (2) storms—lightening, hurricanes, tornadoes, snow; (3) pollution from cars, factories, and burning trash; (4) smoking in public buildings; (5) acid rain; (6) pollution from office equipment—ozone from photocopiers; (7) number of people—crowding, increasing population; (8) fluorescent lighting; (9) water shortage—drought, water depletion; (10) noise pollution; (11) visual pollution—billboards, litter; (12) radioactivity in building materials—radon gas; (13) change to the ozone caused by pollution; (14) earthquakes; (15) soil erosion; (16) impure drinking water; (17) forest fires; (18) floods or tidal waves; (19) germs or microorganisms; (20) radioactive fallout; (21) fumes or fibers from synthetic materials—asbestos, carpets, plastics; (22) chemical dumps; (23) video screen emissions; (24) pesticides and herbicides; (25) groundwater from landfill seepage; (26) air pollution from waste to energy incinerators; (27) surface water contamination from discarded motor oil; and (28) ocean pollution from dumping municipal solid waste.

Fridgen asked people several types of questions with respect to each of these hazards. In one case, for example, people rated the amount of personal responsibility they felt for each hazard on a 7-point Likert scale ranging from *no responsibility*, through *moderate*, to *extreme responsibility*. Fridgen concluded from her results that people tend to perceive themselves to be immune to the effects of most threats to the environment and feel little responsibility for, or ability to control, the threats—even those that clearly result from human behavior.

Although people vary considerably in the extent to which they accept responsibility for environmental problems (Meux, 1973), the results of many public opinion polls have shown that a large majority of Americans consider themselves to be environmentalists or concerned about environmental issues (Dunlap, 1985, 1989, 1992; Erskine, 1972; Gutfeld, 1991; Kempton, Boster, & Hartley, 1995; Milbrath, 1985; Mitchell, 1990; Stern, Dietz, Abel, Guagnano, & Kalof, 1999). Moreover the concern is not limited to the United States, but appears to be strong elsewhere as well (Dunlap, Gallup, & Gallup, 1993; Witherspoon, Mohler, & Harkness, 1995).

A connection sometimes has been found between attitudes on environmental issues and political ideology (Samdahl & Robertson, 1989); some studies have found concern for environmental issues to be most prevalent among people who are political activists and somewhat left of center in orientation (Dunlap, 1975; Koenig, 1975). Some researchers believe that people generally overestimate the ability of the government and industry to solve the problem of environmental pollution (Donohue, Olien, & Tichenor, 1974). Willingness to have the government regulate hazardous technologies appears to depend on people's attitudes toward those technologies (Verplanken, 1989).

Not surprisingly, people's attitudes toward an environmental problem are influenced by the degree to which they identify positively with the cause(s) of the problem. Thus, employees of a factory that contributes to air pollution are likely to be less actively upset about air pollution than are people who do not depend on the polluting agent for their livelihood. Although people in general have shown a great deal of distrust of the government's and industry's policies and practices in managing hazardous wastes (Binney, Mason, Martsolf, & Detweiler, 1996; Kasperson, Golding, & Tuler, 1992; Slovic, Flynn, & Layman, 1991), trust in this regard has been shown to be higher among people who are economically dependent on the waste producer than among those who are not (Williams, Brown, & Greenberg, 1999). Attitudes of affluent people on environmental issues appear to depend in part on the types of industry on which their affluence depends (Althoff & Grieg, 1974).

Sometimes a relationship has been found between environmental attitudes and sociodemographic variables (Hamilton, 1985; Pilisuk & Acredolo, 1988), including age (Lansana, 1992; Van Liere & Dunlap, 1980), gender (Longstreth, Turner, Topliff, & Iams, 1989; Stern, Dietz, & Kalof, 1993), race (Taylor, 1989), education (Lipsey, 1977; Samdahl & Robertson, 1989; Van

Liere & Dunlap, 1980), socioeconomic status (Harry, Gale, & Hendee, 1969; Mohai, 1985), political philosophy (Samdahl & Robertson, 1989), and place of residence (Buttel, Murdock, Feistritz, & Hamm, 1987; Schwepker & Cornwell, 1991), although such relationships tend to account for a relatively small portion of the variance in attitudes.

Stern (1992a) distinguished four types of environmental concern that he sees reflected in the literature and in the various instruments used to study attitudes. *Ecological* concern is "a concern for maintaining the balance of nature as an end in itself" (p. 280.) Anthropocentric *altruism* is based on a concern for people and on the belief that the loss of environmental quality would be harmful for them. *Egoistic* concern focuses on implications of environmental change for one's own well-being or that of one's kin. *Religious* or *ideological* concern is assumed to be rooted in religious or cultural values. Stern noted the possibility that more than one type of concern may be operative simultaneously, and he argued that a better understanding of these distinctions is important because different types of concern may lead to different types of behavior. Commenting on the diversity of views among the delegates to the United Nations Conference on the Human Environment convened in 1971 by then U.N. Secretary-General Maurice Strong, Ward and Dubos (1972) noted that difficulties facing the delegates are more likely to originate "not from uncertainties about scientific facts, but from differences in attitudes toward social values" (p. xvii).

Thompson and Barton (1994) developed a scale for measuring the degree to which one values nature for its own sake (ecocentrism) or for the sake of the benefits it can provide to humans (anthropocentrism). These investigators found that people who scored higher on ecocentrism were less likely to express apathy toward environmental issues and were more likely to conserve and join environmental organizations, but they were able to replicate the results only partially in a second study.

Attitudes regarding proper uses of the natural environment, especially public lands, have received some attention from researchers (de Haven-Smith, 1988). For example, Thurstone scaling techniques have been used, to evaluate the relative acceptability of various possible approaches to the rationing of access to rivers for recreational uses (Wikle, 1991). Although the idea of rationing access to public lands is inherently distasteful to many people, the attractiveness of places of natural beauty may vary inversely with the number of other people one is likely to see there. As Ward and Dubos (1972) put it, "If everyone goes to the same beauty spot, what beauty will there be left to see?" (p. 111)—or more graphically,

> with the surge of visitors rising steadily in national parks and in all well-known areas of great beauty, the visions—of forests, of wild shore and open water—are

> obscured in milling masses of people trampling the turf, parking the cars, shooting across the virgin snow in snowmobiles, and braining the innocent swimmer with their passing speedboats. And once such invasions begin, once hot-dog stands assemble round every Walden Pond, whether can men find nature in her primal state? (p. 113)

I suspect that readers over 50 years of age will find it easy to think of places of natural beauty that they may have frequented as youngsters that are now too crowded to be inviting.

The results of questionnaire and attitude surveys must be interpreted carefully because of the susceptibility of these instruments to unintended effects (Feldman & Lynch, 1988; Schwarz, 1999; Tourangeau & Rasinski, 1988). All attitude surveys are subject to subtle and not-so-subtle effects of question wording (Payne, 1952; Schuman & Scott, 1987), and quality judgments can be affected by the context in which they are made (Helson, 1964). It is often difficult, if not impossible, to tell whether answers to survey queries regarding socially sensitive issues reflect genuine attitudes or simply what respondents believe to be socially correct (Milstein, 1977). The assessment of public attitudes toward environmental issues as well as policies and programs designed to lessen or mitigate detrimental change is a continuing challenge (Dunlap, 1989; Dunlap, Grieneeks, & Rokeach, 1983).

## MEASURING THE PERCEIVED VALUE OF ENVIRONMENTAL RESOURCES

A special aspect of attitude assessment as it pertains to the environment is the problem of determining the value, or perceived value, of environmental resources and features. The problem is not unique to the environmental context, but applies to the determination of values more generally. Bedau (1991) argued that the traditional Western view is that the value of nature is purely instrumental, which is to say that nature has no intrinsic value and that the value it has is by virtue of the means it offers to satisfy human desires and purposes. The results of attempts to measure the perceived value of environmental resources are, in general, consistent with this view.

One method that is used to determine the values that people attach to various things is referred to as *contingent valuation* (CV). People are asked to say what they would be willing to pay for a specified good if it could be purchased in a market (Kahneman & Knetsch, 1992; Kahneman, Ritov, Jacowitz, & Grant, 1993). In the context of environmental matters, one might be asked what one would be willing to pay for a specified change for the better in some environmental condition or to preserve some desirable state.

A problem with this approach is that the values derived from people's responses often depend, to some degree, on precisely how the CV is conducted. Fischhoff, Slovic, and Lichtenstein (1982) illustrated the point with reference to a study that attempted to determine how much visitors to Lake Powell would be willing to pay in increased users' fees not to have an unsightly power plant looming on the opposite shore. Participants were asked whether they would pay $1, $2, $3, and so on until they said "no," whereupon the amount at which they balked was decremented in units of $0.25 until they again said "yes." Fischhoff et al. pointed out that quite different results might have been obtained in the study if, instead of starting with $1 and working up, the investigators had started with a large number—say $100—and worked down. The considerable literature relating to the phenomenon of anchoring and adjustment (Dawes, 1988; Kahneman & Tversky, 1982; Tversky & Kahneman, 1986) supports this claim. Fischhoff et al. (1982) noted too that "the low rates of 'no opinion' responses encountered by surveys addressing diverse and obscure topics suggest that most people are capable of providing some answer to whatever question is put to them" (p. 245). They cautioned, however, that in many instances the responses they provide may reflect a desire to be counted rather than deeply held opinions.

It is not hard to construct situations in which people express preferences and assign values in contradictory ways (Irwin, Slovic, Lichtenstein, & McClelland, 1993). Several studies have demonstrated the phenomenon generally referred to as *preference reversal*, whereby people express a preference of A over B, but when asked how much they would accept from a would-be buyer, put a higher price on B than on A (Goldstein & Einhorn, 1987; Lichtenstein & Slovic, 1971; Loomes & Sugden, 1983; Mellers, Ordóñezm & Birnbaum, 1992; Schkade & Johnson, 1989; Slovic, 1995; Slovic & Lichtenstein, 1983; Tversky, Slovic, & Kahneman, 1990). The reversal has typically been observed in situations involving wagers (choices the outcomes of which are known only probabilistically), but it has been well documented in a variety of such situations and it seems applicable to the problem of assessing environmental variables, at least insofar as environmental outcomes are probabilistically contingent on behavioral choices.

There is also the ubiquitous problem of framing effects, whereby stated preferences among essentially the same alternatives vary as a function of the way the alternatives are expressed (Dawes, 1988; Kahneman & Tversky, 1979, 1984). Such effects are commonly found in public-opinion polls (Moore, 1992; Payne, 1982; Wheeler, 1976). In the environmental context, different results may be obtained depending on whether questions are couched in terms of species lost or species saved (Tversky & Kahneman, 1981) or whether respondents are required to reveal preferences among species by choosing some species or rejecting some (Shafir, 1993).

## ASSESSING ENVIRONMENTAL QUALITY

Much of the work on environmental quality assessment has been motivated by practical needs, especially the need for environmental planners and managers to comply with environmental impact legislation (Holahan, 1986; Zube, Sell, & Taylor, 1982). The National Environmental Policy Act of 1969 requires all U.S. federal agencies to assess potential negative environmental effects of planned agency actions and specify how they intend to mitigate anticipated significant effects. About half of the states have imposed similar requirements on state agencies, and comparable environmental impact assessment approaches have been adopted by several other countries and international organizations (Robinson, 1990).

One objective of the National Environmental Policy Act of 1969 is to ensure "aesthetically pleasing surroundings" for all Americans, but what is an aesthetically pleasing surrounding? Especially relevant to the task of assessing environmental quality is work involving judgments of the beauty of nature scenes, such as forests (Anderson, 1981; Arthur, 1977; Daniel & Schroeder, 1979) and forest roads (Schroeder & Daniel, 1980, 1981), and the perceived quality of less pictorial aspects of the environment, such as the visual quality of air (Malm, Kelley, Molenar, & Daniel, 1981). A few investigators have attempted to relate perceived quality to specifiable objective characteristics of a scene, such as the presence of power lines (Jackson, Hudman, & England, 1978), optical conditions of the atmosphere (Latimer, Daniel, & Hogo, 1980; Latimer, Hogo, & Daniel, 1981), or intended uses of an area viewed (Peterson, 1974).

In general, people appear to prefer natural scenes over man-made scenes (Kaplan, Kaplan, & Wendt, 1972; Purcell, Lamb, Peron, & Falchero, 1994; Ulrich, 1983; Ward, 1977; Wohlwill, 1976), although managed forests are not necessarily less attractive to observers than unmanaged forests (Daniel, Wheeler, Boster, & Best, 1973), and not all observers prefer natural landscapes to those containing built structures (Zube & Pitt, 1981; Zube, Pitt, & Evans, 1983). Purcell et al. (1994) noted that there are different types of natural scenes—strictly natural scenes (lakes and forests) per se, natural vegetation in combination with other attributes, and vegetation that has been cultured in some way (e.g., fields, plantings). They cautioned that the preference for natural over built scenes is more complicated than it might appear to be, and that it is not difficult to find exceptions to this general trend.

Some of this work has involved the use of traditional psychophysical methods or methods derived from them. Rating techniques have been used in some instances (Anderson, 1981; Daniel, Anderson, Schroeder, & Wheeler, 1977; Daniel & Boster, 1976; Schroeder & Daniel, 1980, 1981); paired comparisons have been used in others (Buhyoff & Leuschner, 1978; Buhyoff & Riesenman,

1979; Buhyoff & Wellman, 1980; Buhyoff, Wellman, & Daniel, 1982). Some attempt has been made to develop predictive models of how people respond to environmental scenes (Peterson & Neumann, 1969). Several quality-assessment instruments, collectively referred to as Perceived Environmental Quality Indices (PEQIs), have been developed (Craik, 1981; Craik & Zube, 1976; Daniel & Vining, 1983; Ulrich, 1983; Zube, 1976; Zube, Brush, & Fabos, 1975). Methodological discussions and reviews of studies of environmental quality perception include Redding (1973), Wohlwill (1976), Zube and Craik (1976), Arthur, Daniel, and Boster (1977), Carlson (1977), Palmer (1981), Zube, Sell, and Taylor (1982), Daniel and Vining (1983), and Daniel (1976, 1987, 1990).

A collection of papers dealing primarily with human responses to the natural environment has been assembled by Altman and Wohwill (1983). Topics include the assessment of landscape quality (Daniel & Vining, 1983); aesthetic, affective, or emotional response to the natural environment (Kellert, 1983; Ulrich, 1983); and nature and the wilderness as recreational resources (Driver & Brown, 1983; Kaplan & Talbot, 1983; Knopf, 1983). Ulrich's (1983) paper gives a theoretical account of how emotional and cognitive processes relate in the perception of the environment. Kaplan and Kaplan (1984) reviewed work on cognition as it pertains to environmental matters. Some researchers have stressed the importance of social aspects of recreational uses of natural environments inasmuch as almost all such activities involve groups rather than lone individuals (Knopf, 1983).

Different people can react differently to the same environment—what is inviting to one observer can be threatening to another (Nash, 1973); a campsite that appears to some people to be too open can seem too secluded to others (Foster & Jackson, 1979). Preferences expressed by the general public sometimes differ from those expressed by professionals involved in the design of landscapes or management of natural environments (Buhyoff, Wellman, Harvey, & Fraser, 1978; Kaplan, 1973). The involvement of learning is also indicated by the fact that what scenes people find aesthetically pleasing depends to some degree on the kinds of scenes they typically see in daily life (Sonnenfeld, 1969).

Such differences notwithstanding, the work on environmental quality perception has generally yielded a high degree of consistency, even among judgments obtained from different interest groups and with the use of different methods, as to what constitutes scenic beauty or landscape quality (Buhyoff, Wellman, & Daniel, 1982; Clamp, 1976; Daniel, Anderson, Schroeder, & Wheeler, 1977; Malm, Kelley, Molenar, & Daniel, 1981; Nasar, 1983, 1984; Shafer, Hamilton, & Schmidt, 1969; Ward & Russell, 1981; Zube, 1974; Zube, Pitt, & Anderson, 1975b). Considerable consistency has been found in scenic and landscape preferences even across viewers from a variety of different cultures (Berlyne, 1975; Hull & Revell, 1989; Kwok, 1979; Shafer & Tooby, 1973; Ulrich, 1977; Yang & Brown, 1992; Yang & Tang, 1992); the presence of greenery and water appear to be widely, if not universally, noted elements of preferred scenes. Such hints of cross-cultural consistencies in preferences in nature are consistent with the idea, one version of which is represented by Wilson's (1984) biophilia hypothesis, that human beings have a need for being close to nature and an innate attraction to natural environments. Kaplan and Kaplan (1989) noted that experiences of nature can have restorative effects on people suffering mental fatigue from the demands of daily life.

Many, perhaps most, of the studies of scenic beauty have used photographs of the scenes to be judged. Various types of simulation—scale models, computer-based video presentations—have also been used widely in studies of human response to or interaction with the environment (Marans & Stokols, 1993). Although there seems to be a consensus among investigators that this approach produces valid results (Bosselmann & Craik, 1989; Nausser, 1982; Shuttleworgh, 1980; Zube, Simcox, & Law, 1987) and studies using both photographs and actual scenes have evoked similar reactions (Shafer & Richards, 1974; Stamps, 1990; Zube, Pitt, & Anderson, 1975a), the question is still a topic of debate (Hull & Stewart, 1992).

The problem of ensuring the generalizability of the results obtained with simulations to the corresponding real environments has received some, but not a lot of, attention (Stokols, 1993; Weinstein, 1976). An unanswered question is how accurately people perceive nature when their only experience of it is indirect via media presentations. Some observers have expressed the worry that artificial experiences of nature through TV or virtual-reality technology could devalue and reduce support for preserving the real thing (Levi & Kocher, 1999; McKibben, 1990, 1996).

Considerable effort has been devoted to the identification of aspects or features of a landscape that help determine its aesthetic appeal (Ulrich, 1983). Attempts have been made, often with the use of factor- or cluster-analytic techniques, to develop a theoretical understanding of what makes some environments more attractive to people than others (Herzog, Kaplan, & Kaplan, 1982; Kaplan, 1975, 1977; Kaplan & Kaplan, 1978; Kaplan, Kaplan, & Wendt, 1972), but much remains to be done in this regard.

One set of studies of affective responses to environments has led to the idea that all such responses can be represented by a two-dimensional space, the dimensions of which are pleasantness and arousal (Russell & Pratt, 1980; Russell, Ward, & Pratt, 1981; Ward & Russell, 1981). An environment that would be described as distressing, for example, would be highly arousing and unpleasant, whereas one that would be considered relaxing would be unarousing and pleasant.

The problem of environmental quality perception is complicated by the fact that how people perceive and respond to specific aspects of an environment depends in part on what they are accustomed to or what they have come to consider normal. People who have become accustomed to living in smog, for example, are less sensitive to this form of pollution than are those who are not accustomed to it (Evans, Jacobs, & Frazer, 1982a, 1982b). Recent migrants from rural areas are likely to judge a city to be noisier than are recent migrants from urban areas (Wohlwill & Kohn, 1973). In general, city residents are likely to perceive wilderness differently than do residents of rural areas (Lutz, Simpson-Housley, & de Man, 1999). Experiences with nature appear to be powerful determinants of people's attitudes toward nature and their willingness to protect it (Finger, 1994).

Affective responses to specific scenes can even be influenced by the immediate context in which those scenes are viewed. For example, in keeping with adaptation-level theory (Helson, 1964), a "sad" scene may be judged to be less sad if the previously viewed scene was extremely sad than if it was not (Russell & Lanius, 1984; Wohlwill, 1974); how attractive a particular forest scene is reported to be is likely to depend on the relative attractiveness of other scenes judged in the same session (Brown & Daniel, 1987). How a place is perceived affectively can also be influenced by the perceiver's expectations (Baum & Greenberg, 1975) or prior mood (Gifford, 1980; Sherrod, Armstrong, Hewitt, Madonia, Speno, & Teruya, 1977).

To date, the attention that has been given to the question of what constitutes a high-quality environment has not yielded a simple unequivocal answer that would be widely endorsed by researchers in the area. Yet it is perhaps not reasonable to expect that it would have. It is a hard question and is likely to have a complicated answer. The high degree of consistency found among judgments from diverse groups of people as to what constitutes scenic beauty or landscape quality gives some reason to believe that an answer, undoubtedly with qualifications, is not beyond finding out.

## ATTITUDES TOWARD ANIMALS

An aspect of attitude assessment that deserves special mention in a discussion of environmental issues is that of people's attitudes toward animals and especially undomesticated animals. This subject has received attention from researchers for some time (Kellert, 1974, 1976; King, 1947). People's attitudes toward animals are apparently determined by several factors. Kellert (1983) suggested that the following are among the more influential of them:

- Aesthetic value of the species
- Degree of socioeconomic impact involved in protecting the species
- Phylogenetic relation (similarity) of the species to human beings
- Presumed threat of the species to human health and productivity
- Cultural and historical importance of the species
- Potential and actual economic value of the species.

Other lists of attributes that might be used in species valuation have been proposed (e.g., Adamus & Clough, 1978; Ramsay, 1976). However, as DeKay and McClelland (1996) pointed out, there is a need for empirical investigation to determine which of the potentially relevant attributes actually function as determinants of attitudes.

Large individual differences are to be expected among attitudes of people regarding animals in general and species in particular depending on roles that animals play in their lives. Cattle ranchers are likely to have rather different attitudes than vegetarians in this regard. Attitudes toward hunting not only vary between hunters and nonhunters, but depend on the purpose for which hunting is done, tending to be favorable when a primary purpose is to obtain meat and unfavorable when it is done solely for recreation or to obtain trophies (Kellert, 1978, 1980).

The tendency of people to value species in accordance with their location on the phylogenetic scale (DeKay & McClelland, 1996; Eddy, Gallup, & Polvinelli, 1993) may be a special case of a general similarity bias, according to which we show preference to others depending on their similarity to ourselves (Kellert, 1979; Kellert & Berry, 1980; Plous, 1993). The similarity bias has been observed in the animal preferences of children as well as in those of adults (Kellert & Westervelt, 1983).

It seems more than likely that the way many adults think of animals has been shaped by a mixture of biological facts on the one hand and childhood myths and fantasies on the other. Animals, often with humanlike capabilities and qualities, pervade preschool children's books (Sokolow, 1980). Children fall asleep with teddy bears and other fuzzy, cuddly animal facsimiles; they read comic books in which cats, dogs, and sundry other animal characters talk; they watch TV cartoons in which mice plot clever strategies (that invariably win) against their dull-witted but persistent feline nemeses; some cartoon characters (Mickey Mouse, Bugs Bunny, Porky Pig) have had celebrity status for decades; Big Bird and Kermit the frog have been regular companions for millions of young TV viewers. Stereotypes that we learn early in life—the wise owl, the cunning fox, the menacing wolf, the industrious beaver—stay with us a long time.

Cartmill (1993) attributed much of the current anti-hunting sentiment on the "Bambi myth," deriving from an unrealistic portrayal of animals that romanticizes and anthropomorphizes life in the wild in the fashion of Disney's classic animation of Felix Salten's 1924 novel, *Bambi: A Forest Life*. However that may be, there can be little question of people's common tendency to project human feelings, motivations, intentions, fears, joys, and intelligence to animals of many types. How people conceive of animals and of life in the wild, and how those conceptions are formed, are questions that deserve more attention from researchers than they have received. It would be interesting to know, as a start, what percentage of the information regarding wild life that is received by the average preschool child living in an industrialized country is biologically and behaviorally accurate.

Prevailing attitudes toward wildlife and, in particular, attitudes regarding the relative worth of different species—however worth is defined—are of some practical concern because of the necessity to make priority decisions in allocating limited resources to the preservation of endangered species in accordance with the U.S. Endangered Species Act. On the relatively safe assumption that there are insufficient funds to ensure the survival of every species that is threatened with extinction—and leaving aside the question of whether that would be a desirable objective—it is clear that some priorities need to be established. This need has been recognized, and some attempts to prioritize have been made (Sparrowe & Wight, 1975; U.S. Fish and Wildlife Service, 1983).

When asked to allocate resources to programs aimed at improving the lot of particular species in hypothetical situations, people have shown a sensitivity to a number of variables. It appears that allocations are likely to be greater for species that are highly endangered, but considered savable, than for species not greatly threatened or those believed to be beyond rescuing (Samples, Dixon, & Gowen, 1986).

The extent to which national policy with respect to species preservation efforts should be dictated by species preferences expressed by the general public is debatable, but presumably those preferences should be taken into account in the expenditure of public funds. It is also important, however, that the relative values that people attach to species—or, more to the point, the priorities they give to the allocation of resources to the protection of particular species—not be based on faulty beliefs about the species in question, their degree of endangerment, the probability of their survival with intervention, their importance to other species' well-being, and various other factors (DeKay & McClelland, 1996). Sorting out the determinants of attitudes in this regard is one challenge to psychology; helping to increase the degree to which attitudes rest on a sound objective base is another.

Although people's attraction to nature—animals and plant life—cannot be said to be universal, it is unquestionably widespread, and therefore begs an explanation. Some theorists have hypothesized that this attraction is innate and that the ability to indulge it is essential to mental health and general well-being (Dubos, 1968; Kellert & Wilson, 1993; Wilson, 1984). Much of the research on people's reactions to nature, while not providing conclusive evidence on the suggestion, is compatible with it.

## BELIEFS AND ATTITUDES AS DETERMINANTS OF BEHAVIOR

It seems natural to assume that beliefs and attitudes are major determinants of behavior—that people tend to behave in ways that are consistent with their beliefs and attitudes. On this assumption, if one is interested in modifying behavior, it makes sense to try to change the beliefs and attitudes from which the behavior is assumed to flow. In fact, the question of the validity of the assumption has been a focus of attention from psychologists for many years (Abelson, 1982; Ajzen, 1982; Ajzen & Fishbein, 1977; Cooper & Croyle, 1984; Fishbein & Ajzen, 1975; La Piere, 1934; Wicker, 1969).

The picture that has emerged from studies attempting to link attitudes with other variables and especially with behavior is a cloudy one (Oskamp, Harrington, Edwards, Sherwood, Okuda, & Swanson, 1991; Van Liere & Dunlap, 1980, 1981; Vining & Ebreo, 1990). The difficulty in getting a clearer picture may be due, at least in part, to this fact: The degree to which behavior is influenced by such cognitive variables as attitudes, beliefs, values, and knowledge is much more limited in some contexts than in others by resource limitations and other nonpsychological constraints (Gardner & Stern, 1996; Stern, 1992a). For example, Gardner and Stern (1996) pointed out that environmental damage has been severe even in some cultures where the more prominent religions have explicitly proenvironmental teachings; the proenvironmental beliefs and attitudes are not more effective in inhibiting environmentally destructive behavior, they surmised, because of the strong counteracting influence of other factors and processes. The picture is further clouded because the concerns people reveal about the environment can vary with the specifics of the way in which they are measured (Van Liere & Dunlap, 1981).

Most studies of how attitudes relate to behavior have been correlational; they do not provide evidence on the question of the extent to which the attitudes of interest cause the behavior of interest, but they at least suggest the possibility of causal links that deserve further investigation. Positive attitudes toward recycling have proved to be predictive of participation in a company's paper recycling program (Humphrey, Bord, Hammond, & Mann, 1977). High levels of energy use for indoor temperature control have been found to be correlated with the belief that indoor temperature is an important determinant of health and comfort, but not with belief in the urgency of an energy crisis (Becker, Seligman, Fazio, & Darley, 1981; Seligman, Kriss, Darley, Fazio, Becker, & Pryor, 1979).

We know that beliefs and attitudes about environmental issues, at least as expressed by people when asked about them, are not perfect indicators of how they will act relative to those issues (Bickman, 1972; Eagly & Chaiken, 1990; Geller, 1981a; Howard, Delgado, Miller, & Gubbins, 1993; Hutton, 1982; Oskamp, Harrington, Edwards, Sherwood, Okuda, & Swanson, 1991; Scott & Willits, 1994; Seligman, Kniss, Darley, Fazio, Becker, & Pryor, 1979). It is not safe to assume that people who identify themselves as environmentalists in response to survey questionnaires necessarily have a substantive understanding of the issues or are willing to modify their behavior to make it more environmentally benign if told how to do so (Krause, 1993; O'Riordan, 1976). It is difficult to tell, in the absence of evidence from other sources, the extent to which responses to surveys regarding socially sensitive issues even reflect individuals' real attitudes, let alone predict their behavior. It is hard to rule out the possibility that respondents sometimes give answers they assume the interviewers want to hear or that help convey the socially responsible kind of image they wish to project (DeMaio, 1984; De Oliver, 1999; Fujii, Hennessey, & Mak, 1985; Tedeschi, 1981; Tedeschi, Schenkler, & Bonoma, 1971). It is also possible that people sincerely see their own behavior as more socially responsible than it actually is.

In short, it appears that attitudes are somewhat predictive of behavior, or at least of self-reported behavior, but typically only to a moderate degree, and to a greater degree under some conditions than under others (Hines, Hungerford, & Tomera, 1986; Lipsey, 1977; Mainieri, Barnett, Valdero, Unipan, & Oskamp, 1997; Schuman & Johnson, 1976; Tracy & Oskamp, 1983–1984). How predictive environmental attitudes are of behavior appears to depend in part on their specificity: Attitudes about specific threats to the environment are more predictive of behavior that relates to those threats than general concerns about environmental protection are predictive of generally environmentally friendly behavior (Balderjahn, 1988). For example, attitudes toward recycling are more predictive of (self-reported) recycling behavior than are attitudes representing general concern for the environment (Vining & Ebreo, 1992).

The strength of the relationship between attitudes and behavior appears to depend also on the strength of the barriers to action that exist: The stronger the barriers to action, the less likely are proenvironmental attitudes to affect proenvironmental behavior (Black, Stern, & Elworth, 1985; Guagnano, Stern, & Dietz, 1995). As Gardner and Stern (1996) put it, experimental findings suggest that "external barriers and constraints set limits on what can be accomplished by changing peoples' attitudes. The higher the barriers—expense, inconvenience, technical difficulty, and so on—the less effect proenvironmental attitudes have on behavior" (p. 77). Conversely, to bring about changes in behavior of sufficient magnitude to have substantive benefit to the environment, it may be necessary to remove or mitigate the influence of several such barriers (McKenzie-Mohr, 2000). The availability of personal resources, or lack thereof, can also help determine the degree of correspondence between one's attitudes and actions relative to environmental issues (Mohai, 1985; Prester, Rohrmann, & Schellhammer, 1987). Stern (1992a) stressed the importance of developing a better understanding of the way contextual and psychological variables interact, so as to identify the conditions under which psychological variables make a practical difference in effecting global change.

Inconsistency between people's expressed attitudes toward the environment and their behavior can be due, in some instances at least, to a lack of understanding by people of the environmental implications of their actions. For example, one may be in favor of conserving energy, but fail to conserve because of lack of knowledge of how to do so. In such cases, a reminder of one's expressed attitude and information regarding how to bring one's behavior in line with it may suffice to resolve the inconsistency (Kantola, Syme, & Campbell, 1984).

Discussions of the relationship between attitudes and behavior sometimes have also involved emotions, intentions, and other closely associated concepts. Kals and her colleagues have emphasized the role of emotions as determinants of how one acts with respect to the environment. They have found that environmentally friendly behavior can be motivated by both positive feelings toward nature (Kals, Schumacher, & Montada, 1999) and negative feelings such as guilt, fear, and indignation toward environmentally detrimental behavior by others (Kals, 1996; Kals & Montada, 1994). However, fear and other emotional reactions can evoke a range of behaviors, not always predictable. Fishbein and Ajzen (1975) have stressed the importance of intentions, arguing that they tend to be good predictors of behavior.

Some investigators have found a positive relationship between strength of support for a value in principle and strength of efforts to realize the value in practice, especially among people with higher levels of education. However, studies have also shown that expressions of support of specific values in principle does not ensure support of those same values in practice (Prothro & Grigg, 1960; Stouffer, 1955). Gardner and Stern (1996; Stern, Dietz, Kalof, & Guagnano, 1995) argued that values are especially likely to influence behavior when people need to act in the absence of much relevant knowledge or experience. Sniderman et al. (1991) pointed out that a weak relationship between the support given to a value in principle and in practice can be the consequence of people sometimes having allegiance to values that conflict when applied in specific situations. How personal value systems relate to environmental concerns and find expression in environmentally relevant behavior is likely to continue to be an important focus of research.

The imperfect correlation between behavior and expressed attitudes seen at the level of the individual has its analogue at the level of the behavior of governments and nations as well. There is a sense in which the world as a whole has acknowledged the importance of environmental protection. This claim is supported by the existence of some 170 or more international treaties aimed at protecting various aspects of the global environment. As French (1994) pointed out, however, although it is not always easy to get such treaties signed, it is much more difficult to have them adequately monitored and enforced. Inherent weaknesses in the rules of international diplomacy, he argued, render many of these treaties essentially meaningless.

There have been many studies of the relationship between attitudinal variables and behavior in addition to those that have been mentioned here. In the aggregate, work on this question makes it clear that the relationship is complex and not well understood (Chaiken & Strangor, 1987; Cooper & Croyle, 1984; Tesser & Shaffer, 1990). However, two conclusions, seem safe: (a) People do not always act in accordance with their *expressed* beliefs and attitudes, but (b) changing beliefs and attitudes may, in some cases, be an effective way to change behavior. Assuming that making people more sensitive to the problem of detrimental environmental change is unlikely to promote more environmentally destructive behavior, the approach offers some possibility of benefit with little risk of detrimental effects. Some investigators have argued that attitudes may guide behavior even when the individuals whose behavior is being guided are not aware of the fact (Fazio, 1986, 1989; Fazio & Williams, 1986; Kallgren & Wood, 1986).

Discussions about the relationship between attitudes and behavior usually focus on the relationship between attitudes and the behavior of those who have those attitudes. However, attitudes can have an impact on the environment that is less direct, but no less important, than that which they have through the immediate environmentally relevant behavior of those who hold them. The attitudes of one individual or group can affect the behavior of another individual or group. In a democratic society, elected officials are keenly aware of prevailing attitudes of the general public and especially the attitudes, including those that pertain to environmental issues, of their own constituents (Gil, Crosby, & Taylor, 1986). Hence, strongly expressed attitudes can have an effect on policies that have environmental implications established at all levels of government, even when the holders of those attitudes do not give compelling evidence of the influence of those attitudes on their personal behavior. Merchants and service providers are aware of the effect that the attitudes of their potential customers can have on the choices they make among goods and services they purchase, and the behavior of corporations with respect to the environment can be affected by what corporate decision makers perceive their customers' attitudes to be.

Moomaw and Kildow (1991) described a variety of initiatives that have been taken by corporations in the interest of improving their performance with respect to the environmental impact of their activities. Their explanation of what motivates these initiatives is that corporations are responding to customer attitudes as they understand them.

> Corporations have correctly concluded that a significant fraction of consumers really want to purchase two products from them. The first is the traditional functional item and the second is a clean environment, or at least a clear conscience that the item they have purchased does not contribute significantly to environmental damage. (p. 282)

The corporations' concerns are not lessened, of course, by the assumption that consumers' attitudes are likely to be reflected in their behavior.

> In some cases corporations are forced to respond with 'greener' alternatives when customers walk away from products, as happened with aerosol personal products. In other instances they are responding to threatened or organized boycotts such as were encountered by Exxon after the massive oil spill at Prince William Sound, or by the tuna industry when consumers realized dolphins were being killed. (p. 282)

## EFFECTING CHANGES IN ATTITUDES

Some investigators have distinguished between instrumental and symbolic beliefs, the former being beliefs that serve practical purposes in one's daily life and the latter being less utilitarian and more indicative of abstract values (Abelson & Prentice, 1990). Symbolic beliefs are seen to be less constrained by reality than instrumental beliefs and less likely to motivate behavior. According to this view, it is not surprising to find that people do not always make concerted efforts to bring their behavior into conformity with symbolic beliefs they may hold about the environment (Cary, 1992, 1993).

People who believe—either instrumentally or symbolically—that the problem of environmental change is a fiction are unlikely to be motivated to act in environmentally beneficial ways, at least if doing so is at all inconvenient. How to convince people of the seriousness of the problem—assuming those who would like to do the convincing are convinced that it is indeed a serious one and deserves action—is a question that could benefit from more research than it has received.

Considerable effort has been made to affect beliefs and attitudes about various aspects of environmental change through public service announcements. I am not aware of evidence regarding the effectiveness or ineffectiveness of such announcements. The possibility has been noted that they may sometimes deliver messages other than those intended by their designers. For example, Cialdini (1989) pointed out that antilittering spots that show people tossing trash out car windows, or otherwise inappropriately discarding refuse, can deliver a mixed message even when professionally done with the clear intent of discouraging littering. Although such spots promote the prescriptive norm that people should not litter, they may also inadvertently reinforce the counterbalancing popular norm that doing so is acceptable by conveying that it is common behavior.

Kempton, Darley, and Stern (1992) argued that it is not so much the simple fact of negative environmental effects that drives public concern as it is highly visible and publicized manifestations of these effects. They draw an analogy with the oil crisis of the early 1970s.

> It was not abstract recognition of possible fuel shortages that caused the energy crisis of 1973–1974. The cause was the unprecedented, rapid rise in oil prices made possible by political conditions that allowed a cartel of oil-producing nations to control world markets by withholding oil. Price shocks carried the energy crisis to ordinary consumers. Televised images of long lines at gas pumps were the visible manifestation of shortages. (p. 1214)

The conclusion that Kempton et al. (1992) drew from this analogy is that environmentally concerned social scientists should devise ways to make the effects about which they are concerned "dramatically visible."

An especially challenging aspect of the problem of changing beliefs and attitudes about the environment is the question of how to convince individuals that their personal behavior matters. The natural inclination is to take the attitude that what I, 1 out of 6 billion souls currently on the planet, do cannot possibly have any appreciable impact on the future quality of the environment. It is difficult to argue convincingly to the contrary. However, it is clear that human behavior, in the aggregate, has significant implications for environmental change; if everyone works on the "nothing-I-personally-do-matters" assumption, there seems little chance of changing things for the better.

The importance of little things is illustrated by reference to milk cartons. There is almost twice as much material in two one-quart containers as in one two-quart container, and it takes about as much energy to produce a container of one size as it does to produce one of the other. Given these facts, the consumer who buys a two-quart container instead of two one-quart containers (or a gallon instead of two half-gallons) is behaving in an environmentally beneficial way. According to one estimate, the purchase—once a week by 70 million households—of one half-gallon of milk instead of two quarts would reduce paper and plastic waste by 41.6 million pounds and 5.7 million pounds per year, respectively (Purcell, 1981).

The tendency to see one's own behavior as inconsequential in the grand scheme of things is reinforced by the asymmetry of the cost–benefit equation that pertains to many types of environmentally detrimental behavior, when viewed from a short-term and narrow personal perspective. The situation is captured by Hardin's (1968) metaphor of the *tragedy of the commons*, according to which a herdsman can realize a substantial personal benefit at little personal cost by adding an animal to his herd grazing on common land. The benefit that comes from having an additional animal is his alone, whereas the cost, in terms of slightly less grazing land per animal, is shared by all, so the herdsman with the additional animal realizes a net gain. The problem, of course, is that every herdsman sees the situation the same way, so collectively, with each person working in what appears to be his own best short-term interest, they ruin the land. Many people have written about social dilemmas, for which the tragedy of the commons is the best-known metaphor. More is said on this topic in chapter 12.

Another attitudinal problem that constitutes a continuing major challenge to psychology is the well-known "not-in-my-back-yard" (NIMBY) reaction to measures that are generally acknowledged to be desirable or necessary from a global perspective, but can have undesirable local implications. The siting of hazardous waste treatment facilities is an obvious case in point. Everyone agrees that there is a need for such facilities, but understandably few people want them in their own communities or neighborhoods (Kraft & Clary, 1993; Morell & Magorian, 1980; Portney, 1991b). A similar, albeit perhaps somewhat less extreme, attitude pertains to waste disposal generally. As Hair (1991) succinctly put it, "everybody wants you to pick it up, and nobody wants you to put it down" (p. 88).

Sometimes NIMBY reactions may be based on misunderstanding the costs or risks associated with a specific proposal relative to those associated with alternative courses of action or inaction. In such cases, the problem is, at least in part, one of adequate risk communication. Yet even a good understanding of the costs and risks of various possibilities may not be enough to counter a NIMBY reaction completely because the local participation in the global benefit may not be enough to offset the local cost. Portney (1991a) noted that decision analyses that purport to establish the correctness of a given site for a hazardous waste facility are rarely accepted by the people potentially most affected by the proposed facility.

CHAPTER

# 5

# Changing Behavior

The position can be argued, and it has been argued, that it is sometimes more cost effective to try to change behavior directly than to do so via a change in attitudes, and that attitude change is likely to follow the change in behavior (Geller, 1986, 1992a). The fact that changes in attitude sometimes do follow changes in behavior that have been induced by persuasion or coercion has been a focus of experimentation and theorizing among social psychologists (Tesser & Shaffer, 1990), and supports the belief that attitudes are as likely to be the consequences of behavior as to cause it (Aronson, 1992). Much of the work in this area has been done by psychologists who use the techniques of applied behavior analysis, or behavioral engineering, to study the possibility of modifying behavior in specific ways by the use of incentives or disincentives (antecedent manipulations) and rewards or punishments (contingency management or consequence control) (Geller, 1989; Geller & Lehman, 1986).

There are many ways to attempt to effect changes in the behavior of individuals and corporate entities in addition to that of doing so indirectly through the change of attitudes: legislation and governmental regulations backed up by the threat of civil or criminal sanctions; incentives in the form of tax deductions for the costs of environmental preservation or cleanup activities; disincentives in the form of taxation of pollution-producing activities (in Norway, companies pay a carbon dioxide tax based on the amount emitted to the atmosphere); public recognition and awards for noteworthy environmental activity (or bad press for environmentally detrimental behavior); persuasion, as represented by appeals to moral responsibility or altruism; and the dissemination of information designed to make people aware of problems and what can be done about them.

Geller (1992b) pointed out that environmentally detrimental behavior, such as wasteful use of resources and pollution of air and water, is maintained by a variety of reinforcing consequences, including convenience, comfort, and money. The way to change such behavior, in his view, is to modify the behavioral consequences in such a way that environmentally beneficial behavior gets more positive reinforcement than does environmentally detrimental behavior. Stern and Kirkpatrick (1977) warned, however, that the use of incentives to modify behavior can, under certain circumstances, work against long-term change. They argued that conditioned dependency on immediate rewards can inhibit the development of the kind of farsighted viewpoint that will produce and sustain voluntary constraint. These opinions, in juxtaposition, point up the importance of bearing in mind that the determinants of short- and long-term behavioral change are not necessarily the same.

One innovative attempt to use monetary incentives to modify behavior change at the corporate level in the United States was embedded in the 1990 Amendments to the Clean Air Act in the form of tradeable emission allowances for industries that traditionally have been major emitters of sulfur dioxide to the atmosphere in the production of electric power. The act prescribed that, as of 1995, utilities would receive emission permits for sulfur dioxide, the amounts being determined by past emission data for the industry. The total amount permitted is to decrease gradually over a period of years. The permits are tradeable so that a company that succeeds in lowering its emissions below its allotted amount can receive income from selling its unused credits to other companies that have failed to get their emissions down to the targeted levels (Alper, 1993). This approach has the virtue of simplicity, and it makes the cost of one form of pollution salient while providing a clear incentive for reducing it. Emissions trading was accepted in 2001 by the signatories of the Kyoto Protocol as a viable policy to be used at the international level (Kerr, 2001b).

The use of prices and taxes to influence consumer behavior (e.g., taxes on various forms of energy to decrease unessential use) has received a lot of attention in the press, but opinions differ as to the sensitivity of consumer behavior to price differences, and the evidence is not strong that the use of price adjustments in the past has had major effects on behavior (Hirst, 1976; Lehman & Warren, 1978). The effectiveness of pricing incentives may depend on the size of the cost differential to the buyer between environmentally friendly and environmentally destructive behavior. In my town, the cost to the consumer of water usage is $0.60 per 100 cubic feet for amounts up to 2,000 cubic feet per 6 months; amounts in excess of 2,000 cubic feet are billed at $3.20 per cubic foot. The corresponding sewer charges are $1.50 per 100 cubic feet for up to 2,000 cubic feet and $4.80 per cubic feet thereafter. These are big enough differentials to have a noticeable impact on one's water/sewer bill and, I presume, constitute an effective incentive to conserve. Winter (2000) argued that taxes and prices are unlikely to be major inhibitors of overconsumption unless the taxes are relatively large and product prices are high enough to reflect their actual costs, including the costs of cleanup and/or disposal.

In contrast, Gardner and Stern (1996) sounded a cautionary note against the assumption that the bigger an incentive the better. They pointed out the possibility of making an incentive so large that it may undermine people's intrinsic motive to act. "People can come to believe that they are acting only for the incentive, so that they begin to require large incentives to do things that they might previously have done with only small ones" (p. 116). Much remains to be learned about how to use incentives and disincentives effectively to help motivate environmentally friendly behavior without producing unanticipated and unwanted side effects.

The question of whether to attempt to change attitudes or to attempt to change behavior directly does not require an either–or answer; attitude change may be the appropriate goal in some cases, an attempt to affect behavior more directly may be more appropriate in others, and the targeting of both attitudes and behavior would seem to be the best strategy in general. It may well be that, whichever is targeted first, both attitudes and behavior must be consistent if the desired behavior is to be sustained. Short-term behavior changes may be effected by experimental interventions of various sorts, but they seem unlikely to persist much beyond the durations of the interventions in the absence of attitudes that support them (Dwyer, Leeming, Cobern, Porter, & Jackson, 1993).

## INCREASING ENERGY-CONSERVING BEHAVIOR

Oppenheimer and Boyle (1990) argued that if a three-degree rise in global temperature is to be avoided, 80 trillion kilowatt hours of fossil-fuel energy that the world used annually as of 1990 will have to be decreased by half to 40 trillion kilowatt hours by 2030, despite a growing population and increasing aspirations of people for goods and services everywhere. If the use of fossil-fuel energy is to be reduced, it must be done either by developing alternative energy sources, finding ways to increase energy efficiency, or both. Psychology is probably not likely to play a leading role in developing new energy sources, but it may have something to offer to the problem of finding ways to reduce energy use. Some technologists believe that the technology exists to permit large improvements in the efficiency of energy use and that the main problem is that of convincing people to avail themselves of the possibilities, including that of increasing short-term spending to realize long-term savings (Cherfas, 1991).

The question of how to get people to be more conservative in their use of energy has been of interest to several psychological researchers (Dwyer, Leeming, Cobern, Porter, & Jackson, 1993; Katzev & Johnson, 1987; McClelland & Canter, 1981; Neuman, 1986; Reichel & Geller, 1981; Seligman, Becker, & Darley, 1981). Studies have focused on education, persuasion, inducements and incentives, and feedback regarding the effectiveness of conservation efforts (Coltrane, Archer, & Aronson, 1986; Cook & Berrenberg, 1981; Katzev & Johnson, 1984). The importance of exploration of what can be done with education and feedback is underscored by evidence that people are unlikely to engage in energy-conserving behaviors unless they see the connection between their behavior and the energy savings (Simmons, Talbot, & Kaplan, 1984–1985).

Simply providing consumers with information about ways in which they can reduce their use of energy, or attempting to persuade them to conserve, has resulted in reductions in some, although not all, cases (Dennis, Soderstrom, Koncinski, & Cavanaugh, 1990; Syme, Seligman, Kantola, & MacPherson, 1987). Generally, this has been considered to be a relatively ineffective approach (Hayes & Cone, 1977; Kohlenberg, Phillips, & Proctor, 1976). By way of summarizing studies of efforts to use the media to persuade people to conserve energy, Dwyer, Leeming, Cobern, Porter, and Jackson (1993) concluded that "there is little convincing evidence that mass-media campaigns promoting conservation have had appreciable effects" (p. 291).

Yet, specific modeling, sometimes with videotape, of ways to increase home energy efficiency has had some success (Aronson & O'Leary, 1982–1983; Syme, Seligman, Kantola, & MacPherson, 1987; Winett et al., 1982; Winett, Leckliter, Chinn, & Stahl, 1984; Winett, Leckliter, Chinn, Stahl, & Love, 1985). Helping people to remember—making it difficult for them to forget—to conserve has also been shown to be effective in some instances, especially when the action required is simple; posting of conspicuous signs to turn off unneeded lights, for example, appears to work sometimes (Delprata, 1977; Luyben, 1980, 1982–1983; Winett, 1978; Zolik, Jason, Nair, & Peterson, 1982–1983). In one study, compliance with a request from college administrators for the lowering of venetian blinds at night, so as to inhibit radiative cooling of classrooms, was sustained with the help of thank-you notes from cleaning staff that served as daily reminders of the request (Luyben, 1984).

Incentives to decrease energy consumption have sometimes been effective at least over short periods of time (Foxx & Hake, 1977; Hake & Foxx, 1978; Hake & Zane, 1981; Hayes & Cone, 1977; McClelland & Belsten, 1979–1980; Slavin & Wodarski, 1977; Slavin, Wodarski, & Blackburn, 1981; Stern et al., 1986; Walker, 1979; Winett, Kaiser, & Haberkorn, 1977; Winett & Nietzel, 1975), although the involvement of other variables, such as feedback, has sometimes made the effects of the incentives difficult to isolate. Even a lottery system, involving modest cash payments to winners, coupled with driving-reduction goals and feedback, was enough to reduce automobile driving by participants by roughly 10% over a few weeks but the change in behavior did not persist beyond the duration of the experiment (Foxx & Schaeffer, 1981). In some cases, the cost of incentives has exceeded the immediate monetary value of the energy saved (Hake & Foxx, 1978; McClelland & Cantor, 1981; Newsom & Makranczy, 1977–1978). This might be taken as evidence of the ineffectiveness of incentives from a cost–benefit point of view, but only if one ignores the long-term effects of unnecessary energy use on resources that are at risk of being depleted and on environmental pollution.

Disincentives and penalties can also be used to decrease energy consumption. Much of the debate about the possibility of imposing some type of national tax on energy use has centered on the idea that, in addition to generating revenue for the federal government, such a tax would modify behavior in environmentally beneficial ways. The tenability of the assumption that an energy tax would have the indicated behavioral effect is questionable, however, in the absence of data on the matter. A thought-provoking study that demonstrated the effectiveness of a disincentive for modifying behavior in one context was reported by Van Houten, Nau, and Merrigan (1981); these investigators decreased the amount of elevator use by 31% by simply increasing the door-closing delay from 10 to 26 seconds. In general, however, the question of the effectiveness of disincentives and penalties has not received the same amount of attention from researchers that the question of the effectiveness of incentives and rewards has received.

In the aggregate, the results of energy use studies and efforts to improve the efficiency of that use have demonstrated that changes in behavior in the direction of conservation can be induced, but the effects have typically been small and temporary. The generality of the findings is limited by the fact that the results have usually been obtained with volunteers, and people who volunteer to participate in studies on behavioral effects on the environment may differ in important ways from those who do not (Nietzel & Winett, 1977). Insofar as studies have relied exclusively on questionnaire data, conclusions about behavior must be made with reservations because of the lack of assurance that people's behavior corresponds exactly to their reports of same (Geller, 1981a; Luyben, 1982). Despite these and other problems associated with evaluations of efforts to effect energy-conserving behavior, Stern (1992b) suggested that this may be the area in which psychology has made its greatest practical contribution so far in mitigating global change. Also this area is arguably among the most deserving of attention because of the potential impact that changes in behavior can have (Gardner & Stern, 1996).

Kempton, Harris, Keith, and Weihl (1985) distinguished three types of energy-conserving behaviors: *investment* in energy-efficient equipment (high miles-per-gallon automobiles, low-energy-demand home appliances), efficient *management* of energy use (setting back the thermostat when the house is not in use, planning errands so as to minimize driving), and *curtailment* of energy-demanding amenities or comfort (accommodating to lower indoor temperature, selecting recreation or entertainment that makes low demands on energy over high-demand possibilities). Although all three types of conservation represent opportunities for significant energy savings, Stern and Gardner (1981) noted that actions aimed at increasing efficiency of energy use (improving home insulation or installing more efficient heating equipment, purchasing a fuel-efficient automobile) are generally more effective than action aimed at curtailment of energy use (setting thermostat to lower temperature, carpooling). Kempton, Darley and Stern (1992) pointed out that psychological factors influence all of these behaviors.

## CONSERVING ENERGY IN TRANSPORTATION

Transportation is a major consumer of energy. About one fourth of all energy used in the United States is for transportation, and roughly half of all energy consumed by the household sector of the economy is for private transportation (Stern & Gardner, 1981). An obvious reason for interest in increasing transportation efficiency is the impact this could have on energy conservation. Other compelling environmental reasons for focusing on transportation include the contribution of automotive emissions to air pollution and accumulation of greenhouse gases in the atmosphere, the problem of traffic congestion in many urban areas, and the high incidence of highway fatalities in industrialized countries. As Gibbons, Blair, and Gwin (1989) put it, "If Americans want to hold down oil consumption and attendant carbon dioxide emissions and play a world leadership role, a revision of transportation policy to reflect all energy-related costs would be a good place to start" (p. 141).

The automobile (here to include minivan, sport utility vehicle, and small truck) is, by far, the preferred means of private transportation in the United States, therefore much of the research attention has focused on ways in which the operation of automobiles can be made less detrimental to the environment. Stern and Gardner (1981) argued that investments in energy efficiency (chiefly through the purchase of energy-efficient automobiles) represent the greatest potential for energy savings; other possibilities for conservation include keeping one's automobile properly maintained and practicing driving habits that maximize miles traveled per gallon of fuel. There are reasons to believe that some motor-vehicle driving habits are more environmentally friendly than others, but more needs to be learned about how vehicle emissions are affected by driver behavior (Transportation Research Board, 1997). The other major focus of research has been on the possibility of making greater use of carpooling and public transportation as well as cycling and walking.

Carpooling or ride sharing, especially for commuting to and from work, has been promoted for some time as an effective means of reducing the consumption of gas and oil, decreasing the emission of atmospheric pollutants, and helping relieve the problem of traffic congestion. Despite considerable effort by companies and municipalities to encourage carpooling, the practice has not been adopted as widely as had been hoped. We need to understand why people do or do not participate in carpooling programs. It appears that the decision regarding whether to participate is typically not made strictly on the basis of the economics involved (Margolin & Misch, 1978).

Many municipalities have adopted the practice of reserving one or more lanes on major access highways for vehicles with more than a specified number of passengers. The approach is intended to increase the incidence of carpooling and appears to be effective (MacCalden & Davis, 1972; Rose & Hinds, 1976). However, it is difficult to tell the magnitude of its effect, because the lanes are open to all multipassenger vehicles including those that would have contained multiple passengers even without the incentive the lane access is intended to provide. Other efforts to increase participation in carpooling have involved preferential parking and facilitation of carpooling by providing matching and other services to potential poolers (Geller, Winett, & Everett, 1982).

Reicher and Geller (1981) reviewed the results of attempts to increase participation in carpooling through the use of such approaches. On the basis of this review, these investigators concluded that the assignment of priority lanes has been effective in increasing the average occupancy per vehicle during peak commuting hours, that cost-effective enforcement of priority-lane usage is a problem, that organized efforts to form carpools have been only partially successful, and that social factors are major determinants of individuals' willingness to participate in carpools.

A variant of carpooling that has also received some attention is referred to by Reicher and Geller as *vanpooling*. Vans may be used to transport commuters to their workplaces either from their homes or from parking areas on the outskirts of congested urban centers (Forstater & Twomey, 1976). Like carpooling, vanpooling has the potential of effecting significant savings of automotive fuel and decreasing the environmental burden of passenger transportation.

Some experimentation has been done with the use of token-reinforcement and operant-conditioning techniques to increase the use of public transportation in urban settings (Deslauriers & Everett, 1977; Everett, Deslauriers, Newsom, &

Anderson, 1978; Everett, Hayward, & Meyers, 1974). The results of these studies, which were done primarily with college campus buses, showed that the use of bus transportation can be increased with the help of reinforcement techniques, but they failed to demonstrate that this could be done on a cost-effective basis and in a nonacademic setting or that the increased bus riding was accompanied by a comparable reduction in private vehicle use.

In Trondheim, Norway, transit ridership has been increased through the implementation of a system of time-varying toll pricing on access roads to the city. Toll booths operate electronically so that vehicles equipped with radio tags, provided free by the city, can pass through them without stopping. Making the toll rates higher during rush hours resulted in a switch by some commuters from automobiles to trains (Gibbs, 1997).

One impediment to the use of public transportation, especially by the elderly, appears to be the fear of crime (Patterson, 1985). Research needs to provide a better understanding of other reasons that people choose not to use public transportation when it is available, how it can be made safer and more attractive, and the cost-effectiveness of various approaches (e.g., increasing reliability or upgrading the quality of mass transit service, employer subsidies of rider passes) that might be taken to increase public use. For most automobile owners, the advantages—real or perceived—of using their private vehicle for most of their transportation needs considerably outweigh the advantages—again, real or perceived—of alternative modes of transportation (Everett & Watson, 1987); the question is how to increase the attractiveness of the alternative modes.

## INCREASING RECYCLING

Although a majority of Americans express favorable attitudes toward recycling (Dunlap & Scarce, 1991), the amount of material recycled in the United States falls far short of what is considered possible. People fail to participate in recycling programs for a variety of reasons, including indifference and the perceived nuisance of doing so (Howenstine, 1993; Vining & Ebreo, 1990; Vining, Linn, & Burdge, 1992). Several studies have shown that logistic factors, such as the design and placement of receptacles for deposit of trash or materials for recycling, can have an effect on litter control and recycling behavior (Finnie, 1973; Geller, Brasted & Mann, 1979–1980; Humphrey, Bord, Hammond, & Mann, 1977; Jacobs, Bailey, & Crews, 1984; Luyben & Bailey, 1979; Reid, Luyben, Rawers, & Bailey, 1976).

Not surprisingly, people are more likely to recycle if doing so is convenient (e.g., recyclables picked up at curbside) than if it is not (e.g., recyclables deposited by consumer at collection sites; Derksen & Gartrell, 1993; Guagnano,

Stern, & Dietz, 1995; Schultz & Oskamp, 1996; Scott, 1999). Reasons for recycling also vary; not least among them is the intrinsic satisfaction people get from being frugal or participating in environmentally friendly activities (DeYoung, 1986). Having a neighborhood coordinator of recycling activities has been shown to increase recycling in some instances (Burn, 1991; Hopper & Nielson, 1991).

Several studies have focused on the possibility of increasing the participation of individuals or families in such programs. These studies have shown that participation can sometimes be increased, at least temporarily, through the use of explicit goals or incentives such as contests, prizes, and rewards (Couch, Garber, & Karpus, 1978–1979; Geller, 1981b; Geller, Chafee, & Ingram, 1975; Hamad, Bettinger, Cooper, & Semb, 1980–1981; Hamad, Cooper, & Semb, 1977; Jacobs & Bailey, 1982–1983; Witmer & Geller, 1976).

Perhaps the most obvious attempt to promote recycling through the use of incentives on a broad scale is the requirement for redeemable deposits on certain beverage containers that has been legislatively mandated in some states. Although beverage containers may seem a small part of the problem, the quantities in which they are sold make them significant. According to Hosford and Duncan (1994), makers of beer and soft drink containers in the United States produce about 100 billion cans a year, or about one can per American per day, and that this output accounts for about one-fifth of all aluminum used in the United States. Currently, again according to Hosford and Duncan, somewhat more than 63% of aluminum cans are recycled. An anticipated increase in production by several billion cans per year, resulting presumably from both increased population and development of new markets, makes clear the importance of increasing this percentage and making recycling programs successful globally.

The use of prompting and reminders to recycle has proved to be moderately effective in some cases (Jacobs & Bailey, 1982–1983; Luyben & Bailey, 1979; Luyben & Cummings, 1981–1982; Luyben, Warren, & Tallman, 1979–1980; Reid, Luyben, Rawers, & Bailey, 1976), as has the provision of information regarding the purpose and details of recycling programs (Hopper & Nielsen, 1991; Jacobs et al., 1984), although in some studies the manipulation of these variables produced no effects (Jacobs, Bailey, & Crews, 1984; Pardini & Katzev, 1983–1984; Spaccarelli, Zolik, & Jason, 1989–1990; Witmer & Geller, 1976). In the aggregate, the studies show that prompting, reminding, and information provision can have at least small effects, but they also make it clear that the situation is somewhat more complicated than this claim makes it appear inasmuch as the targeted effects are not always obtained.

In general, successes in motivating participation in resource recovery programs through the use of explicit goals or incentives have been modest. Stern and Oskamp (1987) estimated that behavioral techniques have typically motivated only about 10% to 15% of the people who are eligible to participate in the recycling programs involved to do so. The natural tendency seems to be for early enthusiasm to wane and participation to fall off in time in the absence of continual bolstering (Porter, Leeming, & Dwyer, 1995). In some cases, simple positive reinforcement schemes have even produced unwanted behavior (Geller, 1981b). The results of many studies of recycling behavior, like those of the studies of energy use, are somewhat limited in generality inasmuch as they were obtained with students living in college housing facilities. Among the factors that appear to increase the chances of participation in community-sponsored programs are the scheduling of the pickup of recyclables on the same day as the pickup of the regular trash, the provision of containers by the town, and the minimization of sorting required by residents (Gardner & Stern, 1996). Much remains to be learned about the planning and executing of recycling programs that will effect the lasting changes in behavior that are essential to make real progress on the problem of managing waste in an environmentally sensitive way.

## REDUCING WASTE PRODUCTION

Increasing recycling is unquestionably a worthy objective from an environmental point of view. At least as important an objective, but one that has not received as much attention from researchers, is that of decreasing the production of waste in the first place (DeYoung, 1993; Durning, 1992; West, Lee, & Feiock, 1992). The Municipal Solid Waste Source Reduction and Recycling Act of 1989 focuses on reducing waste at its source and on recycling as the preferred approaches to solid waste management.

The importance of reducing waste production has been recognized by the Environmental Protection Agency (1976) for some time. Relatively little sociopsychological research has been done on how waste reduction might be facilitated, compared with what has been done on recycling behavior and attitudes (Geller, 1981b). It appears that waste reduction is a less salient factor in consumer decision making than is recyclability (Ebreo, Hershey, & Vining, 1999). There is some evidence, however, that corporations are becoming more aware of the importance of reducing waste—especially hazardous waste—and planning for the management of that which they produce. This is probably due, to some degree, to the publicity given to toxic waste production by the Toxic Release Inventory maintained by the Environmental Protection Agency (Baram, Dillon, & Ruffle, 1990). Some industries have also begun to factor long-term costs of waste management into their decision-making processes (General Electric Company, 1987).

Presumably, purchasing decisions and other consumer behavior that showed a preference for producers who gave evidence of minimizing waste in their production or packaging processes would motivate greater attention to this issue among producers. Public concern about waste production does not appear to be strong enough yet to elicit disclosure, in advertising and promotional activities, of information about waste in production or packaging processes, so the consumer who does wish to take this issue into account in making purchasing decisions may find it difficult to do so.

## ANTILITTERING CAMPAIGNS

Psychologists have tried to determine why people litter, and many organized attempts have been made to decrease the incidence of this type of behavior (Finnie, 1973; Huffman, Grossnickle, Cope, & Huffman, 1995; Krauss, Freedman, & Whitcup, 1978; Robinson, 1976). Why people litter is not entirely clear, but apparently the perceived acceptability of littering by peers plays some role inasmuch as people are more likely to litter in an already littered area than in a clean one (Cialdini, Kallgren, & Reno, 1991; Krauss, Freedman, & Whitcup, 1978; Reiter & Samuel, 1980). Numerous publicity campaigns have been mounted by states and municipalities to increase public awareness of the problem, discourage littering, and promote clean-up activities. The Adopt-a-Highway program, first implemented in Texas, is now operating in a majority of the states of the United States. In this program, small citizen groups agree to pick up litter along a specified stretch of roadway several times a year.

There is some evidence that explicit appeals and simple reminders, in the form of signs prompting people to dispose of trash responsibly or thanking them for doing so, can reduce the tendency to litter (Durdan, Reeder, & Hecht, 1985; Geller, Witmer, & Orebaugh, 1976; Hayes, Johnson, & Cone, 1975; Oliver, Roggenbuck, & Watson, 1985; O'Neill, Blanck, & Joyner, 1980). Daily feedback regarding the amount of litter on an elementary school grounds, coupled with the reward of weekly movie viewing when the grounds were clean, effected a significant reduction in littering by school children (Gendrich, McNees, Schnelle, Beagle, & Clark, 1982). Several other studies have shown that incentives and rewards, even of token value, can be effective in reducing littering in campgrounds and other settings (Bacon-Prue, Blount, Pickering, & Drabman, 1980; Burgess, Clark, & Hendee, 1971; Chapman & Risley, 1974; Clark, Burgess, & Hendee, 1972; Kohlenberg & Phillips, 1973; Powers, Osborne, & Anderson, 1973). Daily notices in a newspaper of the amount of litter found in specified areas of a city resulted in reductions in the litter in the target areas during the period of the campaign, although no residual effect was found 1 month following its termination (Schnelle, McNees, Thomas, Gendrich, & Beagle, 1980).

Proponents of the *bottle bills* passed in recent years in some states, mandating refunds on the return of glass, plastic, and aluminum beverage containers, have argued that their enactment would reduce litter and waste and increase participation in recycling. At least one study was done in an effort to determine the effectiveness of the New York bottle bill in reducing the contribution of the refundable bottles to litter in that state. The results, involving a comparison of bottle litter at various locations in New York with bottle litter in comparable locations in New Jersey, which had no bottle bill, showed a significant and persisting reduction in this type of litter in New York, but not in New Jersey after the New York law was enacted (Levitt & Leventhal, 1986).

## EDUCATION AND PERSUASION IN BEHAVIOR CHANGE

Education must be a major component in any approach that has as its aim the influencing of people to behave, intentionally and intelligently, in environmentally beneficial ways. People cannot be concerned about environmental issues if they do not know about them, and they cannot be faulted for behaving in environmentally detrimental ways if they are unaware of the implications of specific forms of behavior.

In many of the studies already mentioned, the main method for trying to effect changes in behavior has been some form of information dissemination or organized attempt at persuasion. There has been considerable interest in determining the effectiveness of information dissemination and advertising campaigns in making behavior more environmentally friendly (Constanzo, Archer, Aronson, & Pettigrew, 1986; Couch, Garber, & Karpus, 1978–1979; Dennis & Soderstrom, 1988; Dennis, Soderstrom, Koncinski, & Cavanaugh, 1990; Ester & Winett, 1982; Geller, Chafee, & Ingram, 1975; Stern & Kirkpatrick, 1977). The most general conclusion that can be drawn from these and similar studies is that simply providing information about the effects of behavior on environmental change and urging people to modify their behavior so as to make it less environmentally detrimental have produced positive, but seldom dramatic, results (Condelli et al., 1984; Dennis, Soderstrom, Koncinski, & Cavanaugh, 1990; Ester & Winett, 1982; Stern & Aronson, 1984). It appears that information campaigns targeting environmentally significant behavior have enjoyed about the same modest level of success as have mass media campaigns aimed at modifying behavior in other areas of public interest (Roberts & Maccoby, 1985; Wallack, 1981).

It is probably important to make a distinction between providing people with information they may lack about alternative ways of doing things that have implications for the environment and trying to persuade them to do something they would rather not do. Persuading people to change their dietary habits by consuming less meat and more grains so as to conserve the energy and water required to produce the meat and meat products may be a hard sell to people who especially like meat. Yet, it seems likely that some environmentally detrimental behavior occurs simply because people are not aware that alternatives to their customary behavior exist. For example, if one would like to make environmentally sensitive purchases, but lacks the information necessary to do so, making such information available should have a positive effect. Results obtained by DeYoung et al. (1993) in a project in which consumers were given information regarding how to reduce waste, or waste toxicity, by purchasing carefully are consistent with this view. Another study showed relevant knowledge about recycling to be a better predictor of participation in a curbside recycling program than several other potential predictors, such as expressed concern for the environment, pressure to participate, and the personal inconvenience of doing so (Gamba & Oskamp, 1994).

How effective information dissemination and persuasion campaigns are in influencing behavior appears to depend on a variety of factors. Those identified include the clarity of the message presented, the degree to which it is personalized, how it is packaged, its emotional content, the specificity and concreteness of recommendations conveyed, and the credibility of its source (Dennis, Soderstrom, Koncinski, & Cavanaugh, 1990; Gonzales, Aronson, & Costanzo, 1988; Leventhal, 1970; Stern, 1986). Daamen, Staats, Wilke, and Engelen (2001) found that messages specifically tailored to their recipients were more effective in causing behavior change than were messages not so specifically tailored. The recipients in this case were workshop managers in garages, and the messages had to do with reduction of oil pollution of waste water. Tailoring has also been found to be effective for messages aimed at changing people's behavior as it relates to personal health (De Vries & Brug, 1999).

Interview data suggest that antilittering campaigns can be effective in raising public awareness of the problem and increasing the expressed expectation that littering would result in a feeling of guilt; whether this translates into an actual decrease in littering behavior is not clear. One study, in which residents of an American city were interviewed before and after an antilittering campaign, showed changes in both attitudes and predictions of own future behavior. The attitudinal changes appeared to be somewhat more substantial than the predicted behavioral changes, however; the percentage of respondents who said they would feel guilty if they littered in the future was 37 before the campaign and 67 after, whereas the percentage who said they probably would litter in the future went from 39 to 31 (Grasmick, Bursik, & Kinsey, 1991). In another study, educational messages about long-term consequences of water conservation and the effectiveness of individual action produced conservation behavior among lower middle-class participants, whereas educational messages focused on the economic consequences of conservation for the participant did not. Neither type of message affected the behavior of upper middle-class participants (Thompson & Stoutemyer, 1991).

Studies involving the dissemination of information for the purpose of effecting changes in energy-use behavior patterns have been reviewed by Dennis, Soderstrom, Koncinski, and Cavanaugh (1990). Although disseminating information about energy use and conservation has increased conservation behavior in some instances, it has not succeeded in doing so in others. Particularly discouraging is that people sometimes fail to act even on information, such as that obtained in a home-energy audit, that deals directly with their specific situation (Hirst, Berry, & Soderstrom, 1981). How successful an information-dissemination effort will be seems to depend, in part, on variables having to do with the substance and form of the information disseminated and the manner of dissemination. Our understanding of how these variables have their effects is fragmentary and could benefit from further research. Stern (1992b) noted the untenability of the simple assumption that technologies that will save their owners money will be adopted once the owners become aware of the benefits.

It appears from several studies, such as those reviewed by Dennis et al. (1990), that in the absence of motivating incentives, the prospects of rewards or punishments, or the extraction of an explicit commitment to participate in an environmental preservation program, information alone is not a reliable effector of lasting behavioral change. However, in most of the studies that support this conclusion, the environmental information was provided in a compressed form (lecture, discussion, pamphlet) over a short period of time. The fact that this approach has not proved to be highly effective does not constitute compelling evidence that providing substantive information over a long period of time about environmental change and the role of human behavior in causing it would be ineffective as well.

It is well known that the effectiveness of an information campaign depends at least as much on the form of the information presented as on its substance. Marketing and advertising firms spend enormous amounts of money on the packaging of the messages they design for the purpose of influencing consumer behavior. If efforts to persuade, or even just inform, through communication are to be successful, they must succeed first in capturing the attention of the target audience and then in holding it long enough to get the message across. The message also must be presented in an understandable and memorable form. Many efforts to inform the public about energy conservation have failed to make use of effective communication techniques (Dennis, Soderstrom, Koncinski, & Cavanaugh, 1990). One technique that has shown promise is that of using televised demonstrations of what constitutes effective energy-conserving behavior (Syme, Seligman, Kantola, & MacPherson, 1987; Winett et al., 1982; Winett, Leckliter, Chinn, Stahl, & Love, 1985).

The effectiveness of persuasion has long been a focus of interest of psychologists across a broad range of contexts, and especially in the context of consumer research (Bettman, 1986). Its relevance to the activity of advertising and to the question of how purchasing behavior is determined is obvious. (We return to this topic in a discussion of consumer behavior.) Progress in producing a consensus on what works and what does not has been slow (Eagly & Himmelfarb, 1978; Himmelfarb & Eagly, 1974). The *sine qua non* of an effective message is that it be understandable, believable, and relevant to the interests of the recipient. Yet many factors play a role in determining how efforts to persuade are perceived and how effective they are (Tesser & Shaffer, 1990).

One important determinant of the persuasiveness of a message is the reliability or credibility of its source, as perceived by the message's recipients (Craig & McMann, 1978; Miller & Ford, 1985). What people who are perceived as experts say is likely to be more persuasive than pronouncements from people who are not seen as experts (Hass, 1981). Messages that come from a source believed to have a direct stake or vested interest in effecting a specific change in the recipients' behavior is likely to be given less credence than those derived from a more disinterested source. In an illustrative study, people were more responsive to a letter suggesting a household energy audit when the letter was printed under a county letterhead than when it was printed under the letterhead of the company that would conduct the audit (Miller & Ford, 1985). Another study reported that a presidential appeal to conserve energy had a more substantial effect than a gubernatorial one (Wodarski, 1982).

What constitutes an effective attempt to persuade appears to depend also on the degree to which the individual toward whom the attempt is made is interested in the issue involved (Chaiken, 1987; Chaiken, Liberman, & Eagly, 1989; Petty & Cacioppo, 1981; Petty, Cacioppo, & Goldman, 1981; Petty, Cacioppo, & Heesacker, 1981). The substance of a message intended to persuade is more likely to be processed deeply if it concerns an issue about which the recipient is already motivated to think than if it concerns one that is of little personal interest. In the latter case, substantive aspects of the message may become less influential while other aspects (e.g., source credibility, message packaging) take on greater significance. Not surprisingly, attitudes based on thinking about issues appear to be more stable and less vulnerable to attack than those molded by more superficial factors (Mackie, 1987; Wu & Shaffer, 1987).

## IMPORTANCE OF CHOICE AND SENSE OF CONTROL

There is evidence from several sources that people are more likely to use systems if they have participated, even minimally, in their design or implementation than if they have not (Castleman, Whitehead, Sher, Hantman, & Massey, 1974; Eason, 1981; Ingersheim, 1976). Similarly, people tend to do better on tasks they have chosen than on those imposed on them (Monty, Geller, Savage, & Perlmutter, 1979; Perlmutter, Scharff, Karsh, & Monty, 1980). This principle appears to be fairly general and should apply to behavior that has environmental implications as well as in other contexts. Evidence that it applies to the case of household energy conservation comes from a study by Yates and Aronson (1983). More generally, survey data indicate that people have a strong preference for conservation measures that are voluntary rather than compulsory and for the use of incentives to motivate conservation behavior rather than penalties for the generation of waste (Milstein, 1977).

In a study of migrant farm workers, Vaughn (1993a, 1993b) found that those who believed they had significant control over the health effects of exposure to pesticides were five times as likely to attempt to protect themselves from exposure than were those who did not share this belief. Other studies have shown that whether people take steps to protect their health depends, to a significant degree, on whether they believe they have control over the situation (Peterson & Stunkard, 1989). The ability to cope effectively with environmental stressors also appears to depend somewhat on the degree to which people perceive the sources of stress to be under their control (Fleming, Baum, & Singer, 1984). Situations that are stressful tend to be less so if one perceives oneself to be in control of them than if one does not, independently of whether one actually does exercise control (Gardner, 1978). Brown and Inouye (1978) also presented evidence that the belief that one has control of a situation may be a more important determinant of one's psychological state than whether one in fact has control.

## IMPORTANCE OF COMMITMENT

Several studies have demonstrated the importance of an overt commitment to an environmental program as a means of ensuring participation in the program (Bachman & Katzev, 1982; Becker, 1978; Burn & Oskamp, 1986; DeLeon & Fuqua, 1995; Katzev & Johnson, 1983, 1984; Katzev & Pardini, 1987–1988; Katzev & Wang, 1994; Pallak, Cook, & Sullivan, 1980; Pallak & Cummings, 1976; Pardini & Katzev, 1983–1984; Van Houwelingen & Van Raaij, 1989; Wang & Katzev, 1990). Commitment is of course a matter of degree, and one would expect that its effectiveness would be proportional to its strength, but sometimes a modest commitment has been enough to have a behavioral effect. Agreement by participants in one household energy-conservation project to have their names appear on a published list was followed by a significant reduction in energy use (Pallak, Cook, & Sullivan, 1980; although for a counterexample, see McCaul & Kopp, 1982). In another study, people who signed pledges to participate in a recycling program did indeed participate at least during the duration of the experiment (Katzev & Pardini, 1987–1988).

There is suggestive evidence that a stronger commitment (e.g., written vs. oral) yields more persistent behavior than a weaker one (Pardini & Katzev, 1983–1984). In one study, a commitment accompanied by an agreement to promote the target behavior among neighbors yielded the desired effect, whereas an expression of commitment by itself did not (Cobern, Porter, Leeming, & Dwyer, 1995). In another study, signing a letter of agreement to participate in a paper recycling program and granting permission for a local newspaper to publish the signers' names did not by itself increase recycling behavior, whereas provision of weekly feedback as to the amount of paper produced by a participating group effected a change, and commitment and feedback in combination effected a larger change. In yet another study, people were asked to respond to from one to three requests regarding recycling; the more requests they were asked to respond to, the more recycling they did during the study and 18 months later (Arbuthnot et al., 1976–1977).

One form that commitment can take is acceptance of a specific goal. In the McCaul and Kopp (1982) study mentioned earlier, agreeing to be identified in a campus newspaper as supporters of energy conservation did not suffice to ensure participation in an aluminum can recycling program, whereas accepting a goal of returning a specific number of cans per day did. The setting of a specific goal also has proved to be effective in a paper-recycling effort (Hamad, Bettinger, Cooper, & Semb, 1980–1981). In general, specific goals appear to be more likely to lead to behavior changes than nonspecific goals (Locke & Latham, 1990).

The finding that an explicit expression of commitment to participate in an environmental program increases the likelihood of actual participation is not surprising. It would be surprising indeed if people who made such a commitment turned out to be less likely than those who did not to engage in the behavior implied by the commitment. Evidence from other studies of the effects of commitment on subsequent behavior suggests that, once having committed oneself to an idea or a position, one tends to take a defensive posture with respect to it and be partial toward it in the interpretation of further data (Geller & Pitz, 1968; Gibson & Nichol, 1964; Nickerson, 1998). To make a commitment is to appropriate the idea or project goal as one's own, to some degree, and to acquire a vested interest in its validation or realization.

In interpreting the results of studies of the effects of commitment as a determinant of environmentally friendly behavior, several facts should be borne in mind. In most of these studies, the levels of commitment involved have been relatively low, compared, say, with the levels probably involved in joining activist environmental organizations, supporting environmental protection projects financially, or campaigning on behalf of a candidate for public office on environmental issues. The general finding that effects are modest in size and perhaps temporary might hold only for small levels of commitment that are temporary. The results of the experiments that have been done lead one to surmise that the effects that major commitments to environmental causes have on environmentally relevant behavior over the long term are probably substantial, but more data on the question are needed.

## IMPORTANCE OF INFORMATION FEEDBACK

People who pay water, fuel, or electricity bills on a regular basis receive feedback about the financial implications of their use of these resources. At least during periods of constant prices, variations in usage are reflected in corresponding variations in costs to the consumer. Consumers understand that the size of their electric utility bill depends on the amount of electrical energy they use in their homes. Yet the kind of feedback the typical bill provides is not detailed. For example, it does not give the consumer a clue as to the relative effectiveness of various possible resource-conserving actions.

Many consumers do not have an accurate understanding of the energy demands of different household appliances or how the electricity used by specific appliances compares with that used for lighting (Costanzo, Archer, Aronson, & Pettigrew, 1986; Kempton, Harris, Keith, & Weihl, 1985; Kempton & Montgomery, 1982). Moreover, misconceptions in this regard can persist in the face of information campaigns designed to dispel them (Stern, 1992b). This is unfortunate because behavior with environmental impact is influenced by assumptions about its cost (Byrne, Rich, Tannian, & Wang, 1985), and misconceptions by consumers of the relative effectiveness of specific energy-conservation behaviors (e.g., turning off unused lights vs. making less frequent use of the clothes dryer) can lead to resistance to conservation programs (Dennis, Soderstrom, Koncinski, & Cavanaugh, 1990).

Gardner and Stern (1996; Stern, 2000) noted the importance of making the effort to effect behavior change commensurate with the potential benefits realized from that change. For example, they pointed out that more than 75% of the energy consumed by the average U.S. household is used to run automobiles and heat homes (and household water); this fact makes effecting conservation in these areas worth much effort. If, because of an overestimation of the relative importance of a particular behavior, modification of that behavior does not produce the expected decrease in energy consumption, participation in other conservation efforts may be resisted. Efforts to motivate people to conserve energy should provide them with the information that will help them form accurate expectations regarding what the effects of specific changes in behavior will be.

The provision of feedback regarding energy use at considerably shorter intervals than those of typical billing procedures—weekly, daily, or continuously—has proved to be effective in reducing energy consumption in some households (Becker, 1978; Dennis & Soderstrom, 1988; Geller, 1992b; Hutton, Mauser, Filiatrault, & Ahtola, 1986; McClelland & Cook, 1979–1980, 1980; Seligman, Becker, & Darley, 1981; Seligman & Darley, 1977; Van Houwelingen & Van Raaij, 1989; Winett, Neale, & Grier, 1979; Winett, Neale, Williams, Yokley, & Kauder, 1978–1979), although in other cases this approach has yielded little or no decrease in consumption (Katzev, Cooper, & Fisher, 1980–1981; Midden, Meter, Weening, & Zieverink, 1983). Becker and Seligman (1978) emphasized the need for feedback to be credible if it is to be effective, and Stern and Gardner (1981) noted the importance of providing, along with feedback about energy consumption, some assistance in effecting the actions necessary to be more efficient.

Several ways of providing feedback have been tried experimentally, including a device for signaling whenever a household's use of electricity exceeds 90% of its peak level, and a metered display of electricity cost. In one study, Sexton, Johnson, and Konakayama (1987) found that, although continuous feedback did not result in a decrease in the total amount of electricity used, it shifted some of the usage to off-peak hours when the cost was low. Hayes and Cone (1981) found that a monthly letter comparing that current month's usage with the amount used during the same month in past years resulted in modest decreases in consumption. In still another study, a daily reporting on an evening TV news program of gasoline purchases in a metropolitan area appeared to be enough to decrease gasoline consumption in that area at least during a few-week period (Rothstein, 1980).

Some experimentation has been done on the possibility of inducing automobile drivers to drive in more fuel-efficient ways by providing them with a daily reckoning (Runnion, Watson, & McWhorter, 1978) or continuous display (Lauridsen, 1977) of some measure of efficiency, such as miles-per-gallon or gallons-per-hour of driving. Although fuel economies were realized by some, but not all, participating drivers, variables in addition to the feedback may have affected driving behavior.

Given the relatively low and decreasing cost of computing elements, it should soon be technically feasible and cost-effective, if it is not so already, to provide consumers with continuous feedback regarding the cumulative costs of the operation of specific electrical appliances. Whether such feedback would influence behavior is a question for research. Some automobiles can already give drivers instantaneous gas mileage and show how this changes on a moment-to-moment basis; I am not aware of data regarding whether this has any effect on driver behavior. Another way to provide knowledge of the energy demands of frequently used devices would be the development of interactive computer programs that would show by simulation the energy-consumption and cost consequences of the operation of various household appliances.

The need for people to understand the environmental implications of their personal behavior is a general one. Many illustrations can be given of feedback being too general and insufficiently coupled to an individual's behavior to have much effect. Homeowners who live in towns providing curbside trash pickup service pay for that service through their taxes, and presumably how much they pay depends on the volume of trash the town produces. There is no direct coupling between an individual's trash production and the amount one pays for the trash removal service, and therefore there is little monetary incentive for one to produce less trash. The situation is quite different for the individual who must pay directly for trash removal by the barrel, say, or the pound. Similarly, people who pay for utilities indirectly through their rent are likely to be less aware of the financial implications of their use of those utilities than are those who pay for them directly. There is some evidence that when renters convert from "utilities-included" rent payment to arrangements that have them paying their utilities directly to the service providers, their usage tends to decrease (McClelland, 1980).

A risk associated with providing people with feedback regarding how their own behavior compares with the behavior of others is that people whose behavior is atypically environmentally beneficial—because of unusually low energy consumption—may discover their atypicality and modify their behavior so as to make it more typical and thus less environmentally beneficial. At least suggestive evidence of this possibility comes from a study by Bittle, Valesano, and Thaler (1979–1980), who found that when people were provided with daily feedback regarding electricity use, those who initially were relatively heavy users decreased their usage, whereas those who initially were relatively light users increased theirs. The result could have reflected a simple regression-on-the-mean phenomenon, but the finding deserves further exploration. A related concern has been expressed regarding the possibility that, to the extent that people believe that specific energy-consuming behaviors are more costly than they actually are, providing them with accurate cost information could have the undesired effect of encouraging greater energy use (Carter, 1977; Craig & McCann, 1977). This possibility, coupled with the fact that energy is a relatively inexpensive commodity for the average consumer, points up the importance of not relying on cost reduction as the sole motivation for energy conservation.

## PEER PRESSURE AND SOCIAL NORMS

The power of peer pressure to influence individual behavior is well documented in the social psychology literature. People's behavior, as it relates to environmental change, is influenced by the behavior of their peers and social norms—what they perceive to be acceptable to others (Black, Stern, & Elworth, 1985; Cialdini, Reno, & Kallgren, 1990; Darley, 1978; Jones, 1990; Kahle & Beatty, 1987; Stern, Dietz, & Black, 1986; Vining & Ebreo, 1990). Social approval and disapproval can play roles much like those of more tangible incentives and disincentives in shaping behavior (Cook & Berrenberg, 1981).

Given that people's behavior relative to specific environmental issues is influenced by what they know or believe the behavior of their peers relative to those issues to be, publicizing average or typical behavior with respect to such matters as electrical energy use, water use, and recycling activity might be expected to help, in some cases, bring atypical behavior more in line with the norm (Pallak, Cook, & Sullivan, 1980). As already noted, however, a risk in publicizing typical behavior is that it would influence those people who are doing better than average, as well as those who are doing worse, to modify their behavior in the direction of typicality. Perhaps what should be publicized are examples not of average behavior but of behavior that is atypical but worthy of emulation from an environmental point of view. How effective the publicizing of exemplary behavior would be in effecting environmentally desirable behavior change is a question for research.

Perhaps even more influential than what is perceived to be socially normative behavior is one's knowledge of the behavior of one's personal friends and acquaintances. With respect to energy conservation, for example, people tend to do what they see those who are close to them do (Darley & Beniger, 1981; Leonard-Barton, 1981). The fact that more people participate in community recycling efforts if recyclables are picked up at curbside than if they have to be deposited at collection centers has been attributed primarily to the greater convenience to participants of the curbside pickup arrangement; another possibly important difference between the two arrangements, however, is that whether one is recycling is more apparent to one's neighbors with curbside pickup than with collection centers, so peer pressure has a greater chance of being effective in the first case.

An approach to behavior change that utilizes peer pressure and social norms and that has shown some success is community-based social marketing (Geller, 1989; Kassirer & McKenzie-Mohr, 1998; McKenzie-Mohr, 2000). A noteworthy aspect of this approach is that it explicitly addresses the problem, emphasized by several investigators (Black, Stern, & Elworth, 1985; Guagnano, Stern, & Dietz, 1995), of the existence of barriers to desired activities. McKenzie-Mohr (2000) saw this aspect of the approach as critical: "It is difficult, if not impossible, to design an effective program to promote an activity without first knowing what inhibits the public from engaging in the activity to be promoted" (p. 533). Psychologists have an opportunity to make an important contribution to behavior-change efforts by identifying such barriers.

## CHANGE VERSUS EFFECTIVE LASTING CHANGE

I have been arguing that it is important to change attitudes and behavior as they relate to various aspects of environmental protection. It should be stressed, however, that what is needed are the kinds of change that will make a real difference in environmental matters. Most studies of the effectiveness of interventions aimed at behavior modification have not included checks for the persistence of effects beyond the intervention period. A typical finding of the few studies that have obtained data on this question is that any behavior changes effected during the intervention have largely disappeared soon after termination of the experiment (DeYoung, 1993; Dwyer, Leeming, Cobern, Porter, & Jackson, 1993; Geller, 1987; Geller, Winett, & Everett, 1982; Katzev & Johnson, 1983; Porter, Leeming, & Dwyer, 1995).

Unfortunately, changes that have little, if any, lasting effect may sometimes be perceived as more efficacious than they are and, consequently, relieve the pressure for substantive and lasting change. Nader (1991) illustrated this point in the context of arguing that whenever there is an "easy exit system" from a problem, people are likely to take it and thereby dissipate the energy that could otherwise be used to effect real change. "People who are concerned about unsafe drinking water buy bottled water, assuming that if it comes in a bottle it's okay. That takes away the people who are most likely to agitate and organize" (p. 15), and it is only citizen agitation and organization, Nader implied, that will ensure implementation of measures that are likely to be environmentally effective in the long run.

Reichel and Geller (1981) argued that, although many experiments have demonstrated that people can be induced to become more conservative in their use of energy for purposes of transportation through the use of incentives and other forms of positive reinforcement, many of the reinforcement schemes used in the experiments would not be cost-effective for long-term use. People are unlikely to voluntarily use energy more conservatively for the long run, they suggested, unless social norms are first changed so that such behavior becomes expected, valued, and socially rewarded on a continuing basis.

Stern (1992a) noted that the most effective efforts to bring about changes in behavior in the interest of environmental preservation have made use of combinations of techniques. There appear to be few instances of effecting substantive lasting change with a unidimensional approach. Neither information dissemination nor the use of incentives seems to work well by itself, for example, but in combination they have produced more promising results. Stern argued that a multifaceted approach to behavior change is needed because it is often necessary to overcome several barriers to such change simultaneously, any one of which could be sufficient to prevent it: "lack of knowledge, money, and attention; mistrust of experts (e.g., the energy auditors who estimate what an expensive action will save); difficulty or inconvenience of taking the necessary action; and lack of social support" (p. 292). If change is to be lasting, such barriers must be overcome for the long term.

Effecting substantive changes in behavior that has environmental implications is made more difficult by the fact that most of the environmental consequences of behavior occur on a time scale that is long relative to that of the goals and objectives that typically motivate behavior. Improvements in the environment that can be expected to result from changes in behavior may not be noticeable for several years or even decades in some cases. Global warming—the most serious of the threats to the environment in the view of some writers—would be unlikely to reveal any changes in progression that resulted from changes in behavior for many decades. A sizable literature on accommodation would lead us to expect it to be much more difficult to motivate people to do something about chronic problems that have slow, long-term, degradative effects than about more attention-getting acute problems that manifest themselves in dramatic ways from time to time, even though the slow, degradative effects may be the more threatening over the long run.

Finally, substantive changes in prevailing attitudes of the general public also often occur only gradually over long periods of time. Effects of such changes on legislation, governmental policies, industrial practices and social mores may be seen clearly only from a retrospective view across many years. It may be unrealistic to expect the modest efforts that have been made to change attitudes and behavior toward the environment to have had a dramatic effect over the relatively short time since environmental change first became an issue of general concern.

## REMAINING QUESTIONS REGARDING HUMAN BEHAVIOR AND ENVIRONMENTAL CHANGE

Probably few people today would question the idea that human behavior is an important cause of environmental change, but realization of how extensive behavioral effects can be was slow in coming. As McKibben (1990) noted, until recently even the most farseeing naturalists could not comprehend that the climate could be drastically altered by human activity. Gardner and Stern (1996) pointed out that many widely held beliefs about how human behavior relates to environmental degradation are based on commonsense notions and need verification—or refutation—from research, and they have noted several such beliefs that they consider to be wrong. Stern (2000) argued that psychology is uniquely positioned to replace unexamined beliefs about human behavior and its environmental effects with empirically established findings.

Some of the research has revealed ways in which specific forms of behavior contribute to specific aspects of that change noted in this chapter. Many details remain obscure, however. A more complete understanding of the causal connections between behavioral and environmental variables would provide a better basis than now exists for prioritizing behavioral change objectives and identifying technological developments that would have significant environmental benefit by virtue of reducing affordances (Gibson, 1977) for detrimental behavioral impact. The National Research Council recognized this need and recommended the development of an electronic information network that would provide researchers with ready access to accumulating data on the human dimensions of environmental change (Stern, Young, & Druckman, 1992).

A better understanding is needed not only of how human behavior causes environmental change, but also of how people respond to policies instituted with the intention of modifying behavior for the better from an environmental point of view. Stern (1993) pointed out that "policy failures repeatedly result from faith in intuitively attractive but mistaken ideas about behavior" (p. 1890) and has called for "a second environmental science—one focused on human–environment interactions—to complement the science of environmental processes" (p. 1897). Such a science would attempt to identify the forces that drive human activities contributing significantly to environmental change, understand the operation and effects of these forces, and determine how environmental change affects human behavior in turn.

An important component of a better understanding of behavioral effects on the environment and how they might be mitigated is an appreciation of the relative magnitudes of the impacts of different behaviors and mitigating actions that might be taken. Without some informed prioritization, there is the danger of focusing research attention and attempts at remediation on aspects of the problem that are relatively inconsequential while neglecting other aspects where the need and potential for effective action are much greater.

## WHAT MOTIVATES ENVIRONMENTALLY BENEFICIAL BEHAVIOR?

We tend to act in our own immediate self-interests. Consumers are more likely to purchase environmentally safe products if they believe environmental problems constitute threats to their personal well-being than if they do not (Baldassare & Katz, 1992). We find it less natural to be concerned about the long-range implications of our actions for others.

> The central lesson of realistic policy-making is that most individuals and organizations change when it is in their interest to change, either because they derive some benefit from changing or because they incur sanctions when they do not—and the shorter the time between change (or failure to change) and benefit (or sanction), the better. (Ruckelshaus, 1989, p. 168)

From a survey of people's attitudes and behavior with respect to home energy use, Seligman (1986) concluded that pleas to conserve are likely to be effective only if people can be told of ways to do so while remaining comfortable.

Numerous activities and programs to protect the environment from degradation have been instituted in recent years. Relatively little is known about what motivates people to participate in or ignore them. For example, we do not know how important beliefs and attitudes are as determinants of people's behavior in this regard. As already noted, many psychologists appear to discount the importance of such variables and advocate attempting to change behavior directly without giving much credence to the idea that it is necessary to change beliefs and attitudes first. However, some have emphasized the importance of a sense of ethical or moral obligation to protect the environment and the personal satisfaction that can come from doing something intended to benefit others as determinants of environmentally protective behavior (Davidson-Cummings, 1977; DeYoung, 1985–1986; DeYoung & Kaplan, 1985–1986; Heberlein, 1972; Thogersen, 1996).

Some investigators have argued that certain types of environmentally beneficial behaviors should be viewed as acts of altruism or reflections of an intrinsic desire to behave in socially beneficial ways (Black, Stern, & Elworth, 1985; Flannery & May, 1994; Geller, 1995a, 1995b; Hopper & Nielsen, 1991; Larsen, 1995; Nielsen & Ellington, 1983). This view is supported when people engage in environmentally protective behavior at some cost or inconvenience to themselves and realize no apparent personal benefit from doing so.

DeYoung (1986) reported survey data suggesting that people can derive significant personal satisfaction from participating in conservation and recycling efforts. What is it that motivates people to act altruistically? To what extent does altruism stem from personal and social mores (Schwartz, 1977)? How can it be cultivated? These questions are of general interest for psychology; they are relevant to an understanding of much environmentally beneficial behavior.

The distinction between extrinsic and intrinsic motivation is a common one in psychology; extrinsic motivation depends on incentives for specific behavior or rewards that can be anticipated for engaging in it, and intrinsic motivation is seen as spontaneous and associated with behavior that is valued for its own sake. Intrinsic motivation is generally considered more likely than extrinsic motivation to move people to engage in environmentally beneficial behavior (Levenson, 1974; Trigg, Perlman, Perry, & Janisse, 1976) and sustain such behavior over the long run (Deci, 1975; Deci & Ryan, 1985). Therefore, another objective for research is to determine what intrinsic motivation people have to preserve their environment and find ways to bolster and reinforce it.

A question of considerable importance is why there is not a greater degree of consistency in the extent to which a given individual's behavior is environmentally friendly across behavioral domains. The evidence suggests that many people show sensitivity to environmental impact in some aspects of their behavior, but not in others. Correlations among different environmentally friendly behaviors tend to be low (Bratt, 1999; Pickett, Kangun, & Grove, 1993). The fact that an individual engages in one form of environmentally-friendly behavior is not a reliable indicator that he or she engages in another (Reams, Geaghan, & Gendron, 1996; Tracy & Oskamp, 1983-1984).

Does this lack of consistency reflect a lack of understanding of what constitutes environmental friendliness in some behavioral domains? Does it mean that people who do understand are willing to behave in ways that are good for the environment in some respects, but not in others? Do some people feel that being conscientious with respect to some aspects of environmental protection entitles them to be lax with respect to others—that they see engaging in environmentally friendly behavior of one sort as compensatory for, or as providing license for, environmentally unfriendly behavior of another sort? Bratt (1999) noted the latter possibility, but found no evidence of it in a questionnaire study of self-reported environmentally-relevant behaviors of various types.

Perhaps people consider some threats to the environment to be more serious than others and are more motivated to do something about the more serious threats than to deal with the less serious ones. That people do consider some threats more serious than others has been shown by their responses to survey questionnaires. For example, they express greater concern, for the toxicity or biodegradability of consumer products than for the way in which the products are packaged (Ebreo, Hershey, & Vining, 1999). Whether the level of people's efforts to help address specific threats to the environment correlate with their perceptions of the relative seriousness of those threats is not clear.

There are many methodological difficulties associated with research on behavior change. One that has been emphasized by Dwyer, Leeming, Cobern, Porter, and Jackson (1993) is that the relative effectiveness of different techniques for bringing such change about is difficult, if not impossible, to infer from existing experimental data because more than two techniques are seldom compared in any given study—many studies compare only one experimental condition with a control condition—and cross-study comparisons are tenuous because of widely differing conditions from study to study.

Another difficulty that one has in interpreting the literature on behavior change stems from the possibility of a bias in the presentation of research results. Almost all published studies report some measurable change in behavior. What is not clear is how the number of attempts to modify behavior that have failed compares with the number of those that have succeeded to some degree. It seems safe to assume that, other things equal, reports of manipulations that have obtained an effect are more likely to be accepted for publication than reports of manipulations that have failed to do so. Even if there were good data regarding the rejection rates of manuscripts reporting negative results relative to rejection rates for those reporting positive results, the question would remain, assuming that researchers are less likely to attempt to publish negative findings than positive ones.

These difficulties notwithstanding, the work on attitude and behavior change has demonstrated the possibility of effecting change of at least modest magnitude and duration through the use of incentives, disincentives, rewards and punishments, and education and persuasion. The promising leads that this work has produced should be followed up with further research. Especially important is the need to continue to find more effective ways to bring about major and lasting change.

The results of work on behavior change also point up the need to find additional ways to bring psychology to bear on the problem of environmental preservation. They demonstrate the riskiness of relying on behavior change alone to solve the problem given our current level of understanding of the variables involved. Other ways in which psychologists can have an impact include helping to make technology and its products more environmentally benign or beneficial, and doing the kind of research that will add to the knowledge base on which future efforts to motivate environmentally friendly behavior can draw.

CHAPTER

# 6

# Technology Enhancement

An approach to the problem of protecting the environment from unnecessary detrimental change that is complementary to that of attempting to modify environmentally damaging behavior is that of making technology more environmentally benign. In focusing on technology here, I do not mean to suggest that technology is the source of all our difficulties. When one begins to consider the various problems that technology has brought us, it is easy to slip into a Luddite mindset and imagine that life was more pleasant when it was simpler and less mechanized. Possibly it was. However, along with its woes, technology has brought many blessings—sanitation, eradication or containment of many diseases, greatly increased life expectancy, mobility, and freedoms of choice unknown in the preindustrialized world.

Moreover, the "good old days" for which people sometimes nostalgically pine were not as good as many romanticized depictions of them suggest. In a little book entitled *The Good Old Days—They were Terrible!,* Bettmann (1974) reminded us of many eminently forgettable aspects of bygone days—involving housing, food, work, crime, health, education, and leisure, among other topics—that the romantic depictions typically fail to reflect. My purpose here is not to disparage technology, but to consider how it might be more protective of the environment and what roles psychology might play in helping to direct it to that end.

Stern (1992b) pointed out that more energy was saved when automobile manufacturers were forced to meet standards of fuel economy than could have been saved by any conceivable effort to change the behavior of automobile purchasers, and that the beneficial effect of forcing appliance manufacturers to provide energy use information on appliance labels came less from the influence the labels had on consumers than on the motivation they provided to manufacturers to produce more energy-efficient models. Stern also noted that the first gains in energy conservation to disappear when energy costs dropped in the 1980s were those that had been realized from resetting home temperatures, and argued that technology choices and policies are better targets of opportunity for energy conservation than are the daily behavior that psychologists tend to look to first. More generally, Stern (2000) argued that adopting environmentally benign technology is a more effective approach to the problem of environmental degradation than is the curtailment of technology use.

Gardner and Stern (1996) contended that despite the prevalence of opposition against governmental regulations, "regulatory solutions that apply across whole industries have been among the most effective of environmental policies" (p. 118). Illustrating the point by reference to the U.S. transportation industry, they mentioned the abolition of leaded gasoline, the mandated installation of catalytic converters on automobile exhaust systems, auto emissions inspections, and the Corporate Average Fuel Economy regulations. Such regulatory policies have resulted in drastic reductions in emissions of certain pollutants from motor vehicles.

Commoner (1991) similarly argued the greater effectiveness of preventive over remedial or clean-up measures in protecting the environment:

> Only in the few instances in which the technology of production has been changed—by eliminating lead from gasoline, mercury from chlorine production, and so on—has the environment been substantially improved. When the technology of production is unchanged, as when you take the same car engine and try to put a control device on it, you don't get very good results. (p. 42)

These observations argue for ways to make the products of technology more environmentally benign. Precisely how to do this, however, is anything but clear. Sometimes technological changes intended to be environmentally beneficial evoke behavior changes that offset the gains that would have been realized had the behavior not changed. In one such instance, installation of water-conserving devices in homes was followed by an increase in durations of showers and frequency of toilet flushings; the investigators saw this behavior change as evidence that the residents felt less inclined to conserve water because they believed the devices were doing it for them (Geller, Erickson, & Buttram, 1983).

It may be that more fuel-efficient cars will motivate people to drive farther and more often, that the availability of cleaner power from renewable sources will encourage the manufacture of more throw-away products, and so on. These are real possibilities, but they do not negate the desirability of increasing the fuel-efficiency of cars, generating power cleanly from renewable sources, and effecting other changes aimed at making the products of technology more environmentally benign. However, it is important to bear in mind that the causes of environmental change are many, that they interact in complex ways, and that no unidimensional approach to the problem is likely to be effective in more than a temporary and limited way.

Ideally, we would like it to be the case that technology provided the means for people to satisfy their needs and desires at minimal expense to the long-term quality of the environment. Realization of such a goal requires a better understanding than we have of the difference between fundamental human needs and desires on the one hand and wants that have been manufactured and sold to consumers for no other reason than to create a market for products of dubious worth. It also requires a better understanding of how technology relates, at a deep level, to fundamental human needs and quality of life.

## INCREASING THE EFFICIENCY OF ENERGY USE

Arguably, technology's most spectacular successes have involved the development of practical ways of producing energy from matter, changing energy from one form to another, and applying the results to human ends. There can be no doubt that we have benefited greatly from these successes. As Ward and Dubos (1972) put it:

> It is difficult to overestimate the degree to which the use of energy and the manipulation of materials has reduced the crushing burdens of physical work, lessened the concentration of human effort on food production, freed men for other pursuits, and extended to millions a wealth and opportunity formerly enjoyed by the smallest elite. (p. 16)

Yet the environmental effects of energy production and use are a legitimate concern and motivate the search for greater efficiencies in this regard.

Increasing the efficiency with which energy is used can be environmentally beneficial in at least two ways: It can increase the yield of goods and services for a given expenditure of natural resources, and it can decrease the magnitude of detrimental environmental effects resulting from a given amount of energy produced or used. It also has the economic benefit of decreasing the cost of energy on a unit basis. Conversely, avoidable inefficiencies in the use of energy are costly in many ways. The importance of increasing the efficiency of energy use is highlighted by the expectation that total worldwide consumption of energy is bound to increase substantially even if aggressive measures of conservation are taken and/or the unit cost is not significantly reduced (World Energy Council, 1994).

Following the mideast oil crisis of the early 1970s, the efficiency of energy use increased substantially in the United States and other industrialized countries (Hamilton, 1990; Rosenfeld & Hafemeister, 1988; Weinberg, 1988–1989). However, the improvements realized fell far short of what is believed to be possible (Department of Energy, 1988; Ross & Williams, 1981; Ross & Steinmeyer, 1990). According to Ross and his colleagues, even after the improvements, basic operations in the most efficient manufacturing plants expended between four and six times as much energy as the minimum possible as dictated by the laws of thermodynamics.

Field studies of energy systems, such as central heating plants, have revealed inefficiencies that are traceable to control displays, operating and maintenance procedures, documentation, and training programs poorly designed from a human factors point of view (Drost, 1992). Commercial buildings are believed to be highly inefficient in their use of energy, the cost of which can be as much as 30% of their total operating costs (Bevington & Rosenfeld, 1990). Gibbons, Blair, and Gwin (1989) estimated that monitoring and control systems that can adjust indoor heating, lighting, and air conditioning, depending on outdoor temperatures, direction of sunlight, and location of people, can reduce energy use by as much as 10% to 20%. Bevington and Rosenfeld believe that the energy efficiency of buildings could be doubled over a couple of decades. Any improvements in efficiency that reduce the use of fossil fuels will not only help conserve these resources, but will also have beneficial environmental effects because of decreased emissions of carbon dioxide and other greenhouse gases.

Changes in work environments that are made for the purpose of increasing the efficiency of energy use should be made, of course, with a sensitivity to the needs of the people who work in those environments. The objective of using energy efficiently and that of providing work environments that are conducive to human safety, comfort, and productivity should be pursued simultaneously and in a coordinated way.

Energy use in the home is affected by the decisions people make when purchasing energy-using appliances and their maintenance and use of what they have purchased. Selecting an appliance on the basis of its energy efficiency is an example of a one-time decision that can have a long-term benefit because the effect continues over the life of the appliance. Keeping major appliances like furnaces, hot water heaters, and air conditioners in efficient running condition also helps conserve energy, although the maximum efficiency that can be realized by any device is limited by its design; for this reason, the initial purchase decision is especially important (Kempton, Darley, & Stern, 1992; Stern & Gardner, 1981). Limiting the use of energy-consuming appliances, like clothes dryers and air conditioners, is obviously helpful.

Inasmuch as the maintenance of comfortable indoor temperatures, through heating and air conditioning, is a major reason for energy consumption in the home, and the primary source of home energy is fossil fuel, measures that permit the realization of the comfort objective with a lower expenditure of energy are environmentally beneficial. Widening the comfort zone by dressing to accommodate larger temperature deviations from the ideal is one effective approach to the extent that people are willing to adopt it. Installing better insulation in houses is an approach that trades immediate costs for long-term savings. Many Americans took advantage of the tax incentives offered by the U.S. government to owners of older homes who were willing to improve their insulation, although according to one survey, 39% of a sample of people who had purchased insulation were unaware of the tax credit and 62% considered it unimportant in their decision to insulate (Pitts & Wittenbach, 1981).

The use of technology that can automatically adjust the demands that heating and cooling systems place on energy resources to reflect changing needs has some advantages over dependence on users to make these adjustments. A thermostat that automatically turns the temperature down at night relieves the homeowner of the need to remember to do so. An air conditioner that automatically lowers its output when the humidity is low can be an energy saver.

Opportunities to increase efficiency of home energy use is not restricted to homes in industrialized countries. Cooking and home heating are needs in the less developed countries as well, and the use of open fires or inefficient stoves for these purposes contributes to deforestation and soil erosion (because of the way wood is sometimes gathered) and to a high incidence of smoke-induced respiratory illnesses as well (Kammen, 1995). The development of efficient, usable, and affordable (which can mean very inexpensive) stoves for heating and indoor cooking is a continuing need.

Another challenge relating to energy use for the future is the energy demand likely to come from leisure pursuits. According to Mayo and Jarvis (1981), almost half of all the money Americans spend on leisure activities is spent on travel. If leisure activities involve travel as much in the future as they do now, and if the number of people engaged in leisure activities at any given time increases faster than the population, as it is expected to do, these activities will become an increasingly important determinant of overall energy utilization. With affluence comes also an opportunity for increasing numbers of people to engage in leisure activities that involve the use of motorized vehicles—motor boats, ski mobiles, jet skies, and all-terrain vehicles. Finding ways to limit the environmental impact of the widespread use of such devices without curtailing human freedoms is a major challenge.

Finally, it is necessary to bear in mind that, as already noted, increasing the efficiency of energy use does not, by itself, guarantee the use of less energy. There is the real possibility that finding ways to make energy use more efficient will, in some cases, stimulate the use of more energy, thus offsetting the increased efficiency. For example, if doubling the fuel efficiency of the U.S. automobile fleet decreased worldwide carbon dioxide emissions by about 2.5% (given the same number of miles traveled; Office of Technology Assessment, 1991), but also had the effect of greatly increasing the amount of traveling done, the possible reduction in carbon dioxide emissions would not be realized. There are many other examples that might be mentioned of how an increase in energy efficiency could stimulate more energy use. The point is that, although increasing energy efficiency is an important goal, it may not have the desired environmental effects unless coupled with other equally important goals.

## DEVELOPING CLEANER MEANS OF ENERGY PRODUCTION

Although improving the efficiency with which energy is used is widely advocated by environmentalists, there is an obvious limit to how effective this can be as a means to protect the environment if the demand for energy continues to grow worldwide as it is expected to do. If the present demand for energy were reduced by 50% through more efficient use, this would have to be considered an extraordinarily successful conservation effort. However, if, following that decrease, the demand grew by 5% per year, it would take only 14 years before it was again at the current level and an additional 14 to be at double that.

At least as important as increases in energy efficiency is the goal of establishing a cleaner means of energy generation. Several industries have convincingly demonstrated that cleaner means of production can be cost-effective even with fossil fuels. Kennecott, for example, has been building a smelter-refinery complex in Bingham, Utah, at about half the cost of existing refineries; it is expected to retain 99.9% of the sulfur produced, compared with 93% retention by the cleanest smelters as of 1995 (Hodges, 1995).

The possibility of separating the carbon from the products of fossil fuel burning and sequestering it in the ocean or geological reservoirs, such as depleted oil and gas sites, is being explored as a means of reducing the build up of $CO_2$ in the atmosphere (Parsons & Keith, 1998; Schneider, 1998). If successful, the techniques represent only a partial answer to the problem, however, because they are likely to be applicable only to the use of fossil fuels in the generation of electric power and not to their use as an energy source for transportation. The long-term solution to energy production must lie in the development of methods that will make cleaner and renewable sources of energy cost-effective alternatives to the burning of fossil fuels.

Alternatives to fossil fuels as energy sources include the wind, water, the sun, the earth's heat (geothermal), and nuclear fission and fusion, among other less obvious possibilities. Some of these alternatives are already in use, although none accounts for as nearly as large a fraction of the total energy produced as does the burning of fossil fuels. In the United States as of 1997, about 53% of electric power came from coal-fueled plants, about 18% from nuclear reactors, about 14% from gas, 3% from petroleum, and the remaining 12% from a variety of renewable sources in combination (Brown, 1999).

Each renewable source has its advantages and liabilities. Major increases in the use of some (e.g., hydropower from dammed rivers) are less than ideal because they can create some environmental problems while addressing others. All are still more expensive than the burning of fossil fuels, if only immediate costs are considered, but the cost-effectiveness of several of them has been improving steadily as a result of continuing research and development. According to recent calculations by Jacobson and Masters (2001), energy generated by wind turbines is already less expensive than that generated by coal when the environmental and health costs resulting from each technology are taken into account. Wind turbines covering large tracts of otherwise scenic areas have been objected to on aesthetic grounds, and they can be hazardous to birds. These problems can be eased by locating turbines outside bird migratory routes and offshore; offshore wind turbine parks are being used successfully by Sweden and Denmark.

The major impediment to a greater use of solar power still appears to be economic. To date, the efficiency of solar panels has not been sufficient to make their use for many purposes—like home heating—cost-competitive with the production of energy from fossil fuels, but making solar technology more cost-effective is a goal toward which many technologists have been working. The gap between the per-unit cost of this technology and that of fossil-fuel energy appears to be narrowing (Beardsley, 1994).

Given the large fraction of gasoline consumption that goes to power automobiles and other private vehicles, it is not surprising that much effort has gone into the search for alternative automotive fuels. Scientists have shown considerable interest in the possibility of replacing gasoline with ethanol (grain alcohol) or methanol (wood alcohol), but especially the latter. Methanol can be produced not only from natural gas, coal and wood, but also from organic garbage, and it could be used on a large scale with relatively modest changes in vehicles and the existing fuel-distribution network. Unfortunately, the benefits that methanol would represent with respect to air pollution are less clear; it would be beneficial in some respects (reduction in ozone emissions), but arguably problematic in others (increase in formaldehyde emission; Gray & Alson, 1989; Seinfeld, 1989; Weinberg & Williams, 1990). Hydrogen is another, but probably less immediate, possible alternative to gasoline as a vehicle fuel (Nadis, 1990; Weinberg & Williams, 1990).

The idea of powering automobiles by electricity has been around for a long time (*Scientific American* reported the appearance of electrically powered cabs in London in 1897 [*Scientific American*, 1997]), and modern electric cars have been on the market for several years. In part, because of their limited range between battery rechargings, they have not yet proved to be sufficiently attractive to the average consumer to compete with conventional gasoline-powered vehicles. Environmental considerations are a major reason for interest in electric cars, and they are often promoted as *zero-emission* vehicles. This designation overlooks that manufacture and reprocessing of lead-acid batteries—the current power source of choice for electric cars—has been estimated to release 60 times as much lead per unit of distance traveled as does a comparable car burning leaded gasoline (Lave, Hendrickson, & McMichael, 1995). One must bear in mind, too, that batteries must be charged and continually recharged, and this represents an increased demand on electric power-generation facilities, which today account for about one third of the $CO_2$ released to the atmosphere. Some technologists believe that the best long-range solution will be the development of practical solar-powered vehicles; the feasibility of such vehicles has been demonstrated convincingly (Wilson, MacCready, & Kyle, 1989), but bringing to market solar-powered cars that can compete effectively with conventional gas burners is likely to take a while.

In the meantime, there is great interest in hybrid electric vehicles (HEVs), which appear to have many of the advantages of both gasoline-powered and electric cars without some of their environmental liabilities (Wouk, 1997). HEVs use battery-stored electricity and gasoline in combination, with a resulting large increase in fuel efficiency and reduction of atmospheric emissions. (According to Wouk, HEVs can be as little as one eighth as dirty, environmentally, as a conventional car with a well-tuned engine; it is not clear that this figure takes account of the environmental costs of manufacture and reprocessing of the batteries noted by Lave, Hendrickson, & McMichael [1995].) The batteries are charged by an onboard generator, so the car does not have the range limitations of a totally battery-powered vehicle, nor does it incur the environmental cost of recharging by a fossil-fueled electricity source. Several manufacturers in the United States, Europe, and Japan have brought HEVs to market, but few sales have been made. Other technological approaches to reduce fossil-fuel consumption by private vehicles and reduce the air pollution such vehicles produce include: development of a vehicle that uses a flywheel to capture and store normally wasted energy for later use (Rosen & Castleman, 1997); and automated or semiautomated highway systems on which specially equipped vehicles can be operated under computer control in such a way as to increase fuel efficiency and safety while easing problems of traffic congestion (Koltnow, 1988; Rillings, 1997; Wright, 1990).

One might argue that psychologists have little to offer to the goal of developing cleaner means of energy production. Yet to the extent that tax money is used to underwrite some portion of the cost of the development, what gets developed is a public policy matter, and there are psychological issues involved in organizing and communicating information that can inform public debate and support the allocation of resources to action alternatives in a rational way. Also efforts on the part of private industry to develop more efficient means of producing energy must take into account the marketability of the results of those efforts. There are a variety of ways to reduce substantially the pollutants emitted by internal combustion engines, but at the present stage of technological know-how, each has certain features that are likely to be seen as drawbacks by consumers, so none has yet been implemented on a large scale. Similarly, demonstrating the technological feasibility of alternatives to gasoline-powered engines for use in private vehicles does not guarantee the acceptance of any of those alternatives by their intended users. Cost is, of course, a major determinant of purchasing decisions, but so are psychological factors not all of which are well understood. The search continues for energy-producing methods that provide the advantages consumers have come to take for granted, but without the environmental problems that conventional methods have often had (Ashley, 2001).

## INCREASING THE EFFICIENCY OF WATER USE

Microirrigation techniques—designed to deliver water directly to the roots of individual plants—are receiving attention as one approach to water conservation in the agricultural context (La Rivière, 1989). Another method of conserving water that is used for agricultural purposes is that of making greater use of reclaimed wastewater (Martindale, 2001b; Postel, 2001).

Among the more notable approaches to the conservation of the domestic use of water have been the development and distribution of low-flow toilets and shower heads. In 1994, New York City launched a rebate program to motivate homeowners and landlords to replace existing toilets that use more than five gallons of water per flush with state-of-the art models that use only 1.6 gallons per flush, which meant that the city picked up most of the cost of the replacements. The result was replacement, over 3 years, of 1.33 million toilets and a 29% reduction in water use per building per year (Martindale, 2001a).

Any technological innovation that could result in greater efficiency of water use will be effective only to the degree that potential users of the innovation actually adopt it. Whether people adopt an innovation is likely to depend on how the consequences of doing so compare—or are believed to compare—with the preinnovation way of doing things. For example, whether one will be satisfied with a *miser* shower head that dispenses much less water per unit time than a conventional head is likely to depend on whether standing under the newer head is as satisfying as standing under the older one.

## IMPROVING MASS TRANSPORTATION FACILITIES

The question of why so many people prefer a privately owned automobile as their primary means of transportation undoubtedly has a many-faceted answer. One factor that must figure large in this preference is the quality of whatever alternatives are available. Efforts aimed at improving the efficiency and attractiveness of public mass transportation to potential users could have beneficial environmental effects of several sorts. One indication of the need for attention to the problem of making public transportation more attractive is the rather dramatic decrease in the number of rides provided by transit systems in the United States from 17.2 billion in 1950 to about 8.3 billion in 1987 (American Public Transit Association, 1987).

It seems unlikely that the popularity of the private vehicle will decrease much in the United States anytime soon because, even if mass transportation facilities are improved a great deal, they will not provide the easy, time-independent, place-to-place access represented by the combination of private vehicles and the U.S. system of highways and roads. Enough improvement in mass transit facilities to induce people to rely more on them for within-city travel and moderate-distance between-city trips, thereby reducing their dependence on private-vehicle travel, would constitute a substantial achievement from an environmental point of view. A major aspect of the problem of public transportation is the need, in many cases, to use more than one mode of conveyance to get from any given origin to a desired destination, which often means walking between and/or waiting at transfer points. Among people who use public transportation for commuting to and from work, there appears to be a correlation between the number of stages in their commute and the frequency of their absence from work (Taylor & Pocock, 1974).

The use of trains for intermediate range travel is considerably more prevalent and successful in Europe and Japan than in the United States. Fast trains—trains that travel in excess of 200 kilometers (approximately 125 hundred miles) per hour—now link major cities in Europe and Japan, and efforts are underway to provide even faster rail service (Raoul, 1997). Experimentation has also been done with high-speed trains that operate by magnetic levitation for some time (Johnson, 1990), but the progress that has been made in increasing the speed of conventional-rail trains has caused interest in maglev technology to decline (Stix, 1997). The United States has made some improvements in rail service, especially along the northeast corridor, but it has not showed much interest in advancing high-speed passenger rail service as a primary means of transportation between major cities around the nation. The expanse of the country is undoubtedly one reason for the relatively low priority that has been given to passenger transportation by rail, but there are political and other reasons as well (Perl & Dunn, 1997). People in positions to provide the private or public funds that would be necessary to greatly improve rail service in the United States need to believe that the public would use rail service if it was provided, and whether they would is likely to be determined, in part, by psychological considerations.

Although the private automobile is seen as a convenient mode of travel from the user's point of view, it is highly inefficient from the perspective of the amount of resources consumed in moving individuals from place to place. The inefficiency stems, in part, from the fact that cars built to carry four to six passengers are frequently used to transport a single person. The development and use of smaller, lighter cars with more efficient engines, including low-emission, two-stroke engines, could have substantial beneficial environmental effects of several types: reduction in energy use, reduction in pollutant emissions, less wear and tear on highway infrastructure (pavement, bridges), and more efficient use of limited parking space. Small, light vehicles are at a disadvantage from the point of view of occupant safety when mixed with larger and heavier vehicles, however, so the problem of gaining the efficiencies that lightness and smallness can represent without incurring the cost of decreased safety is a challenge. Improvements in the safety of small vehicles, including half-size cars, would enhance their attractiveness, and this too would be progress from an environmental point of view.

Other developments that could increase the efficiency of operation of individual vehicles and have beneficial environmental effects might include the provision of aids to drivers or owners that help them keep their cars in top running condition and operate them in ways that make efficient use of fuel and other resources and extend their longevity. Many automobiles can now show the gas mileage being obtained on a moment-to-moment basis, inform the driver when the need for an oil change is approaching, and provide other information that should be helpful in increasing operating efficiency. Automatic navigation systems, point-to-point routing systems, and systems that provide information about accidents or other causes of traffic delays and suggest alternative routing have been under development for some time (Ervine & Chen, 1988–1989; Koltnow, 1988), and initial versions of such capabilities are beginning to appear in automobiles. How driver behavior is or will be affected by any of these innovations remains to be seen.

## IMPROVING THE TECHNOLOGY OF RECYCLING

As already noted, one of the problems associated with collecting recyclable waste—paper, plastics, glass, and various types of metal—is the need to sort it: first to separate the recyclable trash from that which is not currently recyclable, and then separate the recyclable items into several categories for further processing. Usually consumers are expected at least to separate recyclable from nonrecyclable trash and the two types are picked up separately.

Sometimes the recyclable trash is not separated further by the consumer, but is collected all together and transported to a resource-recovery plant, where it is mechanically separated for further processing. In other cases, the consumer sorts the recyclable trash into various types, which are collected separately and transported to separate waste-processing facilities. Geller (1981b) referred to these approaches as high- and low-technology approaches, respectively. The high-technology approach is most convenient for the consumer, but it tends to be the more expensive of the two.

The development of more cost-effective methods for trash separation would improve the technology of recycling. However, methods must be such that consumers will use them or they will defeat the purpose of recycling programs. The design of methods that are both cost-effective and acceptable to consumers will be more difficult as the variety of materials that can be reprocessed grows, as it is likely to do.

The expense of waste recycling, in terms of both dollar and total energy costs, is a major impediment to its wider use. It has been claimed that waste recycling may, in some cases, consume more energy than would the practice of discarding the waste and using only new materials in production (Georgescu-Roegen, 1976). Energy conservation is not the only reason for recycling, but it is an important consideration, and the development of more energy-efficient recycling techniques is a high-priority need. Again, for any techniques to be successful in maximizing material recovery, they must be such that people will participate in the recycling process.

The recycling of organic wastes, such as lawn and yard clippings, in the form of composts for use as soil enrichers and fertilizer has been practiced by some gardeners for a long time. In recent years, communities have collected such wastes and composted them in community facilities. According to Ward and Dubos (1972), in the Netherlands at least 30% of the cities' wastes have been returned to the land as compost for several decades. Technological developments that facilitate the reclamation of waste products of various sorts for productive uses should be a priority objective. However, the effort and investment put into such developments are likely to depend on the extent to which the public can be convinced of the undesirability of the perpetuation of the throw-away mentality that seems to be pervasive in affluent societies.

## RADIOACTIVE WASTE TREATMENT AND CLEANUP TECHNOLOGIES

The treatment and cleanup of radioactive waste have emerged as major societal problems during the latter half of this century, and the technologies involved are still being developed. The U.S. Department of Energy has embarked on a cleanup program, the goals of which are to restore its inventory of previously active nuclear sites to suitability for nonnuclear uses and to bring its currently active sites into compliance with applicable laws and regulations. The cleanup goals are acknowledged to be ambitious and are expected to take three decades to realize. Several interrelated projects have been initiated to facilitate the technology development that will be essential to their realization (Beck, 1992).

A primary focus of this program is the Hanford site in the state of Washington, where weapons-grade radioactive materials have been produced for about 50 years. Planned cleanup and radioactive waste management activities at this site involve a number of unresolved human factors issues (Wise & Savage, 1992). For example, the building of a vitrification plant, in which radioactive liquid wastes will be solidified in preparation for burial, will involve some control-room design questions like, in some respects, those that pertain to the design of nuclear plant control rooms. Because the operation of such plants will require the use of teleoperator material-handling techniques, their design will also involve problems similar to those associated with the design of control facilities for the space station and other space vehicles.

Wise and Savage (1992) emphasized that the waste-handling facilities at the Hanford site will be new, and different in many respects, from anything built before. They will require some new thinking about how to allocate function to people and machines and how to design the requisite human–machine interfaces. Other human factors challenges represented by the Hanford site program include the analysis of risks involved in various aspects of waste treatment and cleanup operations, representation and communication of the results of such analyses, and development of systems that can predict and monitor environmental change in ways that facilitate effective decision making.

The problem of disposing of radioactive material that is no longer serving its originally intended purposes is also seen in the need to dismantle and dispose of thousands of nuclear warheads in the United States and Russia that are obsolete or that are, or soon will be, superfluous under the terms of the Strategic Arms Reduction Treaties.

## ACCIDENT PREVENTION AND AMELIORATION

The total elimination of industrial accidents is not a realistic goal especially in a technologically based society; there simply are too many points in complex systems and processes where failures can occur (Perrow, 1984). The goals of decreasing the probability of such accidents and limiting the severity of the effects of those that do occur, however, are reasonable because there is some hope of attaining them.

Inasmuch as human error is a major cause of industrial accidents that have environmental impact, an obvious way to benefit the environment is to decrease the probability of error in industrial situations and lessen the magnitude of the negative effects of those errors that do occur. These objectives are not new to the human factors community. Human error and the question of how to deal with it in industrial settings have been receiving considerable attention from human factors researchers (Moray & Huey, 1988; Reason, 1990; Senders & Moray, 1991). Much additional research on these topics is clearly desirable from an environmental point of view.

Although most of the psychological research on accidents and accident prevention has focused on industrial accidents, and more recently on accidents in medical contexts (Bogner, 1994), the risk of an accidental firing of nuclear missiles is an ever-present danger as long as thousands of nuclear weapons are poised for launch on very short notice, and especially when the control systems for some of them are of questionable reliability (Blair, Feiveson, & von Hippel, 1997). The psychological problems associated with the reduction of this threat are many and complex.

Based on the assumption that human error cannot be eliminated completely, important aspects of dealing with its occurrence include the design of fail-safe or fail-soft operating procedures to ensure that, when human error occurs, it will not have catastrophic effects either short or long term. Identifying everything that *could* go wrong, and making provision for every contingency, is clearly impossible. In practice, compromises must be made involving the cost of reducing risks and the expected benefit of doing so. It is not always clear how to take long-term environmental considerations properly into account in assessing the costs and benefits of particular situations, but ignoring them can yield results that are grossly unfair to future generations.

The search for more effective ways to prevent human error and ameliorate its effects when it occurs has direct implications for the environment by way of the issue of acceptability by the public of various ways of generating energy. When nuclear power-generating plants function without mishap, they have little effect on the environment, compared, say, with coal-fired plants. The unacceptability to many people of the generation of power by nuclear fission rests in large measure on the problem of the disposal of spent fuel (and of decommissioned plants) and on the fear of accidents in plant operation. The need to find ways to deal effectively with these concerns is likely to become increasingly acute, especially in view of the claim that there is little hope of achieving adequate containment of $CO_2$ and other greenhouse gas emissions without depending on nuclear power for a sizable fraction of the world's projected energy needs through the middle of the 21st century (Sailor, Bodansky, Braun, Fetter, & van der Zwan, 2000).

## HUMAN FACTORS OF FARMING AND FOOD PRODUCTION

Farming has not been the focus of much psychological research. There has been research on activities and tasks performed in farming as well as other contexts and on equipment design principles that would apply to farm and other types of equipment, but whereas one finds many articles in applied psychology and human factors journals dealing explicitly with manufacturing, aviation, office work, and a variety of other topics, there are few that deal in an equally focused way with farming.

Why is this? The practice of farming involves people interacting with machines, and with complicated machines at that. It is an essential occupation and it can be hazardous. One might think it would represent many opportunities for human factors and applied psychology work. Nevertheless, it seems to have been largely ignored by the field.

Perhaps one reason that more attention has not been given to farming is that it directly involves such a small fraction of the total labor force. However, farming is not only critical to the well-being of the global community because of the essential nature of what it produces, but it is the basis of a host of other industries (food processing and packaging, wholesale and retail selling, trucking, refrigeration, fertilizer and pesticide production). Farming is highly efficient in its use of human labor, but with respect to its use of natural resources the picture is quite different. I have already noted that agriculture accounts for about 70% of water usage worldwide. In regions where agriculture is a major activity, the percentage can be higher than that; about 85% of the water usage in California goes to agriculture, and in New Mexico the comparable figure is about 92% (Reisner, 1988–1989). Improvements in the technology for delivering water to plant roots that would minimize loss to evaporation, runoff, and delivery to areas containing no plants could have beneficial effects on the groundwater supply. Similarly, the development of techniques for delivering fertilizers and pesticides in less broadcast ways could reduce the severity of the undesirable side effects of these products on the environment.

Pesticides not only pose a threat to water supplies and, in the form of residues on produce, consumers of foodstuffs, but they can represent a major health hazard to agricultural workers (Coye, 1985; Environmental Protection Agency, 1990; Goldsmith, 1989; Vaughn, 1993a, 1993b). Apparently farm laborers who feel most dependent on farm work for their livelihood, in the sense of having few if any alternatives, are least likely to use available measures to protect themselves against exposure to the toxic chemicals they use (Vaughn, 1993a, 1993b).

Farming is an extremely important occupation. If it fails to do what it is intended to do, the world, or at least major parts of it, suffers from an inadequate food supply. If it succeeds in producing enough food, but does so in an inefficient way, we pay more than we should to eat. If, in meeting the food needs of the present generation, we deplete the capital of natural resources, such as water and tillable soil, we impose a burden on future generations that they should not have to bear.

Recognition that today's farming practices have serious implications for tomorrow's environment has led to the promotion of *sustainable agriculture* (Reganold, Papendick, & Parr, 1990). The term is used in the literature in a variety of ways, relating to such issues as the biophysical limits for agriculture, sustainability of agricultural output levels, supportability of population levels, capacity of agricultural producers to stay in business, and intergenerational equity (the meeting of present needs without creating inequitable burdens for future generations; Brklacich, Bryant, & Smit, 1991). These are complex issues, and more attention from psychologists to farming will not resolve them; such attention should not hurt, however, and it might help considerably in finding ways to make farming not only more efficient in the short run, but less environmentally costly and more sustainable for the long term.

## APPROACHES TO THE HARVESTING OF RENEWABLE FOREST PRODUCTS

There are many renewable forest products in addition to timber that have, or could have, market value. These include many types of plants and animals, fruits, nuts, oils, and fibers. It is believed that, in some cases, the value of such products in a given area could exceed the value of the timber in the same area (Repetto, 1990). However, there is a need for the development of more cost-effective ways of harvesting such renewable products and bringing them to market.

Inasmuch as the harvesting of renewable forest products involves people using tools and interfacing with machines, there may be opportunities here for the application of human factors expertise. To the degree that the harvesting of such products can be done more cost-effectively than can the wholesale harvesting of the forests, the financial pressures that lead to forest destruction would be eased.

There is also a need for the development of timber-harvesting techniques that treat forests as renewable resources. This too is a cost-effectiveness issue. At the present time, timber is harvested most cost-effectively (from a short-range perspective) by techniques that attach little importance to the quality of the land after the harvesting is done. What is needed is the development of techniques that would make it cost-effective (from a short-range perspective) to harvest selectively and in such a way that a forest system, as a whole, is maintained as a productive entity.

## RETHINKING THE NATURE AND PURPOSES OF WORK

Workers see work primarily as a way of making a living, industrialists see labor as a resource to be tapped for purposes of production, and economists see it as a component of cost that must be considered in calculating indexes of productivity. I think it is correct to say that work has been seen, from almost all perspectives, as primarily a means to economic ends. One consequence of this emphasis has been a continuing effort to design jobs so as to maximize the efficiency of labor, which is to say to maximize the output for a given input or minimize the input for a given output in economic terms. This has meant, in many contexts, decomposing the work that is required to yield a specific product, service, or other commodity into simple repetitive tasks that relate only indirectly to the finished good.

This approach has been justified on the grounds that it has made possible through mass production the marketing of consumer goods at prices that are affordable to laborers. Without mass-production techniques, goods like household appliances, automobiles, radios, TV sets, and even many of the countless small items we use every day and take so much for granted would not be ownable except by people of wealth. This argument has great force, but this does not preclude recognition that another effect of mass production has been to provide a surfeit of material goods of dubious worth and to create an entire industry a purpose of which is to convince us that we have a desperate need for many things that we could readily do without.

The great emphasis on efficiency has obscured the fact that work can be viewed as an end in itself independently of its function as a means to other ends. Work is part of living, and people who spend the *working hours* of every day performing boring, meaningless tasks for the sake of making a living are, as it were, suffering a sort of death for a significant fraction of the time allotted to them for the sake of obtaining the wherewithal, hopefully, to live during some portion of the remaining time.

Schumacher (1973) argued that "modern technology has deprived man of the kind of work that he enjoys most, creative, useful work with hands and brains, and given him plenty of work of a fragmented kind, most of which he does not enjoy at all" (p. 160). Regardless of whether Schumacher's sweeping indictment of technology as a degrader of work is fully justified, there can be no question that many of the jobs created by technology fit his description of fragmented and unenjoyable. Human factors, as a discipline, is not blameless, historically, in this regard. Worker efficiency was a major focus of some of the earliest work in the discipline, and time-and-motion studies played a significant role in the fragmentation of workers' tasks.

A challenge for the future is to develop a much better understanding than we now have of what makes a job interesting and intrinsically rewarding independently of its money-making potential, which is not to deny the importance of the latter. We must recognize that work can meet human needs other than strictly economic ones, and we must learn to design jobs that improve the quality of workers' lives—not only indirectly by giving them purchasing power, but directly by making their working hours more interesting and gratifying.

A rethinking of the nature and purposes of work can be justified on strictly humanitarian grounds. There is reason to believe, however, that greater attention to the noneconomic aspects of work could have both economic and environmental benefits. If Schumacher (1973) is right, the best hope of reversing many of the more worrisome economic and environmental trends lies in the creation of millions of new workplaces supporting small-scale industries in rural areas and small towns. The objective, in this view, should not be to maximize output per person, but to provide meaningful employment for everyone who needs it and, to use Schumacher's terminology, give technology a more human face. This is not to suggest that productivity should be of no concern, but that it should not be the single factor considered to the neglect of everything else.

## DEVELOPING MARKETABLE ENVIRONMENTALLY CLEAN TECHNOLOGY

Industrial and environmental interests have been seen as in conflict for the most part. Industry has been viewed by environmentalists as a major cause of detrimental environmental change; environmental concerns have presented themselves to industry mainly in the form of regulations that restrict its activities and impose burdens of record keeping and compliance documentation.

Relatively few American businesses have yet seen the growing global concern for environmental protection as an opportunity to develop new products and processes for an increasingly environment-conscious market. This is unfortunate because the demand for products and processes that are environmentally benign, if not environmentally beneficial, seems likely to be very large. It appears that Japan has a vision of this business opportunity and has initiated a national effort to exploit it (Myers, 1992).

## PROMOTING THE IDEA OF INDUSTRIAL ECOSYSTEMS

As already noted, the problem of environmental change is complex in part because its many aspects are interrelated in numerous ways. The point is especially true with respect to the impact of technology on environmental change. Frosch and Gallopoulos (1989) argued that the traditional model of industrial activity, according to which individual manufacturing processes transform raw materials into products for sale and waste for disposal, should be replaced by a model of an industrial ecosystem.

> In such a system the consumption of energy and materials is optimized, waste generation is minimized and the effluents of one process—whether they are spent catalysts from petroleum refining, fly and bottom ash from electric-power generation or discarded plastic containers from consumer products—serve as the raw material for another process. (p. 144)

Such a model views any particular industrial process as part of a larger system, the overall efficiency of which is what needs to be optimized.

The idea has been realized to a notable degree by an industrial park in Kalundborg, Denmark, where the byproducts of some companies have been piped directly to other companies that use them as industrial inputs.

> For instance, flare gas from an oil refinery heats other factories; a power plant sends gypsum—produced by scrubbing sulfur dioxide from flue gas—to a drywall factory; and a biotech's fermentation waste gets shipped to farmers for fertilizing fields. Cooling water from the refinery is used by the power plant as boiler water, while the power plant's excess steam heats Kalundborg's 4300 homes. (Kaiser, 1999, p. 686)

Whether such a systematic approach to industrial waste recovery would work as well in a less open culture than that of Denmark is a question about which some experts have some doubt. However, the general idea that many of the byproducts of industry that have traditionally been considered waste may have the potential to be used as resources in other processes appears to be getting increasing attention and interest and for good reasons: When industrial uses are found for byproducts that would otherwise be waste, resources (both raw materials and energy) are conserved and the problem of waste disposal is lessened (Iranpour et al., 1999).

CHAPTER

# 7

# Substituting Resource-Light for Resource-Heavy Technologies

The focus, in what follows, is still on the objective of making technology more environmentally benign or beneficial. The substitution of resource-light for resource-heavy technologies is treated as a special case, however, for two reasons: (a) Largely because of the way information technology—computer and communication technology in combination—has developed, this possibility represents an extraordinary opportunity for significant impact on the problem of environmental change. (b) This opportunity may well be missed, or even turned into a disaster, if the possibilities—good and bad—are not recognized.

The desirability of finding effective ways to substitute resource-light for resource-heavy technologies is especially great in view of the increased demands for resources and energy that can be expected from underdeveloped countries as they attempt to catch up with the industrialized world. Consider China alone. According to the National Research Council's Committee on the Human Dimensions of Global Change the future of global climate change depends very much on how energy-intensive the continuing development of this country will be (Stern, Young, & Druckman, 1992). In particular, if both its $CO_2$ emissions—largely from the use of coal—and its total economic output continue to increase at the rate of 4% per year, as they have been doing in recent years, China's contribution to global $CO_2$ emissions will quadruple in less than 40 years.

Similar observations could be made with respect to many countries making concerted efforts to improve their national standard of living through accelerated economic growth. It has been argued that, because developing countries do not yet have much of their industrial infrastructure in place, they do not have the disincentives or encumbrances that such in-place systems can represent; consequently, they have an opportunity, at least in some instances, to engage in "technological leapfrogging," going directly to the adoption of energy-efficient approaches to the provision of goods and services without first adopting the less efficient approaches (Reddy & Goldemberg, 1990). The prospect of this possibility should help establish the urgency of enhancing the utility and usability of resource-light technologies that have the potential to deliver goods or services traditionally delivered by resource-heavy ones.

The basic assumption underlying the following discussion is that there generally are more ways than one to satisfy human needs and desires and that some of the alternatives are harder on the environment than others. In particular, some means of realizing specific objectives are more demanding of energy and material than are alternatives. For example, sometimes it may be possible to accomplish a particular objective equally well either by transporting people and material or by transmitting information from one place to another. If the objective is met equally well either way, the transmission of information would appear to be the preferred alternative from the point of view of protecting the environment. The answer to the question of whether the objective is really met equally well either way is likely to be psychological at least in part.

The idea considered here is that the development of information technology is providing opportunities to accomplish some goals in less energy-and-material-demanding ways than has been feasible in the past. The question is what role, if any, might psychology play in increasing the probability that the use of this technology will constitute a net gain from an environmental point of view.

## INFORMATION TECHNOLOGY

Although computer networks and various types of information systems that depend on them have been in operation since the late 1960s, until relatively recently they were used primarily by scientists and engineers. This situation has been changing as the vision of a networked world has rapidly been becoming more and more fully realized. The dependence of the world's business on information technology is now extensive; if all the world's computers (or networks) suddenly shut down, we would be in serious trouble indeed. The

Internet, the successor to the U.S. Department of Defense's Arpanet and the largest computer network in the world, adds millions of users around the world each year, a decreasing fraction of whom are scientists and engineers. Traffic on this and other networks has been increasing explosively over the past few years, and it is expected to continue to increase at a phenomenal rate as yet greater-capacity transmission facilities—communication satellites, optical fiber networks, and optical switching circuits (Bishop, Giles, & Das, 2001; Blumenthal, 2001; Evans, 1998; Stix, 2001)—are put in place. Already broadband wireless technology permits the transmission of data at more than 10 megabits per second (Grossman, 2001), and it will increasingly be the case that space-based systems deliver information directly to consumers rather than to commercial redistribution facilities (Pelton, 1998).

One of the more impressive promises of this technology is the ability to deliver information in many forms (data, facsimile, voice, motion pictures) from nearly anywhere to nearly anywhere else on Earth more or less instantaneously (Denning, 1989; Forester, 1987). The word that best captures this promise, in my view, is *access*—people will have immediate access to information and information resources on a scale unknown before (Nickerson, 1986, 1995). They will be able to browse through the world's libraries, visit (electronically) the world's museums, and tour (also electronically) many other places of interest. They will be able to direct automatic searches for specific information, dial up movies or TV programs for home viewing on their own schedules, read interactive newspapers and view tell-me-more TV, participate in instantaneous polls and referenda, shop via interactive catalogues and product information services from home, and stay in contact with other individuals and groups to a degree not possible before. Electronic books will contain not only conventional text and graphics, but animations, process simulations, voice and other sound, and question-answering capabilities. Many of these capabilities already exist, at least in rudimentary form, and work currently in progress on new ways to represent knowledge and search large information stores promises to increase the effectiveness of this technology manyfold (Berners-Lee, Hendler, & Lassila, 2001).

These capabilities will not all be unmitigated blessings. There can be no doubt that information technology holds the potential for destructive as well as constructive uses, as does any powerful technology. Even uses that appear to be desirable may, in some cases, turn out to have unanticipated negative effects. (Having immediate access to people all over the world is one thing; people all over the world having immediate access to you is another.) How to ensure that the uses of information technology are, on balance, beneficial for individuals and society is a question that we are likely to be a long time in answering. Information technology has the potential to impact the environment for good and ill;

finding ways to use it to help address the problem of detrimental environmental change is worth considerable effort.

One possibility that information technology seems to offer is that of satisfying some human needs in ways that are more environmentally benign than are the traditional means of satisfying them. Information technology has the potential to provide resource-light alternatives to resource-heavy means of meeting many human needs or desires, and determining how it might be exploited in the interest of helping to address the problem of detrimental environmental change seems a worthy objective of research. I do not claim that greater use of this technology will automatically be good for the environment. There is the distinct possibility that, in the absence of conscious efforts to ensure against it, greater use of the technology could have exactly the opposite effect. Yet the potential for beneficial effect is there, and psychology has something to contribute to its realization, or so I want to argue.

Whenever some need that traditionally has been met by transporting people or material goods from place to place could be met equally well by transmitting information from one place to another, it would seem to be in the interest of environmental protection to substitute transmission for transportation. Transmitting a movie to a home takes less of an environmental toll than does transporting people to a movie theater. More generally, moving electrons through a wire (or photons through an optical cable, or electromagnetic waves through the air) makes lighter demands on resources and contributes less to pollution than does moving people or material goods from place to place. Theoretically, at least, the information that most people now receive via newspapers, magazines, professional journals, and other periodicals could be distributed electronically, and presumably at considerably less cost to the environment in terms of natural resources consumed, pollutants produced, and waste generated.

It would be silly to suggest that electronic transmission of information should substitute for transportation of people and goods in all cases in which such a substitution is feasible; it is hard to imagine that this would be desirable. However, the possibilities of such substitutions should be explored with a view to determining their potential environmental impact, the conditions under which they could be made to good effect and how to promote their judicious use.

## ELECTRONIC DOCUMENTS

An aspect of the possibility of substituting resource-light for resource-heavy technologies that deserves special mention is the problem of making electronic (or photonic) means of storing, conveying, and accessing information at least as acceptable as paper. In my home, I have a modest library of a few thousand books and journals. I am fond of this collection of paper and grudgingly discard existing occupants of limited shelf space to make room for new ones. It is difficult to justify continuing to use paper as a major medium for information storage, however, in light of alternatives becoming available.

The short history of microelectronic technology has been characterized by a steady and rapid increase in the amount of computing power that can be packaged in an area of a given size. According to Moore's law—a trend first noted by Gordon Moore in 1965 and still observable today—the number of transistors that can be placed on a single computer chip doubles about every 18 months. The number went from about 10,000 in 1975 to about 40 million today, and it is expected to go to several billion within the next two decades (Lieber, 2001; Normile, 2001).

Of course, this trend cannot continue indefinitely; with circuit features promising to be as small as 10 to 20 nanometers by around 2015, fundamental limits may soon be encountered. However, it is already possible to store the equivalent of a substantial library in a small device, and devices with much greater capacity will be available before fundamental limitations are reached; experimental arrays are being developed now that can store trillions of bits per square inch (Whiteside & Love, 2001). The widespread use of this technology would greatly reduce the need to collect books and other paper repositories of information as we now do. It is easy to imagine that a considerable savings of energy and material resources used in the production, storage, transportation, and disposal of paper could be realized if electronic storage were used for much of the information now stored not only in books, but in letters, memos, bills, solicitations, advertisements and promotional brochures, catalogues, telephone directories, photos, x-ray images, medical and other records, musical scores, and countless other forms.

Although not motivated by environmental concerns, the general idea that computer technology has the potential to greatly increase people's access to information and make it available to them in far more useful forms than those provided by conventional media has been expressed forcefully by many visionaries, starting more than half a century ago with Vannevar Bush (Bush, 1945; Engelbart, 1963; Lederberg, 1978; Licklider, 1965; Parker, 1973). Access in this context includes the ability to interact with information dynamically—to explore information spaces, as it were, following the interests that the exploration stimulates.

When reading an electronic newspaper, for example, one should be able to browse efficiently by scanning headlines, possibly according to major topical categories, requesting more information on those of special interest—getting first a brief synopsis and then, in response to a request, a more extensive report. One should be able to call up biographical or tutorial information relating to people, events, or concepts about which one is reading. Previously published articles should be easily accessed. Maps, diagrams, still pictures, moving pictures, animations, and process simulations should be available on request.

Serious scholars should be able to access, through the same systems on which they read news, the full bibliographic resources of major information repositories such as libraries and databases. Dozier and Rice (1984) pointed out that the electronic newspaper could provide the reader with access to what might be viewed as "a currently updated newspaper morgue." "The electronic newspaper, when fully implemented," they suggested, "becomes an electronic library with a constantly expanding wealth of instantly updated information" (p. 105).

Not least among the factors likely to determine the future course of the technology for information distribution are those that relate most directly to consumers' needs, preferences and habits. Many people who have access to state-of-the-art equipment and software systems for composing and using electronically stored documents still prefer to work with paper copies of documents. We need a better understanding of why that is so. How do the electronic displays have to be changed so they will be preferred to paper? What would make electronic newspapers, magazines, or books be as acceptable as, or preferred to, their traditional counterparts?

Although display design is undoubtedly an important aspect of the problem, it is not the whole story. Reading is a purposeful activity, but the purposes it serves are not necessarily simple or easy to identify completely. One might assume that people read newspapers for the sake of the information they acquire by doing so, but this is an overly simple view. Newspaper reading is often a highly ritualistic activity, and information acquisition is only one of many reasons that people engage in it (Dozier & Rice, 1984). Attempts to make electronic print media acceptable or preferred substitutes for paper are likely to have only limited success until more effort is made to understand better the reasons that people read what and when they do.

The question of how to increase the acceptability of electronic media as substitutes for paper is more significant, from an environmental point of view, than a casual consideration of it might lead one to think. Not only is paper a major waste problem, but its production is energy intensive, generates toxic emissions, and contributes significantly to deforestation. Moreover, the use of paper as a communication medium requires its transportation from place to place, which is far more detrimental to the environment than is the transmission of information over copper wires, optical cables, or the airways. The question of how to increase the acceptability of electronic print media to users is a kind of problem that human factors specialists and applied psychologists are well qualified to address.

The paperless journal may be thought of as a special case of electronic information distribution. It is special in part because the readership of many professional journals is technically knowledgeable and might be expected to be more receptive than the general public to the idea of receiving information in this way. Scientists, in particular, should find it advantageous to receive technical information in a form that is easily searched and with which they can interact.

Despite the attractiveness of the idea of paperless journals and the fact that the possibility has been of interest for some time, relatively little has been done along these lines. Impediments to faster progress include technical ones (e.g., the problem of handling graphical material given the wide variety of terminals and workstations in use) and psychological ones as well (the strong preference that many people have for reading from paper rather than from a video display terminal; Gardner, 1990; Hunt, 1990).

Yet these problems are not insurmountable, and experimentation with electronic journalism has been underway for some time. For example, the Association for Computing Machinery started experimenting with electronic submissions of articles for publications in its journals and with videotape and CD ROM publishing over a decade ago (Fox, 1990). The Chemistry Online Retrieval Experiment (CORE) got underway at Cornell University in 1993. Other major professional associations, including the American Association for the Advancement of Science and the American Psychological Association, have been developing and expanding systems that provide electronic access to increasing amounts of their archival literatures. Experiments with "virtual libraries" have been conducted at a variety of other places, and several journals are now readily available in electronic form (Krumenaker, 1993).

These ventures should yield some useful data for technologists interested in advancing the idea of electronic publishing. How quickly this idea can become a practical reality is likely to depend, to a substantial degree, on how effectively the psychological impediments to its acceptance and wide use are addressed. Environmental impact is not the only reason that human factors engineers and applied psychologists should be interested in this technology, but it is an important one.

It is time for a caveat. One might hope, if not assume, that greater use of word-processing systems, electronic mail, electronic bulletin boards, and other tools for working with and transmitting text electronically would result in a decrease in the use of paper. The idea of the paperless office lends credence to this notion. However, the use of computers for word processing and information dissemination has increased continually and dramatically over the last few decades, and so has the use of paper. Between 1970 and 1988, total paper consumption increased by over 50% in the United States, and paper for printing and writing more than doubled (Bureau of the Census, 1990). The data do not establish a causal link between increases in the use of information technology and that of paper, but neither do they lend support to the assumption that more use of information technology will automatically result in a decrease in the use of paper. They should caution us against making the assumption that the development of what appears to be an alternative way to meet some need will necessarily result in an immediate decline in the use of the older means. It appears to be possible for the development of new approaches to stimulate greater use of the older means. We need to understand better how new environmentally benign approaches can be used not only to supplement older environmentally detrimental ones, but to replace them.

In discussing the relationship between information technology and the increased consumption of paper in the United States, Herman, Ardekani, and Ausubel (1989) suggested that the reason this caught us by surprise is that we overlooked the fact that the amount of information is not fixed and that the introduction of a technology that makes it much easier to handle large amounts of information is likely to change the demands for information production and use. It is also the case that office computers and related electronic equipment, such as high-speed printers and copiers, make it easy to produce and reproduce paper copies of electronically stored information.

Why people prefer to read a paper document than a computer terminal is not known. Possibly the preference is for paper over currently existing terminals, and this will disappear when technology produces higher quality displays. Perhaps it is a generational phenomenon and people who have grown up with computers will not have the same preference for paper as adults. People who have had decades of experience with books, magazines, and newspapers may react negatively to the idea of "curling up on the couch with a good computer terminal." Research could help answer these questions. Whether it is a matter of improved terminal design or maturing of a generation of readers who have known computers all their lives, it seems likely that the use of electronic devices for acquiring information or reading for pleasure will become increasingly acceptable, especially in view of the interactive capabilities that electronic devices provide that paper does not.

## TELECONFERENCING

Much of the interest in the development and use of teleconferencing facilities stems from the assumption that such facilities could reduce the need for travel. If this assumption is valid, it has obvious implications for the problem of environmental change. Whether teleconferencing systems, and similar approaches to communication and multiperson interaction, will prove to be acceptable substitutes for travel is likely to depend in part on how well they can be made to work. Much remains to be learned about what capabilities and characteristics they need to have to be embraced enthusiastically by potential users. Some of the questions that need to be addressed are the types that human factors researchers tend to ask.

In addition to questions pertaining to the effectiveness and ease of use of teleconferencing systems, there are many questions of a more social-psychological kind that deserve attention as well. How acceptable teleconferencing sessions are likely to be as alternatives to meetings that require travel will depend on a variety of factors relating to the not-always-simple reasons that people attend meetings. When the technology is more mature, teleconferencing may be preferred to in-person meetings in some respects while in-person meetings are preferred in others. Research could help identify the purposes for which, or the conditions under which, each will be preferred.

The expectation that teleconferencing systems, even if advanced to the point that people like to use them, will reduce the amount of traveling that people do should be tempered by the fact that the idea that telecommunications technology could substitute for travel is nearly as old as the telephone. Mokhtarian (1997) pointed out that articles appeared in various London newspapers in the late 1870s that speculated on the potential of the telephone to replace face-to-face meetings, and that an article published in the *Scientific American* in 1914 predicted that telecommunications would reduce transit congestion. Undoubtedly, the telephone does adequately substitute for many face-to-face meetings today, but it is not clear that the (per capita) number of face-to-face meetings that occur per unit time would be greater if the telephone did not exist. The average individual probably communicates with more people because of the existence of the telephone; whether the average person communicates face to face less frequently is another question. Conceivably, if teleconferencing systems become as attractive a means of communication as the telephone became, they could increase the number of virtual meetings that people attend, without decreasing the frequency of face-to-face meetings in the process; but there is at least the hope that the need for face-to-face meetings could be somewhat reduced.

## TELECOMMUTING

Powerful desk- and laptop computers and computer network technology have made it possible for a significant and increasing fraction of the total white-collar workforce to work at home or in other locations outside conventional workplaces. Interest in telecommuting as a possible means of conserving energy and saving transportation costs was sparked by the oil crisis of the early 1970s (Nilles, Carlson, Gray, & Hanneman, 1976a, 1976b). Like teleconferencing, telecommuting has the advantage, from an environmental point of view, of significantly decreasing the need for travel. In theory, at least, it could also decrease the need for office space in urban centers—the costs, financial and environmental, of constructing and maintaining office buildings.

Regarding the last point, Mitchell (1997) suggested that modern skyscrapers became popular beginning in the latter part of the 19th century, in part, "because they satisfied industrial capitalism's growing need to bring armies of office workers together at locations where they could conveniently interact with one another, gain access to files and other work materials, and be supervised by their bosses" (p. 112). He argued, however, that modern telecommunications technology has decreased the importance of centrality:

Digital storage and computer networks have increasingly supported decentralized remote access to databases rather than reliance on centralized paper files. And businesses are discovering that their marketing and public-relations purposes may now be better served by slick World Wide Web pages on the Internet and Superbowl advertising spots than by investments in monumental architecture on expensive urban sites. (p. 112)

Many people are now spending either all or part of their work time at home. Some function as consultants or freelancers, but many are also employees of corporations or government organizations. According to one estimate, 3 million employees of American companies were in this category as of 1995, and this number was increasing by about 20% per year (Jaroff, 1995). There are many obvious advantages to working at home from the worker's point of view—greater control over one's working hours, avoidance of commuting hassle and saving of commuting time, and availability to meet family needs. There are also drawbacks, and what one worker (or employer) sees as a plus, another may consider a minus (Huws, Korte, & Robinson, 1990). There is much to be learned about what makes or could make telecommuting an acceptable substitute for physical commuting for purposes of work.

## DEVELOPMENT OF VIRTUAL-REALITY TECHNOLOGY

The objective of virtual-reality technology is to create simulations of objects or situations with which one can interact, much as one would with the real-world objects or situations that are simulated, except without the inconvenience or danger that interacting with the real-world objects or situations might involve (Foley, 1987). Interest in virtual-reality technology is high among computer scientists and other researchers (Durlach & Mavor, 1995; Foley, 1987; Hamilton, 1992b; Pool, 1992; Thomas & Stuart, 1992), but it is a relatively new area of research. Its potential is not known, but believed by some to be great.

An objective of some researchers in this area is to create simulated environments that give one the sense of sharing a space with other (remotely-located) participants in a conversation or multi-person gathering. In such a telepresence or teleimmersion situation, all participants would see the same space, but each from his or her own perspective, which would change appropriately as he or she moved around in it. Lanier (2001), a pioneer in the field, speculated that "business travel might be replaced to a significant degree by teleimmersion in 10 years," although he cautioned that few are likely to claim that it will be just as good as being there in person. Accomplishing teleimmersion is a much more ambitious goal than teleconferencing as currently realized and will require large amounts of computing power by comparison.

This technology could make available many services and capabilities not possible before. For example, researchers may be able to investigate virtual worlds that are too small or too large to interact with directly. There is also the possibility of representing as virtual realities abstract entities and things that have no physical counterparts, such as mathematical relationships and models of possible but never-realized structures. The main point to be argued here is that virtual-realtity technology may represent possibilities for substituting energy-light and material-light resources for energy-heavy and material-heavy ones, or for contributing to the problem of controlling detrimental environmental change in other ways. Developing this technology to the point of practical usefulness will require research on perception, motor control, cognition, and other areas of psychology as well.

Much of a visionary nature has been written about the implications of the information revolution for the future (Dertouzos, 1998; Lucky, 1989). I find some of the projections and speculations about the impact that information technology is likely to have on our lives to be exciting and inviting, and some to be disconcerting. I have been surprised and disappointed not to find more emphasis given by visionary writers to the implications—good or bad—that uses of information technology could have for the environment.

There can be no doubt that information technology will enable great changes in our lives. The enormous potential of this technology, especially as represented by computer networks, for both good and bad uses, is only beginning to be realized. Ensuring that the technology benefits society on balance will require the continuing development not only of socially desirable applications, but also the means to limit realization of the predatory and destructive possibilities for uses that also exist. How the uses of it will affect the environment in particular remains to be seen. One can imagine significant beneficial effects resulting from the substitution of resource-light for resource-heavy ways of satisfying human needs and desires. Yet it is also easy to imagine uses of the technology that would exacerbate the current situation. They could accelerate an increase in consumption in the worst sense and amplify the detrimental effects of behavior now being realized. I am guardedly optimistic that the changes that will be affected will, on balance, be positive. Yet it seems to me unwise to assume that they will be in the absence of considerable effort on the part of people of good will to make them so.

CHAPTER

# 8

# Artifact Design and Evaluation

Human factors specialists and engineering psychologists have put a great deal of emphasis on the importance of designing products so they are functional, safe, and convenient to use. These are unquestionably important design criteria, and many improvements in the functionality, safety, and usability of machines and appliances must be credited to the attention brought to these issues. A related focus of these disciplines has been the design and evaluation of tools intended to enable or facilitate the performance of specific tasks. I argue here that the interest of human factors and allied disciplines in artifact design and evaluation also has the potential of being turned to environmental benefit.

## DESIGNING FOR LONGEVITY, RECYCLABILITY, AND DISPOSABILITY

In addition to functionality, safety, and usability, other objectives of equipment design that deserve attention—especially from an environmental point of view—include maintainability, repairability, recyclability, and disposability. In the interest of environmental preservation, products could also be evaluated in terms of the efficiency with which they use natural resources—both those from which they are made and those that are used up in their making—taking their full life cycles and subsequent status, as recycled material or disposable trash, into account. Other things being equal, products that can be easily recycled are to be preferred to those that cannot; those that are destined to cause disposal problems should be given especially low marks.

The objective of designing with environmental impact in mind should also extend to the design of packages and product packaging practices. Packaging materials make up nearly half of the municipal solid waste in industrialized countries (Organization of Economic and Cooperative Development, 1991), and much of this material is plastic, which represents special disposal problems because of its durability.

Product design is not only a concern of human factors engineers. Designers more generally are being urged to consider the environmental impact of product or process designs and to give preference to those for which the impacts are the most favorable. The term *industrial ecology* is sometimes used to reflect this interest (Marshall, 1993b).

## PRODUCT EVALUATION FROM AN ENVIRONMENTAL PERSPECTIVE

Recognition that some products are more environmentally benign than others is beginning to give rise to consumer guides and product- or company-certification programs intended to help consumers choose among competing products on the basis of environmental impact. The comparisons required can involve numerous factors in addition to the products, including packaging, production processes, materials recyclability, and manufacturers' practices as they pertain to the environment (Welter, 1990).

The problem of making environmentally beneficial choices in retail buying is likely to turn out to be more complicated than it would appear to be at first glance. The environmental salience of certain product characteristics, coupled with the relative invisibility of others, will lend themselves to opportunistic advertising and consumer choices based on partial and inadequate information. The point is illustrated by a comparison of paper and polystyrene as disposable hot-drink containers.

In recent years, the use of polystyrene for disposable cups and other food containers has received considerable criticism—enough to convince some major fast-food companies to discontinue it—largely because of the nonbiodegradable nature of the material. A fair environmentally sensitive comparison of paper and polystyrene as materials for disposable food containers would take many factors in addition to ultimate disposability into account, including the environmental implications of their production (raw materials consumed, energy used, waste effluents and atmospheric emissions produced) and recyclability. A comparison that considered all these factors (Hocking, 1991a, 1991b) showed polystyrene to be superior to paper with respect to many of them. How one would judge the relative merits of the two options overall would depend on how one weighted the several individual factors. Yet it is difficult to imagine any reasonable weighting that would make paper the undisputed winner that consideration of biodegradability alone has made it in the past.

This example illustrates what may be a pervasive problem relating to human choice involving options that differ in many ways—namely, the problem of single-issue focus. If one of the ways in which the choice options differ is particularly salient or if it has received an unusual amount of attention from the media, it can become the dominant, if not the only, one considered. How to get people not to be one-issue decision makers in situations in which many issues are relevant is a psychological question with applicability beyond the matter of behavioral implications for environmental change, but nowhere is its applicability more apparent than here.

It would be difficult to overstate the importance of this question. The ease with which decisions made with the best of intentions, but with inadequate attention to all the relevant issues, can turn out to be problematic is illustrated by the well-known story, already mentioned, of how CFCs came to be so widely used and for such a long period of time. In the words of a National Research Council report,

> They [chlorinated fluorocarbons] reduced the occupational hazard of compressor explosions, they all but ended toxic pollution (and deaths) from refrigerant gases, and they dramatically increased the variety and safety of the human food supply. For 50 years, they seemed a perfect example of a benign technical solution to environmental and engineering problems, with no negative side effects of any kind. (Stern, Young, & Druckman, 1992, p. 59)

The NRC report points out that use of CFCs so enhanced the technology of refrigeration and cooling that it had a major impact on the evolution of modern urban life styles and on the growth of warm-climate population centers, thus creating a continuing and increasing demand for this technology. It notes too the unhappy recent realization that the quality that made CFCs seem so safe—their stability—ensures that their destructive presence in the stratosphere will continue for a long time even if their production and use were discontinued immediately.

This is not a criticism of the people who perceived CFCs to be preferred alternatives to other possible chemicals for use as refrigerants in the 1930s; perhaps the knowledge of atmospheric physics was inadequate to allow the effects of emissions of these substances into the atmosphere to be foreseen. My point is simply that evaluation—especially predictive evaluation—of the long-term effects of specific products on the environment can be a complex matter. Conclusions drawn on the basis of consideration of a narrow subset of the issues involved should be seen as tentative and in need of frequent review from a broad perspective.

## DATABASE DESIGN AND INFORMATION ACCESS

The proliferation of databases is a natural consequence of the increasing availability of computer and communication resources. There now exist several databases that contain data relating to one or another aspect of environmental change, and more are in preliminary stages of development. There also exist large collections of data amassed over many years for military and intelligence purposes. Some of the information in these collections could be useful in assessing the changes that have occurred during the last few decades in the world's forests, wetlands, deserts, arable lands, and ice caps, and they could contribute to a better understanding of other environmental issues as well. Some steps have been taken to bring this information store to bear on environmental concerns (Richelson, 1998).

One of the national-challenge areas targeted by the government's High Performance Computing and Communications (HPCC) and National Information Infrastructure (NII) initiatives is the environment (NIST, 1994; OSTP, 1994). What is wanted is a system that will support monitoring of environmental change and effective response to environmentally detrimental events. Important aspects of this objective are the design and operation of databases containing information gathered from many sources on various aspects of environmental status and making it available to users.

The existence of databases does not guarantee ease of access to the information they contain by the people who need or desire it. There are a host of issues—some technological, some political, some psychological—that collectively determine ease of access and use. There is a pressing need for tools to help compile, manage, and use large databases that hold information pertaining to environmental change. The National Research Council's Committee on the Human Dimensions of Global Change has emphasized the need for improved access to existing data as well as the collection of critical new data. It has also recommended that social scientists from a variety of disciplines be involved at every stage of the design and implementation of national data and information systems pertaining to human dimensions of global change to ensure the usefulness of those systems (Stern, Young, & Druckman, 1992).

Illustrative of the need both for additional data and better methods of accessing the data that exist is the need, noted by the Office of Technology Assessment (1987) relative to the problem of decreasing biodiversity, for more complete biological databases and for more effective techniques for collecting, storing, and accessing biological data. There are several times as many candidates for the endangered species list as are on it; better databases could speed up the process of determining which of them are sufficiently threatened to warrant action (Gibbons, 1992). Widely accessible databases could also greatly facilitate the screening of plant species for pharmaceutical value.

Another example of a need for database design is the Earth Observing System Data and Information System (EOSDIS). This system is composed of a collection of earth-orbiting observational satellites (Marshall, 1993a). The fourth satellite, and the flagship of this system, Terra, was launched in December 1999. It collects data on 16 of 24 factors identified by the EOS team as major determinants of climate (aerosols, air temperature, clouds, fires, glaciers, land temperature, land use, natural disasters, ocean productivity, ocean temperature, pollution, radiation, sea ice, snow cover, vegetation, and water vapor). Together the EOS satellites transmit to Earth tens of trillions of bytes of information every week (King & Herring, 2000).

Other databases dealing with specific aspects of environmental change are maintained by government agencies such as the Department of Energy, the Department of the Interior, and the Environmental Protection Agency. Whether the data in these and other databases will be used to advantage or languish in archival repositories will depend, to a large degree, on the effectiveness of the tools developed to give scientists easy access to them and help them work with them. An international network providing global access to ecological databases is part of the vision of the signatories to the 1992 biodiversity treaty—the Convention on Biological Diversity—but realization of the vision will require successful negotiation of such issues as the protection of developing countries against uncompensated exploitation of their genetic resources (Stone, 1994b).

Even if it were not for the expectation of the development of databases that are many times larger than those that now exist, database design would still pose a significant challenge to human factors engineering with its interest in making it easier for people to use technology. Most of the databases that currently exist leave something to be desired from the point of view of ease of use. As Wulf (1993) put it, "scientists are mostly struggling with database technology designed for employees' records and automated teller machines" (p. 854).

An obvious problem associated with the existence of many databases with similar or overlapping data is that of multiple interfaces. Database developers all have their own ideas as to what constitutes a user-friendly interface, so the interfaces of different databases are likely to differ in various ways. This may mean that a person who wants the greatest possible access to data in a particular problem area has to learn how to interact with several databases, and this can be a nontrivial task.

At least two approaches can be taken to solve this problem. The first is the development of interface standards or guidelines. Database developers may see the imposition of standards as an unwelcome constraint; people who are capable of developing new systems typically believe they can improve on existing systems. Standards, which represent maintenance of the status quo, may be seen as impediments to progress.

Another approach to the problem of multiple interfaces is that of developing a meta-interface—one high-level interface through which a user can communicate with all the databases of interest. The meta-interface would function like a translator between the user and various systems in the complex. Ensuring the usability of such facilities will require the collaboration of software engineers and human factors specialists in their development and refinement.

## MODEL DEVELOPMENT AND EVALUATION

Much of the research that is aimed at providing a better understanding of environmental change and the factors that contribute to it makes use of computer-based simulation models of various types. For example, scientists who study acid rain would like to determine where precipitated depositions at specific sites originated. This requires an understanding of how emissions are dispersed in the atmosphere and how the dispersion depends on atmospheric and climatic conditions, underlying terrain, and the nature of the emitted matter. Simulation modeling techniques are being used on this problem, but the situation is still not well understood.

Scientists who study air quality for the purpose of ensuring the healthfulness of air also use simulation models to predict and monitor the distribution of specific pollutants in space and time. The importance of such models' accuracy of is obvious. The possibility that models have sometimes yielded overestimates of the progress made in reducing the concentration of certain pollutants has been a matter of some concern (Seinfeld, 1989).

Ecosystem models are widely used as tools to facilitate decision making in many contexts that have relevance for environmental change (Halfon, 1979). These models come in many forms, some deterministic, some stochastic, and they have been applied to a wide range of phenomena (Levine, 1991). Computer technology has made possible the construction of complex simulations of ecological systems. Levine cautioned that if the results of modeling are to be meaningful, the models must account for all important components of the system modeled and the interactions among them. The most difficult aspect of modeling, he noted, is deciding which components and interactions are important.

Models are the fundamental tool used to develop predictions of climate change and its potential effects (Keeling, Bacastow, Carter, Piper, & Whorf,

1989; MacDonald, 1989; National Research Council, 1987). Largely because of uncertainty about the effects of the oceans and clouds, the accuracy of the predictions that climate models make, at least with respect to increases in temperature resulting from increases in the concentration of carbon dioxide in the atmosphere, is unknown to within a factor of three (Cess et al., 1993; La Brecque, 1989). Models also differ by a factor of two or three in their retrospective projections of actual trend data for the past 100 years (Grotch, 1988; Schlesinger & Mitchell, 1987; Wigley & Schlesinger, 1985). Because of the complexity of the models and differences in the assumptions that underlie different models, predictions tend to become increasingly disparate as the time period for which they are made increases. Model-based predictions of sea-level rise due to global warming by the middle of the 21st century, for example, vary around 1 foot (Meier, 1990); predictions for the amount of rise by the end of the 21st century vary over a range of less than a foot to 6 or 7 meters (Titus, 1991).

The complexity and computational demands of climate modeling are such that, until quite recently, no single model could incorporate all the relevant variables; different models focused on different aspects of the problem. The need for models that not only can project trends with respect to greenhouse gas concentrations but also provide cost–benefit information regarding possible preventive or accommodation measures is becoming recognized, and efforts to develop such integrated models are being made (Dowlatabadi & Morgan, 1993). Climate models push the limits of even the largest of today's computers; this application is seen as one of the primary uses of *hypercomputers*—machines that are expected to run at *transpetaflop* rates (more than a quadrillion floating point operations per second) or more than 1,000 times as fast as today's fastest machines (Sterling, 2001).

The use of models to predict the propagation of aircraft noise illustrates what is possible when the important parameters of the situation being modeled are well known and the modeling technique is relatively mature. Although noise propagation models have been used since the early 1970s (Galloway & Bishop, 1970), until recently their application was limited primarily to the vicinity of airports and relatively flat terrain. The availability of greatly increased amounts of computing power has enabled the development of programs that can generate equal-noise-level or equal-annoyance contours—much like the equal-altitude contours used on topographical maps—produced by en-route flights over extremely irregular terrain, such as that of the Grand Canyon and other national parks. There now exist software packages that can color code a relief map to show such contours, given a set of flyover parameters, such as flight paths, altitudes, speeds, and aircraft types (Fidell & Finegold, 1991).

Modeling is not this advanced in most areas of environmental application, but the approach is widely used as a major basis for planning and decision making. Environmental economists make much use of mathematical models to infer the effects of various approaches to resource management and pollution control on economic steady states (see e.g., any issue of the *Journal of Environmental Economics and Management*). Understanding better the limitations of models and their probable margins of error is an important goal. Better techniques are also needed for evaluating the strengths and weaknesses of decision processes that rely heavily on the predictions and projections of such models. This becomes increasingly important as policymaking entities, such as the U.S. Congress, are called on more and more to base environmental policy decisions on the expected long-term effects of those decisions. As Russell (1990) put it, "as Congress provides more and more detail in the environmental legislation it passes, it faces ever more difficulty in understanding the full implications of its actions—and ever more responsibility to do so" (p. 16).

The challenges involved in model building and use in the context of efforts to understand climate change have been clearly articulated by Dowlatabadi and Morgan (1993). These writers also pointed out the importance of taking human preferences and judgment into account in the modeling approach.

> Whereas the arguments for integrated assessment are intellectually compelling, current understanding of the natural and social sciences of the climate problem is so incomplete that today it is not possible to build traditional analytical models that incorporate all the elements, processes, and feedbacks that are likely to be important. Faced with similar problems in the past, the policy research community has typically modeled what was understood and waved their hands at the rest. The result has often been that the policy discussion has focused on what we know, rather than what is important. To avoid this difficulty in the climate problem, it will be necessary to evolve a new class of policy models that allows an integration of subjective expert judgment about poorly understood parts of the problem with formal analytical treatments of the well-understood parts of the problem. (p. 1932)

Dowlatabadi and Morgan noted that work on the development of integrated models of the type they envision is underway at several institutions.

Several large complex—global—models were developed in the 1960s and 1970s to influence the formulation of policies dealing with major societal problems, such as population growth and its attendant demands on natural resources and social systems. There appears to be a consensus that most of these models fell short of the original expectations for them. As to why they did so, Morgan and Henrion (1990) gave the following reasons:

> (1) inadequate and incomplete understanding of the systems being modeled and a concomitant lack of attention to model verification; (2) failure to be suffi-

> ciently specific about the objectives of the modeling project, (3) failure to examine carefully the implications of uncertainty in input variables and model time constants; (4) inability to deal with the stochastic elements in the systems being modeled; and (5) difficulties arising from the ideological perspectives of the analysis. (p. 297)

The failure to deal adequately with the uncertainty inherent to many situations is seen as a particularly serious matter: "The key point to remember is that without thorough and systematic modeling and analysis of the uncertainty of the problem, we can not be sure that the results of a model, especially a very large and complex one, mean anything at all" (p. 304).

Another especially important aspect of modeling relates to the expectations and perspectives of their users. On the basis of interviews of both experienced and inexperienced modelers following their use of a model for policy analysis under conditions of uncertainty, Morgan and Henrion (1990) concluded that "most users do not view the process of model building, refinement, and use as an iterative process of exploration and learning whose objective is insight.... Rather they see it more as a linear 'one-shot' process of building something that produces answers" (p. 275). Given the complexity of the models used in the attempt to understand environmental change, expecting answers seems far less appropriate than looking for insights and ideas for exploration.

A critical aspect of model development and use is that of model evaluation. Models are useful only to the degree that they are valid; grossly inaccurate predictions may well be worse than no predictions at all. Although claims of validity are frequently made in literature promoting the use of specific models, validation is extremely difficult and, in the case of numerical models of complex natural systems, perhaps impossible in any complete way. Oreskes, Shrader-Frechette, and Belitz (1994) argued that models should be used only as heuristic aids to thought—to challenge existing policy formulations, say, rather than to justify them. The risk in using models for policy justification is in the ease with which they can, unwittingly, be used to reinforce preexisting beliefs or biases.

## TOOLS FOR INTERDISCIPLINARY AND INTERNATIONAL COLLABORATION AND COOPERATION

Environmental change and its many ramifications involve numerous interacting variables. A clear picture of the problem is unlikely to be produced or even fully understood by the members of any single discipline. Similarly, no single discipline is likely to be able to develop plans for dealing with the various aspects of the problem in a comprehensive way.

The need for interdisciplinary collaboration is more easily recognized, however, than met. Cross-discipline communication is difficult under the best of circumstances; specialists find it easier to talk with other specialists who share their background knowledge, interests, specialized language, and orientation than with those who do not. Finding ways to facilitate communication and cooperation across disciplinary boundaries is a continuing challenge for research.

Many of the most threatening aspects of environmental change are global in extent, and their solutions will require worldwide efforts. Moreover, parts of the world that have contributed in only minor ways to certain aspects of environmental change in the past will become major contributors in the foreseeable future. In the past, about 80% of the greenhouse gases have been produced by the industrialized nations (Fulkerson, Judkins, & Sanghvi, 1990), but the situation is rapidly changing as more of the world is becoming industrialized. Some observers believe that $CO_2$ emissions from developing countries could soon exceed those of the already industrialized world (Fulkerson et al., 1989).

The concept of *sustainable agriculture* has been generalized to *sustainable development* to convey the need for resource management policies that will permit worldwide economic development in a way that will not cause irremediable environmental damage. The idea has not escaped criticism. For example, Beckerman (1994) claimed that the concept is not useful, but that, as usually defined, it is "either morally repugnant or logically redundant" (p. 191). The definition used in *Our Common Future*, the 1987 report of the World Commission on the Environment and Development, equates sustainable development with "development that meets the needs of the present without compromising the ability of future generations to meet their own needs." The fatal flaw in this definition, Beckerman argued, is the subjective nature of *needs*. One person's needs are another's luxuries; this is especially apparent when one contrasts what are considered needs in industrial societies with what are considered needs in undeveloped countries. The point is well taken, but it does not negate the legitimacy of the concern behind the idea of sustainable development—namely, that the current generation should not wittingly engage in behavior that appears to have a good chance of degrading the quality of life of generations to come.

Research aimed at creating a better understanding of cultural determinants of technological feasibility is needed. As Schumacher (1973) pointed out, economic neocolonialism can be accomplished deliberately or inadvertently, and it is more insidious and harder to combat when done unintentionally than when intentionally pursued. "Poor countries slip—and are pushed—into adoption of production methods and consumption standards which destroy the possibilities of self-reliance and self-help. The results are unintentional neocolonialism and hopelessness for the poor" (p. 207).

Awareness of the global nature of many aspects of environmental change and of the need for internationally coordinated efforts to address the problem is keen among many policymakers (Silver & DeFries, 1990; World Commission on Environment and Development, 1987). International agreements have been signed with respect to several aspects of environmental change, including nuclear testing, ocean dumping, stratospheric ozone protection, and endangered species. Yet parties involved in collaborative decision making sometimes make decisions that not only fail to achieve a possible outcome that would have been desirable from all participants' points of view, but may even be detrimental to all (Olson, 1965). Tools are needed that would decrease the probability of such outcomes and help collaborative decision makers to achieve mutually desirable results. Especially needed are tools that can facilitate communication and collaboration across linguistic, national, and cultural boundaries.

CHAPTER

# 9

# Consumption, Consumerism, and Environmental Economics

In this chapter and several that follow, some topics are considered that represent opportunities, I believe, for psychological research motivated by an interest in finding ways to decrease the detrimental impact of human behavior on the environment. This chapter focuses on consumer behavior and closely related topics such as advertising and consumer education. Subsequent chapters deal with the perception and communication of risk, the psychology of prevention, cost–benefit and trade-off analyses, competition, cooperation, negotiation, and policymaking, among other topics that relate to environmental change and the role of behavior in effecting it.

## CONSUMER BEHAVIOR

The term *consumer* is a misnomer; we consume little of what we purchase or otherwise acquire. More typically we use something for a while, possibly transforming it in one way or another in the process of wearing it out, and eventually dispose of it as waste. But *consumer* is the word used to refer to people who purchase, or use, goods and services, and *consumption* is the term used to denote the behavior in which consumers, as consumers, engage, so those are the terms used here.

Consumer behavior has been a major interest of psychologists for several decades. A chapter on consumer psychology was included in the *Annual Review of Psychology* in 1965 (Twedt, 1965), and the subject has been covered in the same publication several times since then. Research in this area has focused on a broad range of topics, including consumer attitude assessment and change; processing of product information; physiological, affective, or cognitive reactions to specific advertisements; complaint behavior; persuasion; finding predictors of purchasing behavior; and assessing the effectiveness of advertisements in evoking purchasing behavior. Traditional subareas of psychology such as perception, memory, decision making, and motivation have been investigated as they relate to consumer behavior with the objective of understanding better why consumers make the choices they do (Bettman, 1979, 1986; Kassarjian, 1982).

For the most part, consumer psychology takes consumption as a given. The objective is to understand why people make the purchasing choices they do; little attention has been given to the question of whether consumption, at any given level, is good or bad from some specific perspective. As Bettman (1986) put it, "The focus of consumer psychology is on understanding and explaining the psychological factors that influence ... choice, purchase, and usage behaviors" (p. 258). With the exception of the work on energy consumption, I found almost no mention in several reviews of consumer psychology of environmental implications of consumer behavior. Perhaps this type of question is seen as outside the purview of the area and more appropriately the concern of economists, earth scientists, or social philosophers. Yet consumer behavior clearly has implications for the environment, and psychological research should be useful in finding ways to make consumption more environmentally friendly. There can be little doubt that findings from research on consumer behavior can be, and are, used to influence that behavior. Advertisement and marketing agencies pay attention to the results of consumer research and apply them with considerable effect.

A better understanding of consumerism as a life style is a fundamental challenge to psychological research. What makes people attach such great importance to the acquisition of ever more material possessions? Why do acquisitions seem almost invariably to lead to the desire for additional acquisitions? Is it a matter of the inherent insatiability of human avarice? Does it reflect the effectiveness of the advertising industry promoting the idea that happiness depends on consumption? Is there any evidence of such a dependence?

If contentment with one's lot is a function of the difference between what one has and what one wants, there is something to be said for giving some attention to the possibility of decreasing the difference by diminishing the *wants* term in this equation, at least in the case of people who have a great deal already. Schumacher (1973) made a similar point this way: "Since consumption is merely a means to human well-being, the aim should be to obtain the maximum of well-being with the minimum of consumption" (p. 61). This is not the canonical business perspective, but it is a provocative idea especially if it is true, as Schumacher claimed, that as a society we have been guilty of "systematically cultivating greed and envy and thus building up a vast array of totally unwarranted wants" (p. 38). In any case, psychology has a lot to learn about the relationship between human contentment and material possessions. If, as Durning (1992) argued, only population growth rivals high consumption as a cause of ecological decline, a better understanding of what drives consumption is critical from an environmental point of view.

The promotion of a high level of consumption is often justified on the grounds that it is essential to a strong economy. I do not mean to argue that this claim has no merit; it is difficult to imagine, however, that it can be unqualifiedly true that the greater the level of consumption, the better. Moreover, to refer to Durning again, even granting that changing from a high- to a low-consumption economy would require some difficult adjustments, not doing so may ensure more severe economic problems later; in his words, "business ... will not do well on a dying planet" (p. 107).

A high level of consumption is not unique to the United States, but it is apparent here. We use more energy, purchase more goods, and generate more waste, per capita, than any other country in the world. We need to understand better why this is so. We also need to know why societies, even industrialized societies, vary as much as they do with respect to their energy use and consumptive behavior.

There can be little doubt that overconsumption is a serious problem from an environmental point of view, but for a given overall level of consumption there is also an issue of the selectivity in consumer behavior. Some consumer goods and products are more environmentally friendly than others. Environmentally responsible consumer behavior is sometimes defined in terms of such selectivity: "We define environmentally responsible consumer behavior as the purchase of products that benefit or cause less harm to the environment than do more conventional consumer goods" (Ebreo, Hershey, & Vining, 1999, p. 108).

Several efforts have been made to determine whether environmentally responsible consumers share any distinguishing personality characteristics as a group (Balderjahn, 1988; Henion, 1976; Rotter, Chance, & Phares, 1972; Schwepker & Cornwell, 1991). My sense is that no major personality trait emerges as a reliable predictor, although the results of all of these studies suggest that internal locus of control tends to be correlated with environmentally friendly behavior. Other correlational studies have found a relationship between environmentally responsible behavior and one's belief that actions under one's control have implications for the environment (Allen & Ferrand, 1999).

## FASHION, STYLE, AND RESOURCE UTILIZATION

Sometimes we discard and replace items not because they are no longer serviceable, but because they are no longer in fashion—they have gone out of style. This is most obviously true, perhaps, in the case of clothing. There is an opportunity for some important research focused on the question of how fashion and style, and the psychology that attends these concepts, influence behavior that has long-term implications for the utilization of resources and consequently for environmental change.

Fashion-driven buying can be viewed as a special case of the more general problem of overconsumption mentioned before. From this perspective, it is an extravagance that works against resource conservation and environmental preservation. Yet, many jobs depend on that consumption or at least so it would appear. Figuring out how the critical variables relate and how to make rational trade-offs is a task for research, and the problem has significant psychological dimensions.

A more-than-superficial understanding of the relationships of interest and how consumer attitudes and behavior should be changed, if they should, can not be attained quickly or easily. It is easy to jump to the conclusion that our attitudes, as consumers, are formed by fashion promoters, style setters, and advertisers, and that they should be modified so as to bring our wants more in line with our actual needs. Yet a complete picture of the situation must include the implications of major changes in consumer behavior for the numerous industries and many workers that that behavior supports.

## ADVERTISING

Considerable attention has been given by researchers to questions pertaining to advertising. What makes advertising effective (in the sense of influencing purchasing behavior in intended ways)? How are the effects of advertising mediated? Do advertisements change people's beliefs about products and influence their purchases via a cognitive path? Is their impact more affective in nature, influencing purchasing through changes in emotional reactions to products? Is advertising that does nothing more than increase the familiarity or salience of a brand name effective?

It has been suggested that less thought typically goes into purchasing decisions than is generally assumed (Olshavsky & Granbois, 1979; Ray,

1974). This could be due, in part, to the difficulty people have in extracting precisely the product information they need from that which is provided—which generally is intended to make the product look as good as possible. Apparently people do put some effort into seeking product information for major purchases like an automobile, calibrating the effort on the basis of what they think the information is worth relative to the cost of its acquisition (Furse, Punj, & Stewart, 1984; Punj & Staelin, 1983). Whether the information that is acquired is used to make a selection or rationalize a decision already made can be difficult to determine in individual instances (Soelberg, 1967).

The cognition of advertisement processing has been the focus of numerous studies and is likely to continue to be so (Harris, 1983; Percy & Woodside, 1983). The evidence makes it clear that advertising can be effective in more than one way. Some advertisements engage some consumers cognitively and affect their beliefs about products. However, advertisements that do not evoke high-involvement processing may also be effective perhaps simply by increasing consumers' awareness of the advertised products or creating purchase-promoting associations involving them (Batra & Ray, 1983; Cacioppo & Petty, 1984; Deighton, 1983). Much remains to be learned about the role of affective variables as determinants of consumer behavior (Hirschman & Holbrook, 1982; Holbrook & Hirschman, 1982).

Some advertising is explicitly identified by the advertisers as such, whereas some is not. Products are promoted indirectly through media presentations that have ostensible purposes other than advertising. Direct and explicit advertising has received considerable attention from researchers, but primarily for determining what works and what does not. Much less interest has been shown in the question of the extent to which consumer behavior is influenced by values that are promoted directly and indirectly in TV and other media when they are ostensibly used for purposes of entertainment, as distinct from explicit advertising. More focus by researchers on implicit advertising could contribute to a better understanding of the determinants of consumer behavior.

## ALTERNATIVE WAYS OF SATISFYING NEEDS AND DESIRES

Means are easily confused with ends. I may say that I would like the temperature in my house to be at about 70° in the winter. What I really want is for the house to be a comfortable place, and I say I would like the temperature to be such and so because I believe that to be essential to comfort. If I could be convinced that it could be made quite comfortable at a lower temperature, through the manipulation of other variables such as relative humidity, air circulation, and choice of clothing, I might give up the 70° objective readily.

Many of the things we often perceive to be ends may better be considered as means to more fundamental ends, such as safety, health, comfort, mobility, peer acceptance, security, and productivity. Explicitly recognizing something as a means to an end—a way to satisfy some other desire or more fundamental need—rather than an end, encourages one to consider the possibility of satisfying the need or desire involved in some other way. The implications of this distinction for environmental change lie in the fact that not all the means of satisfying the same fundamental needs have the same environmental consequences.

Consumer products, few if any of which can be considered ends, presumably are valued because of the basic needs they help to satisfy. This is easily overlooked, however, and products are treated as if they were ends. Help from psychologists in sharpening this distinction and increasing our consciousness of it might motivate choices of environmentally benign ways to satisfy basic needs as alternatives to more environmentally detrimental ways of satisfying those needs when such alternatives exist. It could also facilitate the development of such alternatives when they do not yet exist.

It would be good not only to have a better understanding of human needs and preferences at a fundamental level, but also to understand better why people make the choices they make when alternative means of satisfying a given need exist. The relative roles of physiological and psychological variables, and the interactions between them, in determining human comfort and satisfaction are not well understood. The fact that thermal comfort depends, in part, on symbolic and other nonphysical factors (Heijs & Stringer, 1988) is the kind of finding that should caution us against uncritically accepting causal accounts of need satisfaction that do not take psychological variables into consideration.

## CONSUMER EDUCATION GENERALLY

People need reliable, precise, and understandable information regarding the environmental implications, in quantitative terms, of specific practices and behaviors. Of the variety of choices that each of us makes more or less continuously, we need to know which of them can have major significance for environmental change. It does not suffice to take the position that everything is important even if it is; people need some feeling for relative magnitudes of effects. If one is prepared to put effort into effecting change, one wants some assurance that the time and energy will be well spent.

The challenge is not simply that of providing people with more information, but that of providing them with factual information presented in a form that ensures its accessibility and helps people make decisions consistent with their goals. With respect to purchasing decisions, it has been suggested that consumers already receive more product information than they can effectively use

(Jacoby, Speller, & Berning, 1974; Jacoby, Speller, & Kohn, 1974); whether they do has been a matter of debate (Russo, 1974; Wilkie, 1974). Yet in purchasing situations, the goals of sellers are unlikely to be the same as those of buyers, and it is the sellers who, within certain regulatory limits, decide what information is presented and how it is packaged. Generally, consumers are not given information about future costs—resulting from long-term environmental implications—of current purchasing decisions. To be sure, such costs are not easily quantified, but sellers have little incentive to attempt to quantify or publicize them to the extent that they can be estimated.

One compelling reason for making public education regarding environmental issues a high priority is that public policy is often influenced, if not dictated, by public opinion as revealed in polls, referenda, and political action of citizen groups. To the extent that public opinion on specific issues is based on unfounded assumptions or misinformation, it can promote policies that may have effects different from those intended. Many investigators and theorists have expressed concern about this possibility (Fischhoff & Furby, 1988; Gregory, Lichtenstein, & Slovic, 1993; Hammond & Adelman, 1976; Lazo, Schulze, McClelland, & Doyle, 1992).

A second important reason for attempting to increase public understanding of environmental issues is the assumption that beliefs motivate behavior and accurate beliefs about the environmental effects of behavior are more likely than inaccurate ones to motivate environmentally beneficial or benign behavior. There is some evidence that people are more willing to pay to rectify environmental damage caused by humans than to take care of that which has other causes (DeKay & McClelland, 1996; Kahneman, Ritov, Jacowitz, & Grant, 1993). This being the case, it is important that people have an accurate understanding of the various ways in which environmental problems have their roots in human behavior.

There exist many readily accessible books that describe specific aspects of the problem of detrimental environmental change in considerable detail and in lay terms (Carson, 1962; Durning, 1992; Gore, 1992), as well as others that give many suggestions regarding what average citizens can do to help solve the problem (American Automobile Association, 1975; Federal Energy Administration, 1977; Purcell, 1980; The EarthWorks Group, 1989, 1991a, 1991b). Unfortunately, there is little evidence regarding what effect, if any, this literature has had on people's behavior.

Despite the growing literature and considerable attention that environmental change has received from the press and other media, it is doubtful that the general public has a detailed understanding of the various aspects of the problem. The public is concerned about the quality of the environment in general (Tyson, 1992), but there are reasons to believe that knowledge of specifics is not precise. For example, there appears to be confusion between the issue of the atmospheric accumulation of greenhouse gases that may be contributing to global climate change and that of air pollution (Kempton, 1990). Many people are not aware of what causes air pollution or the effects that such pollution can have on human health (Kromm, Probald, & Wall, 1973). Many do not have an accurate understanding of the relative effectiveness of various forms of energy conservation (Kempton, Harris, Keith, & Weihl, 1985; Milstein, 1977). Apparently consumers are likely to identify products that come in recyclable containers but not those that use least wasteful packaging (Linn, Vining, & Feeley, 1994). Many other examples of limited understanding of environmental issues could be given.

There also is little evidence that the ideas people have about the causal connections between their behavior and environmental effects are accurate. Probably most of us understand that our behavior often has environmental implications, and are aware, in specific instances, of the direction in which we would have to modify that behavior to make it more environmentally friendly. What we typically do not know, in any precise way, is how much effect any given change in behavior is likely to have. This knowledge is important because without it well-intentioned people may put effort into activities that have little effect while failing to do other things the impact of which could be significant. For example, people need to know that the major users of energy in the home are furnaces, air conditioners, water heaters, and refrigerators, and that a minor adjustment in the use of one of these appliances can have a considerable effect relative, say, to careful turning off of unnecessary lights (Seligman, Becker, & Darley, 1981).

It was noted in chapter 5 that attempts to inform people about the problem of environmental change or persuade them to modify their behavior in the interest of environmental preservation have been only marginally successful. These efforts have typically been of short duration, however, and have focused on attempts to induce participation in particular experimental programs. It remains to be seen what could be accomplished by sustained attempts to educate the public about the general problem of environmental change and to provide it with solid information regarding the implications of specific types of behavior relative to the problem.

## THE MEDIA AND PUBLIC OPINION

Most of what the average citizen knows today about the environment, or about any other newsworthy topic, has been learned through the media—TV, radio, newspapers, and news magazines. The role of the media in shaping public attitudes about environmental issues, and especially about various risks posed by technology has been emphasized by some writers (e.g., Kasperson et al., 1988; Krimsky & Golding, 1991; Renn, Burns, Kasperson, Kasperson, & Slovic, 1992; Vincent, 1990). If the media present a biased or distorted view on any particular subject, that view is likely to be pervasively held throughout a society. Do the media present biased views on issues relating to environmental change? Some observers claim they do—not necessarily intentionally, but simply because of the nature of their business.

For example, Melnick (1990) suggested that the media tend to dramatize and exaggerate health risks that can be personalized and photographed. Personal interest stories, especially those that have a strong emotional component, capture and hold viewer or reader attention, whereas the cold objective reporting of statistics does not. The tendency of the media to give disproportionate time to the reporting of sensational items may make for good ratings at the expense of presenting an accurate view of what is going on in the world. According to Rothman and Lichter (1987), the media, by giving disproportionate attention to the views of scientists who are most opposed to the use of nuclear power, have created the impression that the scientific community is closely divided on the issue of the safety of this industry, whereas in fact most scientists who are familiar with it believe it to be relatively safe.

Regardless of whether the media lack balance in their representation of the news as it pertains to environmental matters, we need to understand better than we do the role the media play in shaping public opinion, attitudes, beliefs, and actions. Informing public opinion by a balanced presentation of facts relating to controversial issues is a proper function of news media, shaping public opinion by presenting systematically biased or distorted accounts of the facts, whether intentionally or as a consequence of the need to maintain ratings and sales, is not.

A more difficult and sensitive question already mentioned relating to the media's role in environmental change pertains to the shaping of values and attitudes, both through direct advertising and the portrayal of what constitute desirable life styles. The inordinate amount of time that American children spend watching TV during their formative years has been highly publicized; although the effects of this experience on the attitudes, beliefs, and values of the viewers is a matter of continuing debate, it is difficult to imagine that they are not great. The fact that young children have stereotypes of people on the basis of the products they own (Belk, Bahn, & Mayer, 1982) is a thought-provoking finding—one that deserves further study in the context of trying to develop a better understanding of consumer behavior.

Much of the information that people receive about the environment comes from environmental organizations. The tendency to present one-sided arguments and views is pervasive and independent of the side of an issue an individual or organization wishes to defend. There is little reason to expect environmental organizations, whether within government or the private sector, to be any more immune to vested interests and empire building than are other organizations. The interests of the people running the organization, and benefiting personally from its existence, may wander considerably from those of the organization's founders and even current supporters. How is the general public to judge the effectiveness of organizations? To distinguish accomplishments from promotional claims? To determine whether the ostensible purposes of the organizations are really being well served by their leaders? To judge the accuracy, balance, and completeness of the information it disseminates?

## ENVIRONMENTAL PROTECTION AND ECONOMIC DEVELOPMENT

The relationship between economic development and the impact of human activity on the environment is not well understood. Experts often express diametrically opposing views on the subject. Free trade, as represented by the General Agreement on Tariffs and Trade (GATT) and the North American Free Trade Agreement (NAFTA), for example, has been described as both threatening to the environment (Daly, 1993) and facilitative of its protection (Bhagwati, 1993). Experts also disagree on the environmental effects of factors such as national debt and level of government spending on domestic programs (Pearce, Adger, Maddison, & Moran, 1995).

According to one view, the relationship is described by an inverted U: When per capita income is increased above minimal levels the degradative environmental effect increases, but as income grows further the relationship reverses and the degradative effect begins to decrease (Dietz & Rosa, 1997; Grossman & Krueger, 1995). The idea is that, in the early stages of economic development of an undeveloped country, the emphasis is totally on economic growth, and little concern is shown for any degradative environmental impact of this growth. Yet as the standard of living reaches a certain level, the citizenry begins to pay more attention to environmental issues because it can afford to do so (Beckerman, 1992). Some writers have pointed out positive relationships between specific indicators of environmental concern or quality and per-capita income levels at least for levels above some minimum value (Vincent & Panayotou, 1997).

The generality of this inverted-U relationship has been questioned, in part, on the grounds that

> it has been shown to be valid for pollutants involving local short-term costs (for example, sulfur, particulates, and fecal coliforms), not for the accumulation of

stocks of waste or for pollutants involving long-term and more dispersed costs (such as $CO_2$), which are often increasing functions of income. (Arrow et al., 1995, p. 520)

Arrow et al. pointed out that the relationship has been shown to hold for emissions of pollutants, but not for resource stocks such as soil, forests, and other ecosystems. Economic development, these authors argued, does not guarantee environmental protection. "The solution to environmental degradation lies in such institutional reforms as would compel private users of environmental resources to take account of the social costs of their actions" (p. 520).

Some people assume that economic development not only fails to guarantee environmental protection, but more or less ensures the opposite. Environmentalists and economic developers have often been seen as natural adversaries; what has been desirable to the one group has been presumed to be anathema to the other. Some environmentalists have viewed developers as greedy opportunists so focused on profits as to be oblivious to the effects of their activities on the long-term quality of the environment. Some developers have viewed environmentalists as impractical fanatics who put personal esthetic tastes and the protection of obscure species of questionable value ahead of jobs and the economic security of their fellow human beings.

There appears to be a growing belief, however, that environmental protection and economic development are not necessarily opposing interests. Water utilization has been a policy concern from an environmental point of view in the United States for a long time (Burges, 1979; Loucks, Stedinger, & Haith, 1981). The application of economics to water resource management has been part of governmental policy at least since the Flood Contol Act of 1936, and formal cost–benefit analyses of management policies were undertaken at least as early as the 1950s (Eckstein, 1958; Rogers, 1991). Increasingly, economists are attempting to assess the value of environmental variables in monetary terms. Although attaching a monetary value to the maintenance of a specified standard of clean air or water is difficult, it is clear that such things are worth a great deal indeed. Getting a better understanding of the true values of resources and services provided by natural systems and of the real costs incurred when their effectiveness is diminished is a major challenge facing economists at the present time.

In summing up a review of the application of economic analyses to water resource management, Rogers (1991) noted that it "could be read as an assertion of the futility of attempting economic analysis on a subject as complicated as environmental policy." As to why, in view of this, attention should be given to economic aspects of environmental decision making, his answer is:

economic thinking and conceptualization appear to be the only alternative to a chaotic political battle with no concepts of the public good, but only "log roll-

> ing" and "pork barreling." ... Although it by no means solves all the problems in the field, economic analysis and economic thinking on the part of environmental managers and consumers is essential if a coherent environmental policy is to emerge in the United States. (p. 153)

Environmental economics appears to be coming into its own as a bridging discipline (Costanza, 1992; Dixon & Hufschmidt, 1986; Galbraith, 1991; Kiessling & Landberg, 1994; Kneese, 1977; Krutilla & Fisher, 1985; Tietenberg, 1988).

Environmentalists and economists have many common interests and an increasing willingness to work together on the problem of better understanding environmental economics. This was indicated by the formation of the International Society for Ecological Economics in 1988 and the launching of the society's journal *Ecological Economics* (Holden, 1990). This is not to suggest that all economists and environmentalists now see eye to eye regarding environmental and economic policy and that disputes between environmentalists and economic developers are things of the past. However, the fact that collaborations between environmentalists and economists aimed at improving their common understanding of economic development and environmental change are occurring (Costanza, 1992) is encouraging.

Another promising development is the emergence of industrial ecology as a field of endeavor, the objectives of which are "to examine the environmental impacts of modern industrial society" and "to discover new methods of production and consumption that will lead—when all the consequences, good and bad, are fully accounted for—to fewer harmful side effects" (Lifset, 2000, p. 32). Effective pursuit of these objectives means viewing manufacturing in a much broader context than that in which it has typically been viewed. It means considering not only the manufacturing process, but also the premanufacturing processes involved in acquiring the raw materials used and the postmanufacturing problems associated with the disposal of products when they no longer serve their intended purposes.

One hope is that viewing consumer society as an ecosystem will (a) lead to a better understanding of how human activities affect the flow of substances on a comprehensive scale, and (b) reduce the chances of effecting innovations that are environmentally beneficial if seen from a narrow perspective, but may do more harm than good if seen in a broader context. The variables are many and the interactions among them complex, but the goal of coming to a better understanding of how to meet the needs of the present generation without mortgaging the quality of life of future generations is one on which there should be wide agreement.

Quality of life is the issue. The basic question is how to increase it or at least ensure that it does not decrease, for people in general, those who are alive now and those of future generations. We cannot look far into the future—which is not to say that our current actions can have no impact on the distant future—but we can have some plausible ideas about what life could possibly be like for our children's children and theirs. We know enough about environmental change to have legitimate concerns about how current behavior could reflect itself in a lower quality of life during the future that is close enough for us to be able to identify with it. Yet we need a much better understanding than we now have of what constitutes quality of life, of how this varies with sociocultural context, and of the environmental implications of the various ways in which it can be enhanced.

Precisely how the quality of the environment affects the quality of life of its inhabitants is an important question for continuing research. It would be naive in the extreme to assume that a high-quality environment would ensure happiness to all who live in it, but it seems obvious that the quality of life cannot be independent of the quality of the environment in which it exists. Other things equal, a pleasant healthful environment must be greatly preferred to a polluted one.

CHAPTER

# 10

# Risk and the Psychology of Prevention

Risk[1] is an unavoidable fact of life; specific risks may be reduced, but seldom can they be eliminated. This is true of environmental as well as other types of risks. The unavoidability of risk is implicit in the notion of risk management, the objective of which is to limit risk and make it commensurate with the benefits to be obtained from taking it.

## RISK ASSESSMENT

To work effectively on the objectives of managing specific risks—getting them to acceptable levels and keeping them there—requires first that they be assessed for what they are. A reasonably accurate understanding of what the risks are is essential to a wise allocation of resources to their reduction and control. Both governments and individuals tend to act in accordance with what they believe risks to be (Gould et al., 1988; Russell &

[1]Sometimes a distinction is made between a *risk* and a *hazard*—a risk being a measure of harm and a hazard the source of the risk (Krimsky & Golding, 1991). Here it suffices to give risk a sufficiently broad connotation to encompass both ideas.

Gruber, 1987), and their actions may be dysfunctional to the degree that their beliefs are wrong. (For an introduction to risk analysis, see Kammen & Hassenzahl [1999] and for a history of efforts to understand and manage risk, see Bernstein [1996].) As critics of some environmental programs have rightly pointed out, the overestimation of risks can have costly consequences just as their underestimation can. There are many evidences that people do overestimate risks in some instances and underestimate them in others. Gardner and Stern (1996) discussed several psychological factors that have been identified as possible contributors to over- and underestimates.

The assessment of risk has received considerable attention from psychological researchers (Fischhoff, Lichtenstein, Slovic, Derby, & Keeney, 1981; Fischhoff, Sverson, & Slovic, 1987; Glickman & Gough, 1990; Kates & Kasperson, 1983; Krimsky & Plough, 1988; Wilson & Crouch, 1987.) This will continue to be an important area of research in connection with the problem of understanding the risks associated with various policies that might be adopted or actions taken for the purpose of limiting detrimental environmental change (Krimsky & Golding, 1991).

People often underestimate their personal vulnerability to various types of risk (Weinstein, 1984, 1989; Weinstein, Klotz, & Sandman, 1988; Weinstein, Sandman, & Roberts, 1991). Personal beliefs about fate and luck relate to this tendency. For example, automobile drivers tend to consider themselves more expert and safer than average (Svenson, 1981) and estimate their chances of being involved in an automobile accident to be higher when they are a passenger in an automobile than when driving it (Greening & Chandler, 1997; McKenna, 1993; McKenna, Stanier, & Lewis, 1991). The seriousness of a medical risk is sometimes discounted by people who have reason to believe themselves to be especially susceptible to it (Block & Keller, 1995; Ditto, Jemmott, & Darley, 1988; Ditto & Lopez, 1992; Jemmott, Ditto, & Croyle, 1986; Kunda, 1987).

In general, it appears that people tend to consider specified positive events to be more likely to happen to themselves than to another person, and to consider specified negative events to be more likely to happen to someone else than to themselves (Bauman & Siegel, 1987; Harris & Guten, 1979; Perloff & Fetzer, 1986; Robertson, 1977; Svenson, 1981; Zakay, 1983, 1984). A bias toward optimism with respect to one's future is arguably beneficial in certain ways (Alloy & Ahrens, 1987; Taylor, 1989), but it does not help ensure accurate appreciation of threats to or from the environment.

## PROBLEMS IN QUANTIFYING RISK

Quantitative risk assessment is an imprecise and controversial activity (Cohrssen & Covello, 1989; Fischhoff, 1977; Krimsky & Golding, 1991; Primack, 1975; Sjoberg, 1980). It is an example of the problem of estimation of probabilistic variables more generally. When frequency-of-incidence data exist in sufficient quantity, they may be used as the basis for risk estimates. This approach is effective for certain purposes, such as the setting of premiums for insurance against specific eventualities. The interpretation of the relative frequencies in large data sets as reflective of the probabilities of the occurrence of specific events is widely accepted among people who study risks. Some of the risks that are of concern, however, cannot be estimated this way because they are low-frequency events or have never occurred in the past (a thermonuclear holocaust; accidental development of a lethal virus from genetic experimentation; release of high-level radioactive waste from any of the various proposed long-term storage sites). Estimating the probabilities of such events must involve expert judgment, and there are conflicting opinions as to what probabilities based on such judgments mean.

There is also the problem that many risks are unknown simply because of a lack of knowledge of a fundamental nature. The effects of long-term exposure to many (perhaps most) chemicals used in industrial, agricultural, medical, military or other contexts are not known. Krimsky and Golding (1991) referred to the quantification of the long-term cumulative effects of low doses of a toxin as one of the most refractory problems in toxicological risk assessment. Experts are not agreed on what the nature of the risk of global warming is, either in the sense of whether or to what extent it will occur or in that of what the consequences of a given increase in average temperature would be. Lack of consistency among geologists in the way probabilities are used in deriving estimates of crude oil reserves has resulted in enormous variability in the numbers that reach policymakers and the general public (Campbell & Laherrère, 1998).

Policy decisions must be made, if only by default, on the basis of current knowledge, even if it is inadequate simply because there must be policy: Either use of pesticide X is permitted or it is not. Obviously, getting a better scientific understanding of the relative seriousness of specific risks is an important goal, as is that of conveying to the general public accurate information regarding those risks.

## EXPERT VERSUS LAY PERCEPTIONS OF RISK

Several studies have shown disparities between the perceived riskiness of specific situations and the actual riskiness of those situations as reflected in incidence statistics (Lichtenstein, Slovic, Fischhoff, Layman, & Combs, 1978;

Litai, Lanning, & Rasmussen, 1983; Slovic, Fischhoff, & Lichtenstein, 1979). Other studies have shown that the general public perceives environmental risks differently, in many cases, than do the experts (Bell, Fisher, Baum, & Greene, 1990; Burton, Kates, & White, 1978; Gardner & Gould, 1989; Gould, Gardner, DeLuca, Tiemann, Doob, & Stolwijk, 1988; Kamieniecki, O'Brien, & Clarke, 1986; Kempton, 1991; Lewis, 1980, 1990).

Portney (1991b) contended that the discrepancy between expert and lay opinions about risks has found its way into many environmental policy decisions, among which are:

> whether or where to site and license nuclear-power plants; license or ban specific pesticides, fertilizers, other agricultural chemicals, food additives, industrial chemicals, and pharmaceutical products; shut solid-waste landfills; regulate emissions to the air and water from industrial plants and automobiles; clean up existing hazardous-waste sites; and many others. The recurring pattern is of a positivist analysis that demonstrates the risks from some action are quite low—and of the public disagreeing. (p. 208)

Slovic, Fischhoff, and Lichtenstein (1980, 1981) suggested that the availability heuristic (Tversky & Kahneman, 1973) may account for many of the general public's misperceptions of risks: Risks are judged to be more severe the more readily they come to mind, and how readily they come to mind is likely to depend, in large measure, on the kind of coverage they receive in the press, which does not necessarily reflect the degree of threat they represent. There is reason to believe that sensational events are considerably more likely to be covered by the press and other media—and therefore more in the public eye—than unspectacular events that could have equally or more serious consequences (Greenberg, Sachsman, Sandman, & Salomone, 1989). Consistently with the availability heuristic, the perceived likelihood by the public of the occurrence of an event, such as a nuclear power plant accident, appears to increase following the occurrence of such an event (Drottz-Sjoberg & Sjoberg, 1990; Midden & Verplanken, 1990, Renn, 1990). Risk perception can also be distorted by the sensitivity of current laboratory testing techniques, which permit detection of impurities in human biologics such as blood or urine, as well as in air, water, and soil at the parts-per-trillion level. Awareness of contaminants that exist in very small amounts can cause concern even when these levels are too low to constitute a real threat (Gute, 1991).

An accurate perception of risks by the general public is made difficult to ensure in some cases because of emotional reactions of people on all sides of a controversial issue. The point is illustrated by the long-standing and continuing public debate about nuclear power generation (Dupont, 1980; Fischhoff, Slovic, Lichtenstein, Read, & Combs, 1978; Hughey, Sundstrom, & Lounsbury, 1985;

Kasper, 1979; Levi & Holder, 1986; Reicher, Podpadec, Macnaghten, Brown, & Eiser, 1993; Sundstrom, Lounsbury, DeVault, & Peele, 1981; Van der Pligt, Eiser, & Spears, 1986a, 1986b). However, people appear to accept or ignore some risks despite the fact that they are highly publicized and readily brought to mind (e.g., living in an earthquake-prone area) while being highly adverse to accepting others that may be considerably smaller.

Strangely, despite the considerable attention that psychologists have given to the study of risk perception, and the fact that energy production has been a focus of much public concern, relatively little is known about the social-psychological determinants of public responses to risks from energy production systems. Slovic, Fischhoff, and Lichtenstein (1980) pointed out this paucity of knowledge and attributed it to lack of research addressed to this particular question. One finding, not surprising, is that people who express more favorable attitudes toward nuclear power plants are more likely than those who do not to see the benefits of such plants (jobs, inexpensive power), whereas those who express more negative attitudes are more focused on the hazards they believe they represent (Sundstrom, Lounsbury, DeVault, & Peele, 1981; Sundstrom, Lounsbury, Schuller, Fowler, & Mattingly, 1977).

The problem of ensuring that the public's perception of risk is reasonably accurate is also made difficult because it is often unclear how to determine what the actual risk is (Fischhoff, 1977; Holdren, 1976; Primack, 1975). Considering only those cases in which either frequency statistics or a consensus among technical experts would be considered an appropriate basis for assigning relative risks, it would be good if the public's perceptions corresponded to the degrees of risk thus derived. It appears that the bases of public reactions to some policy issues have little to do with either incidence statistics or experts' opinions (Slovic, Flynn, & Layman, 1991; Weart, 1988). Specific risks can easily be exaggerated by reports of incidents involving individuals in an emotionally charged way. As Krimsky and Golding (1991) pointed out, people respond strongly to singular, dramatic events, which means that a single dramatic reporting on TV of the effects on an individual of long-term exposure to a toxin used, say, for agricultural purposes can have more impact on the viewing public than many pages of objective and compelling, but cold, statistics.

The Environmental Protection Agency has considered assessing the risks that chemicals, human actions, and other stressors represent for specific ecological systems, with a view to publishing guidelines for assessing such risks (Hamilton, 1992a). Both the assessment of these risks and the communication of the results to the public represent numerous psychological challenges.

## LIMITATIONS OF EXPERT OPINION

That experts can and often do disagree on matters pertaining to their areas of expertise is obvious. Among the topics that relate to environmental change, none has evoked more debate among experts than that of greenhouse warming. Although many—perhaps most—Earth and atmospheric scientists consider the possibility of gradually increasing temperature to be a real and serious threat, the opposite opinion has been strongly expressed and a spirited debate has occurred (Ellsaesser, 1991; Kerr, 1989; Lindzen, 1990; Roberts, 1989; Seitz, Jastrow, & Nierenberg, 1989).

The opinions of climate change experts are based on historical data and the outputs of complicated global circulation models. Experts contribute to the design of the models, of course, but what can be done by way of modeling is constrained by both the status of climatology as a science and the computational facilities available to modelers. Model outputs must be interpreted by individual scientists in the light of their own theoretical understanding of climatology and their awareness of the models' capabilities and limitations. It would be good to understand better how expert opinion on matters as complex as climate change gets formed and how it should be factored into policy decisions when there is a lack of unanimity or strong consensus on significant issues.

Even when there is a strong consensus among experts, the possibility of erroneous estimates is not ruled out. There are many examples in science of estimates that have been made by experts and that have been shown in time to have been far less accurate than they were initially believed to be (Henrion & Fischhoff, 1986). Expert opinion formation deserves much more careful study than it has received—not only in the context of climate change, but more generally. Experts are not immune from having greater confidence in their opinions than is justified (Arkes, Dawes, & Christensen, 1986/1988; Einhorn & Hogarth, 1978; Lichtenstein, Fischhoff, & Phillips, 1977, 1982).

Among the most well-documented findings of psychology is the operation of a confirmation bias in many guises (Nickerson, 1998). People, including scientists, tend to see what they are looking for and find it easy to ignore or discount evidence that runs counter to established beliefs. It would be surprising indeed if this bias did not operate among participants on all sides of the various debates regarding environmental change (Swann & Giuliano, 1987). How else are we to explain that experts looking at the same evidence can come to such disparate conclusions regarding the nature of the problem and even as to whether there is one. Kates (1994) suggested that there is an apparent bias in environmental research that encourages the identification of harmful effects rather than negative feedback cycles that moderate environmental damage. It is easy to imagine that this is true. However, it is equally easy to imagine that there are also biases among people who find the idea of environmental protection burdensome to discount or explain away evidence of detrimental environmental change. More objective research on the uses of evidence in this highly charged area would be helpful.

## FALLIBILITY OF PREDICTIVE BEHAVIOR

One of the things that policymakers do is predict the effects of the implementation of various policies. Support for or opposition to possible policy changes is often based on the predictions of experts regarding the effects such changes would have. It is not uncommon for the predictions of different experts to differ dramatically. For example, one will say, in support of a proposed tax increase that it will create jobs and improve the economy, whereas another, in opposition to the same increase, will predict that it will make less money available for industrial expansion and, consequently, increase unemployment and be detrimental for the economy generally. People may, of course, sometimes say things they do not believe to accomplish specific goals. Yet one must assume that, for the most part, experts who make predictions about the effects of possible policy changes believe what they say. There is a need for better understanding of the psychology of prediction and how it is that knowledgeable people, considering the same sets of facts in their areas of expertise, can come to such disparate conclusions about what they portend.

There are many examples of detrimental environmental change resulting from human activities undertaken with the best of intentions; the problem has been a failure, or inability, to foresee the unwanted consequences of the activities. The widespread use of DDT and CFCs are two well-known cases; there are many others. When the damage becomes apparent in such cases, it may also be discovered that reversing it—if reversing it is possible—is extremely costly. The planned restoration of the Kissimmee River in Florida to something like its original (103-mile) rambling trajectory following its straightening (to a 56-mile canal) by the Army Corps of Engineers illustrates the point. According to Holloway (1994), the restoration was expected to cost about 100 times as much as the straightening. This also illustrates the need for predictive techniques that are especially sensitive to possible consequences of a planned activity other than the intended ones.

For over 100 years, dams have been built on rivers to generate electric power; they have been built longer to capture water for irrigation. There are now about 70,000 dams in the United States alone and many more around the world, some of which are noted as marvels of engineering. The generation of electric power by the capture of falling water has much to recommend it from an environmental point of view. However, detrimental effects on ecosystems have become clear during the last few decades (Gleick, 2001). Again, the lesson to be learned is that it appears to be easier to predict the benefits realized from activities planned with good intentions than to anticipate potentially countervailing problems that those activities might cause.

A major challenge is that of being prepared to deal with unpredicted—perhaps inherently unpredictable—events. Major developments sometimes catch even the experts unprepared. Who among the experts, for example, foresaw by a significant time the dissolution of the USSR, the development of the Internet, or the emergence of the AIDS epidemic? There undoubtedly will be events in the future that have implications for environmental change that no one now foresees.

## COMMUNICATION OF RISK

Whether acting as individuals or communities, people respond to what they perceive the threats to their security and comfort to be. If the responses are to be appropriate, it would seem to be important that the perceptions be relatively accurate. As already noted, there is much evidence that they often are not, at least to the extent that either incidence statistics or experts' opinions are taken to represent actual risks. This is one of the reasons for researchers' interest in how to assess risks and how to effectively communicate the results of those assessments (Allen, 1987; Hance, Chess, & Sandman, 1988; National Research Council, 1989b).

An aspect of risk communication that deserves emphasis is the problem of communicating to people who are at immediate risk, as the result of a natural disaster or industrial accident, the nature of the risk and information regarding any actions they can take to limit their exposure to potentially injurious consequences. The Three Mile Island incident serves as a compelling illustration of the need for work on this problem. Immediately following that accident, area residents received a barrage of inconsistent and sometimes contradictory information from a variety of sources regarding exactly what had happened, the kinds of risks the incident entailed, and what they should do. The result was considerable confusion and a loss of confidence in the information sources (Goldsteen, Schorr, & Goldsteen, 1989). One indication of a prevailing fear that authorities were understating the seriousness of the risks is that about 200,000 people fled the area following the issuing of a gubernatorial advisory that pregnant women and preschool children living within 5 miles of the plant (an estimated 3,500 people) might want to evacuate, and that everyone living within 10 miles should consider staying indoors (Erikson, 1990).

A full understanding of risk communication and its effect on people's behavior must also take into account instances in which people appear to underreact to the information they are given. People often choose to remain in areas in which the risk of personal injury is believed to be exceptionally high for a short period because of a predicted natural disaster such as a hurricane, flood, or volcanic eruption. Many people refused to leave the vicinity of Mt. Saint Helens, for example, before its eruption in May 1980 (Saarinen, 1980).

Over- or underreaction to a communication about risk could be due to misunderstanding the intended message or lack of confidence in its source. There is some evidence that misestimation of readers' comprehension ability has been a problem in brochures intended to help people make informed decisions about specific environmental risks (Atman, Bostrom, Fischhoff, & Morgan, 1994). Source credibility was noted in chapter 5 as affecting the effectiveness of efforts to evoke behavior change through information dissemination and persuasion, and this is likely to be as true when the topic is risk as when it is anything else.

The communication of risk is especially problematic when the risks to be communicated are not easily quantified. The issue of radioactive waste storage illustrates the point. Experts are of many minds regarding the riskiness of the various methods proposed for addressing this problem. Indeed, it is questionable whether it is appropriate to speak of *experts* in this context given that even the people who know most about the matter have to base their opinions largely on theory and speculation because empirical data regarding the long-term dependability of any of the proposed solutions do not exist. Nevertheless, the public has a right to be informed with respect not only to the opinions of the experts, but to the bases on which they are held. How to convey the situation in objective, accurate, and understandable terms is a nontrivial psychological challenge.

## HUMAN RESPONSE TO RISK

Let us ignore for the moment the daunting problem of ensuring the correspondence of perceived and actual risks. Rather, let us consider the question of whether people typically respond appropriately to risks—as they are represented by incidence statistics, say—and, if not, what might be done to encourage more appropriate behavior. For present purposes, *appropriate* is given the narrow connotation of consistency with one's self-interest: One is said to be responding appropriately when one selects that action from a set of alternatives that is most consistent with the goal of balancing the benefit of acting to avoid threats to one's security or comfort with the cost of doing so.

An abiding puzzle is that people often willingly engage in certain types of relatively high-risk behavior (smoking, driving an automobile while drinking or without the use of safety restraints) while being averse to putting themselves in situations that—in terms of incidence statistics—pose much smaller threats (flying, living within a few miles of a nuclear power plant). This is sometimes seen as evidence of irrationality in dealing with threats (Nelkin, 1989; Wandersman & Hallman, 1993).

Vlek and Stallen (1980) identified a large number of factors they believe to be involved in determining behavior in risky situations; they argued that the perception of risk is predictable when these factors are taken adequately into account. Wandersman and Hallman (1993) took the position that people's responses to environmental threats are predictable and not as irrational as they sometimes have appeared to be: "Risk perceptions … are supported by a set of beliefs that are sensible and not simply composed of senseless or irrational fears and unbridled emotions" (p. 684). They focused specifically on the risk of developing cancer from exposure to one or another form of toxic waste, and noted that, although there is no comprehensive model of individual or community response to risks from toxic wastes, there are several models that can deal with aspects of it. They pointed particularly to work by Baum, Fleming, and Singer (1983), Cvetkovich and Earle (1992), and Hallman and Wandersman (1992).

People's responses to risks are determined not only by the perceived likelihood of a threat being realized, but also by a variety of other factors (Litai, Lanning, & Rasmussen, 1983; Portney, 1991b; Rowe, 1977; Wandersman & Hallman, 1993). Citing the distinction made by Hance, Chess, and Sandman (1988) between hazard factors, which are those usually measured objectively if possible, and outrage factors, which tend to be more social, political, or ethical in nature, Wandersman and Hallman (1993) suggested that

> the more outrage factors that surround a risk, the more likely people will be concerned (or outraged) about it, despite scientific data indicating that a risk is low … given two risks of equal magnitude, a risk that is voluntary is more acceptable than an involuntary risk. Similarly, risks under individual control are seen as more acceptable than those under government control. Risks that seem fairly distributed are more acceptable than those that seem unfairly distributed. Natural risks are more acceptable than artificial risks. Familiar risks are more acceptable than exotic risks. Risks that are detectable are more acceptable than risks that are undetectable. Risks that are well understood by science are more acceptable than those that are not. Risks that are associated with other memorable events (like Love Canal or Chernobyl) are seen as more risky. Risks that seem ethically wrong are less acceptable. (p. 683)

A similar, but not identical, set of variables is given by Portney (1991b) and is reproduced as Table 10.1.

The importance of whether exposure to a risk is voluntary is seen in the finding by Starr (1969) that, for the same level of benefit, people were willing to accept risks from voluntary activities such as skiing that were roughly 1,000 times as great as those they would accept from involuntary risks such as those

TABLE 10.1
Nine Dimensions of Risk Acceptance

| *Dimension of Risk Acceptance* | *Features That Enhance Acceptability* | *Features That Diminish Acceptability* |
|---|---|---|
| 1. Volition | Voluntary | Involuntary |
| 2. Severity | Ordinary or incremental | Catastrophic |
| 3. Origin | Natural | Human-made |
| 4. Effect manifestation | Delayed effect | Immediate effect |
| 5. Exposure pattern | Occasional or sporadic exposure | Continuous exposure |
| 6. Controllability | Uncontrollable | Controllable |
| 7. Familiarity | Old/familiar | New/unfamiliar |
| 8. Personal benefit | Clear benefit in return | Unclear benefit |
| 9. Necessity | Necessary | Luxury |

*Note:* From Portney (1991b).

associated with food additives. Other discussions of the various factors that help determine the acceptability or unacceptability of risks include those of Fischhoff, Slovic, Lichtenstein, Read, and Combs (1978), Slovic (1987), and Slovic, Fischhoff, and Lichtenstein (1979).

Responses to perceived risks are bound to be affected by personal values; to the extent that individuals differ with respect to what they value, they are likely to respond to the same perceived risk in different ways (Brody, 1984; Office of Technology Assessment, 1987). Values and attitudes toward risks are strongly influenced by the sociocultural contexts in which people live (Bradbury, 1989; Covello & Johnson, 1987; Douglas & Wildavsky, 1982; Short, 1984; Vaughn & Nordenstam, 1991). The perception of risks to the environment is influenced by people's attitudes and beliefs about nature (Steg & Sievers, 2000).

Another issue relating to how people respond to risks involves the well-known *framing effect* observed in many contexts in a variety of forms. The basic finding is that the choices people make between or among alternatives in situations in which at least some of the outcomes are known only probabilistically strongly depend on how the outcome possibilities are described or framed. Thus, an individual's selection in a given situation is likely to depend on whether the options are represented in terms of potential gains or potential losses, survival rates or mortality rates, or gambles or insurance (Kahneman & Tversky, 1984; Kahneman, Slovic, & Tversky, 1982; Tversky &

Kahneman, 1981). People are more likely to see risk data as relevant to themselves when they are framed in terms of personal risks than when presented as population statistics (Jeffery, 1989; Sharlin, 1986).

Independently of the objective reality of specific risks, the perception of risk can be injurious. Apparently living in the proximity of a nuclear power plant, a hazardous landfill, or land known or believed to be contaminated by industrial toxins can produce stress-related symptoms in some people who worry about the perceived threat (Baum & Fleming, 1993; Baum, Gatchel, & Schaeffer, 1983; Baum, Weiss, & Davidson, 1988; Davidson & Baum, 1986; Davidson, Fleming, & Baum, 1986; Matthies, Höger, & Guski, 2000). People who live in an environmentally threatened community, as evidenced by being on the EPA's National Priority List, tend to report more illness and less satisfaction with community life than do those living in communities not on the list (Adeola, 2000). As Levi, Kocher, and Aboud (2001) put it, "From a community perspective, long-term disasters can have a double impact: that arising from the event itself and the social disruptions that are generated over time" (p. 80).

The possibility has also been noted that health-promotion programs may, in some cases, cause epidemics of apprehension about the risks targeted by the programs (Thomas, 1983). Although such effects should not be ignored, it is not entirely clear how best to take them into account (Baum & Fleming, 1993). The authors of a report commissioned by the California Environmental Protection Agency included risks to social welfare—as represented by potential harm to mental health and personal relationships, among other problems—and, perhaps not surprisingly, the inclusion proved to be controversial (Stone, 1994a).

Human response to risk is an active area of psychological research. Much of what is being learned is undoubtedly relevant to the perception of and reaction to risks associated with environmental change. In many cases, the relevance needs to be articulated, however. Also, more needs to be learned about how to increase the accuracy with which environmental risks are comprehended by both experts and the general public. Slovic (1987) cautioned against assuming uncrictically that when experts and the public disagree, the experts' perceptions are invariably the more accurate. Portney (1991b) argued the importance of dialogue as a means of getting expert and lay opinions regarding risk to converge. When risk communication is a one-way process—from experts to the public—it appears not to have the intended result (Krimsky & Plough, 1988). More promising, Portney contended, is "a two-way process, where citizens and experts exchange views and ideas to reach a mutually acceptable understanding of the risks that a particular set of decisions poses. Seen this way, risk communication results in much greater public acceptance" (p. 212). Trettin and Mushman (2000) argued that probably even more important to the effective communication of risk than a high level of trust is the establishment of procedures and standards that the public understands and accepts.

## THE PSYCHOLOGY OF PREVENTION

Inasmuch as prevention tends to be more cost-effective than cleanup or cure, the question of how to generate and sustain public interest in the prevention of environmental problems before they occur is especially important. Although the advantages of prevention over cleanup are widely recognized (Cortese, 1993; Geller, 1986; Hirschhorn & Oldenburg, 1991; Leutwyler, 1995), people tend not to participate in organized attempts to prevent threats that are not perceived to be imminent (Cook, 1983). Preventive actions are as difficult to motivate when the goal is protection of the environment as they are in general (Burton, Kates, & White, 1978).

There is a fundamental problem associated with creating and sustaining public enthusiasm for preventive measures stemming from the fact that blame is relatively easy to assign, in retrospect, for failure to have taken preventive measures, but the benefits of having taken them tend not to be very salient. For example, if I neglect to clear ice from my walkway and someone falls and breaks a leg there, my negligence becomes apparent. Yet if I clear the walkway of ice and people make it safely to my door, the fact that no one broke a leg in my yard is probably not going to get a lot of notice. In general, victims of failures to take preventive measures are relatively easy to identify, but beneficiaries of successful acts of prevention are not. It seems safe to assume that many people who are alive today would not be if any of a variety of preventive vaccines had not been developed, but the beneficiaries of these developments have no way of knowing who they are. It is in part because of the relative difficulty of pointing to specific beneficiaries of successful measures, I suspect, that it is easier to energize the public to respond to societal problems after they have arisen and approached crisis proportions than to create enthusiasm for measures that are designed to prevent them from occurring. The question of how to make the importance and cost-effectiveness of preventive measures salient deserves more attention than it has received.

The importance of prevention, from a cost–benefit point of view, may also be unappreciated because the cost of failing to prevent a specific event may be impossible to estimate until the event has actually occurred. It may not even be possible to anticipate with any confidence that, in the absence of preventive measures, the event will occur. To compound the problem, the successfulness of a preventive measure may be difficult to substantiate. If Measure A is taken for the purpose of preventing Event B and B does not occur, proponents of A may find it difficult to convince opponents of the measure that B would have occurred if the measure had not been taken. Opponents may remain convinced that A was unnecessary and resent having had to spend money on it.

CHAPTER

# 11

# Cost–Benefit and Trade-Off Analyses

Actions that are, or could be, taken in the interest of protecting the environment have costs, and so do failures to take action in many cases. Presumably actions are taken because they are believed to have benefits that outweigh their costs, and sometimes actions are not taken because the benefits that might be realized are believed not to justify the costs that would be incurred. Sometimes decision makers are faced with choice situations in which one desired end can be realized only at the expense of not realizing another desired end—one type of benefit can be increased only by accepting a decrease in another type of benefit. In such cases, trade-offs are said to be involved. This chapter deals with cost–benefit and trade-off analyses as they pertain to the problem of environmental change.

## COST–BENEFIT ANALYSES

Cost–benefit analysis is a tool much used by economists. Its applicability to environmental issues seems obvious from an economic point of view. As Arrow et al. (1996) put it, "Most economists would argue that economic efficiency, measured as the difference between benefits and costs, ought to be one of the fundamental criteria for evaluating proposed environmental, health, and safety regulations" (p. 221). The function of such analysis is to lay out explicitly the consequences of the various options in a decision situation—or in Russell's (1990) words, to "illuminate the ramifications of choices" (p. 19).

Attempting to take long-term environmental costs and benefits into account in decision making with respect to the environment has not been the norm. In the manufacturing context; economic analyses typically take into account only the immediate effects of production decisions (Frosch & Gallopoulos, 1989), but the tendency to neglect long-term costs and benefits applies much more generally. Ward and Dubos (1972) put it this way:

> Modern industrial systems still do not normally include in the cost of what they produce such diseconomies of production and distribution as the spewing off of effluents into the air or the overloading of the land with solid waste or the lack of any charge for eventual disposal of the used-up goods. Thus they pass on a hidden and heavy cost to the community where it is either met by higher taxation and public spending or by the destruction of amenity. (p. 49)

The same writers pointed out that cost–benefit analyses are often distorted by our tendency to treat certain resources, such as air and water, as free goods, which ignores the costs involved in maintaining the quality of these resources.

The position I want to promote here is not that all policy or regulatory decisions should be based solely on the results of cost–benefit analyses, but that, as Arrow et al. (1996) argued, such analyses, if properly done, have an important role to play in informing such decisions. Getting agreement regarding what constitutes being properly done may not be easy, but in the absence of any knowledge or estimates of the costs and benefits associated with the action possibilities in a decision situation, it is hard to see how rational choices can be made.

## THE DIFFICULTY OF QUANTIFYING COSTS

The centrality of the issue of costs and benefits to the question of how to deal with environmental change is clear. No one is against environmental protection in principle. No one enjoys pollution or argues that we need more of it. "If environmental benefits were costless, regulation would generate virtually no controversy" (Melnick, 1990, p. 50). However, environmental benefits are not costless, although the costs, in many cases, are hard to quantify. Some of the costs are direct, such as the cost of building a state-of-the-art sulfur-retaining refinery or that of cleanup of a toxic waste dump; yet many of the costs that must be considered are not so direct but no less real. For example, Melnick (1990) noted the political reality of opportunity costs. The question of interest, he argued, is what is given up in reducing water pollution or protecting the snail darter or creating a national wilderness area. Another fundamental problem stems from the fact that many of the costs of environmental protection (or lack thereof) are paid indirectly through taxes, insurance premiums, fees to health care providers, and the purchases of goods and services and are difficult to track.

Consider what would appear to be a relatively straightforward practical problem—namely, that of determining the costs of various ways to increase the efficiency of electricity production and use. Increased energy efficiency can have such benefits as decreasing the rate at which limited natural resources are consumed and reducing the amount of carbon dioxide and other troublesome emissions to the atmosphere. Improvements in efficiency typically come at some cost, but whenever the cost of a gain in efficiency is less than the cost of the energy saved (the energy that would have had to be supplied if the gain had not been realized), the cost of realizing the increased efficiency is justified in two ways: The total cost to the consumer is decreased and detrimental impact on the environment is lessened.

Unfortunately, determining the cost of specific conservation measures that could be taken has proved to be surprisingly difficult to do. Estimates of such costs made by the Rocky Mountain Institute and the Electric Power Research Institute differ by substantial amounts and have been challenged as too low in both cases. Joskow and Marron (1993) argued, on the basis of an analysis of the costs of some conservation programs, that the actual costs were higher and the energy savings lower than the estimates indicated. Other studies, they pointed out, have shown energy savings realized by specific conservation programs to have commonly been only 50% to 60% of engineering estimates. Joskow and Marron noted that their findings do not mean that policies that promote energy conservation are undesirable; the point is simply that the costs and benefits of such policies can be difficult to quantify especially in advance of their implementation.

In the context of environmental concerns, cost–benefit analyses are usually applied to the costs of possible approaches that could be taken to protect the environment against detrimental change and the benefits that are expected to be realized if they are taken. There is also a need to better understand the costs and benefits of specific goods and services that industry and, in some cases, the government produces and sells. The total cost of a particular consumer product includes not only the costs of manufacturing, marketing, sales, and transportation to points of sale, which are usually considered, but also the costs of use (e.g., fuel), effects of use (e.g., on the environment), maintenance, and disposal, which often are not considered. Not all of the costs of goods and services are reflected in purchase prices, and not all are always borne by purchasers and users.

A few years ago, I received one mail delivery a day at my home. One truck came down the street on which I live once a day and delivered all the mail that people received. It typically stopped at every house on the street. Now four or five trucks come down that street to deliver mail on some days. Most of them stop at one or a very few houses. In addition to the U.S. Postal Service, organizations delivering mail include Federal Express, Airborne Express, United Parcel Service, Guaranteed Overnight Delivery, and several smaller delivery and courier services. As a consumer, I appreciate the convenience of being able to send or receive a parcel with a guaranteed short delivery time. I understand that the proliferation of delivery-service companies has provided jobs for many people, and I believe in the free-enterprise system that encourages competition. I am not arguing, necessarily, against the existence of multiple mail delivery organizations, but simply want to make the point that, to determine the full cost of doing business this way, one would have to take into account its long-term impact on the environment. One must wonder whether, if such costs were considered, a system that requires the operation of several vehicles to deliver what probably could be delivered, albeit not quite as quickly, by a single one would prove to be cost-effective.

In general, there is a considerably less-than-perfect match between the people who realize the benefits from goods and services and those who pay the costs of their production, use, and, in the case of durable goods, eventual disposal. Usually when one purchases something, one pays for the cost of its manufacture and distribution, but one does not pick up the cost of any effects the item might have on the environment as a consequence of either its use or disposal when it is no longer serviceable. The implication of this fact for present purposes it that the quantification of costs and benefits needs to take into account not only the easily identified costs of getting an item to a consumer, but also those less obvious, but no less real, costs that will be incurred—and paid by someone—as a consequence of its existence and use.

Among the more difficult aspects of doing cost–benefit analyses is that of giving due weight to the long-term costs of *not* taking steps at the present time to halt or reverse some environmentally detrimental trend. Immediate costs of specific possible actions are relatively easy to quantify by comparison. Perhaps for that reason they are likely to weigh heavily in decision making regarding actions addressed to environmental problems (Nikolai, Bazley, & Brummet, 1976), but such costs are only part of the equation. Costs of long-term consequences of inaction should also be considered. That inaction can result in significant costs can hardly be doubted, but how to identify those costs and quantify them is a matter of considerable complexity. If the costs of inaction are not estimated, however, the acceptability of the costs of specific possible actions can not be determined. Suppose it is true, as suggested, that the cost of meeting the need for home fuel in Third World countries through the use of fuelwood plantations would be about $12 billion per year; this figure is hard to evaluate in the abstract, but looks attractive when compared with an estimated cost of $50 billion or more a year of the status quo alternative of foraging fuelwood in natural forests (Myers, 1995).

The need for better ways to quantify the costs of specific environmental measures is generally recognized, at least within the various government agencies that have the responsibility of establishing regulatory policies aimed at protecting human life and well-being, because, as a recent National Research Council report pointed out, "Regulatory agencies regularly confront difficult trade-offs among important values, such as health, safety, longevity, and the monetary and nonmonetary costs and benefits associated with protecting human health and well-being against the hazards of modern life" (Hammond & Coppock, 1990, p. 3). It needs to be remembered too that regulation is not without significant costs, that these costs can exceed the worth of the benefits that accrue in specific cases, and that overregulation is a possibility that should not be ignored. According to one report, the number of federal regulations increased about twelve-fold (from 16,502 to 200,000) between 1954 and 1992 (Ray & Guzzo, 1994).

## THE DIFFICULTY OF QUANTIFYING BENEFITS

The quantification of benefits can also be extremely difficult. Sometimes benefits are overlooked completely. Much attention has been given in this book and elsewhere to fossil fuel-burning motor vehicles as a primary source of air pollution, but it is easy to overlook that replacement of horsedrawn vehicles with motor cars in the United States during the early part of the 20th century brought some nontrivial benefits in addition to increased mobility. Horses were a major source of pollution in city streets (Ausubel, 1989), and tuberculosis rates dropped precipitously when they were displaced (Gibbs, 1997). An article published in the July 1899 issue of *Scientific American* predicted that the adoption of the motor car would result in improvement in city conditions—clean, dustless, odorless, and less noisy streets—that could hardly be overestimated. This prediction looks ironic today when we are constantly reminded of the environmental and other costs associated with extensive reliance on the automobile for personal travel. On the benefit side, we are aware of the great mobility that the automobile represents, but have largely forgotten the role it played in decreasing respiratory diseases transmitted by airborne bacteria.

The complexity of the problem of quantifying benefits is making itself evident in the medical arena as a consequence of the keen interest in controlling increasing health care costs. The costs of health care are relatively easy to quantify in many cases, but the benefits are not. Even when it is possible to get plausible estimates of the consequences of health care programs and services (e.g., broad-based screening for specific diseases, vaccination programs) in terms of number of years of life saved or prolonged, how these measures should be translated into financial terms is a matter of controversy (Leutwyler,

1995). Nevertheless, benefit to public health is a major motivator for environmental initiatives (Chivian, McCally, Hu, & Haines, 1993; Rogers, 1991). According to figures published by Myrick (1982) and reported also in Rogers (1991), 78% of an estimated $21 billion of benefit being realized as a consequence of air pollution control as of 1978 was due to improved public health. This was in contrast to the situation with water pollution control, for which only 10% of the estimated benefit was attributed to improved public health and 50% was attributed to improved recreational facilities. Rogers made the point that threats to public health are more effective motivators of political action than is interest in providing better recreational facilities.

As it relates to environmental change, the problem of determining the value of any benefits that are to be expected from a planned or contemplated intervention is compounded by the difficulty of putting a value on specific benefits derived from the natural environment as it exists. For example, how much are clean air and clean water worth (Kneese, 1984)? How does one quantify the benefits of climate stabilization (Nordhaus, 1992; Peck & Teisberg, 1992)? How does one attach a value to the benefits derived directly or indirectly from the world's forests (Pearce, 1992)? How does one determine the value of avoidance of chronic stress and stress-related disorders that have been observed among people who live with the threat or actuality of industrial or agricultural toxins in their neighborhoods (Fowlkes & Miller, 1982; Gatchel & Newberry, 1991; Gibbs, 1986)?

Especially problematic is the quantitative valuation of the emotional and affective benefits that people may derive from natural environments. The importance of trees and plants for the maintenance of a life-supporting atmosphere, through their production of oxygen and absorption of carbon dioxide, is widely recognized; their importance from a psychological point of view is much less well known, but some investigators have noted it (Alexander, Ishikawa, & Silverstein, 1977; Lewis, 1979; Thayer & Atwood, 1978). Studies of recreational uses of the natural environment have focused on a variety of specific activities such as hiking (Brown & Haas, 1980; Knopf, 1983), tenting and camping (LaPage & Ragain, 1974; Lime, 1971), hunting (Kellert, 1980; Potter, Hendee, & Clark, 1973), fishing (Driver & Cooksey, 1977), cross-country skiing (Haas, Driver, & Brown, 1980), and river running (Schreyer & Nielson, 1978).

It seems only reasonable to expect that what people see when they look out their windows would have some effect on their moods and feelings. Data indicate that people have preferences for some out-of-window views over others and that trees, woods, and other forms of vegetation are valued elements of the views of people who can see them (Herzog, 1989, 1992; Herzog, Kaplan, & Kaplan, 1982; Im, 1984; Kaplan, 1979a, 1979b, 1983). Some investigators believe that views of natural settings from hospital windows may have some therapeutic value (Ulrich, 1981, 1984; Verderber, 1986; Verderber & Reuman, 1987). Many people derive satisfaction from gardening and caring for plants (Clark & Manzo, 1987; Langer & Rodin, 1976) and not only because of the practical usefulness of growing vegetables and other food. The basis of this satisfaction is not well understood, although there has been some speculation as to what it might be (Lewis, 1979; Kaplan, 1973, 1983).

There is some evidence that a well-kept nature park in one's vicinity can be a source of pleasure and satisfaction even when it is not part of one's daily view, and that ease of access to nature is a major determinant of how satisfied many people are with their residences (Fried, 1982; Kaplan, 1981; Ulrich & Addoms, 1981). This is not to deny that under certain conditions (especially those that lead to disuse [Whyte, 1980]), parks and wooded areas in urban settings have been scenes of violence and personal assaults. In general, *nearby nature* appears to be valued by urban residents for a variety of reasons, aesthetic appreciation and recreation among them (Clark & Manzo, 1987; Kaplan, 1985; Talbot, Bardwell, & Kaplan, 1987).

Experience of natural environments and especially the wilderness is considered by several researchers to have health-enhancing or restorative value (Driver & Brown, 1975; Hartig, Mang, & Evans, 1991; Kaplan, 1974; Kaplan & Kaplan, 1989; Kaplan & Talbot, 1983; Knopf, 1983; Stokols, 1990; Turner, 1976). Although questions have been raised by Gibson (1979) about the methodological adequacy of some of the relevant studies, many of which have focused on organized wilderness-experience programs, the same reviewer concluded that the weight of evidence favors the conclusion that such effects are real. Natural environments are seen by some investigators as providing experiences of peacefulness, tranquillity, relief from tension, and escape or respite from frenetic aspects of many man-made environments (Driver & Knopf, 1976; Driver & Tocher, 1970; Mandell & Marans, 1972; Stillman, 1977) and opportunities to resolve problems that are difficult to deal with in one's workaday world (Knopf, Driver, & Basset, 1973).

How are we to attach a monetary value to emotional benefits that people realize from recreational uses of wilderness areas (Rossman & Ulehla, 1977; Shafer & Meitz, 1969)? What are the restorative or well-being benefits that people are believed to get from wilderness experiences and the natural environment more generally worth? What is it about natural scenes that prompt people to respond so positively to them (Ulrich, 1981; Zuckerman, 1977), and how does one attach a value to their preservation? How do we quantify the importance to physical and mental health of trees, nature parks, and plants (Gold, 1977; Kaplan, 1983) and of birds and other wildlife (Hounsome, 1979) in urban areas?

Although there is little doubt that biological ecosystems provide an array of essential services—from emitting oxygen to the atmosphere to maintaining the fertility of soil—precise quantification of the value of the services provided by a single species, or by a specified degree of biodiversity, is beyond the current state of the art. Yet somehow decisions must be made regarding how much to spend, or how much economic development to forego, to preserve a regional ecosystem or a threatened species. It seems unlikely that such decisions will be more rational if decision makers ignore benefit and cost considerations than if they explicitly attempt to take them into account.

To some extent, benefits are in the eye of the beneficiary. What one person sees as a benefit (e.g., the preservation of pristine forests or species diversity) may be viewed with indifference or even disdain by another (Fischhoff, 1991; Pearce & Turner, 1990). It is also the case that sometimes people who value the environment do so for reasons that can come into conflict. A natural resource like water, for example, has many uses, and estimating the benefit of preserving it must take account of the various benefits it provides (Desvogues & Smith, 1983). People who like to fish and those who enjoy white-water rafting have an interest in preserving rivers in their natural state, but the two activities, in some instances, may be seen as incompatible with each other. People who value the quiet and tranquillity they can find in the wilderness may find themselves at odds with those who enjoy exploring with trail bikes and all-terrain vehicles.

That the interests of operators of power boats conflict with those of sailors and canoeists is well known (Lucas, 1964); snowmobilers and cross-country skiers can also find themselves at odds with each other (Rosenthal, Driver, & Rauhauser, 1980). Conflicts arise from the interest in exploiting forests and other natural resources for immediate economic purposes and the desire to preserve them for long-term uses (Babbitt, 1995). The use of water for generating electric power has the environmental benefit of not contributing to air pollution, but river dams modify the natural terrain in ways that many naturalists find destructive: They create a variety of other problems ranging from the blockage of fish from their spawning grounds to the accumulation of problematic amounts of silt in the reservoirs of water that they create.

## THE CONTROVERSIAL NATURE OF COST–BENEFIT ANALYSIS

There are wide differences of opinion with regard to the specifics of how cost–benefit analyses should be conducted and their results applied. According to the Hammond and Coppock (1990) report, "there is no single approach or set of methods for cost-benefit analysis now in use in any federal regulatory agency with responsibility for health and safety" (p. 9). A major challenge, therefore, is the development of approaches to cost-benefit analyses, and rationales for those approaches, that will be widely accepted by both social scientists and people in positions of decision-making and policy-setting responsibility. Some standardization is needed as well if meaningful cross-study comparisons are to be made.

The need for better techniques for the quantification of costs and benefits of activities aimed at environmental improvement or preservation is illustrated by an attempt by Krupnick and Portney (1991) to do a cost–benefit assessment of controls proposed for improving air quality, especially in the Los Angeles area, by decreasing the concentration of tropospheric ozone and particulates. The publication of the investigators' conclusion that the expected costs of the proposed controls would probably exceed their benefits evoked a number of criticisms (Chapman, 1991; Friedman, 1991; Lents, 1991; Lippert & Morris, 1991; Miller, 1991). Objections were raised both regarding the benefits mentioned—some critics thought important ones had been overlooked—and about the monetary values assigned to those that were considered.

The assignment of monetary values to such factors as human life and health is a delicate matter that often evokes strong objections. As MacLean (1990) put it, "People ... feel uncomfortable with even rationally defensible procedures for making difficult decisions if those procedures make finding an exchange rate for life a prominent feature" (p. 102). Regarding the implicitness of value-of-life quantification in policy decisions, the value given (implicitly) to life can be calculated by computing the ratio of the cost of an intervention to the estimated number of lives saved (premature deaths prevented) by it. One survey yielded $2 million as the average implicit per-life-saved value of several federal cancer risk management programs (Travis, Richter, Crouch, Wilson, & Klema, 1987).

The resistance to the idea of attaching a value to human life is sufficiently strong in some instances to translate into resistance against the use of cost–benefit analyses as a basis for decision making or policy setting at all. Thus, one sometimes sees objections by congressional committees to any consideration of costs in the setting of, for example, air quality standards. The same attitude is sometimes reflected in the responses of people to public opinion polls. For example, consider the statement that appeared in a *New York Times*/CBS poll: "Protecting the environment is so important that requirements and standards cannot be too high, and continuing environmental improvements must be made regardless of cost." Ruckelshaus (1989) noted that the percentage of polled Americans who agree with this statement went from about 45 in 1981 to about 80 in 1989, the latter figure probably being a reaction to the *Exxon Valdez* oil spill. Of course, such extreme positions cannot be translated into any feasible policy. This may not be obvious as long as one is in the realm of hypotheticals, but it becomes clear when cost-inducing decisions must be made. As Melnick (1990) put it, "faced with abstract policy questions, the public often advocates paying 'any price' for a clean environment; faced with the prospect of actually bearing these costs, most people change their mind" (p. 46).

Melnick (1990) noted that the very members of congress who take untenable positions when debating pending legislation sometimes find themselves pleading later for a relaxed interpretation or enforcement of unrealistic legislation that their efforts allowed to be passed. This state of affairs illustrates the paradox of the controversy regarding the use of cost–benefit analyses: "The widespread hostility to the use of benefit-cost and risk assessment analysis is based on an absolutist health-only position that virtually no one is willing to embrace in the real world. To put it more bluntly, almost no one really believes what many informed people emphatically maintain in public" (p. 25). Melnick attributed the hostility that many congressmen, jurists, and managers of regulatory agencies show to cost–benefit analyses to the fact that such analyses were devised by economists, whereas congress, the courts, and the upper echelons of most regulatory agencies are dominated by lawyers. "Economists think in terms of opportunity costs and incentives; lawyers think in terms of rules and penalties and of defeating their adversary" (p. 27).

The difficulty of assessing costs and benefits is also seen in the ongoing debates in the international arena regarding who should bear the costs of limiting the emission of greenhouse gases in developing countries. The argument that industrialized countries should bear most of these costs rests, in part, on the fact that these countries have contributed more than their fair per-capita share to the creation of the problem and, in part, on the assumption that they stand to benefit from any steps that developing countries take to limit further emissions because warming is a global phenomenon. Not surprisingly, opinions differ as to how to quantify these ideas. Moreover, it is to be expected that different countries will attach different values to the same benefit depending on their stage of economic development and standard of living (Bhagwati, 1993).

## ETHICS VERSUS ECONOMICS IN COST–BENEFIT ANALYSIS

As MacLean (1990) pointed out, although society considers each of the various benefits on which environmental preservation programs are focused to be valuable, there has yet to be developed a satisfactory way to weight them on a common metric, and the underlying issues are not strictly economic but ethical: "The appropriateness of discounting the value of future lives, the application of benefit-cost analysis as a method of setting environmental policies more generally, and other issues that remain central and contentious in the environmental policy arena are essentially moral disputes" (p. 85). Morowitz (1991) made a similar point and argued that trying to determine the value, or benefit, of a given biological species, for example, involves not only issues of economics, but also of ethics, and the *good* of economics and ethics are not necessarily the same. Kneese and Schulze (1985) also distinguished ethical from economic issues as they relate to environmental concerns. The role that ethics should play in environmental decision making has not received as much attention as economics, but ethical issues abound (Bedau, 1991; Partridge, 1981).

A particular ethical complication in the use of cost–benefit analysis ins that costs and benefits are often not distributed in the same way. Those who stand to benefit most (least) from any given activity aimed at addressing some aspect of detrimental environmental change are not necessarily the same as those who will have to pick up the largest (smallest) fraction of its cost. What is done in one part of the world for the benefit of the inhabitants of that area can impose costs on people in other parts of the world who do not receive the same benefits. Also benefits that are enjoyed by one generation may incur costs that must be borne by another generation. Simply deferring costs to a future generation is beneficial to the generation that does the deferring, but not to the one to which the costs are deferred. Postponing action aimed at reversing or slowing an environmentally detrimental trend—say global warming—on the grounds that the need for action is not yet indisputably clear ensures deferral of the cost of any action that eventually proves to be necessary.

Especially vexing are decisions that cause dislocations or other inconveniences to individuals or groups of people to allow development considered to be for the common good. The law of eminent domain recognizes the principle that sometimes the general benefit derived justifies the specific harm that is caused. The use of falling water to generate electric power has advantages over the burning of fossil fuels, from an environmental point of view, because water is a renewable resource, and this means of generating electricity does not pump hydrocarbons into the atmosphere. However, the building of dams for hydroelectric plants frequently requires the dislocation of people who live in the vicinity of the dam site and often against their will (Ezell, 2001). How to weigh the cost to one group against the benefit to another (even when the larger group includes the smaller) and ensure equitable decision making in such cases is far from being an exact science.

Costs that are deferred may escalate as a consequence of the deferral, and there is the possibility that what is a manageable cost at one point in time may become an unmanageable one later. As Railton (1990) put it,

> reflecting on the environmental problems of toxic wastes, atmospheric pollution and warming, nonrenewable resources, ozone layer depletion, and so forth, raises the real possibility that future generations will be worse off than today's. It is simply not clear that the economic growth made possible by rapid exploitation of the environment will be great enough to enable future societies to make up the losses connected with resource exhaustion and environmental degradation. (p. 78)

The problem of comparing costs and benefits across generations is an especially controversial one. One issue that is debated is whether future benefits or problems should be valued differently than present ones. A common practice is to apply a "social discount rate" to consequences that are expected to occur in the future, the amount of the discount being the greater, the further in the future the expected consequence (MacLean, 1990):

> The reasons for discounting can appeal to the opportunity costs of capital, the reasons for wanting returns on investments sooner rather than later; or they can appeal to rates of time preference, the claim that people tend to care less about consumption in the future or about the remote effects of their actions and policies. (p. 93)

These are different kinds of justification for discounting, but they often are not differentiated. Regardless of how one justifies it, if discounting is done, small differences in the discount rate that is used can have large effects on present values of future benefits.

In part for such reasons, Railton (1990) argued that cost–benefit analyses should be used to yield information but not to make decisions. In his view, decision making must also involve considerations of possible conflicts between the well-being of the majority and the rights of individuals or minorities, and other issues that can only be resolved by appeal to one or another concept of justice. A similar view is defended in the concluding section of the National Research Council conference report in which Railton's argument appears.

> Benefit-cost analysis cannot now be considered to be a formal decision-making mechanism accounting, for example, for the need for symbolic action or the full range of qualitative costs and benefits associated with policy alternatives. Cost-benefit analysis is more appropriately used in conjunction with other factors as a set of information-gathering and organizing tools that may be used to support both decision making and the presentation of information to the public. (Hammond & Coppock, 1990, p. 190)

Another conclusion coming out of the same conference was that there is a need for improvement of cost-benefit analysis as a practical set of tools for policymaking. Emphasis was placed on the need to extend the range of factors, including nonquantitative ones, that can be taken into account and for better approaches to making comparisons across time.

Cost–benefit analyses are undoubtedly seen as the province of economics, and economists have been the primary developers and users of them. However, establishing costs and benefits, in any but the most superficial of senses, must take human values and preferences into account. The measurement of human values and preferences, especially as they pertain to characteristics of the environment that contribute to the quality of life, is a psychological problem of considerable complexity.

Presumably human behavior is motivated by basic human needs and desires. Behavior that is intended to accomplish a specific objective is not necessarily the only, or even the best, way that that objective can be realized. Often the benefits, especially the immediate benefits, that derive from a specific type of behavior are much more apparent than its costs especially its long-term costs. We need more effective ways to quantify the costs and benefits of proposed approaches to realizing objectives, as well as to identify what alternative approaches are possible and quantify the costs and benefits of them as well.

## TRADE-OFF ANALYSES

Closely associated with cost–benefit analysis is the concept of *trade-offs*. The idea is that, to realize or increase one good, one must be willing to forego or decrease another. An illustration of the need to understand trade-offs better relates to energy consumption. Perhaps most people would agree that the rate of growth of energy use worldwide should be slowed at least so long as energy is produced and used in ways that have detrimental environmental effects. Yet how to achieve a sustainable level of energy consumption remains an open question, especially in view of the enormous disparity in current use across nations and the understandable desire of less-developed countries to approach the standard of living of the more developed ones.

> The simplistic idea that energy conservation and the enhanced use of renewables could solve the world's sustainability and environmental problems, particularly those of the developing countries, by the year 2020 is entirely unrealistic. All sources of energy will be needed, despite energy conservation efforts in LCDs [less-developed countries] and industrialized countries. The alternative for developing countries would be to remain at a dismally low level of development which, ironically, would generate additional, serious political problems and an unchecked population growth that would aggravate the problems of sustainability.... A delicate balance between economic paralysis, with its grievous consequences, and development has to be sought and ways will have to be found to promote development while minimizing, but not completely avoiding, environmental problems. (Goldemberg, 1995, p. 1059)

Trade-offs are often involved in resource-allocation decisions. However one feels about the merits of the objections raised about their analysis of proposed air pollution control measures, one must share Krupnick and Portney's (1991) conviction that careful analyses are essential to effective decision making about the allocation of limited resources.

> It is unpleasant to have to weigh in such a calculating manner the pros and cons of further air pollution control efforts. We would prefer limitless resources so that every pollution control measure physically possible could be pursued. Because resources are scarce, however, the real cost of air pollution control is represented by the government programs or private expenditures that we forego by putting our resources into reducing VOC [volatile organic compound] emissions. (p. 526)

Precisely the same point can be made about any expenditure from a cache of resources that is inadequate to meet all the demands placed on it.

Resource-allocation problems can often be seen as social dilemmas, the solutions to which require the balancing of competing and interacting resources. As one means to deal with the complexity of such problems, Vogel (1991) argued for the application of a systems approach. This generally means attempting to identify the important variables, develop conceptual process models of how these variables interrelate, and apply mathematical or programming techniques to these models to explore the effects of the introduction of constraints or forcing functions at various points in the process. As Vogel pointed out, however, agreeing on what the objectives of the resource allocation should be often turns out to be the most challenging aspect of such problems. The quality of the outcome of the application of a systems approach to a specific problem is limited by the validity of the assumptions underlying the model that is used and by the accuracy with which the various model components are quantified. However, even when the attempt to take this approach does not lead to an optimal solution, the discipline of structuring the problem and focusing on its details can provide useful insights into the trade-offs involved and what the nature of an acceptable solution might be.

A specific illustration of a trade-off involving an environmental concern is that of exposure to ultraviolet (UV) radiation. Discussions of the problem of stratospheric ozone depletion often emphasize the role of UV radiation in causing skin cancer as a compelling reason to maintain the ozone layer. However, others have pointed out that UV radiation has certain beneficial effects, its carcinogenic properties notwithstanding; it plays a critical role in the synthesis of vitamin D, an inadequate supply of which can result in brittle bones or, in extreme cases, rickets. Moreover, Ray and Guzzo (1994) argued that if an equally inexpensive and effective replacement for freon as a refrigerant is not developed, the effects of higher cost refrigeration could include increased hunger and food-borne diseases in some parts of the world.

A related example involves the replacement of CFCs with compounds that do not have the destructive effect on stratospheric ozone that they do. Browne (1989) contended that some of the candidate substitutes for CFCs are likely to be more hazardous for workers and equipment than the CFCs they would replace. A not dissimilar trade-off is sometimes involved in decisions regarding the use or banning of certain pesticides, fumigants, and food additives. Although some of the agents in question have been shown to cause cancer when given in sufficiently large doses to animals, they also are known to be effective in controlling damage to crops and stored food from insects, mold, or fungi. The problem is to limit the one type of risk without creating a yet more serious one.

Like cost–benefit analyses, trade-off analyses sometimes involve the need to quantify the value of human life, implicitly if not explicitly, and this is an exceedingly difficult thing to do. Russell (1990) spoke of the "almost visceral reaction against the open consideration of any trade-off regarding human health and the environment [that he encountered within the EPA], even though such trade-offs are implicit in every decision" (p. 17). He illustrated the need to consider such trade-offs by reference to the problem of deciding where to put sewage sludge. Assuming the decision is made to put it in the ocean (similar trade-offs would arise if the decision were to put it in the ground or, via incineration, in the air),

> protecting fish has to be balanced against protecting humans. Is the probability of avoiding one excess premature death worth reducing the risk to fish in one cubic mile of ocean? A hundred cubic miles? The North Atlantic? Or, with respect to timing, is avoiding one probable excess premature death now worth as much as avoiding one next year? or avoiding 500, let us say, 1,000 years from now? (p. 20)

The problem can be ignored, but only by closing one's eyes to reality. As Russell noted, "the sludge has to go somewhere. When it gets there, the fabric of consequences are real, and the trade-offs will have been made" (p. 21).

Trade-offs sometimes become an issue because an action intended to encourage behavioral change that would be beneficial to the environment has some unforeseen costs to which the people who have to bear them object. The practice of reserving certain traffic lanes for use only by vehicles with more than a specified number of passengers, for example, has been discontinued in some instances because of other drivers' objection to the fact that the reduction of number of lanes available to all vehicles meant more traffic delays for those not traveling in the reserved lanes (Zerega, 1981).

Regulatory measures aimed at protecting the environment sometimes involve reductions in personal freedoms. Ordinances that restrict smoking in workplaces or public buildings limit the freedom of smokers to smoke wherever they wish. The imposition of such limitations is defended on the grounds that it is necessary to protect the rights of others. This is but one of many examples in which the rights, or at least desires, of different groups conflict and compromises involving trade-offs must be struck.

It is possible for steps taken in the interest of improving the environment to incur costs of unforeseen effects that offset, or more than offset, the gains realized from an environmental point of view. The possibility for well-intentioned decisions to have undesired side effects is illustrated by the fact that widespread use of antibiotics has facilitated the emergence of strains of bacteria that are resistant to antibacterial agents in common use (Levy, 1998). Few would argue that antibiotics have not done enormous good in the past or that they should never be used in the future. However, recognition of the undesirable side effects of overly liberal use has come slowly and only after the acquisition of compelling evidence that certain serious diseases are no longer responsive to specific antibiotics that once were used effectively in their treatment.

In a variety of contexts, concern has been expressed that programs that have been implemented for the express purpose of benefiting the environment could have ended up actually harming it. For example, some have worried that the establishment of recycling programs might, even if successful in getting wide participation, increase the total amount of waste as a consequence of making people less motivated to control consumption. Bratt (1999) found no evidence of this sort of trade-off—or compensatory behavior—at least as indicated in responses to a survey regarding recycling, use of cars, energy consumption, and selection of consumer items, but the possibility is not ruled out in all instances.

There is also the possibility that steps taken to reduce environmental pollution from one source can have the unanticipated effect of increasing pollution from another source. Ward and Dubos (1972) illustrated this possibility with an example involving water resources.

> If waters are cleansed of impurities by sewage systems which then burn the final product off as noxious gases in the air, the environmental return on the cost of the treatment plant can be nil or may even be negative if the gas in the atmosphere is more pervasive than the water-borne wastes and can, by combining with a wider range of pollutants, produce more lethal damage. (p. 50)

Other examples of trade-offs that yield nil or net negative returns on efforts to protect the environment can be found. They point up the ease with which narrowly focused thinking can overlook unwanted results from well-intentioned actions.

Trade-offs can be subtle and difficult to anticipate. The term *dematerialization*, is sometimes used to characterize a decline over time in the weight of the materials used in industrial end products or a decrease in the energy embedded in those products (Herman, Ardekani, & Ausubel, 1989). Looked at from one perspective, a trend in this direction is good news for people concerned about the environmental impact of production processes; the manufacture of lighter automobiles by using plastics and aluminum instead of steel in many places means the expenditure of less energy in the manufacturing process and the burning of less gasoline in operating the resulting vehicles. However, steel is considerably easier to recycle than plastics, so the net gain, from an environmental point of view, is not clear (Frosch & Gallopoulos, 1989).

A trade-off that deserves special attention is that between the costs of prevention and the costs of cleanup. Successful prevention programs reduce the need for cleanup activities and thereby decrease the costs of the latter. Yet prevention programs can be costly, so, from a strictly economic point of view, the problem is to derive plausible estimates of both types of cost. Estimating future cleanup costs requires extrapolation of actual current costs of cleanup (or estimates of what adequate cleanup would currently cost if undertaken) given various assumptions about relevant trends. Determining actual current costs of cleanup activities is not straightforward because only a small percentage of them are incurred by visible government programs; most are borne by the private sector. In 1990, for example, the Environmental Protection Agency's direct expenditures for pollution cleanup were about $5.5 billion, whereas the total amount spent by the country was estimated at $115 billion (Roberts, 1991b).

Not least among the reasons for attempting to understand trade-offs better is the importance of distinguishing between situations in which a gain with respect to one desired objective can be realized only at the cost of a loss with respect to another and situations in which it may be possible to find a way to work effectively toward competing objectives simultaneously. This is the distinction, in game-theory terms, between *zero-sum* and *non-zero-sum* games. Many of the trade-off relationships that are receiving attention in the context of environmental concerns are typically treated as if they involve zero-sum situations. Examples include energy conservation versus economic development, species habitat preservation versus job protection, and reduction in consumption versus maintenance of a high-quality life style. It is important to understand whether the opposing goals in such cases necessarily have a zero-sum relationship; to the extent that they do not, effort can profitably be devoted to finding win–win solutions to the apparent conflicts.

We tend to associate cost–benefit and trade-off analyses with large projects and major industrial or governmental programs. However, they are also applicable to the behavior of the individual citizen or consumer. The question of what an individual is or should be willing to pay to obtain a particular benefit is germane to a variety of environmental issues. The feasibility of reducing the use of chemical fertilizers or pesticides in the growing of crops is somewhat tied, for example, to the willingness of consumers to pay more for organically grown produce or purchase produce with modest amounts of insect damage (Zilberman, Schmitz, Casterline, Lichtenberg, & Siebert, 1991).

CHAPTER

# 12

# Competition, Cooperation, Negotiation and Policymaking

The problem of detrimental environmental change is everyone's problem. It does not follow that everyone recognizes it as such or that everyone is naturally motivated to do what he or she can to help solve it. Real progress on the problem will require cooperative behavior at all levels—among individuals, communities, and nations. For this reason, research on competition, cooperation, and negotiation should have important implications for making policy with respect to environmental issues.

## THE NATURE OF SOCIAL DILEMMAS

The detrimental effects of behavior that characterizes the "tragedy of the commons" (Hardin, 1968) in its numerous guises establishes the importance of developing a better understanding of the conditions under which cooperative behavior relating to problems of general interest can be evoked and sustained. Hardin illustrated the conflict that can occur between self-interest and the common good in what must be one of the most widely cited articles ever published about the environment. According to his metaphor, a herdsman can realize a substantial personal benefit at little personal cost by adding an animal to his herd that is grazing on common land. The benefit that comes from having an additional animal is that herdsman's alone; the cost, in terms of slightly less grazing land per animal is shared by all users of the common. The dilemma is that every herdsman sees the situation the same way; when each works in what appears to be his own best short-term interest, they collectively ruin the land. A conventional analysis of the herdsman's optimal behavior as a function of what the other herdsmen do shows that his own payoff is maximized by adding the additional animal whether the other herdsmen also add one or not, and the same analysis shows this is true for every herdsman (Swap, 1991).

The general idea finds another graphic illustration in the response of designers of fossil fuel-burning power-generation plants to concern about the polluting emissions that such plants make to the atmosphere—namely, the specification of ever taller smokestacks. (Over the twenty-year period between 1956 and 1976, the average height of new smokestacks almost tripled, increasing from slightly over 200 feet to about 600 feet [Patrick, Binetti, & Halterman, 1981].) The intended effect of this policy is to disperse one part of the cost of the energy produced by a single plant—the environmental cost of poorer air quality—over an adequately large area that none of the individuals who share that cost will find it sufficiently intolerable to rebel strongly against absorbing it. The tragedy of the commons becomes evident when one considers the many variations on the taller-smokestack theme that are played in major urban areas and their cumulative effect on the quality of the regional environments.

The tragedy of the commons illustrates the more general idea of a social trap (Platt, 1973) or social dilemma (Glance & Huberman, 1994; Komorita & Parks, 1996). The general situation of interest is one in which individuals or groups seek short-term benefits by doing things that, if done by many, would eventually have undesirable consequences for all. The costs of the benefits realized by the few are borne by the many. Of course, the benefits evaporate if the many begin to emulate the few.

Galbraith (1991) pointed out that the tourist industry "has an extraordinary capacity for destroying the very attractions that created the industry in the first place" (p. 30). If all of us succeed in making our way to those idyllic vacation spots to which the tourist industry attempts to lure us, what we will see when we get there is mainly each other. Few exotic spots can maintain their genuine exoticism in the face of excessive tourism. As Galbraith put it, "What is advantageous for the individual enterprise in seeking a share of the business culminates in disaster for all enterprises" (p. 30). Galbraith noted that a similar consideration applies to real estate development. "The unspoiled landscape, the unspoiled environment, initially sustains and encourages the development. But that development, particularly if it is unwise, then repels the people who were initially attracted" (p. 31).

Sociologists and economists have identified many situations in which members of a group acting in their individual self-interest appear to be acting against the best interests of the group. Hollis, Sugden, and Weale (excerpted in Fisher, 1988) characterized such situations in which enlightened self-interest is self-defeating as those in which your order of preferences is as follows (X in this example stands for not paying and Y stands for paying):

1 You do X, others do Y.

2 You do Y, others do Y.

3 You do X, others do X.

4 You do Y, others do X. (p. 163)

They illustrated the distinction between individual and collective self-interest by reference to public goods, which are goods supplied to all members of a group if they are supplied to any of them: roads, public transportation facilities, public radio broadcasts. "Once a public good is supplied, anyone can enjoy it whether he pays anything towards the costs or not: so why would anyone pay?"

When, in such situations, everyone acts in one's self interest, narrowly conceived, no one benefits. The practical problem for the species stems from the fact that life presents many situations in which behavior that is beneficial to the individual who engages in it is disadvantageous to the individual's community or society in general, and may be devastating if done on a large scale. Gardner and Stern (1996) argued that one or another form of the tragedy of the commons underlies most environmental problems.

## DEALING WITH SOCIAL DILEMMAS

Various ways to deal with the commons dilemma or facilitate escape from social traps have been proposed. Hardin (1968) saw only two feasible approaches—socialism or the privatism of free enterprise. His own preference was for a social pact among users of the common resource, provided agreement could be obtained on rules for use and sanctions for cheating. The possibility of privatizing—partitioning the commons into smaller units, each of which is used by only a subset of the population—has attracted considerable attention from other researchers. The theory behind this approach is that relatively small groups of users of a shared resource should find it easier than large groups to cooperate in the management of the resource and to share responsibility for its preservation. One reason for this expectation is that it is easier for members of a small group to monitor each others' behavior than for members of a large group to do so. Ostrom et al. (1999) pointed out, however, that several aspects of modern technology, including citizen-band radios, the Internet, and geographic information systems, are making it increasingly easy even for members of large groups to monitor each others' behavior. Conceivably this could facilitate cooperative common-pool resource sharing within large groups.

Berkes, Feeney, McCay, and Acheson (1989) made a distinction between *open-access* systems and *communal property.* They argued that there are many examples of the latter that have been managed well for sustainable use by their owners. The results of both laboratory studies and real-world experiments have shown that the approach can work (Leavitt & Saegert, 1989; Stern, 1978; Stern & Kirkpatrick, 1977), although it is not feasible in all cases (e.g., it is hard to privatize air and water) and is not without problems even when it is feasible (Feeney, Berkes, McCay, & Acheson, 1990). Other writers, including Ophuls (1977), Messick and Brewer (1983), Swap (1991), Ostrom (1990), Gardner and Stern (1996), and Van Vugt (1997), have described a variety of approaches to the resolution of social dilemmas. Suggested approaches include governmental initiatives (laws to regulate commons uses, enforcement of compliance), education and persuasion, appeal to religious beliefs and moral convictions regarding responsibility for environmental preservation, privatization, and providing incentives for cooperative behavior.

In laboratory research with analogs of commons problems, Yamagishi (1988) showed that coercion is likely to be more palatable to users if they see evidence of lack of cooperation and the stakes (gains from cooperation and incentive to defect) are high. Platt (1973) mentioned making long-term negative consequences of behavior more salient, offsetting short-term benefits by increasing the behavior's immediate cost and encouraging alternative behavior that does not have long-term negative consequences.

Swap (1991) pointed out that how easy it is to manage a common resource is likely to depend on a number of specifics, such as the natural rate of renewal of the resource, the reversibility of exceeding a resource's carrying capacity (depletion), and the value attached to the resource by its users. It is also likely to depend, to some degree, on the number of its users, one reason being that free loading or free riding is less noticeable, the larger the group (Stroebe & Frey, 1982).

The tragedy of the commons metaphor illustrates one form of freeloading—an individual benefiting at community expense. A complementary form of freeloading is that of avoiding the payment of one's fair share of the cost of a community good. This is illustrated by the voluntary sharing, by the users of a private road, of the costs of keeping the road in good repair. If a small fraction of the users opt not to contribute, they get the benefit of the road at no expense. As in the case of the tragedy of the commons, this form of freeloading works only so long as the fraction of the community that practices it is relatively small. If a sufficiently large percentage of the beneficiaries of the good refuse to pay, it is likely to go away.

Despite the widely shared view that social dilemmas are hard to deal with effectively without the imposition of top–down controls and sanctions, there are examples in history of communities that have developed effective cooperative approaches to the management of common-pool resources (Cox, 1985; Ostrom, Burger, Field, Norgaard, & Policansky, 1999). Ostrom et al. argued that more solutions of commons problems exist than Hardin realized (and that the solutions that Hardin proposed sometimes fail), and they described several approaches that have worked well and for a long time at the local level. They noted too, however, that solutions that work at a local level may not transfer directly to global-scale problems because size and complexity can introduce issues not found at the local level. The members of small groups seem more likely than members of large ones to share normative values, identify with the group, and be motivated by interest in the group's well-being rather than by fear of the consequences of noncompliance with externally imposed regulations. Cooperative behavior sometimes arises spontaneously in social groups, but often it does not. Glance and Huberman (1994) suggested that it is more likely to occur in small groups than in large ones, and that how long it is sustained depends in part on how long the participants expect the group to exist. They also noted that the group behavior can change rapidly under some conditions.

Edney (1980) considered existing theories of social behavior to be inadequate to the task of identifying effective approaches to the problem of protecting common resources. He argued "that human beings probably have greater capacities for both socially constructive and destructive behaviors around resources than is generally recognized" (p. 148), and he suggested that the important questions for research have to do with how these capacities vary and what conditions elicit them. The kind of theory that is most likely to lead to effective resolutions of commons problems, he suggested, will be multifaceted, combining dispositional factors, environmental factors, and group and community dynamics. Relatively little is known about how to address the commons tragedy effectively or about precisely why people behave noncooperatively on commons maintenance problems in the first place.

Ostrom et al. (1999) contended that the prediction of the inevitability of the destruction of common-pool resources by their users is based on the assumption that all people are "selfish, norm-free, and maximizers of short-run results." They argued the need to recognize four types of users of such resources:

> (i) those who always behave in a narrow, self-interested way and never cooperate in dilemma situations (free-riders); (ii) those who are unwilling to cooperate with others unless assured that they will not be exploited by free-riders;

> (iii) those who are willing to initiate reciprocal cooperation in the hopes that others will return their trust; and (iv) perhaps a few genuine altruists who always try to achieve higher returns for a group. (p. 279)

Ostrom et al. concluded from their consideration of instances of effective management of common-pool resources that "tragedies of the commons are real, but not inevitable" (p. 281). A major challenge for future research is to find ways to apply what has been learned in the management of relatively small commons (local communities and regional groups) to global commons that involve many cultures, different resources interlinked in various ways, and accelerating rates of change.

## SOCIAL DILEMMA RESEARCH

Much of the research on social dilemmas has used computer simulations or other laboratory analogues of real-life problems (Brechner & Linder, 1981; Cass & Edney, 1978; Dawes, 1975, 1980; Edney & Harper, 1978; Fusco, Bell, Jorgensen, & Smith, 1991; Gifford & Wells, 1991). A major goal of this research has been to distinguish the conditions under which people will cooperate or behave in ways that advance the common good from those in which they will compete or work strictly in their own best interests, narrowly conceived. Researchers have often used one or another version of the prisoner's dilemma, which puts people in the position of deciding whether to cooperate (for mutual good) or defect (to gain at another's expense; Dawes, 1988; Orbell, van de Kragt, & Dawes, 1988). The prisoner's dilemma is seen as prototypical of all situations that are characterized by the "temptation to better one's own interests in a way that would be ruinous if *everyone* did it" (Poundstone, 1992, p. 126).

Cooperative behavior has been increased in some instances by the use of rewards for cooperation (Birjulin, Smith, & Bell, 1993; Martichuski & Bell, 1991) and/or punishments for defection (Bell, Peterson, & Hautaluoma, 1989; Harvey, Bell, & Birjulin, 1993). The likelihood of cooperating in the situations of interest is greatly influenced by one's expectations regarding the behavior of others. If one has no hope of influencing the behavior of others, the motivation for cooperation is likely to be low (Dawes, van de Kragt, & Orbell, 1988).

Among the more thought-provoking findings of psychologists relating to the modification of behavior in the interest of environmental concerns is the importance of mutual trust among people in responding effectively to commons-tragedy type problems (Edney, 1980; Lindskold, 1978; Mosler, 1993; Parks, 1994; Rotter, 1971). That mutual trust would play a key role in the resolution of such problems is not surprising. An ongoing challenge to research is to discover how the trust that is needed can be developed in commons-dilemma situations.

An important distinction in research on behavior in prisoner's dilemma situations is between situations in which the same participants play the same prisoner's-dilemma game an unspecified number of times and those in which they face the situation only once or a specified number of times. For present purposes, a finding of special interest is that when the game is played an unspecified number of times, without a prespecified stopping place, consistent cooperative (competitive) play on the part of one participant tends to evoke the same type of play on the part of the other (Axelrod, 1984). This finding is believed by some investigators to provide some insight into the evolution of cooperative (reciprocally altruistic) or competitive behavior (Boyd, 1988; Trivers, 1971). A strategy that has proved to be effective in repeated-play prisoner's dilemma situations is the tit-for-tat strategy in which the tit-for-tat player always selects the option (cooperate or defect) chosen by the opponent on the preceding trial (Axelrod, 1980a, 1980b; Nowak & Sigmund, 1992; Rapoport & Chammah, 1965).

The concept of a social dilemma is familiar to social psychologists and others who do related research, but it is probably unfamiliar to many, if not most, lay people. It is a concept that, arguably, should have a greater presence in the public consciousness. How best to convey the notion to people has been considered by some investigators. Some have suggested the use of simulations of commons dilemmas and other social traps to educate people to the existence of such situations and to the relative effectiveness of alternative ways of dealing with them (Brechner & Linder, 1981; Powers, Duus, & Norton, 1979).

## NEGOTIATION AND CONFLICT RESOLUTION

The problem of protecting the environment is an intrinsically difficult one because many of the more obvious steps that might be taken to that end conflict, or at least appear to conflict, with economic interests and the goal of industrial development. Debates about public policy pertaining to environmental issues often become highly polarized with environmentalists and developers taking equally inflexible stands on opposite sides of the question. Conflicts also arise between groups that appear to be equally interested in environmental preservation; the U.S. Department of Agriculture's Forest Service and the U.S. Department of the Interior's National Park Service, for example, have often found themselves in conflict regarding programs and policies (Grumbine, 1991).

Archer, Pettigrew, and Aronson (1992) described the conflict they encountered in an evaluation study of several large-scale efforts to modify energy-related attitudes and behavior as "a collision of cultures."

> It is clear that the conflict we encountered was an inevitable by-product of three colliding cultures: the basic research world of the academic, the dollar-driven corporate world, and the routinely adversarial world of public regulation. These

> worlds are poorly matched in many ways. The academic world values (or at least pays lip service to) criticism, and the conclusions of most scholarly research projects have no fiscal consequences. By contrast, in the corporate world, decisions are often associated with enormous costs, leading to fierce defense of past expenditures and thin-skinned hostility to suggested improvements. Finally, in the adversarial world of public regulation, the fear of perceived impropriety is endemic. Just as regulated monopolies depend on looking good in front of their regulatory agency, the regulatory agency is itself apprehensive at any suggestion that public funds may have been fruitlessly spent. For both the regulated and the regulator, this amplifies enormously sensitivity to all criticism and, particularly, to public criticism. (p. 1236)

Several efforts by communities to deal with conflicting interests relating to environmental change (e.g., logging vs. recreational use of land, agricultural development vs. land conservation, water use vs. aquifer protection) have been analyzed by Crowfoot and Wondolleck (1991). The conflict-resolution process involved assumed voluntary participation by all parties with vested interests in the outcome and made use of an independent negotiator. Crowfoot and Wondolleck emphasized the importance of flexibility and a willingness to compromise if such a process is to work and noted that these ingredients are often lacking, especially in radical special-interest groups.

The problem of detrimental environmental change is global in extent. It affects, and will continue to affect, people everywhere. Yet different nations contribute to it in different ways and to different degrees, and the roles they play in addressing it are bound to differ as well. Attitudes that prevail in the industrialized world differ from those widely held in Third World countries. Generally speaking, public concern about long-range environmental change is more prevalent in relatively affluent societies than in countries struggling to raise the economic standard of living of their citizenry (Ward & Dubos, 1972).

Because of the global nature of the problem of environmental change, it represents one of the most important opportunities psychologists have for international collaboration (Pawlik, 1991). Such collaboration should be actively sought because global problems can only be solved with global involvement. It can also be argued that development of collegial relationships among scientists from different cultures and different parts of the world can contribute much to the objective of maintaining world peace.

Conflicts are inevitable as agreements are sought for effective cooperative action. Conflicts can arise for many reasons, not the least of which are poorly understood cultural differences. It may be especially easy for Western-trained scientists and technologists to overestimate the likely effectiveness of technological solutions to problems in developing countries and to underestimate the importance of customizing imported technology to local values, mores, and knowledge (Sperling, Loevinsohn, & Ntabomvura, 1993).

There is a need for better techniques both for resolving conflicts—for negotiating compromise—and anticipating conflicts so they can be avoided or, if not avoided altogether, at least controlled so they do not escalate to crisis proportions. Research on conflict resolution and conflict avoidance should make use of the best predictive models of environmental change available and experiment with situations that are patterned, as nearly as possible, on those believed likely to arise. In this way, experience can be gained not only on the effectiveness of specific negotiation techniques in the abstract, but on their effectiveness in situations similar to those that are likely to have to be faced. There is also a need for training people in the art of negotiation. Computer simulations of conflict situations can be useful to this end (Sheer, Baeck, & Wright, 1989).

## POLICY FORMULATION AND DECISION MAKING

Policy formulation is a human activity undertaken by individuals and groups in positions of authority. It depends on human perception and cognition, and consequently it is subject to all the limitations of perceptual and cognitive processes. Because it often involves negotiations among people representing different, perhaps conflicting, perspectives and interests, it is also affected by the dynamics of group behavior (Portney, 1991b). Policy formulation and decision making with respect to environmental issues tend to be complicated because typically there are many kinds of factors to consider—physical, psychological, economic, ethical, political—as well as the often-conflicting vested interests of different groups. Indeed, the complexity of environmental decision problems is such that they may appear to defy rational analysis (Vogel, 1991). There can be little question that efforts to establish environmental policies encounter controversy on many issues (Kamieniecki, O'Brien, & Clarke, 1986).

The ease with which decisions can be made on the basis of salient aspects of a situation while overlooking less obvious, but important, facts is illustrated by the problem of assessing the relative merits of polystyrene and paper as materials for making disposable food containers. Pesticide use is another challenge to cost–benefit analysis; benefits in terms of crop protection are salient, whereas long-term costs are less immediately apparent, but no less real. For example, the beneficial effects of DDT in controlling pests are seen quickly, whereas its toxicity on other life forms, including humans, becomes detectable only as a result of its accumulation in the food chain over long periods of time.

MacNeill (1989) argued that the most important condition for sustainable development to be realized is that environmental and economic issues be merged in decision making. He claims, however, that policy decisions are often taken with little understanding of their environmental implications.

> Tax and fiscal incentives, pricing and marketing policies and exchange-rate and trade-protection policies all influence the environment and the resource content of the growth that takes place. Yet the people responsible for setting these policies seldom consider their impact on the environment or on stocks of resource capital.... It is surprising how few government and corporate leaders are aware of the ecologically and economically perverse nature of the incentive systems created by these policies and the often enormous budgets they command. Even the environmental movement is only dimly aware of it. (p. 163)

The situation is further complicated by the high degree of uncertainty associated with many predictions of environmental change. Delaying policy decisions in the hope of reducing uncertainties through further research has its risks; not only can problems worsen over time and become more difficult to address, but delay also provides time during which investments in prevailing technologies can be increased and the stakes that inhibit change raised (Harris, 1990). Further complicating the process is that both executive and legislative branches of government participate in the establishment of policy at the national level, and issues of national interest become clouded with regional and political concerns.

Chechile (1991a) argued that decisions pertaining to the environment tend to differ from decisions made in other contexts in several ways, their generally greater complexity and degree of incertitude being only two of them. Others he listed are the delay of feedback regarding the effectiveness of decisions because of the inertia that is typical of environmental systems, involvement of citizens stimulated by hazards and risks, challenges posed by environmental decision demands to certain ideas regarding utility in orthodox economic models, some challenges to classical Western thought about corporate and individual conduct, and rapidity of technological development that undercuts the effectiveness of normal diplomacy among nations as a way of dealing with environmental problems of international scope. A point that Chechile (1991b) made that strikes me as especially important is that there is no absolute utility that is independent of the perspective of the decision maker, so the application of the idea of utility to decision making regarding the environment—or anything else—is likely to give different results depending on the values of the one making the application.

The point is illustrated by the current debate about the possibility of drilling for oil in the Arctic National Wildlife Reserve. Gibbs (2001) pointed out that there is no shortage of scientists on either side of this question, although biologists tend to be opposed to drilling because of the assumed negative effect it would have on wildlife, whereas petroleum geologists insist that the damage caused by recovery of the oil would be cosmetic only. Gibbs's conclusion is: "In a fundamentally political dispute, scientists' opinions should carry no more weight than anyone else's" (p. 65). Similarly, scientists in favor of genetically modified crops argue that such crops are helpful to the environment because they can be grown with fewer or less toxic pesticides than can conventional crops, whereas opponents point out the many uncertainties about the long-term environmental effects—the possibility that genetically modified crops could pollinate related noncrop plants, thus creating superweeds that would also be pest-resistant, the expectation that pests would evolve so that genetic modification of crops would no longer provide an effective defense against them, and so on (Brown, 2001; Kaiser, 2001). This debate is being informed by ongoing research on how genes can be transferred laterally between organisms in the environment (Levy & Miller, 1989; Miller, 1998).

Portney (1991b) distinguished between the positivist approach to policy formulation and the public policymaking process. According to this distinction, the positivist approach assumes that there exists a single correct decision, or a small number of them, to be made and that it, or they, can be identified by analysis performed by experts. In contrast, the public policymaking process does not assume a single or small set of correct decisions and does not see decision making as the responsibility of experts. "It suggests that the range of answers to a specific environmental problem can be wide, and that it is rather the process our public decision makers go through that will ultimately determine the kind of decision made" (p. 198). The positivist approach involves, at least in theory, application of objective methods by a value-neutral researcher; the public policymaking approach

> accepts as inevitable that "politics," or interpersonal value-based interactions, will determine which decisions are made.... The fundamental premise of the policymaking-process approach is that no analytical technique will necessarily produce the best course of action. Indeed, there is no best course of action to be found; there are only courses of action that can be agreed upon, courses of action that are politically acceptable, and these are the correct decisions. (p. 200)

Portney illustrated the tension between the positivist and public policymaking approaches with the problem of citing of hazardous-waste treatment facilities.

Decisions are made and policies established by many different entities ranging from individuals to corporations to governmental bodies at all levels (local, state, and national) and multi-nation governmental organizations such as the European Economic Community, the United Nations, and the World Bank. Moomaw and Kildow (1991) noted that new units of power have been emerging in recent years, including multinational corporations (some of which have higher revenues than some nations) and nongovernmental organizations (e.g., the World Resources Institute, WorldWatch, the Environmental Defense Fund), that exercise considerable influence in national and international policymaking.

> What has clearly changed in recent international environmental decision making is that the nation-state has ceased to be the exclusive initiator and implementor of responses to environmental threats.... A new, complex set of international environmental and economic groups is setting the policy agenda and forcing decisions and actions to meet emerging environmental challenges. (p. 282–283)

We need to understand better, from a psychological point of view, the processes by which policies are formed and adopted. It would be useful to have not only explicit normative models of rational policy-formulation procedures, but also more objective data on how they actually are formed. For example, it would be helpful to know in specific instances the degree to which individual policymakers understand particular aspects of the issues their policies address, their level of comprehension of probabilistic concepts, their method of dealing with conflicting information, and their attitude toward compromise.

We need a better understanding too of how policymakers become aware of environmental concerns that deserve their attention. To what extent are their interests overly influenced by especially vivid representations of specific aspects of environmental change by the media (Vincent, 1990)? What determines how politically salient any particular environmental problem will be (Merkhofer, 1987)? As Machina (1990) pointed out, if people's choices depend on the manner in which probabilistic information is presented, "the manner of presentation *itself* becomes a public policy issue over which interest groups may well contend" (p. 176).

CHAPTER

# 13

# Concluding Comments

In an article based on her 1997 presidential address to the American Association of the Advancement of Science, Lubchenco (1998), who referred to the coming century as the "century of the environment," proposed a new social contract for science

> predicated upon the assumptions that scientists will (i) address the most urgent needs of society, in proportion to their importance; (ii) communicate their knowledge and understanding widely in order to inform decisions of individuals and institutions; and (iii) exercise good judgment, wisdom, and humility. The Contract should recognize the extent of human domination of the planet. It should express a commitment to harness the full power of the scientific enterprise in discovering new knowledge, in communicating existing and new understanding to the public and to policy-makers, and in helping society move toward a more sustainable biosphere. (p. 495)

Lubchenco was quick to stress that the suggestion was not intended to be a call to abandon fundamental research, which she argued is more needed than ever before. However, she did urge a greater direction of fundamental research on the development of knowledge needed to address pressing social problems, of which environmental change was emphasized as one.

Lubchenco's sentiments echo, and have been echoed by, those of many other scientists. Assessments of the situation by some (Commoner, 1991; Dubos, 1970; Ehrlich, 1968; McKibben, 1990; Meadows, Meadows, & Randers, 1992) are not pleasant reads. Wilson (1998) characterized the challenge the situation represents this way: "Like it or not, we are entering the century of the environment, when science and politics will give the highest priority to settling humanity down before we wreck the planet" (p. 2049). Gell-Mann's (1994) assessment is similar:

> In negative terms, the human race needs to avoid catastrophic war, widespread tyranny, and the continued prevalence of extreme poverty, as well as disastrous degradation of the biosphere and destruction of biological and ecological diversity. The key concept is the achievement of quality of human life and of the state of the biosphere that is not purchased mainly at the expense of the future. (p. 348)

This book is predicated on the assumption that there is much that can be done to address the many concerns that have been expressed, and that psychologists have opportunities to contribute to that end. Some of those opportunities have been pursued by researchers, and many of the results they have obtained have been noted in the preceding chapters. However, much more could be done if the problem of environmental change were higher on the priority list for the psychological research community as a whole.

Inattention to the problem could be due to a variety of reasons. Undoubtedly some psychologists, like many people more generally, are not convinced that there is a serious problem to be addressed. Others may feel that addressing any politically sensitive problem is risky. There appears to be tension among many scientists, including ecologists and conservation biologists, who are likely to be more knowledgeable than most about environmental problems, between the belief that those who understand what is happening to the environment have a responsibility to try to do something about it and the fear that scientists who become too closely identified with causes risk losing their credibility as objective investigators (Kaiser, 2000).

There is also the possibility that some researchers consider the environmental situation to be so complicated that effective action to prevent further degradation is not possible. Ehrenfeld (1981) expressed the view, with considerable persuasiveness, that human planning with respect to the environment is futile and that even the effort to undertake it is evidence of human arrogance. He argued the necessity of coming to terms "with our irrational faith in our own limitless power, and with the reality that is the widespread failure, in their largest context, of our inventions and processes, especially those that aspire to environmental control" (p. 5). The message of Ehrenfeld's book, as he described it,

> is that people are spending too much valuable time and causing too much damage by pretending that our efforts in politics, economics, and technology usually have the effects we intend them to have, especially when there are strong environmental interactions involved. We have been fooled by our own humanist cant into thinking that we are actually learning how to steer the planet in its orbit. (p. 16)

> In no important instance have we been able to demonstrate comprehensive, successful management of our world, nor do we understand it well enough to be able to manage it in theory. Only in those few cases in which small, remote systems could, in effect, be treated as if they were isolated, have management and control worked at all; but one cannot run an entire world this way. (p. 105)

I find much in Ehrenfeld's view thought provoking and helpful, but believe the general picture he paints is too pessimistic. To be sure, efforts to preserve the environment or protect it from disastrous change should be tempered by a sober recognition of the complexity of the problem and resistance of the temptation to assume lightly that technology is up to any challenge, but "absolute faith in our ability to control our own destiny," which Ehrenfeld described as "a dangerous fallacy" (p. 10), is not essential to belief in the rationality of efforts to address specific aspects of the problem of detrimental environmental change. If it is clear that human behavior can affect the environment adversely, why should we not assume that changing that behavior in specific ways could mitigate those adverse effects or even have beneficial ones? Even if the assumption proved to be wrong, what rational alternative is there to making it?

The idea of managing the planet raises two questions: "What kind of planet do we want? What kind of planet can we get?" (Clark, 1989, p. 48). I believe that both of these questions should be asked on a continuing basis and that the answer to each is likely to change as more is learned about the causes of environmental change and what might be done about them. The question of what kind of planet we want must be asked with respect to more than one time frame. What kind of planet do we want for ourselves, here and now? What kind of planet do we want for our children and theirs? The rub comes from the fact that ensuring a planet that is hospitable to future generations may mean settling for one that serves less than optimally our current wants and desires. This trade is one we appear to find extraordinarily difficult to make.

Peterson (1991) argued that our preoccupation with the near term and our excessive dedication to material progress constitute the major obstacles to facing up to what he sees as the *impending crisis*.

> Decision makers are primarily concerned with improving this quarter's financial statement, getting reelected next election, gaining tenure, or obtaining funding. What is needed are more people, and especially leaders, who think comprehensively and globally, who weigh the impact of today's decisions on the quality of life of future generations, and who gain job satisfaction primarily from contributing to the welfare of others. (p. 191)

An important question for psychology is that of how people—government policymakers, business leaders, academics, all of us—can be induced to take a long-range view, think in terms of the future implications of today's actions, and be motivated to work toward long-range goals.

Even considering only the present, it is not clear that we value a quality environment enough to be willing to sacrifice much in the way of material possessions to help ensure it. As Dubos (1970) put it, "We dislike polluted and cluttered environments, but we like economic prosperity and gadgets even more" (p. 127). For this reason, Dubos expressed doubt that we will take the actions necessary to control the environment until forced to do so by catastrophic events. Here is another challenge to psychology: how to get people to place a higher value on unpolluted air, clean water, open space, tolerable climate, uncongested places of natural beauty, which we are likely to take too much for granted when we are not keenly aware of the threat to their existence.

I am not prepared to argue that psychology, as a discipline, has more to offer to the fight against environmental degradation than do other disciplines. However, I see many opportunities for its perspective and methods to have an impact that is unlikely to be realized from other quarters. More active involvement of the profession in work on the problem seems likely to lead to recognition of opportunities not now appreciated.

There are two ways to make research useful in a practical sense. One is to start with what has been learned from research motivated by other than practical concerns and try to find practical problems to which it can be applied. The other is to start with a practical problem and try to design some research that can help solve that problem. Both approaches could be applied beneficially to the problem of detrimental environmental change. There are many findings of research that has been done for reasons other than environmental concerns that nevertheless could have implications in this context. These implications have to be spelled out, however, and communicated to people who can put them to use. Those who have done the research may not always be the best people to articulate the practical implications of their findings. This means that there is a need for people to bridge the gap between the applicable research findings on deposit in the technical literature and the people who are in positions to make the applications. This is not an easy role. To play it effectively, one must be knowledgeable with respect to both the psychological literature and the problem area of application.

Doing research addressed explicitly to specific practical problems is not easy either. It requires researchers to become familiar with the problems to be addressed and determine ways in which psychological research could be useful. It is easy enough to identify relatively general objectives of a psychological nature that relate to environmental change:

- Generation of a better understanding of why people engage in behavior that degrades the environment and of how technology and social customs enable or facilitate environmental harm.
- Motivation of environmentally beneficial or benign behavior by individuals, corporations, and geopolitical entities.
- Development of environmentally friendly devices and processes, and the kind of technology that will make it harder, less pleasant, more costly (immediately) to pollute the environment than to treat it well.
- Identification of environmentally friendly ways to satisfy human needs and desires that could be effective alternatives to environmentally unfriendly ways to satisfy them, and of the factors that determine the extent to which people will opt to use them.
- Development of more effective approaches to risk assessment, decision making, negotiation, interdisciplinary collaboration, and policymaking for application to environmental problems.
- Development of usable database-management systems and other tools to facilitate the monitoring of environmental change and the effectiveness of attempts to improve the situation.
- Development of approaches to the assessment of consumer products in terms of total costs, including those expected to be incurred in the future to remediate environmental damage caused by their use or disposal.
- Encouragement of a greater willingness to challenge old assumptions: that continual unlimited growth is essential to a strong economy, that increasing the quality of life is dependent on the production and consumption of ever more material goods, that technology is capable of solving all environmental problems, and so on

The challenge is to find within these and other objectives research problems of manageable size.

Other challenges to which psychologists might respond are the needs for theory development and research integration. Several efforts have been made to determine what people want from outdoor recreation experiences and quantify the demand for such experiences (Driver & Brown, 1983), some of which have been mentioned in this book. Knopf (1983) pointed out that although there are scores of in-depth analyses of what people are seeking from recreational experiences in natural environments, there is a paucity of theoretical accounts of the findings: "Although data abound, theory does not" (p. 210). The analyses he cited include backcountry hiking, cross-country skiing, fishing, hunting, off-road vehicle and snowmobile use, and river running. Studies typically involve an effort to get insights about human preferences by obtaining and perusing large amounts of descriptive data and are seldom theory driven. One consequence of such a totally empirical approach is the inability to predict human reactions to environmental situations and comparisons other than those explicitly studied.

A better theoretical understanding of the bases for the pleasure and satisfaction that people get from nature and their various interactions with it not only is necessary for any reasonably comprehensive theory of human psychology, it also could be applied usefully to the practical goal of fostering interests in activities that have the dual benefit of providing satisfaction to those who engage in them and that have positive, or at worst neutral, environmental effects. It would be useful to know, for example, the extent to which people's reactions to natural environments are learned, as some investigators have suggested (Knopf, 1983; Moore, 1979; Tuan, 1974), as opposed to being innate, as the data that indicate preference consistencies across cultures might suggest (Kwok, 1979; Shafer & Tooby, 1973).

Second only to the problem of the lack of theory is the fragmentation of research. Knopf (1983) also articulated this problem by pointing out the importance of the perspective that the researcher brings to the task of determining how people perceive nature.

> Recreation sociologists concentrate almost exclusively on developing appreciation for the social system. Those with a natural-resource management perspective in their efforts to understand demand for backcountry experiences have tended to focus on the motivation effects of conditions in nonleisure environments. Researchers with physical education and recreation health perspectives have concentrated on the personality system as they seek to understand the mental health benefits of leisure participation. Only infrequently does collaboration reach across these disciplinary lines; it is rare to find cross-citation between the three bodies of literature.... As students of the recreation literature, our image of why people visit recreation areas differs according to who is doing the teaching—a sociologist, a forester, a psychologist, or a personologist. Without the benefit of debate and critique, individual investigators have not been inclined to place their information in the context of that being generated by others, leaving us with a view of the recreationist that is disjointed, incomplete, and possibly erroneous. (p. 226–228)

Knopf's comments regard research on human uses of and interactions with the natural environment, but similar observations could be made regarding research on the relationship between people and the environment more generally and especially on that which is most relevant to human involvement in environmental change. Theory development and integration of research results are major needs of the larger field.

A growing interest in this general objective is seen in the emergence of "sustainability science," which "seeks to understand the fundamental character of interactions between nature and society," as a scientific discipline (Kates et al.,

2001). Given the importance of human needs, desires, decisions, and actions as determinants of environmental change, there should be many opportunities for psychologists to participate in this discipline.

Finally, communicating the practical implications of research results—regardless of whether the research was motivated by practical concerns—is also a challenge. In responding to it, one can go wrong in either of two ways. One can fail to articulate the implications with sufficient specificity or in language that potential users of the findings will readily comprehend. One can overstate the case—claim potential applications that, realistically, do not exist. Failure to communicate practical implications explicitly and clearly more or less ensures that the results will not be used; and overstating the practical impact of research findings harms the credibility of the field.

The evidence seems compelling that the quality of the environment is seriously threatened in a variety of ways. It also seems clear that the extent to which the threats are realized will depend on how people—individually and corporately—respond to them. I have tried to make the case in this book that psychology has something to contribute to the goal of maintaining or improving the quality of the environment. Psychological studies have addressed some aspects of the problem, but there are many opportunities for relevant research beyond what has yet been done.

# References


Abelson, P. H. (1995a). Low-level radioactive waste. *Science, 268,* 1547.

Abelson, P. H. (1995b). Response [to letters to the editor]. *Science, 269,* 1566, 1567.

Abelson, R. P. (1982). Three modes of attitude-behavior consistency. In M. P. Zanna, E. T. Higgins, & C. P. Herman (Eds.), *Consistency in social behavior: The Ontario Symposium* (Vol. 2, pp. 131–146). Hillsdale, NJ: Lawrence Erlbaum Associates.

Abelson, R. P. , & Prentice, D. A. (1990). Beliefs as possessions: A functional perspective. In A. R. Pratkanis, S. J. Breckler, & A. G. Greenwald (Eds.), *Attitude structure and function.* Hillsdale, NJ: Lawrence Erlbaum Associates.

Adamus, P. R, & Clough, G. C. (1978). Evaluating species for protection in natural areas. *Biological Conservation, 13,* 165–178.

Adeola, F. O. (2000). Endangered community, enduring people: Toxic contamination, health, and adaptive response in a local context. *Environment and Behavior, 32,* 209–249.

Ajdukovic, D. (1990). Psychosocial climate in correctional institutions. *Environment and Behavior, 22,* 420–432.

Ajzen, I. (1982). On behaving in accordance with one's attitudes. In M. P. Zanna, E. T. Higgins, & C. P. Herman (Eds.), *Consistency in social behavior: The Ontario Symposium* (Vol. 2, pp. 3–15). Hillsdale, NJ: Lawrence Erlbaum Associates.

Ajzen, I., & Fishbein, M. (1977). Attitude-behavior relations: A theoretical analysis and review of empirical research. *Psychological Bulletin, 84,* 888–918.

Aldous, P. (1993). Tropical deforestation: Not just a problem in Amazonia. *Science, 259,* 1390.

Aldwin, C., & Stokols, D. (1988). The effects of environmental change on individuals and groups: Some neglected issues in stress research. *Journal of Environmental Psychology, 8,* 57–75.

Alexander, C., Ishikawa, S., & Silverstein, M. A. (1977). *Pattern language.* New York: Oxford University Press.

Allen, F. W. (1987). Towards a holistic appreciation of risk: The challenges for communicators and policy makers. *Science, Technology, and Human Values, 12,* 138–143.

Allen, J. B., & Ferrand, J. L. (1999). Environmental locus of control, sympathy, and proenvironmental behavior: A test of Geller's actively caring hypothesis. *Environment and Behavior, 31,* 338–353.

Alloy, L. B., & Ahrens, A. H. (1987). Depression and pessimism for the future. *Journal of Personality and Social Psychology, 52,* 366–378.

Alper, J. (1993). Protecting the environment with the power of the market. *Science, 260,* 1884–1885.

Althoff, P., & Grieg, W. H. (1974). Environmental pollution control policy-making: An analysis of elite perceptions and preferences. *Environment and Behavior, 6,* 259–288.

Althuis, T. (1995). Letter to editor re radioactive waste at Ward Valley. *Science, 269,* 1655.

Altman, I. (1970). Territorial behavior in humans: An analysis of the concept. In L. Pastalan & D. H. Carson (Eds.), *Spatial behavior of older people* (pp. 1–24). Ann Arbor, MI: University of Michigan-Wayne State University Press.

Altman, I. (1975). *The environment and social behavior.* Monterey, CA: Brooks-Cole.

Altman, I. (1977). Privacy regulation: Culturally universal or culturally specific? *Journal of Social Issues, 33,* 66–84.

Altman, I. (1979). Privacy as an interpersonal boundary process. In M. von Cranach, K. Foppa, W. Lepenies, & D. Ploog (Eds.), *Human ethology: Claims and limits of a new discipline* (pp. 45–132). Cambridge, UK: Cambridge University Press.

Altman, I., & Wohlwill, J. F. (Eds.). (1983). *Behavior and the natural environment.* New York: Plenum.

Alvo, R. (1986). Lost loons of the northern lakes. *Natural History, 95*(9), 58–65.

Alward, R. D., Detling, J. K., & Milchunas, D. G. (1999). Grassland vegetation changes and nocturnal global warming. *Science, 283,* 229–231.

American Automobile Association. (1975). *Gas watchers' guide.* Falls Church, VA: Author.

American Public Transit Association. (1987). *1988 transit fact book.* Washington, DC:Author.

Anderson, C. A. (1989). Temperature and aggression: Ubiquitous effects of heat on occurrence of human violence. *Psychological Bulletin, 106,* 74–96.

Anderson, C. A., & DeNeve, K. M. (1992). Temperature, aggression, and the negative affect escape model. *Psychological Bulletin, 111,* 347–351.

Anderson, L. M. (1981). Land use designations affect perception of scenic beauty in forest landscapes. *Forest Science, 27,* 392–400.

Anderson, R. N. (1998). Oil production in the 21st century. *Scientific American, 278*(3), 86–91.

Andreae, M. O., & Crutzen, P. J. (1997). Atmospheric aerosols: Biogeochemical sources and role on atmospheric chemistry. *Science, 276,* 1052–1058.

Arbuthnot, J., Tedeschi, R., Wayner, M., Turner, J., Kressel, S., & Rush, R. (1976–1977). The induction of sustained recycling behavior through the foot-in-the-door technique. *Journal of Environmental Systems, 6,* 353–366.

Archer, D., Pettigrew, T. F., & Aronson, E. (1992). Making research apply: High stakes public policy in a regulatory environment. *American Psychologist, 47,* 1233–1236.

Arkes, H. R., Dawes, R. M., & Christensen, C. (1988). Factors influencing the use of a decision rule in a probabilistic task. In J. Dowie & A. Elstein (Eds.), *Professional judgment: A reader in clinical decision making* (pp. 163–180). Cambridge, England: Cambridge University Press. (Originally published in *Organizational Behavior and Human Decision Processes, 37,* 93–110.)

Aronson, E. (1992). The return of the repressed: Dissonance theory makes a comeback. *Psychological Inquiry, 3,* 303–311.

Aronson, E., & O'Leary, M. (1982–83). The relative effectiveness of models and prompts on energy conservation: A field experiment in a shower room. *Journal of Environmental Systems, 12,* 219–224.

Arrow, K., Bolin, B., Costanza, R., Dasgupta, P., Folke, C., Holling, C. S., Jansson, B.-O., Levin, S., Mäler, K.-G., Perrings, C., & Pimentel, D. (1995). Economic growth, carrying capacity, and the environment. *Science, 268,* 520–521.

Arrow, K. J., Cropper, M. L., Eads, G. C., Hahn, R. W., Lave, L. B., Noll, R. G., Portney, P. R., Russell, M., Schmalensee, R., Smith, V. K., & Stavins, R. N. (1996). Is there a role for benefit-cost analysis in environmental, health, and safety regulations? *Science, 272,* 221–222.

Arthur, L. M. (1977). Predicting scenic beauty of forest environment: Some empirical tests. *Forest Science, 23,* 151–160.

Arthur, L. M., Daniel, T. C., & Boster, R. S. (1977). Scenic assessment: An overview. *Landscape Planning, 4,* 109–129.

Ashley, S. (2001). A low-pollution engine solution. *Scientific American, 284,* 90–95.

Askins, R. A. (1995). Hostile landscapes and the decline of migratory songbirds. *Science, 267,* 1956–1957.

Atman, C. J., Bostrom, A., Fischhoff, B., & Morgan, M. G. (1994). Designing risk communications: Completing and correcting mental models of hazardous processes, Part I. *Risk Analysis, 14,* 779–788.

Ausubel, J. H. (1989). Regularities in technological development: An environmental view. In J. H. Ausubel & H. E. Sladovich (Eds.), *Technology and environment* (pp. 70–91). Washington, DC: National Academy Press.

Axelrod, R. (1980a). Effective choice in the prisoner's dilemma. *Journal of Conflict Resolution, 24,* 3–25.

Axelrod, R. (1980b). More effective choice in the prisoner's dilemma. *Journal of Conflict Resolution, 24,* 379–403.

Axelrod, R. (1984). *The evolution of cooperation.* New York: Basic Books.

Ayers, R. U. (1989). Industrial metabolism. In J. H. Ausubel & H. E. Sladovich (Eds.), *Technology and environment* (pp. 23–69). Washington, DC: National Academy Press.

Azar, C., & Rodhe, H. (1997). Targets for stabilization of atmospheric $CO_2$. *Science, 276, 1818–1819.*

Babbitt, B. (1995). Science: Opening the next chapter of conservation history. *Science, 267,* 1954–1955.

Bachman, W., & Katzev, R. (1982). The effects of non-contingent free bus tickets and personal commitment on urban bus ridership. *Transportation Research, 16A,* 103–108.

Bacon-Prue, A., Blount, R., Pickering, D., & Drabman, R. (1980). An evaluation of three litter control procedures—Trash receptacles, paid workers, and the marked item technique. *Journal of Applied Behavior Analysis, 13,* 165–170.

Baker, L. A., Herlihy, A. T., Kaufmann, P. R., & Eilers, J. M. (1991). Acidic lakes and streams in the United States: The role of acidic deposition. *Science, 252,* 1151–1154.

Baker, M. B. (1997). Cloud microphysics and climate. *Science, 276,* 1072–1078.

Baldassare, M., & Katz, C. (1992). The personal threat of environmental problems as predictor of environmental practices. *Environment and Behavior, 24,* 602–616.

Balderjahn, I. (1988). Personality variables and environmental attitudes as predictors of ecologically responsible consumption patterns. *Journal of Business Research, 17,* 51–56.

Baram, M., Dillon, P., & Ruffle, B. (1990). *Management of chemical risks: Corporate response to SARA Title III.* Medford, MA: Center for Environmental Management, Tufts University.

Barker, R. G. (1960). Ecology and motivation. *Nebraska symposium on motivation* (Vol. 8, pp. 1–48). Lincoln, NB: Nebraska University Press.

Barker, R. G. (1968). *Ecological psychology: Concepts and methods for studying the environment of human behavior.* Stanford, CA: Stanford University Press.

Barker, R. G., & Associates. (1978). *Habitats, environments, and human behavior.* San Francisco, CA: Jossey-Bass.

Barnett, T. P., Pierce, D. W., & Schnur, R. (2001). Detection of anthropogenic climate change in the world's oceans. *Science, 292,* 270–274.

Barnola, J. M., Raynaud, D., Korotkevich, Y. S., & Lorius, C. (1987). Vostok ice core provides 160,000 year record of atmospheric $CO_2$. *Nature, 329,* 408–414.

Barrett, E., & Brodin, G. (1955). The acidity of Scandanavian precipitation. *Tellus, 7,* 251–257.

Baskin, Y. (1993). Ecologists put some life into models of a changing world. *Science, 259,* 1694–1696.

Baskin, Y. (1994). Ecologists dare to ask: How much does diversity matter?

Batra, R., & Ray, M. L. (1983). Advertising situations: The implications of differential involvement and accompanying affect responses. In R. J. Harris (Ed.), *Information processing research in advertising* (pp. 127–151). Hillsdale, NJ: Lawrence Erlbaum Associates.

Baum, A. (1987). Toxins, technology, and natural disasters. In G. R. VandenBos & B. K. Bryant (Eds.), *Cataclysms, crises, and catastrophes* (pp. 5–53). Washington, DC: American Psychological Association.

Baum, A. (1990). Stress, intrusive imagery, and chronic stress. *Health Psychology, 9,* 653–675.

Baum, A., & Fleming, I. (1993). Implications of psychological research on stress and technological accidents. *American Psychologist, 48,* 665–672.

Baum, A., Fleming, R., & Davidson, L. (1983). Natural disaster and technological catastrophe. *Environment and Behavior, 15,* 333–354.

Baum, A., Fleming, R., & Singer, J. E. (1983). Coping with victimization by technological disaster. *Journal of Social Issues, 39,* 117–138.

Baum, A., & Gatchel, R. J. (1981). Cognitive determinants of reaction to uncontrollable events: Development of reactance and learned helplessness. *Journal of Personality and Social Psychology, 40,* 1078–1089.

Baum, A., Gatchel, R. J., & Schaeffer, M. A. (1983). Emotional, behavioral, and physiological effects of chronic stress at Three Mile Island. *Journal of Consulting and Clinical Psychology, 51,* 565–572.

Baum, A., & Greenberg, C. I. (1975). Waiting for a crowd: The behavioral and perceptual effects of anticipating crowding. *Journal of Personality and Social Psychology, 32,* 671–679.

Baum, A., & Singer, J. E. (Eds.). (1982). *Advances in environmental psychology: Volume 4. Environment and health.* Hillsdale, NJ: Lawrence Erlbaum Associates.

Baum, A., Singer, J. E., & Baum, C. S. (1982). Stress and the environment. In G. W. Evans (Ed.), *Environmental stress* (pp. 15–44). Cambridge, UK: Cambridge University Press.

Baum, A., Weiss, L. M., & Davidson, L. M. (1988, August). *Chronic stress in victimized communities.* Paper presented at the 96th annual convention of the American Psychological Association, Atlanta, GA.

Bauman, L. J., & Siegel, J. (1987). Misperception among gay men of the risk of AIDS associated with their sexual behavior. *Journal of Applied Social Psychology, 17,* 329–350.

Bazzaz, F. A., & Fajer, E. D. (1992). Plant life in a $CO_2$–rich world. *Scientific American, 266*(1), 68–74.

Beardsley, T. (1994). Hot property. *Scientific American, 270*(4), 115.

Beaton, S. P., Bishop, G. A., Zhang, Y., Ashbaugh, L. L., Lawson, D. R., & Stedman, D. H. (1995). On-road vehicle emissions: Regulations, costs, and benefits. *Science, 268,* 991–992.

Beck, D. (1992). U.S. DOE's Office of Technology Development solves environmental restoration and waste management problems. *Proceedings of the Human Factors Society 36th annual meeting* (pp. 633–635). Santa Monica, CA: Human Factors Society.

Becker, L. J. (1978). Joint effect of feedback and goal-setting on performance: A field study of residential energy conservation. *Journal of Applied Psychology, 63,* 428–433.

Becker, L. J., & Seligman, C. (1978). Reducing air-conditioning waste by signalling that it is cool outside. *Personality and Social Psychology Bulletin, 4,* 412–415.

Becker, L. J., Seligman, C., Fazio, R. H., & Darley, J. M. (1981). Relating attitudes to residential energy use. *Environment and Behavior, 13,* 590–609.

Beckerman, W. (1992). Economic growth and the environment. Whose growth? Whose environment? *World Development, 20,* 481–496.

Beckerman, W. (1994). "Sustainable development": Is it a useful concept? *Environmental Values, 3,* 191–210.

Bedau, H. A. (1991). Ethical aspects of environmental decision making. In R. A. Chechile & S. Carlisle (Eds.), *Environmental decision making: A multidisciplinary perspective* (pp. 176–194). New York: Van Nostrand Reinhold.

Belk, R. W., Bahn, K. D., & Mayer, R. N. (1982). Developmental recognition of consumption symbolism. *Journal of Consumer Research, 9,* 4–17.

Bell, P. A., Fisher, J. D., Baum, A., & Greene, T. C. (1990). *Environmental psychology.* Fort Worth, TX: Holt, Rinehart & Winston.

Bell, P. A., Peterson, T. R., & Hautaluoma, J. E. (1989). The effect of punishment probability on overconsumption and stealing in a simulated commons. *Journal of Applied Social Psychology, 19,* 1483–1495.

Belsie, L. (1990, July 18). Recycling rebounds across America. *Christian Science Monitor,* p. 8.

Berkes, F., Feeney, D., McCay, B. J., & Acheson, J. M. (1989). The benefits of the common. *Nature, 340,* 91–93.

Berlyne, D. E. (1975). Extension to Indian subjects of a study of exploratory and verbal responses to visual patterns. *Journal of Cross-Cultural Psychology, 6,* 316–330.

Berners-Lee, T., Hendler, J., & Lassila, O. (2001). The semantic web. *Scientific American, 284*(5), 34–43.

Bernstein, P. L. (1996). *Against the gods: The remarkable story of risk.* New York: Wiley.

Bertine, K. K., & Goldberg, E. D. (1971). Fossil fuel combustion and the major sedimentary cycle. *Science, 173,* 233–235.

Bettman, J. R. (1979). *An information processing theory of consumer choice.* Reading, MA: Addison-Wesley.

Bettman, J. R. (1986). Consumer psychology. *Annual Review of Psychology, 37,* 257–289.

Bettmann, O. L. (1974). *The good old days—They were terrible!* New York: Random House.

Bevington, R., & Rosenfeld, A. H. (1990). Energy for buildings and homes. *Scientific American, 263*(3), 76–86.

Bhagwati, J. (1993). The case for free trade. *Scientific American, 269*(5), 42–49.

Bickman, L. (1972). Environmental attitudes and actions. *Journal of Social Psychology, 87,* 323–324.

Binney, S. E., Mason, R., Martsolf, S., & Detweiler, J. H. (1996). Credibility, public trust, and the transport of radioactive waste through local communities. *Environment and Behavior, 28,* 283–302.

Birjulin, A. A., Smith, J. M., & Bell, P. A. (1993). Monetary reward, verbal reinforcement, and harvest strategy of others in the commons dilemma. *Journal of Social Psychology, 133,* 207–214.

Bishop, D. J., Giles, C. R., & Das, S. R. (2001). The rise of optical switching. *Scientific American, 284*(1), 88–96.

Bittle, R. G., Valesano, R. M., & Thaler, G. M. (1979–1980). The effects of daily feedback on residential electricity usage as a function of usage level and type of feedback information. *Journal of Environmental Systems, 9,* 275–287.

Black, J. S., Stern, P. C., & Elworth J. T. (1985). Personal and contextual influences on household energy adaptations. *Journal of Applied Psychology, 70,* 3–21.

Blair, B. G., Feiveson, H. A., & von Hippel, F. N. (1997). Taking nuclear weapons off hair-trigger alert. *Scientific American, 277*(5), 74–81.

Bleviss, D. L., & Walzer, P. (1990). Energy for motor vehicles. *Scientific American, 263*(3), 102–109.

Block, L. J., & Keller, P. A. (1995). When to accentuate the negative: The effects of perceived efficacy and message framing on intentions to perform a health-related behavior. *Journal of Marketing Research, 32,* 192–203.

Bloom, D. E. (1995). International public opinion on the environment. *Science, 269,* 354–358.

Blumenthal, D. J. (2001). Routing packets with light. *Scientific American, 284*(1), 97–99.

Bogner, M. S. (Ed.). (1994). *Human error in medicine.* Hillsdale, NJ: Lawrence Erlbaum Associates.

Bolin, B. (1998). The Kyoto negotiations on climate change: A science perspective. *Science, 279,* 330–331.

Bolin, B., & Doos, B. R. (1986). *The greenhouse effect: Climatic change and ecosystems.* New York: Wiley.

Bongaarts, J. (1994a). Can the growing human population feed itself? *Scientific American, 270*(3), 36–42.

Bongaarts, J. (1998). Demographic consequences of declining fertility. *Science, 282,* 419–420.

Bosselmann, P., & Craik, H. K. (1989). Perceptual simulations of environments. In R. Bechtal, R. Marans, & W. Michelson (Eds.), *Methods in environmental and behavioral research* (pp. 162–190). New York: Van Nostrand Reinhold.

Bowles, I. A., Rice, R. E., Mittermeier, R. A., & da Fonseca, G. A. B. (1998). Logging and tropical forest conservation. *Science, 280,* 1899–1900.

Boyd, R. (1988). Is the repeated prisoner's dilemma a good model of reciprocal altruism? *Ethology and Sociobiology, 9,* 211–222.

Bradbury, J. A. (1989). The policy implications of differing concepts of risk. *Science, Technology, and Human Values, 14,* 380–399.

Bradley, R. (2000). 1000 years of climate change. *Science, 288,* 1353–1355.

Bratt, C. (1999). Consumers' environmental behavior: Generalized sector based, or compensatory? *Environment and Behavior, 31,* 28–44.

Bray, F. (1994). Agriculture for developing nations. *Scientific American, 271*(1), 30–37.

Brechner, K. C., & Linder, D. E. (1981). A social trap analysis of energy distribution systems. In A. Baum & J. E. Singer (Eds.), *Advances in environmental psychology: Vol. 3. Energy conservation: Psychological perspectives* (pp. 27–51). Hillsdale, NJ: Lawrence Erlbaum Associates.

Briffa, K. R., & Osborn, T. J. (1999). Seeing the wood from the trees. *Science, 284,* 926–927

Brklacich, M., Bryant, C. R., & Smit, B. (1991). Review and appraisal of concept of sustainable food production systems. *Environmental Management, 15,* 1–14.

Brody, C. J. (1984). Differences by sex in support for nuclear power. *Social Forces, 63,* 209–228.

Bronfenbrenner, U. (1977). Toward an experimental ecology of human development. *American Psychologist, 32,* 513–531.

Bronfenbrenner, U. (1979). *The ecology of human development.* Cambridge, MA: Harvard University Press.

Brown, I., & Inouye, D. K. (1978). Learned helplessness through modeling: The role of perceived similarity in competence. *Journal of Personality and Social Psychology, 36,* 900–908.

Brown, K. (2001). Seeds of concern. *Scientific American, 285*(1), 52–57.

Brown, K. S. (1999). Bright future—or brief flare—for renewable energy? *Science, 285,* 678–680.

Brown, L. R. (1991). The battle for the planet. In A. B. Wolbrast (Ed.), *Environment in peril* (pp. 154–187). Washington, DC: Smithsonian Institution Press.

Brown, L. R., & Kane, H. (1994). *Full house: Reassessing the earth's population carrying capacity.* New York: Norton.

Brown, P. J., & Haas, G. E. (1980). Wilderness recreation experiences: The Rawah case. *Journal of Leisure Research, 12,* 229–241.

Brown, T. C., & Daniel, T. C. (1987). Context effects in perceived environmental quality assessment: Scene selection and landscape quality ratings. *Journal of Environmental Psychology, 7,* 233–250.

Browne, M. W. (1989, March 7). In protecting the atmosphere, choices are costly and complex. *New York Times,* Section C, p. 1.

Brune, W. H., Anderson, J. G., Toohey, D. W., Fahey, D. W., Kawa, S. R., Jones, R. L., McKenna, D. S., & Poole, L. R. (1991). The potential for ozone depletion in the Arctic polar stratosphere. *Science, 252,* 1260–1266.

Bryant, D., Nielsen, D., & Tangley, L. (1997). *The last frontier forests: Ecosystems and economics on the edge.* Washington, DC: World Resources Institute.

Budin, W. (1995). Letter to editor re radioactive waste at Ward Valley. *Science, 269,* 1655–1656.

Budyko, M. I., Ronovn, A. B., & Yanshin, A. L. (1987). *History of the Earth's atmosphere.* Berlin: Springer-Verlag.

Buhyoff, G. J., & Leuschner, W. A. (1978). Estimating psychological disutility from damaged forest stands. *Forest Science, 24,* 424–432.

Buhyoff, G. J., & Riesenman, M. F. (1979). Experimental manipulation of dimensionality in landscape preference judgments: A quantitative validation. *Leisure Sciences, 2,* 221–238.

Buhyoff, G. J., & Wellman, J. D. (1980). The specification of a non-linear psychophysical function for visual landscape dimensions. *Journal of Leisure Research, 12,* 257–272.

Buhyoff, G. J., Wellman, J. D., & Daniel, T. C. (1982). Predicting scenic quality for mountain pine beetle and western spruce budworm damaged vistas. *Forest Science, 28,* 827–838.

Buhyoff, G. J., Wellman, J. D., Harvey, H., & Fraser, R. A. (1978). Landscapes architects' interpretations of people's landscape preferences. *Journal of Environmental Management, 6,* 255–262.

Burges, S. J. (1979). Water resource systems planning in the USA: 1776–1976. *Journal of the Water Resources Planning and Management Division, ASCE, 105* (WR1), 91–111.

Burgess, R. L., Clark, R. N., & Hendee, J. C. (1971). An experimental analysis of anti-litter procedures. *Journal of Applied Behavior Analysis, 4,* 71–75.

Burn, S. M. (1991). Social psychology and the stimulation of recycling behaviors: The block leader approach. *Journal of Applied Social Psychology, 21,* 611–629.

Burn, S. M., & Oskamp, S. (1986). Increasing community recycling with persuasive communication and public commitment. *Journal of Applied Social Psychology, 16,* 29–41.

Burner, R. A., & Lasaga, A. C. (1989). Modeling the geochemical carbon cycle. *Scientific American, 260*(3), 74–81.

Burton, I., Kates, R. W., & White, G. R. (1978). *The environment as hazard.* New York: Oxford University Press.

Bush, V. (1945, July). As we think. *The Atlantic Monthly.* (pp. 101–108).

Buttel, F. H., Murdock, S. H., Feistritz, F. L., & Hamm, R. R. (1987). Rural environments. In E. H. Zube & G. T. Moore (Eds.), *Advances in environment, behavior, and design* (Vol. 1, pp. 107–128). New York: Plenum.

Byrne, J., Rich, D., Tannian, F. X., & Wang, Y. (1985). Rethinking the household energy crisis: The role of information in household energy conservation. *Marriage and Family Review, 9,* 83–113.

Cacioppo, J. T., & Petty, R. E. (1984). The elaboration likelihood model of persuasion. *Advances in Consumer Research, 11,* 673–675.

Caldwell, J. C., & Caldwell, P. (1990). High fertility and sub-Saharan Africa. *Scientific American, 262*(5), 118–125.

Callendar, G. S. (1938). The artificial production of carbon dioxide and its influence on temperature. *Quarterly Journal of the Royal Meteorological Society, 64,* 223–237.

Callendar, G. S. (1949). Can carbon dioxide influence climate? *Weather, 4,* 310–314.

Calvert, J. G., Heywood, J. B., Sawyer, R. F., & Seinfeld, J. H. (1993). Achieving acceptable air quality: Some reflections on controlling vehicle emissions. *Science, 261,* 37–45.

Campbell, C. J., & Laherrère, J. H. (1998). The end of cheap oil. *Scientific American, 278*(3), 78–83.

Canter, D. (1983a). The purposive evaluation of places: A facet approach. *Environment and Behavior, 15,* 659–698.

Canter, D. (1983b). Way-finding and signposting: Penance or prosthesis? In R. Easterby (Ed.), *Information design: The design and evaluation of signs and printed material* (pp. 245–264). Chichester, UK: Wiley.

Carlson, A. A. (1977). On the possibility of quantifying scenic beauty. *Landscape Planning, 4,* 131–172.

Carp, F. M. (1987). Environment and aging. In D. Stokols & I. Altman (Eds.), *Handbook of environmental psychology* (Vol. 1, pp. 329–360). New York: Wiley.

Carpenter, S. R., Chisholm, S. W., Krebs, C. J., Schindler, D. W., & Wright, R. F. (1995). Ecosystem experiments. *Science, 269,* 324–327.

Carson, R. (1962). *Silent spring.* Boston, MA: Houghton-Mifflin.

Carter, J. L. (1977, November). Saving energy, saving dollars: How young couples—North and South—do it. *Redbook,* pp. 118, 121, 184–186, 188.

Cartmill, M. (1993, June). The Bambi syndrome. *Natural History,* pp. 6–12.

Cary, J. W. (1992). Belief and behavior related to improved land management. *Proceedings of the 7th International Soil Conservation Organization Conference, 2,* 377–383.

Cary, J. W. (1993). The nature of symbolic beliefs and environmental behavior in a rural setting. *Environment and Behavior, 25,* 555–576.

Cass, B. C., & Edney, J. J. (1978). The commons dilemma: A simulation testing resource visibility and territorial division. *Human Ecology, 6,* 371–386.

Castleman, P. A., Whitehead, S. F., Sher, L. D., Hantman, L. M., & Massey, L. D., Jr. (1974). *An assessment of the utility of computer aids in the physician's office* (Report No. 3096). Cambridge, MA: Bolt Beranek & Newman.

Catalano, R. (1979). *Health, behavior, and the community: An ecological perspective.* Elmsford, NY: Pergamon.

Cess, R. D., Zhang, M. H., Minnis, P., Corsetti, L., Dutton, E. G., Forgan, B. W., Garber, D. P., Gates, W. L., Hack, J. J., Harrison, E. F., Jing, X., Kiehl, J. T., Long, C. N., Morcrette, J.-J., Potter, G. L., Ramanathan, V., Subasilar, B., Whitlock, C. H., Young, D. F., & Zhou, Y. (1995). Absorption of solar radiation by clouds: Observations versus models. *Science, 267,* 496-499.

Cess, R. D., Zhang, M.-H., Potter, G. L., Barker, H. W., Colman, R. A., Dazlich, D. A., Del Genio, A. D., Esch, M., Fraser, J. R., Galin, V. Gates, W. L., Hack, J. J., Ingram, W. J., Kiehl, J. T., Lacis, A. A., Le Treut, H., Li, Z.-X., Liang, X.-Z., Mahfouf, J.-F., McAvaney, B. J., Meleshko, V. P., Morcrette, J.-J., Randall, D. A., Roeckner, E., Royer, J.-F., Sokolov, A. P., Sporyshev, P. V., Taylor, K. E., Wang, W.-C., Wetherald, R. T.

(1993). Uncertainties in carbon dioxide radiative forcing in atmospheric general circulation models. *Science, 262,* 1252–1255.

Cezeaux, A. (1991). East meets West to look for toxic waste sites. *Science, 251,* 620–621.

Chaiken, S. (1987). The heuristic model of persuasion. In M. P. Zanna, J. M. Olson, & C. P. Herman (Eds.), *Social influence: The Ontario Symposium* (pp. 3–39). Hillsdale, NJ: Lawrence Erlbaum Associates.

Chaiken, S., Liberman, A., & Eagly, A. H. (1989). Heuristic and systematic information processing within and beyond the persuasion context. In J. S. Uleman & J. A. Bargh (Eds.), *Unintended thought: Limits of awareness, intention, and control* (pp. 212–252). New York: Guilford.

Chaiken, S., & Stangor, C. (1987). Attitudes and attitude change. *Annual Review of Psychology, 38,* 575–630.

Chameides, W. L., Saylor, R. D., & Cowling, E. B. (1997). Ozone pollution in the rural United States and the new NAAQS. *Science, 276,* 916.

Chandler, W. U., Makarov, A. A., & Dadi, C. (1990). Energy for the Soviet Union, Eastern Europe, and China. *Scientific American, 263*(3), 120–126.

Chapman, C., & Risley, T. R. (1974). Anti-litter procedures in an urban high-density area. *Journal of Applied Behavior Analysis, 7,* 377–384.

Chapman, D. (1991). Letter to the editor (Air pollution benefit-cost assessment). *Science, 253,* 608.

Charlson, R. J., & Wigley, T. M. L. (1994). Sulfate aerosol and climate change. *Scientific American, 270*(2), 48–57.

Chazdon, R. L. (1998). Tropical forests—Log 'em or leave 'em? *Science, 281,* 1295–1296.

Chechile, R. A. (1991a). Introduction to environmental decision making. In R. A. Chechile & S. Carlisle (Eds.), *Environmental decision making: A multidisciplinary perspective* (pp. 1–13). New York: Van Nostrand Reinhold.

Chechile, R. A. (1991b). Probability, utility, and decision trees in environmental decision analysis. In R. A. Chechile & S. Carlisle (Eds.), *Environmental decision making: A multidisciplinary perspective* (pp. 64–91). New York: Van Nostrand Reinhold.

Chechile, R. A., & Carlisle, S. (Eds.). (1991). *Environmental decision making: A multidisciplinary perspective.* New York: Van Nostrand Reinhold.

Cherfas, J. (1991). Skeptics and visionaries examine energy saving. *Science, 251,* 154–156.

Chivian, E., McCally, M., Hu, H., & Haines, A. (1993). *Critical condition: Human health and the environment.* Cambridge, MA: The MIT Press.

Cialdini, R. B. (1989). Littering: When every litter bit hurts. In R. E. Rice & C. K. Atkin (Eds.), *Public communication campaigns* (2nd ed., pp. 221–223), London: Sage.

Cialdini, R. B., Kallgren, C. A., & Reno, R. R. (1991). A focus theory of normative conduct: A theoretical refinement and re-evaluation. *Advances in Experimental Social Psychology, 24,* 201–234.

Cialdini, R. B., Reno, R. R., & Kallgren, C. A. (1990). A focus theory of normative conduct: Recycling the concept of norms to reduce littering in public places. *Journal of Personality and Social Psychology, 58,* 1015–1026.

Cifuentes, L., Borja-Aburto, V. H., Gouveia, N., Thurston, G., & Davis, D. L. (2001). Hidden health benefits of greenhouse gas mitigation. *Science, 293,* 1257–1259.

Clamp, P. (1976). Evaluating English landscapes—Some recent developments. *Environment and Planning, 8,* 79–92.

Clark, R. N., Burgess, R. L., & Hendee, J. C. (1972). The development of anti-litter behavior in a forest campground. *Journal of Applied Behavior Analysis, 5,* 1–5.

Clark, H., & Manzo, L. (1987). Community gardens: Factors that influence participation. In D. Lawrence, R. Habe, A. Hacker, & D. Sherrod (Eds.), *Proceedings of the 19th*

*Annual Environmental Design Research Association Conference* (pp. 57–62). Washington, DC: Environmental Design Research Association.

Clark, W. C. (1989). Managing planet earth. *Scientific American, 261*(3), 47–54.

Cobern, M. K., Porter, B. E., Leeming, F. C., & Dwyer, W. O. (1995). The effect of commitment on adoption and diffusion of grass recycling. *Environment and Behavior, 27,* 213–232.

Cogbill, C. V., & Likens, G. E. (1974). Acid precipitation in the northeastern United States. *Water Resources Research, 10,* 1133–1137.

Cohen, J. (1994). California's disposal plan goes nowhere fast. *Science, 263,* 912.

Cohen, J. E. (1995). Population growth and earth's human carrying capacity. *Science, 269,* 341–346.

Cohen, S. (1984). Defusing the toxic time bomb: Federal hazardous waste programs. In N. J. Vig & M. E. Kraft (Eds.), *Environmental policy in the 1980s: Reagan's new agenda* (pp. 273–291). Washington, DC: Congressional Quarterly Press.

Cohen, S., Evans, G. W., Stokols, D., & Krantz, D. S. (1986). *Behavior, health and environmental stress.* New York: Plenum.

Cohen, S., & Spacapan, S. (1984). The social psychology of noise. In D. M. Jones & A. J. Chapman (Eds.), *Noise and society* (pp. 221–245). New York: Wiley.

Cohrssen, J. J., & Covello, V. T. (1989). *Risk analysis: A guide to principles and methods for analyzing health and environmental risks.* Washington, DC: U.S. Council on Environmental Quality.

Coltrane, S., Archer, D., & Aronson, E. (1986). The social-psychological foundations of successful energy conservation programmes. *Energy Policy, 14,* 133–148.

Commoner, B. (1991). The failure of the environmental effort. In A. B. Wolbrast (Ed.), *Environment in peril* (pp. 38–63). Washington, DC: Smithsonian Institution Press.

Compton, W. D., & Gjostein, N. A. (1986). Materials for ground transportation. *Scientific American, 255*(4), 92–100.

Condelli, L., Archer, D., Aronson, E., Curbow, B., McLeod, B., Pettigrew, T., White, L., & Yates, S. (1984). Improving utility conservation programs: Outcomes, interventions, and evaluations. *Energy, 9,* 485–494.

Cone, J. D., & Hayes, S. C. (1980). *Environmental problems/behavioral solutions.* Monterey, CA: Brooks/Cole.

Conner, J. (1988). Empty skies: Where have all the songbirds gone. *Harrowsmith, 3*(16), 35–45.

Constanzo, M., Archer, D., Aronson, L., & Pettigrew, T. (1986). Energy conservation behavior: The difficult path from information to action. *American Psychologist, 41,* 521–528.

Cook, J. (1983). Citizen response in a neighborhood under threat. *American Journal of Community Psychology, 11,* 459–471.

Cook, S. W., & Berrenberg, J. L. (1981). Approaches to encouraging conservation behavior: A review and conceptual framework. *Journal of Social Issues, 37*(2), 73–107.

Cooper, J., & Croyle, R. T. (1984). Attitudes and attitude change. *Annual Review of Psychology*, 35, 395–426.

Cortese, A. D. (1993). Introduction: Human health, risk, and the environment. In E. Chivian, M. McCally, H. Hu, & A. Haines (Eds.), *Critical condition: Human health and the environment* (pp. 1–11). Cambridge, MA: MIT Press.

Costanza, R. (Ed.). (1992). *Ecological economics: The science and management of sustainability.* New York: Columbia University Press.

Costanza, R., d'Arge, R., de Groot, R., Farber, S., Grasso, M., Hannon, B., Limburg, K., Naeem, S., O'Neill, R. V., Paruelo, J., Raskin, R. G., & Sutton, P. (1997). The value of the world's ecosystem services and natural capital. *Nature, 387,* 253–260.

Costanzo, M., Archer, D., Aronson, E., & Pettigrew, T. (1986). Energy conservation behavior: The difficult path from information to action. *American Psychologist, 41,* 521–528.

Couch, J. V., Garber, T., & Karpus, L. (1978–1979). Response maintenance and paper recycling. *Journal of Environmental Systems, 8,* 127–137.

Cousteau, J. (1991). A global view of environmental problems. In A. B. Wolbrast (Ed.), *Environment in peril* (pp. 96–109). Washington, DC: Smithsonian Institution Press.

Covello, V. T., & Johnson, B. B. (1987). The social and cultural construction of risk: Issues, methods, and case studies. In B. B. Johnson & V. T. Covello (Eds.), *The social and cultural construction of risk* (pp. vii–xiii). Dordrecht, Netherlands: D. Reidel.

Cox, P. A., & Balick, M. J. (1994). The ethnobotanical approach to drug discovery. *Scientific American, 270*(6), 82–87.

Cox, S. J. (1985). No tragedy on the commons. *Environmental Ethics, 7,* 49–61.

Cox, V. C., Paulus, P. B., McCain, G., & Karlovac, M. (1982). The relationship between crowding and health. In A. Baum & J. E. Singer (Eds.), *Advances in environmental psychology: Volume 4. Environment and health* (pp. 271–294). Hillsdale, NJ: Lawrence Erlbaum Associates.

Coye, M. J. (1985). The health aspects of agricultural production: The health of agricultural workers. *Journal of Public Health Policy, 6,* 349–370.

Craig, C. S., & McCann, J. M. (1977). *Marketing energy conservation to residential consumers of electricity: Report to the Federal Energy Administration.* Ithica, NY: Graduate School of Business and Public Administration, Cornell University.

Craig, C. S., & McCann, J. M. (1978). Assessing communication effects on energy conservation. *Journal of Consumer Research, 5,* 82–88.

Craik, K. H. (1970). Environmental psychology. In K. H. Craik, B. Kleinmuntz, R. L. Rosnow, R. Rosenthal, J. R. Cheyne, & R. W. Walters (Eds.), *New directions in psychology* (pp. 1–121). New York: Holt, Rinehart & Winston.

Craik, K. H. (1973). Environmental psychology. *Annual Review of Psychology, 24,* 403–422.

Craik, K. H. (1981). Environmental assessment and situational analysis. In D. Magnusson (Ed.), *Toward a psychology of situations* (pp. 37–48). Hillsdale, NJ: Lawrence Erlbaum Associates.

Craik, K. H., & Zube, E. H. (Eds.). (1976). *Perceiving environmental quality.* New York: Plenum.

Creer, R., Gray, R., & Treshow, M. (1970). Differential responses to air pollution as an environmental health problem. *Journal of the Air Pollution Control Association, 20,* 814–818.

Crossen, P. R., & Rosenberg, N. J. (1989). Strategies for agriculture. *Scientific American, 261*(3), 128–135.

Crowfoot, J. E., & Wondolleck, J. M. (1991). *Community involvement in conflict resolution.* Washington, DC: Island Press.

Crowley, T. J. (2000). Causes of climate change over the past 1000 years. *Science, 289,* 270–277.

Crowley, T. J., & North, G. R. (1991). *Paleoclimatology.* New York: Oxford University Press.

Crutzen, P. J. (1970). The influence of nitrogen oxides on the atmospheric ozone content. *Quarterly Journal of the Royal Meteorological Society, 96,* 320–325.

Crutzen, P. J., & Andreae, M. O. (1990). Biomass burning in the tropics: Impact on atmosphere chemistry and biogeochemical cycles. *Science, 250,* 1669–1678.

Crutzen, P. J., Grooß, J.-U., Brühl, C., Müller, R., & Russell, J. M., III. (1995). A reevaluation of the ozone budget with HALOE UARS data: No evidence for the ozone deficit. *Science, 268,* 705–708.

Csikszentmihalyi, M., & Rochberg-Halton, E. (1981). *The meaning of things: Domestic symbols and the self.* New York: Cambridge University Press.

Cvetkovich, G., & Earle, T. C. (Eds.). (1992). Public responses to environmental hazards. *Journal of Social Issues, 48*(4), 1–187.

Daamen, D. D., Staats, H., Wilke, H. A. M., & Engelen, M. (2001). Improving environmental behavior in companies: The effectiveness of tailored versus nontailored interventions. *Environment and Behavior, 33,* 229–248.

Dahl-Jensen, D. (2000). The Greenland ice sheet reacts. *Science, 289,* 404–405.

Daily, C. C. (1995). Restoring value to the world's degraded lands. *Science, 269,* 350–354.

Daly, H. E. (1993). The perils of free trade. *Scientific American, 269*(5), 50–57.

Daniel, T. C. (1976). Criteria for development and application of perceived environmental quality indices. In E. H. Zube & K. Craik (Eds.), *Perceived environmental quality indices* (pp. 27–45). New York: Plenum.

Daniel, T. C. (1987). The legendary beauty of the Rocky Mountain region: Is it more than skin deep? *Journal of the History of the Behavioral Sciences, 24,* 18–23.

Daniel, T. C. (1990). Measuring the quality of the natural environment—A psychological approach. *American Psychologist, 45*(5), 633–637.

Daniel, T. C., Anderson, L. M., Schroeder, H. W., & Wheeler, L. W., III. (1977). Mapping the scenic beauty of forest landscapes. *Leisure Sciences, 1,* 35–53.

Daniel, T. C., & Boster, R. S. (1976). *Measuring landscape aesthetics the scenic beauty estimation method* (USDA Forest Service Research Paper, 167). Fort Collins, CO: Rocky Mountain Forest and Range Experiment Station.

Daniel, T. C., & Schroeder, H. W. (1979). Scenic beauty estimation model: Predicting perceived beauty of forest landscapes. In *Our national landscape* (USDA Forest Service Technical Report PSW–35, pp. 514–523). Berkeley, CA: Pacific Southwest Forest and Range Experiment Station.

Daniel, T. C., & Vining, J. (1983). Methodological issues in the assessment of landscape quality. In I. Altman & J. F. Wohlwill (Eds.), *Behavior and the natural environment* (pp. 39–84). New York: Plenum.

Daniel, T. C., Wheeler, L., Boster, R. S., & Best, P. (1973). Quantitative evaluation of landscapes: An application of signal detection analysis to forest management alterations. *Man-Environment Systems, 3,* 330–344.

Daniels, J. E. (Ed.). (1992). *1993 earth journal: Environmental almanac and resource directory.* Boulder, CO: Buzzworm Books.

Darley, J. M. (1978). Energy conservation techniques as innovations and their diffusion. *Energy Building, 1,* 339–343.

Darley, J. M., & Beniger, J. R. (1981). Diffusion of energy-conserving innovations. *Journal of Social Issues, 37,* 150–171.

Dasgupta, P. S. (1995). Population, poverty and the local environment. *Scientific American, 272*(2), 40–45.

Davidson, L. M., & Baum, A. (1986). Chronic stress and post-traumatic stress disorders. *Journal of Consulting and Clinical Psychology, 54,* 303–308.

Davidson, L. M., Fleming, I., & Baum, A. (1986). Post-traumatic stress as a function of chronic stress and toxic exposure. In C. P. Figley (Ed.), *Trauma and its wake* (pp. 55–77). New York: Brunner/Mazel.

Davidson-Cummings, L. (1977). Voluntary strategies in the environmental movement: Recycling as cooptation. *Journal of Voluntary Action Research, 6,* 153–160.

Davis, C. E., & Lester, J. P. (Eds.). (1988). *Dimensions of hazardous waste politics and policy.* Westport, CT: Greenwood.

Davis, G. R. (1990). Energy for planet earth. *Scientific American, 263*(3), 54–62.

Dawes, R. M. (1975). Formal models of dilemmas in social decision-making. In M. Kaplan & S. Schwartz (Eds.), *Human judgment and decision processes* (pp. 87–107). New York: Academic Press.

Dawes, R. M. (1980). Social dilemmas. *Annual Review of Psychology, 31,* 169–193.

Dawes, R. M. (1988). *Rational choice in an uncertain world.* New York: Harcourt Brace Jovanovich.

Dawes, R. M., van de Kragt, A. J. C., & Orbell, J. M. (1988). Not me or thee but we: The importance of group identity in eliciting cooperation in dilemma situations: Experimental manipulations. *Acta Psychologica, 68,* 83–97.

Deci, E. L. (1975). *Intrinsic motivation.* New York: Plenum.

Deci, E. L., & Ryan, R. M. (1985). *Intrinsic motivation and self-determinism in human behavior.* New York: Plenum.

DeCicco, J., & Ross, M. (1994). Improving automotive efficiency. *Scientific American, 271*(6), 52–57.

Deevey, E. S. (1960). The human population. *Scientific American, 203*(3), 194–203.

Deffeyes, K. S. (2001). *Hubbert's peak: The impending world oil shortage.* Princeton, NJ: Princeton University Press.

de Haven-Smith, L. (1988). Environmental belief systems: Public opinion on land use regulation in Florida. *Environment and Behavior, 20,* 176–199.

Deighton, J. (1983). How to solve problems that don't matter: Some heuristics for uninvolved thinking. *Advances in Consumer Research, 10,* 314–319.

DeKay, M. L., & McClelland, G. H. (1996). Probability and utility components of endangered species preservation programs. *Journal of Experimental Psychology: Applied, 2,* 60–83.

DeLeon, I. G., & Fuqua, R. W. (1995). The effects of public commitment and group feedback on curbside recycling. *Environment and Behavior, 27,* 233–250.

Delprata, D. J. (1977). Prompting electrical energy conservation in commercial users. *Environment and Behavior, 9,* 433–440.

DeMaio, T. J. (1984). Social desirability and survey measurement: A review. In C. F. Turner & E. Martin (Des.), *Surveying subjective phenomena* (pp. 257–282). New York: Russel Sage.

Deming, D. (1995). Climatic warming in North America: Analysis of borehole temperatures. *Science, 268,* 1576–1577.

Denning, P. J. (1989). The science of computing: Worldnet. *American Scientist, 77,* 432–434.

Dennis, M. L., & Sonderstrom, E. J. (1988). Application of social psychological and evaluation research: Lessons from energy information programs. *Evaluation and Program Planning, 11,* 77–84.

Dennis, M. L., Soderstrom, E. J., Koncinski, W. S., Jr., & Cavanaugh, B. (1990). Effective dissemination of energy-related information: Applying social psychology and evaluation research. *American Psychologist, 45,* 1109–1117.

De Oliver, M. (1999). Attitudes and inaction: A case study of the manifest demographics of urban water conservation. *Environment and Behavior, 31,* 372–394.

Derksen, L., & Gartrell, J. (1993). The social contexts of recycling. *American Sociological Review, 58,* 434–442.

Dertouzos, M. (1998). *What will be: How the new world of information will change our lives.* San Francisco: Harper.

Deslauriers, B. C., & Everett, P. B. (1977). Effects of intermittent and continuous token reinforcement on bus ridership. *Journal of Applied Psychology, 62,* 369–375.

Desvogues, W. H., & Smith, N. K. (1983). *Benefit-cost assessment handbook for water programs* (Vol. 3). Durham, NC: Research Triangle Institute.

DeVries, H., & Brug, J. (1999). Computer tailored interventions motivating people to adopt health promoting behaviours: Introduction to a new approach. *Patient Education and Counseling, 36,* 99–105.

DeYoung, R. (1985–1986). Encouraging environmentally appropriate behavior: The role of intrinsic motivation. *Journal of Environmental Systems, 15,* 281–292.

DeYoung, R. (1986). Some psychological aspects of recycling: The structure of conservation satisfactions. *Environment and Behavior, 18,* 435–449.

DeYoung, R. (1989). Exploring the difference between recyclers and non-recyclers: The role of information. *Journal of Environmental Systems, 18,* 341–351.

DeYoung, R. (1993). Changing behavior and making it stick: The conceptualization and management of conservation behavior. *Environment and Behavior, 25,* 485–505.

DeYoung, R., Duncan, A., Frank, J., Gill, N., Rothman, S., Shenot, J., Shotkin, A., & Zweizig, M. (1993). Promoting source reduction behavior: The role of motivational information. *Environment and Behavior, 25,* 70–85.

DeYoung, R., & Kaplan, S. (1985–1986). Conservation behavior and the structure of satisfactions. *Journal of Environmental Systems, 15,* 233–242.

Dickinson, R. E., & Cicerone, R. J. (1986). Future global warming from atmospheric trace gases. *Nature, 319,* 109–115.

Dickson, D., & Marshall, E. (1989). Europe recognizes the ozone threat. *Science, 243,* 1279.

Dietz, T., & Rosa, E. A. (1997). Effects of population and affluence on $CO_2$ emissions. *Proceedings of the National Academy of Sciences, 94,* 175–179.

Ditto, P. H., Jemmott, J. B., & Darley, J. M. (1988). Appraising the threat of illness: A mental representational approach. *Health Psychology, 7,* 183–201.

Ditto, P. H., & Lopez, D. F. (1992). Motivated skepticism: Use of differential decision criteria for preferred and nonpreferred conclusions. *Journal of Personality and Social Psychology, 63,* 568–584.

Dixon, J. A., & Hufschmidt, M. M. (Eds.). (1986). *Economic valuation techniques for the environment.* Baltimore, MD: Johns Hopkins University Press.

Dobson, A. P., Bradshaw, A. D., & Baker, A. J. M. (1997). Hopes for the future: Restoration ecology and conservation biology. *Science, 277,* 515–522.

Donohue, G. A., Olien, C. N., & Tichenor, P. J. (1974). Communities, pollution, and the fight for survival. *Journal of Environmental Education, 6,* 29–37.

Dorf, R. C. (1974). *Technology and society.* San Francisco: Boyd & Fraser.

Douglas, M., & Wildavsky, A. (1982). *Risk and culture.* Berkeley, CA: University of California Press.

Dowlatabadi, H., & Morgan, M. G. (1993). Integrated assessment of climate change. *Science, 259,* 1813, 1932.

Downs, R. M., & Stea, D. (1977). *Maps in minds: Reflections on cognitive mapping.* New York: Harper & Row.

Doyle, R. (1997). Access to safe drinking water. *Scientific American, 277*(5), 38.

Doyle, R. (2001). In a dry land. *Scientific American, 285*(1), 30.

Dozier, D. M., & Rice, R. E. (1984). Rival theories of electronic newsreading. In R. E. Rice (Ed.), *The new media: Communication, research, and technology.* London: Sage.

Drablös, D., & Tollan, A. (Eds.). (1980). *Ecological impact of acid precipitation* (International conference proceedings). Oslo-Aas, Norway: SNSF Project.

Driver, B. L., & Brown, P. J. (1975). A social-psychological definition of recreation demand, with implications for planning. In *Assessing demand for outdoor recreation* (Appendix A). Washington, DC: National Academy Press.

Driver, B. L., & Brown, P. J. (1983). Contributions of behavioral scientists to recreation resource management. In I. Altman & J. F. Wohlwill (Eds.), *Behavior and the natural environment* (pp. 307–339). New York: Plenum.

Driver, B. L., & Cooksey, R. W. (1977). Preferred psychological outcomes of recreational fishing. In R. A. Barnhart & T. D. Roelofs (Eds.), *Catch and release fishing as a management tool: A national sportfishing symposium* (pp. 27–40). Arcata, CA: Humboldt State University.

Driver, B. L., & Knopf, R. C. (1976). Temporary escape—One product of sport fisheries management. *Fisheries, 1,* 24–29.

Driver, B. L., & Tocher, S. R. (1970). Toward a behavioral interpretation of recreation, with implications for planning. In B. L. Driver (Ed.), *Elements of outdoor recreation planning* (pp. 9–31). Ann Arbor, MI: University Microfilms International.

Drost, M. K. (1992, October 12–16). *Impact of operation and maintenance on the performance of energy systems.* Paper presented at the 36th Human Factors Society 36th annual meeting, Atlanta, GA.

Drottz-Sjoberg, B. M., & Sjoberg, L. (1990). Risk perception and worries after the Chernobyl accident. *Journal of Environmental Psychology, 10,* 135–149.

Dubos, R. (1968). *So human an animal.* New York: Scribner.

Dubos, R. (1970). *Reason awake: Science for man.* New York: Columbia University Press.

Dunlap, R. E. (1975). The impact of political orientation on environmental attitudes and actions. *Environment and Behavior, 7,* 428–454.

Dunlap, R. E. (1985). Public opinion: Behind the transformation. *EPA Journal, 11,* 15–17.

Dunlap, R. E. (1989). Public opinion and environmental policy. In J. P. Lester (Ed.), *Environmental politics and policy: Theories and evidence* (pp. 87–134). Durham, NC: Duke University Press.

Dunlap, R. E. (1992). Trends in public opinion toward environmental issues: 1965–1990. In R. E. Dunlap & A. G. Mertig (Eds.), *American environmentalism: The environmental movement, 1970–1990* (pp. 89–116). Washington, DC: Taylor & Francis.

Dunlap, R. E., Gallup, G. H., Jr., & Gallup, A. M. (1993, November). Global environmental concern: Results from an international public opinion survey. *Environment, 35*(9), 6–15, 33–39.

Dunlap, R. E., Grieneeks, J. K., & Rokeach, M. (1983). Human values and pro-environmental behavior. In W. D. Conn (Ed.), *Energy and natural resources: Attitudes, values, and public policy* (AAAS Selected Symposium 75, pp. 145–168). Boulder, CO: Westview.

Dunlap, R. E., & Scarce, R. (1991). The polls and poll trends: Environmental problems and protection. *Public Opinion Quarterly, 55,* 651–672.

Dunlap, R. E., & Van Liere, K. D. (1978). The "new environmental paradigm": A proposed measuring instrument and preliminary results. *Journal of Environmental Education, 9,* 10–19.

Dupont, T. (1980). *Nuclear phobia: Phobic thinking about nuclear power.* Washington, DC: The Media Institute.

Durdan, C. A., Reeder, G. D., & Hecht, P. R. (1985). Litter in a university cafeteria: Demographic data and use of prompts as an intervention strategy. *Environment and Behavior, 17,* 387–404.

Durlach, N. I., & Mavor, A. S. (1995). *Virtual reality: Scientific and technological challenges.* Washington, DC: National Academy Press.

Durning, A. (1992). *How much is enough?* New York: W. W. Norton.

Dwyer, W. O., Leeming, F. C., Cobern, M. K., Porter, B. E., & Jackson, J. M. (1993). Critical review of behavioral interventions to preserve the environment: Research since 1980. *Environment and Behavior, 25,* 275–321.

Eagly, A. H., & Chaiken, S. (1990). *The psychology of attitudes.* New York: Harcourt Brace.

Eagly, A. H., & Himmelfarb, S. (1978). Attitudes and opinions. *Annual Review of Psychology, 29,* 517–554.

Eason, K. D. (1981). A task-tool analysis of manager-computer interaction. In B. Shackel (Ed.), *Man-computer interaction: Human factors aspects of computers and people* (pp. 289–307). Rockville, MD: Sijthoff & Noordhoff.

Ebreo, A., Hershey, J., & Vining, J. (1999). Reducing solid waste: Linking recycling to environmentally responsible consumerism. *Environment and Behavior, 31,* 107–135.

Eckstein, O. (1958). *Water resource development and the economics of project evaluation.* Cambridge, MA: Harvard University Press.

Edney, J. J. (1974). Human territorially. *Psychological Bulletin, 81,* 959–975.

Edney, J. J. (1980). The common problem: Alternative perspectives. *American Psychologist, 35,* 131–150.

Edney, J. J., & Harper, C. S. (1978). The effects of information in a resource management problem: A social trap analysis. *Human Ecology, 6,* 387–395.

Eddy, T. J., Gallup, G. G., Jr., & Polvinelli, D. J. (1993). Attribution of cognitive states to animals: Anthropomorphism in comparative perspective. *Journal of Social Issues, 49,* 87–101.

Ehrenfeld, D. (1981). *The arrogance of humanism.* New York: Oxford University Press.

Ehrlich, P. R. (1968). *The population bomb.* New York: Ballentine Books.

Ehrlich, P. R. (1987). Habitats in crises: Why we should care about the loss of species. *Wilderness, 50,* 12–15.

Ehrlich, P. R. (1991). Can we respond to the growing environmental threat to civilization? In A. B. Wolbrast (Ed.), *Environment in peril* (pp. 110–139). Washington, DC: Smithsonian Institution Press.

Ehrlich, P. R., & Ehrlich, A. H. (1991). *Healing the planet.* New York: Addison-Wesley.

Ehrlich, P. R., & Holdren, J. (1971). Impact of population growth. *Science, 171,* 1212–1217.

Ehrlich, P. R., & Wilson, E. O. (1991). Biodiversity studies: Science and policy. *Science, 253,* 758–762.

Einhorn, H. J., & Hogarth, R. M. (1978). Confidence in judgment: Persistence of the illusion of validity. *Psychological Review, 85,* 395–416.

Elgin, D. (1993). *Voluntary simplicity: Toward a way of life that is outwardly simple, inwardly rich* (rev. ed.). New York: Quill.

Ellsaesser, H. W. (Winter, 1991). Setting the 10,000 year climate record straight. *21st Century Science and Technology,* pp. 52–58.

Engelbart, D. C. (1963). A conceptual framework for the augmentation of man's intellect. In P. W. Howerton & D. C. Weeks (Eds.), *Vistas in information handling* (Vol. I, pp. 1–29). Washington, DC: Spartan.

Environmental Protection Agency. (1976). *Report to the Congress: Minimization of hazardous waste.* Washington, DC: Environmental Protection Agency, Office of Solid Waste.

Environmental Protection Agency. (1990). *Reducing risk: Setting priorities and strategies for environmental protection: Report of the Science Advisory Board.* Washington, DC: U.S. Government Printing Office.

Environmental Protection Agency. (1992). *National ambient air quality and emissions trend report, 1991* (EPA Report 450–R–92–001). Research Triangle Park, NC: Author.

Epstein, S. S., Brown, L. O., & Pope, C. (1982). *Hazardous waste in America.* San Francisco, CA: Sierra Club Books.

Eriksen, M. P., LeMaistre, C. A., & Newell, G. R. (1988). Health hazards of passive smoking. In L. Breslow, J. E. Fielding, & L. B. Lave (Eds.), *Annual Review of Public Health, 9,* 47–70.

Erikson, K. (1990, Fall). The fear you can't ignore. *Best of Business Quarterly,* pp. 52–59.

Erskine, H. (1972). The polls: Pollution and its costs. *Public Opinion Quarterly, 36,* 120–135.

Ervine, R. D., & Chen, K. (1988–1989). Toward motoring smart. *Issues in Science and Technology, 5*(2), 92–97.

Ester, P. A., & Winett, R. A. (1982). Toward more effective antecedent strategies for environmental programs. *Journal of Environmental Systems, 11,* 201–221.

Evans, G. W., & Cohen, S. (1987). Environmental stress. In D. Stokols & I. Altman (Eds.), *Handbook of environmental psychology.* New York: Wiley.

Evans, G. W., & Howard, R. (1973). Personal space. *Psychological Bulletin, 80,* 334–344.

Evans, G. W., Jacobs, S. V., & Frager, N. B. (1982a). Adaptation to air pollution. *Journal of Environmental Psychology, 2,* 99–108.

Evans, G. W., Jacobs, S. V., & Frager, N. B. (1982b). Behavioral responses to air pollution. In A. Baum & J. E. Singer (Eds.), *Advances in environmental psychology: Vol. 4. Environment and health* (pp. 237–270). Hillsdale, NJ: Lawrence Erlbaum Associates.

Evans, G. W., Kliewer, W., & Martin, J. (1991). The role of the physical environment in the health and well-being of children. In H. Schroeder (Ed.), *New directions in health psychology: Assessment* (pp. 127–157). New York: Hemisphere.

Evans, G. W., Palsane, M. N., Lepore, S. J., & Martin, J. (1989). Residential density and psychological health. *Journal of Personality and Social Psychology, 57,* 994–999.

Evans, J. V. (1998). New satellites for personal communications. *Scientific American, 278*(4), 70–77.

Everett, P. B., Deslauriers, B. C., Newsom, T., & Anderson, V. B. (1978). The differential effect of two free ride dissemination procedures on bus ridership. *Transportation Research, 12,* 1–6.

Everrett, P. B., Hayward, S. C., & Meyers, A. W. (1974). The effects of a token reinforcement procedure on bus ridership. *Journal of Applied Behavior Analysis, 7,* 1–10.

Everett, P. B., & Watson, B. (1987). Psychological contributions to transportation. In D. Stokols & I. Altman (Eds.), *Handbook of environmental psychology* (Vol. 2, pp. 987–1008). New York: Wiley.

Ezell, C. (2001). The Himba and the dam. *Scientific American, 284*(6), 80–89.

Farman, J. C. (1987, November 12). What hope for the ozone layer now? *New Scientist,* pp. 50–54.

Farman, J. C., Gardiner, G. B., & Shanklin, J. D. (1985). Large losses of total ozone in Antarctica reveal seasonal $ClO_x/NO_x$ interaction. *Nature, 315,* 207–210.

Fawcett, J. T. (1970). *Psychology and population: Behavioral research issues in fertility and family planning.* New York: The Population Council.

Fawcett, J. T. (Ed.). (1973). *Psychological perspectives on population.* New York: Basic Books.

Fazio, R. H. (1986). How do attitudes guide behavior? In R. M. Sorrentino & E. T. Higgins (Eds.), *The handbook of motivation and cognition: Foundations of social behavior* (pp. 204–243). New York: Guilford.

Fazio, R. H. (1989). On the power and functionality of attitudes: The role of attitude accessibility. In A. R. Pratkanis, S. J. Breckler, & A. G. Greenwald (Eds.), *Attitude structure and function* (pp. 153–179). Hillsdale, NJ: Lawrence Erlbaum Associates.

Fazio, R. H., & Williams, C. J. (1986). Attitude accessibility as a moderator of the attitude-perception and attitude-behavior relations: An investigation of the 1984 presidential election. *Journal of Personality and Social Psychology, 51,* 505–514.

Federal Energy Administration. (1977). *Tips for energy savers.* Washington, DC: U.S. Government Printing Office.

Feeney, D., Berkes, F., McCay, B. J., & Acheson, J. M. (1990). The tragedy of the commons: Twenty-two years later. *Human Ecology, 18,* 1–19.

Feldman, J. M., & Lynch, J. G., Jr. (1988). Self-generated validity and other effects of measurement on belief, attitude, intention, and behavior. *Journal of Applied Psychology, 71,* 421–435.

Fickett, A. P., Gellings, C. W., & Lovins, A. B (1990). Efficient use of electricity. *Scientific American, 263*(3), 64–74.

Fidell, S., Reddingius, N., Smyth, J., & Sneddon, M. (1991, October). Presented at the 122nd meeting of the Acoustical Society of America, Houston, TX.

Fielding, J. E., & Phenow, K. J. (1988). Health effects of involuntary smoking. *The New England Journal of Medicine, 319,* 1452–1460.

Finger, M. (1994). From knowledge to action? Exploring the relationships between environmental experiences, learning, and behavior. *Journal of Social Issues, 50,* 141–160.

Finlayson-Pitts, B. J., & Pitts, J. N., Jr. (1997). Tropospherеic air pollution: Ozone, airborne toxics, polycyclic aromatic hydrocarbons, and particles. *Science, 276,* 1045–1051.

Finnie, W. C. (1973). Field experiments in litter control. *Environment and Behavior, 5,* 123–144.

Fischetti, M. (2001). Drowning New Orleans. *Scientific American, 285*(4), 76–85.

Fischhoff, B. (1977). Cost-benefit analysis and the art of motorcycle maintenance. *Policy Sciences, 8,* 177–202.

Fischhoff, B. (1991). Eliciting values: Is there anything in there? *American Psychologist, 46,* 835–847.

Fischhoff, B., & Furby, L. (1983). Psychological dimensions of climatic change. In R. S. Chen, E. Boulding, & S. H. Schneider (Eds.), *Social science research and climate change: An interdisciplinary appraisal* (pp. 180–203). Doredrecht, The Netherlands: Reidel.

Fischhoff, B., & Furby, L. (1988). Measuring values: A conceptual framework for interpreting transactions with special reference to contingent valuation of visibility. *Journal of Risk and Uncertainty, 1,* 147–184.

Fischhoff, B., Lichtenstein, S., Slovic, P., Derby, S. L., & Keeney, R. L. (1981). *Acceptable risk.* New York: Cambridge University Press.

Fischhoff, B., Slovic, P., & Lichtenstein, S. (1982). Lay foibles and expert fables in judgments about risks. *The American Statistician, 36,* 241–255.

Fischhoff, B., Slovic, P., Lichtenstein, S., Read, S., & Combs, B. (1978). How safe is safe enough? A psychometric study of attitudes towards technological risks and benefits. *Policy Sciences, 9,* 127–152.

Fischhoff, B., Sverson, O., & Slovic, P. (1987). Active responses to environmental hazards: Perception and decision making. In D. Stokols & I. Altman (Eds.), *Handbook of environmental psychology* (pp. 1089–1133). New York: Wiley.

Fishbein, M., & Ajzen, I. (1975). *Belief, attitude, intention, and behavior: An introduction to theory and research.* Reading, MA: Addison-Wesley.

Fisher, A. (1988). *The logic of real arguments.* New York: Cambridge University Press.

Flannery, B. L., & May, D. R. (1994). Prominent factors influencing environmental activities: Application of the Environmental Leadership Model (ELM). *Leadership Quarterly, 5,* 201–221.

Fleishman, J. A. (1988). The effects of decision framing and others' behavior on cooperation in a social dilemma. *Journal of Conflict Resolution, 32,* 162–180.

Fleming, R., Baum, A., & Singer, J. E. (1984). Toward an integrative approach to the study of stress. *Journal of Personality and Social Psychology, 46,* 939–949.

Foley, J. D. (1987). Interfaces for advanced computing. *Scientific American, 257*(4), 126–135.

Forester, T. (1987). *High-tech society: The story of the information technology revolution.* Cambridge, MA: MIT Press.

Forstater, I., & Twomey, E. (1976). *Vanpooling: A summary and description of existing vanpool programs.* Washington, DC: U.S. Environmental Protection Agency.

Foster, R. J., & Jackson, E. L. (1979). Factors associated with camping satisfaction in Alberta provincial park campgrounds. *Journal of Leisure Research, 4,* 292–306.

Fourier, J. B. J. (1827). Mémoire sur les températures du globe terrestre et des espaces planétaires. *Memoires de l'Académie Royal des Sciences de l'Institut de France, (Memorandum on temperatures of the terrestrial globe and planetary spaces) 7,* 569–604.

Fowlkes, M. R., & Miller, P. (1982). *Love Canal: The social construction of disaster.* Washington, DC: Federal Emergency Management Agency.

Fox, E. A. (1990). How to precede toward electronic archives and publishing. *Psychological Science, 1,* 355–358.

Foxx, R. M., & Hake, D. F. (1977). Gasoline conservation: A procedure for measuring and reducing the driving of college students. *Journal of Applied Behavior Analysis, 10,* 61–74.

Foxx, R. M., & Schaeffer, M. H. (1981). A company-based lottery to reduce the personal driving of employees. *Journal of Applied Behavior Analysis, 14,* 273–285.

Franck, K. (1987). Phenomenology, positivism, and empiricism as research strategies in environment-behavior research and in design. In E. Zube & G. T. Moore (Eds.), *Advances in environment, behavior and design* (Vol. 1, pp. 59–67). New York: Plenum.

French, H. F. (1994). Making environmental treaties work. *Scientific American, 271*(6), 94–97.

Fridgen, C. C. (1994). Human disposition toward hazards: Testing the environmental appraisal inventory. *Journal of Environmental Psychology, 14,* 101–111.

Fried, M. (1982). Residential attachment: Sources of residential and community satisfaction. *Journal of Social Issues, 38,* 107–119.

Friedli, H., Lötscher, H., Oeschger, H., Siegenthaler, U., & Stauffer, B. (1986). Ice core record of the $^{13}C/^{12}C$. Ratio of atmospheric $CO_2$ in the past two centuries. *Nature, 324,* 237–238.

Friedman, R. M. (1991). Letter to the editor (Air pollution benefit-cost assessment). *Science, 253,* 607.

Frosch, R. A., & Gallopoulos, N. E. (1989). Strategies for manufacturing. *Scientific American, 261*(3), 144–152.

Fujii, E. T., Hennessey, M., & Mak, J. (1985). An evaluation of the validity and reliability of survey response data on household electricity conservation. *Evaluation Review, 9,* 93–104.

Fulkerson, W., Judkins, R.R., & Sanghvi, M. J. (1990). Energy from fossil fuels. *Scientific American, 263*(3), 128–135.

Fulkerson, W., Reiser, D. B., Perry, A. M., Crane, A. T., Cash, D. E., & Auerbach, S. I. (1989). Global warming: An energy technology R&D challenge. *Science, 246,* 868–869.

Furse, D. J., Punj, G. N., & Stewart, D. W. (1984). A typology of individual search strategies among purchasers of new automobiles. *Journal of Consumer Research, 10,* 417–431.

Fusco, M. E., Bell, P. A., Jorgensen, M. D., & Smith, J. M. (1991). Using a computer to study the commons dilemma. *Simulation Games, 22,* 67–74.

Galbraith, J. K. (1991). The economic case for the environment. In A. B. Wolbrast (Ed.), *Environment in peril* (pp. 26–37). Washington, DC: Smithsonian Institution Press.

Galloway, W., & Bishop, D. (1970). *Noise exposure forecasts: Evolution, evaluation, extensions, and land use interpretations* (FAA Report NO–70–9).

Gamba, R. J., & Oskamp, S. (1994). Factors influencing community residents' participation in commingled curbside recycling programs. *Environment and Behavior, 26,* 587–612.

Gardner, G. T. (1978). Effects of federal human subjects regulations on data obtained in environmental stressor research. *Journal of Personality and Social Psychology, 36,* 628–634.

Gardner, G. T., & Gould, L. C. (1989). Public perceptions of the risks and benefits of technology. *Risk Analysis, 9,* 225–242.

Gardner, G. T., & Stern, P. C. (1996). *Environmental problems and human behavior.* Boston: Allyn & Bacon.

Gardner, W. (1990). The electronic archive: Scientific publishing for the 1990s. *Psychological Science, 1,* 333–341.

Gärling, A., & Gärling, T. (1990). Parent's residential satisfaction and perceptions of children's accident risk. *Journal of Environmental Psychology, 10,* 27–36.

Gärling, T. (1989). The role of cognitive maps in spatial decisions. *Journal of Environmental Psychology, 9,* 269–278.

Gärling, T., Book, A., & Lindberg, E. (1984). Cognitive mapping of large-scale environments: The interrelationship of action plans, acquisitions, and orientation. *Environment and Behavior, 16,* 3–34.

Gatchel, R. J., & Newberry, B. (1991). Psychophysiological effects of toxic chemical contamination exposure: A community field study. *Journal of Applied Social Psychology, 21,* 1961–1976.

Gatchel, R. J., Schaeffer, M. A., & Baum, A. (1985). A psychophysiological field study of stress at Three Mile Island. *Psychophysiology, 22,* 175–181.

Geller, E. S. (1981a). Evaluating energy conservation programs: Is verbal report enough? *Journal of Consumer Research, 8,* 331–335.

Geller, E. S. (1981b). Waste reduction and resource recovery: Strategy for energy conservation. In A. Baum & J. E. Singer (Eds.), *Advances in environmental psychology: Vol. 3. Energy: Psychological perspectives* (pp. 115–154). Hillsdale, NJ: Lawrence Erlbaum Associates.

Geller, E. S. (1986). Prevention of environmental problems. *Handbook of prevention* (pp. 361–383). New York: Plenum.

Geller, E. S. (1987). Environmental psychology and applied behavior analysis: From strange bedfellows to a productive marriage. In D. Stokols & I. Altman (Eds.), *Handbook of environmental psychology* (pp. 361–388). New York: Wiley.

Geller, E. S. (1989). Applied behavior analysis and social marketing: An integration for environmental preservation. *Journal of Social Issues, 45,* 17–36.

Geller, E. S. (1990). Behavior analysis and environmental protection: Where have all the flowers gone? *Journal of Applied Behavior Analysis, 23,* 269–273.

Geller, E. S. (1992a). Comment: It takes more than information to save energy. *American Psychologist, 47,* 814–815.

Geller, E. S. (1992b). Solving environmental problems: A behavior change perspective. In S. Staub & P. Green (Eds.), *In our hands: Psychology, peace and social responsibility* (pp. 248–268). New York: New York University Press.

Geller, E. S. (1995a). Actively caring for the environment: An integration of behaviorism and humanism. *Environment and Behavior, 27,* 184–195.

Geller, E. S. (1995b). Integrating behaviorism and humanism for environmental protection. *Journal of Social Issues, 51,* 179–195.

Geller, E. S., Brasted, W., & Mann, M. (1979–80). Waste receptacle designs as interventions for litter control. *Journal of Environmental Systems, 9,* 145–160.

Geller, E. S., Chaffee, J. L., & Ingram, R. (1975). Promoting paper recycling on a university campus. *Journal of Environmental Systems, 5,* 39–57.

Geller, E. S., Erickson, J. B., & Buttram, B. A. (1983). Attempts to promote residential water conservation with educational, behavioral and engineering strategies. *Population and Environmental Behavioral and Social Issues, 6,* 96–112.

Geller, E. S., & Lehman, G. R. (1986). Motivating desirable waste management behavior: Applications of behavior analysis. *Journal of Resource Management and Technology, 15,* 58–68.

Geller, E. S., & Pitz, G. F. (1968). Confidence and decision speed in the revision of opinion. *Organizational Behavior and Human Performance, 3,* 190–201.

Geller, E. S., Winett, R. R., & Everett, P. B. (1982). *Preserving the environment: New strategies for behavior change*. Elmsford, NY: Pergamon.

Geller, E. S., Witmer, J. F., & Orebaugh, A. L. (1976). Instructions as a determinant of paper-disposal behaviors. *Environment and Behavior, 8,* 417–439.

Gell-Mann, M. (1994). *The quark and the jaguar: Adventures in the simple and the complex*. New York: Freeman.

Gendrich, J. G., McNees, M. P., Schnelle, J. F., Beagle, G. P., & Clark, H. B. (1982). A student-based anti-litter program for elementary schools. *Education and Treatment of Children, 5,* 321–335.

General Electric Company. (1987). *Financial analyses of waste management*. Washington, DC: Environmental Law Institute.

Georgescu-Roegen, N. (1976). *Energy and economic myths: Institutional and analytical essays*. New York: Basic Books.

Getz, W. M., Fortmann, L., Cumming, D, du Toit, J., Hilty, J., Martin, R., Murphree, M., Owen-Smith, N., Starfield, A. M., & Westphal, M. I. (1999). Sustaining natural and human capital: Villagers and scientists. *Science, 283,* 1855–1856.

Gibbons, A. (1992). Mission impossible: Saving all endangered species. *Science, 256,* 1386.

Gibbons, J. H., Blair, P. D., & Gwin, H. L. (1989). Strategies for energy use. *Scientific American, 261*(3), 136–143.

Gibbs, M. S. (1986). Psychopathological consequences of exposure to toxins in the water supply. In A. H. Lebovits, A. Baum, & J. E. Singer (Eds.), *Advances in environmental psychology: Vol. 6. Exposure to hazardous substances: Psychological parameters*. Hillsdale, NJ: Lawrence Erlbaum Associates.

Gibbs, W. W. (1995). The treaty that worked—Almost. *Scientific American, 273*(3), 18–19.

Gibbs, W. W. (1997). Transportation's perennial problems. *Scientific American, 277*(4), 54–57.

Gibbs, W. W. (2001). The Arctic oil wildlife refuge. *Scientific American, 284*(5), 62–69.

Gibson, R. S., & Nichol, E. H. (1964). *The modifiability of decisions made in a changing environment* (ESD–TR–64–657). Bedford, MA: Electronic Systems Division, USAF.

Gibson, J. J. (1977). The theory of affordances. In R. Shaw & J. Bransford (Eds.), *Perceiving, acting and knowing*. Hillsdale, NJ: Lawrence Erlbaum Associates.

Gibson, P. M. (1979). Therapeutic aspects of wilderness programs: A comprehensive literature review. *Therapeutic Recreational Journal, 13,* 21–33.

Gifford, R. (1980). Environmental dispositions and the evaluation of architectural interiors. *Journal of Research in Personality, 14,* 386–399.

Gifford, R., & Wells, J. (1991). FISH: A common dilemma simulation. *Behavioral Research Methods, Instrumentation and Computing, 23,* 437–441.

Gill, J. D., Crosby, L. A., & Taylor, J. R. (1986). Ecological concern, attitudes, and social norms in voting behavior. *Public Opinion Quarterly, 50,* 537–554.

Glance, N. S., & Huberman, B. A. (1994). The dynamics of social dilemmas. *Scientific American, 279*(3), 76–81.

Glanz, J. (1999). Sharp drop seen in soil erosion rates. *Science, 285,* 1187–1189.

Glas, J. P. (1989). Protecting the ozone layer: A perspective from industry. In J. H. Ausubel & H. E. Sladovich (Eds.), *Technology and environment* (pp. 137–155). Washington, DC: National Academy Press.

Gleason, J. F., Bhartia, P. K., Herman, J. R., McPeters, R., Newman, P., Stolarski, R. S., Flynn, L., Labow, G., Larko, D., Seftor, C., Wellemeyer, C., Komhyr, W. D., Miller, A. J., & Planet, W. (1993). Record low global ozone in 1992. *Science, 260,* 523–526.

Gleick, P. H. (2001). Making every drop count. *Scientific American, 284*(2), 40–45.

Glickman, T. S., & Gough, M. (Eds.). (1990). *Readings in risk*. Washington, DC: Resources for the Future.

Gold, S. M. (1977). Social benefits of trees in urban environments. *International Journal of Environmental Studies, 10,* 85–90.

Goldemberg, J. (1995). Energy needs in developing countries and sustainability. *Science, 269,* 1058–1059.

Goldsmith, J. R., & Landow, S. A. (1968). Carbon monoxide and human health. *Science, 162,* 1352–1359.

Goldsmith, M. F. (1989). As farmworkers help keep America healthy, illness may be their harvest. *Journal of the American Medical Association, 26,* 3207–3213.

Goldsteen, R., Schorr, J. K., & Goldsteen, K. S. (1989). Longitudinal study of appraisal at Three Mile Island: Implications for life event research. *Social Science and Medicine, 28,* 389–398.

Goldstein, W., & Einhorn, H. (1987). Expression theory and the preference reversal phenomena. *Psychological Review, 94,* 236–254.

Gonzales, M. H., Aronson, E., & Costanzo, M. A. (1988). Using social cognition and persuasion to promote energy conservation: A quasi-experiment. *Journal of Applied Social Psychology, 18,* 10491–1066.

Goodman, B. (1993). Drugs and diversity threaten diversity in Andean forests. *Science, 261,* 293.

Gopal, S., Klatzky, R. L., & Smith, T. R. (1989). Navigator: A psychologically-based model of environmental learning through navigation. *Journal of Environmental Psychology, 9,* 309–331.

Gore, A. (1992). *Earth in the balance: Ecology and the human spirit*. New York: Penguin.

Gould, L. C., Gardner, G. T., DeLuca, D. R., Tiemann, A. R., Doob, L. W., & Stolwijk, J. A. J. (1988). *Perceptions of technological risks and benefits*. New York: Russell Sage Foundation.

Graedel, T. E., & Crutzen, P. J. (1989). The changing atmosphere. *Scientific American, 261*(3), 58–68.

Graham, N. E. (1995). Simulation of recent global temperature trends. *Science, 267,* 666–671.

Grasmick, H. G., Bursik, R. J., Jr., & Kinsey, K. A. (1991). Shame and embarrassment as deterrents to compliance with the law: The case of an antilittering campaign. *Environment and Behavior, 23,* 233–251.

Gray, C. L., Jr., & Alson, J. A. (1989). The case for methonal. *Scientific American, 261*(5), 108–114.

Greenberg, M., Lowrie, K., Krueckeberg, D., Mayer, H., & Simon, D. (1997). Bombs and butterflies: A case study of the challenges of post Cold War environmental planning and management for the U.S. nuclear weapons sites. *Journal of Environmental Planning and Management, 40,* 739–750.

Greenberg, M., Sachsman, D., Sandman, P., & Salomone, K. (1989). Network evening news coverage of environmental risk. *Risk Analysis, 9,* 119–126.

Greenberg, M. R., Sandman, P. M., Sachsman, D. B., & Salomone, K. L. (1989, March). Network evening news coverage of environmental risks. *Environment, 31*(2), 16–20, 40–44.

Greenberg, M., & Schneider, D. (1994). Hazardous waste site recommendation, neighbor change, and neighborhood quality. *Environmental Health Perspectives, 102,* 542–547.

Greenberg, M., & Schneider, D. (1996). *Environmentally devastated neighborhoods: Perceptions, realities, and policies*. New Brunswick, NJ: Rutgers University Press.

Greenberg, M., Schneider, D., & Choi, D. (1994). Neighborhood quality. *The Geographical Review, 84,* 1–15.

Greening, L., & Chandler, C. C. (1997). Why it can't happen to me: The base rate matters, but overestimating skill leads to underestimating risk. *Journal of Applied Psychology, 82,* 760–780.

Gregory, R., Lichtenstein, S., & Slovic, P. (1993). Valuing environmental resources: A constructive approach. *Journal of Risk and Uncertainty, 7,* 177–197.

Greve, M. S., & Smith, F. L., Jr. (1992). *Environmental politics: Public costs, private rewards.* New York: Praeger.

Grime, J. P. (1997). Biodiversity and the ecosystem function: The debate deepens. *Science, 277,* 1260–1261.

Grossman, C. M. (1995). Letter to editor re radioactive waste at Ward Valley. *Science, 269,* 1656.

Grossman, G., & Krueger, A. (1995). Economic growth and the environment. *Quarterly Journal of Economics, 110,* 353–377.

Grossman, W. M. (2001). Wireless wonder. *Scientific American, 285*(2), 20.

Grotch, W. L. (1988). *Regional intercomparisons of general circulation model predictions and historical climate data* (Report #DOE/NBB 0084). Washington, DC: U.S. Department of Energy.

Grumbine, R. E. (1991). Cooperation or conflict? Interagency relationship and the future of biodiversity for U.S. parks and forests. *Environmental Management, 15,* 27–37.

Guagnano, G. A., Stern, P. C., & Dietz, T. (1995). Influences on attitude-behavior relationships: A natural experiment with curbside recycling. *Environment and Behavior, 27,* 699–718.

Gute, D. M. (1991). Regulatory environmental decisions. In R. A. Chechile & S. Carlisle (Eds.), *Environmental decision making: A multidisciplinary perspective* (pp. 217–237). New York: Van Nostrand Reinhold.

Gutfeld, R. (1991). Eight of 10 Americans are environmentalists, at least so they say. *Wall Street Journal, 218*(24), A1–A4.

Haas, G. E., Driver, B. L., & Brown, P. J. (1980). A study of ski touring experiences on the White River National Forest. *Proceedings of the North American Symposium on dispersed winter recreation* (pp. 25–30). St. Paul, MN: College of Forestry, University of Minnesota.

Haigh, J. D. (1996). The impact of solar variability on climate. *Science, 272,* 981–984.

Hair, J. D. (1991). Should EPA have cabinet status? In A. B. Wolbrast (Ed.), *Environment in peril* (pp. 82–95). Washington, DC: Smithsonian Institution Press.

Hake, D. F., & Foxx, R. M. (1978). Promoting gasoline conservation: The effects of reinforcement schedules, a leader and self-recording. *Behavior Modification, 2,* 339–369.

Hake, D., & Zane, T. (1981). A community-based gasoline conservation project: Practical and methodological considerations. *Behavior Modification, 5,* 435–458.

Hales, S. (1738). *Vegetable staticks* (3rd ed.). London: Innys & Manby.

Halfon, E. (Ed.). (1979). *Theoretical systems ecology.* New York: Academic Press.

Hall, E. T. (1966). *The hidden dimension.* New York: Doubleday.

Hall, J. V., Winer, A. M., Kleinman, M. T., Lurmann, F. W., Brajer, V., & Colome, S. D. (1992). Valuing the health benefits of clean air. *Science, 255,* 812–817.

Hallman, W. K., & Wandersman, A. H. (1992). Attribution of responsibility and individual and collective coping with environmental threats. *Journal of Social Issues, 48*(4), 101–118.

Hamad, C. D., Bettinger, R., Cooper, D., & Semb, G. (1980–1981). Using behavioral procedures to establish an elementary school paper recycling program. *Journal of Environmental Systems, 10,* 149–156.

Hamad, C. D., Cooper, D., & Semb, G. (1977). Resource recovery: The use of a group contingency to increase paper recycling in an elementary school. *Journal of Applied Psychology, 62,* 768–772.

Hamilton, D. P. (1990). Briefings: Growth without new energy. *Science, 248,* 1486.
Hamilton, D. P. (1992a). Environmental agency launches a study in "Ecological risk assessment." *Science, 255,* 1499.
Hamilton, D. P. (1992b). Envisioning research with virtual reality. *Science, 256,* 603.
Hamilton, L. C. (1985). Concern about toxic wastes. *Sociological Perspectives, 28,* 463–486.
Hammond, K. R., & Adelman, L. (1976). Science, values and human judgment. *Science, 194,* 389–396.
Hammond, P. B., & Coppock, R. (Eds.). (1990). *Valuing health risks, costs, and benefits for environmental decision making.* Washington, DC: National Academy Press.
Hance, B. J., Chess, C., & Sandman, P. M. (1988). *Improving dialogue with communities: A risk communication manual for government.* Trenton, NJ: Department of Environmental Protection.
Hardin, G. (1968). The tragedy of the commons. *Science, 162,* 1243–1248.
Harris, D. M., & Guten, S. (1979). Health protective behavior: An exploratory study. *Journal of Health and Social Behavior, 20,* 17–29.
Harris, J. E. (1990). Act now or wait for more information? In P. B. Hammond & R. Coppock (Eds.), *Valuing health risks, costs, and benefits for environmental decision making* (pp. 107–133). Washington, DC: National Academy Press.
Harris, R. J. (Ed.). (1983). *Information processing: Research in advertising.* Hillsdale, NJ: Lawrence Erlbaum Associates.
Harris, R. N., & Chapman, D. S. (1997). Borehole temperatures and a baseline for 20th-century global warming estimates. *Science, 275,* 1618–1621.
Harrison, H. (1970). Stratospheric ozone with added water vapor: Influence of high-altitude aircraft. *Science, 170,* 734–736.
Harry, J., Gale, R., & Hendee, J. (1969). Conservation: An upper-middle class social movement. *Journal of Leisure Research, 1,* 246–254.
Hartig, T., Mang, M., & Evans, G. W. (1991). Restorative effects of natural environment experiences. *Environment and Behavior, 23,* 3–26.
Harvey, J. (Ed.). (1981). *Cognition, social behavior, and the environment.* Hillsdale, NJ: Lawrence Erlbaum Associates
Harvey, M. L., Bell, P. A., & Birjulin, A. A. (1993). Punishment and type of feedback in a simulated commons dilemma. *Psychological Reports, 73,* 447–450.
Hass, R. G. (1981). Effects of source characteristics on cognitive responses in persuasion. In R. E. Petty, T. M. Ostrom, & T. C. Brock (Eds.), *Cognitive responses in persuasion* (pp. 141–172). Hillsdale, NJ: Lawrence Erlbaum Associates.
Hasselmann, K. (1997). Are we seeing global warming? *Science, 276,* 914–915.
Hatch, M. C., Wallenstein, S., Beyea, J., Nieves, J. W., & Susser, M. (1991). Cancer rates after the Three Mile Island nuclear accident and proximity of residence to the plant. *American Journal of Public Health, 81,* 719–724.
Hayduk, L. A. (1978). Personal space: An evaluative and orienting overview. *Psychological Bulletin, 85,* 117–134.
Hayes, S. C., & Cone, J. D. (1977). Reducing residential electrical energy use: Payments, information, and feedback. *Journal of Applied Behavior Analysis, 10,* 425–435.
Hayes, S. C., & Cone, J. D. (1981). Reduction of residential consumption of electricity through simple monthly feedback. *Journal of Applied Analysis of Behavior, 14,* 81–88.
Hayes, S. C., Johnson, V. S., & Cone, J. D. (1975). The marked item technique: A practical procedure for litter control. *Journal of Applied Behavior Analysis, 8,* 381–386.
Heberlein, T. A. (1972). The land ethic realized: Some social psychological explanations for changing environmental attitudes. *Journal of Social Issues, 28,* 79–87.
Hedge, A. (1989). Environmental conditions and health in offices. *International Review of Ergonomics, 3,* 87–110.

Heft, H. (1985). High residential density and perceptual-cognitive development: An examination of the effects of crowding and noise in the home. In J. F. Wohwill & W. Van Vliet (Eds.), *Habitats for children: The impacts of density* (pp. 39–75). Hillsdale, NJ: Lawrence Erlbaum Associates.

Heft, H., & Wohlwill, J. F. (1987). Environmental cognition in children. In D. Stokols & I. Altman (Eds.), *Handbook of environmental psychology* (Vol. 1, pp. 175–204). New York: Wiley.

Heijs, W., & Stringer, P. (1988). Research on residential thermal comfort: Some contributions from environmental psychology. *Journal of Environmental Psychology, 8,* 235–248.

Heimstra, N. W., & McFarling, L. H. (1974). *Environmental psychology.* Monterey, CA: Brooks Cole.

Helson, H. (1964). *Adaptation level theory.* New York: Harper & Row.

Henion, K. (1976). *Ecological marketing.* Columbus, OH: Grid.

Henrion, M., & Fischhoff, B. (1986). Assessing uncertainty in physical constants. *American Journal of Physics, 54,* 791–798.

Herman, R., Ardekani, S. A., & Ausubel, J. H. (1989). Dematerialization. In J. H. Ausubel & H. E. Sladovich (Eds.), *Technology and environment* (pp. 50–69). Washington, DC: National Academy Press.

Hershkowitz, A. (1990). Without a trace: Handling medical waste safely. *Technology Review, 93*(6), 35–40.

Herzog, H., Eliasson, B., & Kaarstad, O. (2000). Capturing greenhouse gases. *Scientific American, 282*(2), 72–79.

Herzog, T. R. (1989). A cognitive analysis of preference for urban nature. *Journal of Environmental Psychology, 9,* 27–43.

Herzog, T. R. (1992). A cognitive analysis of preference for urban spaces. *Journal of Environmental Psychology, 12,* 237–248.

Herzog, T. R., Kaplan, S., & Kaplan, R. (1982). The prediction of preference for unfamiliar urban places. *Population and Environment, 5,* 43–59.

Hibbard, W. R. (1986). Metals demand in the United States: An overview. *Materials and Society, 10*(3), 251–258.

Hileman, B. (1999, August 9). Case grows for climate change. *Chemical and Engineering News,* pp. 16–33.

Himmelfarb, S., & Eagly, A. H. (Eds.). (1974). *Readings in attitude change.* New York: Wiley.

Hines, J. M., Hungerford, H. R., & Tomera, A. N. (1986). Analysis and synthesis of research on responsible environmental behavior: A meta-analysis. *Journal of Environmental Education, 18,* 1–8.

Hirschhorn, J. S., & Oldenburg, K. U. (1991). *Prosperity without pollution: The prevention strategy for industry and consumers.* New York: Reinhold.

Hirschman, E. C., & Holbrook, M. B. (1982). Hedonic consumption: Emerging concepts, methods and propositions. *Journal of Marketing, 46,* 92–101.

Hirst, E. (1976). Transportation energy conservation policies. *Science, 192,* 15–20.

Hirst, E., Clinton, J., Geller, H., & Kromer, W. (1986). *Energy efficiency in buildings: Progress and promise.* Washington, DC: American Council for an Energy-Efficient Economy.

Hirst, E., Berry, L., & Soderstrom, J. (1981). Review of utility home energy audit programs. *Energy, 6,* 621–630.

Hirtle, S. C., & Hudson, J. (1991). Acquisition of spatial knowledge for routes. *Journal of Environmental Psychology, 11,* 335–345.

Hocking, M. B. (1991a). Paper versus polystyrene: A complex choice. *Science, 251,* 504–505.

Hocking, M. B. (1991b). Relative merits of polystyrene foam and paper in hot drink cups: Implications for packaging. *Environmental Management, 15,* 731–747.

Hodges, C. A. (1995). Mineral resources, environmental issues, and land use. *Science, 268,* 1305–1312.

Hoffman, M. S. (Ed.). (1992). *The world almanac and book of facts.* New York: Pharos.

Holahan, C. (1986). Environmental psychology. *Annual Review of Psychology, 37,* 381–407.

Holbrook, M. B., & Hirschman, E. C. (1982). The experiential aspects of consumption: Consumer fantasies, feelings, and fun. *Journal of Consumer Research, 9,* 132–140.

Holden, C. (1990). Multidisciplinary look at a finite world. *Science, 249,* 18–19.

Holding, C. S. (1992). Clusters and reference points in cognitive representations of the environment. *Journal of Environmental Psychology, 12,* 45–55.

Holding, C. S. (1994). Further evidence of the hierarchical representation of spatial information. *Journal of Environmental Psychology, 14,* 137–147.

Holdren, J. P. (1976). The nuclear controversy and the limitations of decision making by experts. *Bulletin of the Atomic Scientists, 32*(3), 20–22.

Holdren, J. P. (1990). Energy in transition. *Scientific American, 263*(3), 156–163.

Hollister, C. D., & Nadia, S. (1998). Burial of radioactive waste under the seabed. *Scientific American, 278*(1), 60–65.

Holloway, M. (1994). Nurturing nature. *Scientific American, 270*(4), 98–108.

Holmes, B. (1993). Can sustainable farming sin the battle of the bottom line? *Science, 260,* 1893–1895.

Hopper, J. R., & Nielsen, J. McC. (1991). Recycling as altruistic behavior: Normative and behavioral strategies to expand participation in a community recycling program. *Environment and Behavior, 23,* 195–220.

Horiuchi, S. (1992). Stagnation in the decline of the world population growth rate during the 1980s. *Science, 257,* 761–765.

Hosford, W., & Duncan, J. L. (1994). The aluminum beverage can. *Scientific American, 271*(3), 48–53.

Houghton, H. (1955). On the chemical composition of fog and cloud water. *Journal of Meteorology, 12,* 355–357.

Houghton, J. T., Jenkins, G. J., & Ephraums, J. J. (Eds.). (1990). *Climate change: The IPCC scientific assessment.* Cambridge, UK: Cambridge University Press.

Houghton, R. A., & Woodwell, G. M. (1989). Global climatic change. *Scientific American, 260*(4), 36–44.

Hounsome, M. (1979). Bird life in the city. In I. C. Laurie (Ed.), *Nature in cities* (pp. 179–203). Chichestire, England: Wiley.

Howard, G. S. (2000). Adapting human lifestyles for the 21st century. *American Psychologist, 55,* 509–515.

Howard, G. S., Delgado, E., Miller, D., & Gubbins, S. (1993). Transforming values into actions: Ecological preservation through energy conservation. *Counseling Psychologist, 21,* 581–595.

Howenstine, E. (1993). Market segmentation for recycling. *Environment and Behavior, 25,* 86–102.

Hueber, R. B., & Lipsey, N. W. (1981). The relationship of three measures of locus of control to environmental activism. *Basic and Applied Social Psychology, 2,* 45–58.

Huffman, K. T., Grossnickle, W. F., Cope, J. G., & Huffman, K. P. (1995). Litter reduction: A review and integration of the literature. *Environment and Behavior, 27,* 153–183.

Hughey, J. B., Sundstrom, E., & Lounsbury, J. W. (1985). Attitudes toward nuclear power: A longitudinal analysis of expectancy-value models. *Basic and Applied Social Psychology, 6,* 75–91.

Hull, R. B., & Revell, G. R. B. (1989). Cross-cultural comparison of landscape scenic beauty evaluations: A case study in Bali. *Journal of Environmental Psychology, 9,* 177–191.

Hull, R. B., & Stewart, W. P. (1992). Validity of photo-based scenic beauty judgments. *Journal of Environmental Psychology, 12,* 101–114.

Humphrey, C. R., Bord, R. J., Hammond, M. M., & Mann, S. (1977). Attitudes and conditions for cooperation in a paper recycling program. *Environment and Behavior, 9,* 107–124.

Hunt, E. (1990). People, pitfalls, and the electronic archive. *Psychological Science, 1,* 346–349.

Hutton, R. B. (1982). Advertising and the Department of Energy's campaign for energy conservation. *Journal of Advertising, 11*(2), 27–39.

Hutton, R. B., Mauser, G. A., Filiatrault, P., & Ahtola, O. T. (1986). Effects of cost-related feedback on consumer knowledge and consumption behavior: A field experimental approach. *Journal of Consumer Research, 13,* 327–336.

Huws, U., Korte, W. B., & Robinson, S. (1990). *Telework: Towards the elusive office.* New York: Wiley.

Im, S. (1984). Visual preferences in enclosed urban spaces: An exploration of a scientific approach to environmental design. *Environment and Behavior, 16,* 235–262.

Inamdar, A., de Jode, H., Lindsay, K., & Cobb, S. (1999). Capitalizing on nature. *Science, 283,* 1856–1857.

Ingersheim, R. H. (1976). Managerial response to an information system. *Proceedings of the National Computer Conference, 45,* 877–882.

Intergovernmental Panel on Climate Change. (1990). *Policymakers' summary of the scientific assessment of climate change.* Geneva: World Meteorological Organization.

Intergovernmental Panel on Climate Change. (1996). *Climate change 1995: The science of climate change.* New York: Cambridge University Press.

Intergovernmental Panel on Climate Change. (2001). *Climate change 2001: The scientific basis.* (*www.ipcc.ch*)

International Energy Agency. (1987). *Energy usage in IEA countries.* Paris: Organization of Economic Cooperation and Development.

Iranpour, R., Stenstrom, M., Tchobanoglous, G., Miller, D., Wright, J., & Vossoughi, M. (1999). Environmental engineering: Energy value of replacing waste disposal with resource recovery. *Science, 285,* 706–710.

Irwin, J., Slovic, P., Lichtenstein, S., & McClelland, G. (1993). Preference reversals and the measurement of environmental values. *Journal of Risk and Uncertainty, 6,* 5–18.

Ittelson, W. H. (1989). Notes on theory in environment and behavior research. In E. H. Zube & G. T. Moore (Eds.), *Advances in environment, behavior, and design* (Vol. 2, pp. 71–83). New York: Plenum.

Jablonski, D. (1991). Extinctions: A palentological perspective. *Science, 253,* 754–757.

Jackson, R. H., Hudman, L. E., & England, J. L. (1978). Assessment of the environmental impact of high voltage power transmission lines. *Journal of Environmental Management, 6,* 153–170.

Jacobs, H. E., & Bailey, J. S. (1982–1983). Evaluating participation in a residential recycling program. *Journal of Environmental Systems, 12,* 141–152.

Jacobs, H. E., Bailey, J. S., & Crews, J. I. (1984). Development and analysis of a community-based resource recovery program. *Journal of Applied Behavior Analysis, 17,* 127–145.

Jacobson, M. Z., & Masters, G. M. (2001). Exploiting wind versus coal. *Science, 293,* 1438.

Jacoby, J., Speller, D. E., & Berning, C. A. K. (1974). Brand choice behavior as a function of information load: Replication and extension. *Journal of Consumer Research, 1,* 33–42.

Jacoby, J., Speller, D. E., & Kohn, C. A. (1974). Brand choice behavior as a function of information load. *Journal of Marketing Research, 11,* 63–69.

Jaroff, L. (1995). Age of the road warrior. (Special Issue: Welcome to Cyberspace) *Time*, pp. 38–40.

Jastrow, R. (1990). Global warming report (Letter to the Editor). *Science, 247,* 14, 15.

Jeffery, R. W. (1989). Risk behaviors and health: Contrasting individual and population perspectives. *American Psychologist, 44,* 1194–1202.

Jemmott, J. B., Ditto, P. H., & Croyle, R. T. (1986). Judging health status: Effects of perceived prevalence and personal relevance. *Journal of Personality and Social Psychology, 50,* 899–905.

Johannessen, O., Shalina, E. V., & Miles, M. W. (2000). Satellite evidence for an arctic sea ice cover in transformation. *Science, 286,* 1937–1939.

Johnson, L. R. (1990). Putting maglev on track. *Issues in Science and Technology, 6*(3), 71–76.

Johnson, N. L. (1998). Monitoring and controlling debris in space. *Scientific American, 279*(2), 62–67.

Johnston, H. S. (1971). Reduction of stratospheric ozone by nitrogen oxide catalysts from supersonic transport exhausts. *Science, 173,* 517–522.

Jones, A., Roberts, D. L., & Singo, A. (1994). A climate model of study of indirect radiative forcing by anthropogenic sulphate aerosols. *Nature, 370,* 450–453.

Jones, R. E. (1990). Understanding paper recycling in an institutionally supportive setting: An application of the theory of reasoned action. *Journal of Environmental Systems, 19,* 307–321.

Jones, P. D., & Wigley, T. M. L. (1990). Global warming trends. *Scientific American, 263*(2), 84–91.

Jones, P. D., Wigley, T., & Wright, P. (1986). Global temperature variation between 1861 and 1984. *Nature, 322,* 432–434.

Joos, F., Plattner, G.-K., Stocker, T. F., Marchal, O., & Schmittner, A. (1999). Global warming and marine carbon cycle feedbacks on future atmospheric $CO_2$. *Science, 284,* 464.

Joskow, P. L., & Marron, D. B. (1993). What does utility-subsidized energy efficiency really cost? *Science, 260,* 281, 370.

Kahle, L. R., & Beatty, S. E. (1987). Cognitive consequences of legislating postpurchase behavior: Growing up with the bottle bill. *Journal of Applied Social Psychology, 17,* 828–843.

Kahneman, D., & Knetsch, J. L. (1992). Valuing public goods: The purchase of moral satisfaction. *Journal of Environmental Economics and Management, 22,* 57–70.

Kahneman, D., Ritov, I., Jacowitz, K. E., & Grant, P. (1993). Stated willingness to pay for public goods: A psychological perspective. *Psychological Sciences, 4,* 310–315.

Kahneman, D., Slovic, P., & Tversky, A. (Eds.). (1982). *Judgment under uncertainty: Heuristics and biases*. Cambridge, UK: Cambridge University Press.

Kahneman, D., & Tversky, A. (1979). Prospect theory: An analysis of decisions under risk. *Econometrika, 47,* 262–291.

Kahneman, D., & Tversky, A. (1982). On the study of statistical intuitions. *Cognition, 11,* 123–141.

Kahneman, D., & Tversky, A. (1984). Choices, values and frames. *American Psychologist, 39,* 341–350.

Kaiser, J. (1998). Pollution permits for greenhouse gases. *Science, 282,* 1025.

Kaiser, J. (1999). Turning engineers into resource accountants. *Science, 285,* 685–686.

Kaiser, J. (2000). Ecologists on a mission to save the world. *Science, 287,* 1188–1192.

Kaiser, J. (2001). Breeding a hardier weed. *Science, 293,* 1425–1427.

Kallgren, C. A., & Wood, W. (1986). Access to attitude-relevant information in memory as a determinant of attitude-behavior consistency. *Journal of Experimental Social Psychology, 22,* 328–338.

Kals, E. (1996). Are proenvironmental commitments motivated by health concerns or by perceived justice? In L. Montada & M. Lerner (Eds.), *Current societal concerns about justice* (pp. 231–258). Hingham, MA: Kluwer Academic Publishers.

Kals, E., & Montada, L. (1994). Umweltschutz und die verantwortung der bürger (Environmental protection and the responsibility of the citizen). *Zeitschrift für Sozialpsychologie, 25,* 326–337.

Kals, E., Schumacher, D., & Montada, L. (1999). Emotional affinity toward nature as a motivational basis to protect nature. *Environment and Behavior, 31,* 178–202.

Kamieniecki, S., O'Brien, R., & Clarke, M. (Eds.). (1986). *Controversies in environmental policy.* Albany, NY: SUNY Press.

Kammen, D. M. (1995). Cookstoves for the developing world. *Scientific American, 273*(1), 72–75.

Kammen, D. M., & Hassenzahl, D. M. (1999). *Should we risk it? Exploring environmental, health, and technological problem solving*. Princeton, NJ: Princeton University Press.

Kantola, S. J., Syme, G. J., & Campbell, N. A. (1984). Cognitive dissonance and energy conservation. *Journal of Applied Psychology, 69,* 416–421.

Kaplan, R. (1973). Predictors of environmental preference: Designers and clients. In W. Preiser (Ed.), *Environmental design research* (pp. 265–274). Stroudsburg, PA: Dowden, Hutchinson & Ross.

Kaplan, R. (1974). Some psychological benefits of an Outdoor Challenge program. *Environment and Behavior, 6,* 101–116.

Kaplan, R. (1975). Some methods and strategies in the prediction of preference, In E. H. Zube, R. O. Brush, & J. G. Fabos (Eds.), *Landscape assessment: Values, perceptions and resources* (pp. 118–129). New York: Van Nostrand Reinhold.

Kaplan, R. (1977). Preference and everyday nature: Method and application. In D. Stokols (Ed.), *Perspectives on environment and behavior* (pp. 235–250). New York: Plenum.

Kaplan, R. (1979a). A methodology for simultaneously obtaining and sharing information. In *Assessing amenity resource values* (pp. 58–66). (USDA Forest Service General Technical Report RM–68). Fort Collins, CO: USDA Forest Service.

Kaplan, R. (1979b). Visual resources and the public: An empirical approach. In *Proceedings of our national landscape conference* (pp. 209–216). (USDA Forest Service General Technical Report PSW–35). Berkeley, CA: USDA Forest Service.

Kaplan, R. (1981). *Evaluation of an urban vest-pocket park* (USDA Forest Service, North Central Forest Experiment Station Research Paper NC–195). St. Paul, MA: USDA Forest Service.

Kaplan, R. (1983). The role of nature in the urban context. In I. Altman & J. F. Wohlwill (Eds.), *Behavior and the natural environment* (pp. 127–161). New York: Plenum.

Kaplan, R. (1985). Nature at the doorstep: Residential satisfaction and the nearby environment. *Journal of Architectural Planning Research, 2,* 115–128.

Kaplan, R., & Kaplan, S. (1989). *The experience of nature: A psychological perspective.* New York: Cambridge University Press.

Kaplan, S., & Kaplan, R. (Eds.). (1978). *Humanscape: Environments for people.* Belmont, CA: Duxbury.

Kaplan, S., & Kaplan, R. (1984). *Cognition and environment.* New York: Praeger.

Kaplan, S., Kaplan, R., & Wendt, J. S. (1972). Rated preference and complexity for natural and urban visual material. *Perception and Psychophysics, 12,* 354–356.

Kaplan, S., & Talbot, J. F. (1983). Psychological benefits of a wilderness experience. In I. Altman & J. F. Wohlwill (Eds.), *Behavior and the natural environment* (pp. 163–203). New York: Plenum.

Karl, T. R., Heim, R. R., & Quayle, R. G. (1991). The greenhouse effect in central North America: If not now, when? *Science, 251,* 1058–1061.

Karl, T. R., Knight, R. W., Kukla, K. G., & Gavin, J. (1995). Evidence for radiative effects of anthropogenic sulfate aerosols in the observed climate record. In R. J. Charlson & J. Heintzenberg (Eds.), *Aerosol forcing of climate* (pp. 363–382). Chichester, UK: Wiley.

Kasl, S. V., White, M., Will, J., & Marcuse, P. (1982). Quality of the residential environment and mental health. In A. Baum & J. E. Singer (Eds.), *Advances in environmental psychology: 4. Environment and health* (pp. 1–30). Hillsdale, NJ: Lawrence Erlbaum Associates.

Kasper, R. G. (1979). Perceived risk: Implications for policy. In G. Goodman & W. D. Rowe (Eds.), *Energy risk management* (pp. 87–95). London: Academic Press.

Kasperson, R. E., Golding, D., & Tuler, S. (1992). Social distrust as a factor in siting hazardous facilities and communicating risks. *Journal of Social Issues, 48,* 161–187.

Kasperson, R. E., Renn, O., Slovic, P., Brown, H., Emel, J., Goble, R., Kasperson, J., & Ratick, S. (1988). The social amplification of risk: A conceptual framework. *Risk Analysis, 8,* 177–187.

Kassarjian, H. H. (1982). Consumer psychology. *Annual Review of Psychology, 33,* 619–649.

Kassirer, J., & McKenzie-Mohr, D. (1998). *Tools of change: Proven methods for promoting environmental citizenship.* Ottawa, Ontario, Canada: National Round Table on Environment and the Economy.

Kates, R. W. (1994). Sustaining life on the earth. *Scientific American, 271*(4), 114–122.

Kates, R. W., Clark, W. C., Corell, R., Hall, J. M., Jaeger, C. C., Lowe, I., McCarthy, J. J., Schellnhuber, H. J., Bolin, B., Dickson, N. M., Faucheux, S., Gallopin, G. C., Grübler, A., Huntley, B., Jäger, J., Jodha, N. S., Kasperson, R. E., Mabogunje, A., Matson, P., Mooney, H., Moore, B., III, O'Riordan, T., & Svedin, U. (2001). Sustainability science. *Science, 292,* 641–642.

Kates, R. W., & Kasperson, J. X. (1983). Comparative risk analysis of technological hazards (a review). *Proceedings of the National Academy of Sciences, 80,* 7027–7038.

Katzev, R. D., Cooper, L., & Fisher, P. (1980–81). The effect of feedback and social reinforcement on residential electricity consumption. *Journal of Environmental Systems, 10,* 215–227.

Katzev, R. D., & Johnson, T. R. (1983). A social-psychological analysis of residential electricity consumption: The impact of minimal justification techniques. *Journal of Economic Psychology, 3,* 267–284.

Katzev, R. D., & Johnson, T. R. (1984). Comparing the effects of monetary incentives and foot-in-the-door strategies in promoting residential energy conservation. *Journal of Applied Social Psychology, 14,* 12–27.

Katzev, R. D., & Johnson, T. R. (1987). *Promoting energy conservation: An analysis of behavioral research.* Boulder, CO: Westview.

Katzev, R. D., & Pardini, A. U. (1987–88). The comparative effectiveness of reward and commitment approaches in motivating community recycling. *Journal of Environmental Systems, 17,* 93–113.

Katzev, R. D., & Wang, T. (1994). Can commitment change behavior? A case study of environmental actions. *Journal of Social Behavior and Personality, 9,* 13–26.

Kauppi, P. E. (1995). The United Nations climate convention: Unattainable or irrelevant. *Science, 270,* 1454.

Keeling, C. D. (1986). Atmospheric $CO_2$ concentrations—Maunaloa Observatory, Hawaii, 1958–1986. Scripts Institute of Oceanography CDIAC NDP–001/R1.

Keeling, C. D., Bacastow, R. B., Carter, A. F., Piper, S. C., & Whorf, T. P. (1989). A three-dimensional model of atmospheric $CO_2$. *Aspects of Climate Variability in the Pacific and the Western Americas.* Geophysical Monograph 55 (Appendix A), American Geophysical Union.

Keep America Beautiful, Inc. (1968). *Who litters and why: Summary of survey findings concerning public awareness and concern about the problem of litter.* New York: Author.

Keep America Beautiful, Inc. (1970). *Fact sheet: Litter is a national disgrace*. New York: Author.

Kellert, S. R. (1974). *From kinship to mastery: A study of American attitudes toward animals.* A report to the U.S. Fish and Wildlife Service, Yale University.

Kellert, S. R. (1976). Perceptions of animals in American society. *Transactions of the North American Wildlife and Natural Resources Conference, 41,* 533–545.

Kellert, S. R. (1978). Attitudes and characteristics of hunters and anti-hunters. *Transactions of the North American Wildlife and Natural Resources Conference, 43,* 412–423.

Kellert, S. R. (1979). *American attitudes, knowledge and behaviors toward wildlife and natural habitats: Phase I. Public attitudes toward critical wildlife and natural habitat issues.* Washington, DC: U.S. Government Printing Office.

Kellert, S. R. (1980). Public attitudes, knowledge and behaviors toward wildlife and natural habitats. *Transactions of the North American Wildlife and Natural Resources Conference, 45,* 111–124.

Kellert, S. R. (1983). Affective, cognitive, and evaluative perceptions of animals. In I. Altman & J. F. Wohlwill (Eds.), *Behavior and the natural environment* (pp. 241–267). New York: Plenum.

Kellert, S. R., & Berry, J. K. (1980). *American attitudes, knowledge and behaviors toward wildlife and natural habitats: Phase III. Knowledge, affection and basic attitudes toward animals in American society.* Washington, DC: U.S. Government Printing Office.

Kellert, S. R., & Westervelt, M. O. (1983). *American attitudes, knowledge and behaviors toward wildlife and natural habitats: Phase V. Children's attitudes, knowledge and behaviors toward animals.* Washington, DC: U.S. Government Printing Office.

Kellert, S. R., & Wilson, E. O. (Eds.) (1993). *The biophilia hypothesis.* Washington, DC: Island Press.

Kellogg, W. W., & Schware, R. (1981). *Climate change and society: Consequences of increasing atmospheric carbon dioxide.* Boulder, CO: Westview.

Kelly, T. J., Mukund, R., Spicer, C. W., & Pollack, A. J. (1994). Concentrations and transformations of hazardous air pollutants. *Environmental Science and Technology, 28,* 378A–387A.

Kempton, W. (1990). Lay perspectives on global climate change (PU/CEES Report No. 251). Princeton, NJ: Princeton University, Center for Energy and Environmental Studies.

Kempton, W. (1991). Lay perspectives on global climate change. *Global Environmental Change, 1,* 183–208.

Kempton, W., Boster, J., & Hartley, J. (1995). *Environmental values in American culture.* Cambridge, MA: MIT Press.

Kempton, W., Darley, J. M., & Stern, P. C. (1992). Psychological research for the new energy problems: Strategies and opportunities. *American Psychologist, 47,* 1213–1223.

Kempton, W., Harris, C. K., Keith, J. G., & Weihl, J. S. (1985). Do consumers know what works in energy conservation? *Marriage and Family Review, 9,* 115–133.

Kempton, W., & Montgomery, L. (1982). Folk quantification of energy. *Energy, 7,* 817–827.

Kendall, H. W., Arrow, K. J., Borlaug, N. E., Ehrlich, P. R., Lederberg, J., Vargas, J. I., Watson, R. T., & Wilson, E. O. (1996). *Meeting the challenge of population, environment, and resources: The costs of inaction.* Washington, DC: The World Bank.

Kerr, J. B., & McElroy, C. T. (1993). Evidence for large upward trends of ultraviolet-B radiation linked to ozone depletion. *Science, 262,* 1032–1034.

Kerr, R. A. (1988). Stratospheric ozone is decreasing. *Science, 239,* 1489–1491.
Kerr, R. A. (1989). Research news: Hanson vs. the world on the greenhouse threat. *Science, 244,* 1041–1043.
Kerr, R. A. (1990). New greenhouse report puts down dissenters. *Science, 249,* 481–482.
Kerr, R. A. (1991). Ozone destruction worsens. *Science, 252,* 204.
Kerr, R. A. (1992a). Greenhouse science survives skeptics. *Science, 256,* 1138–1140.
Kerr, R. A. (1992b). New assaults seen on Earth's ozone shield. *Science, 255,* 797–798.
Kerr, R. A. (1994a). Antarctic ozone hole fails to recover. *Science, 266,* 217.
Kerr, R. A. (1994b). Climate modeling's fudge factor comes under fire. *Science, 265,* 1528.
Kerr, R. A. (1994c). Did Pinatubo sent climate-warming gases into a dither? *Science, 263,* 1562.
Kerr, R. A. (1995a). Is the world warming or not? *Science, 267,* 612.
Kerr, R. A. (1995b). It's official: First glimmer of greenhouse warming seen. *Science, 270,* 1565–1567.
Kerr, R. A. (1996). Ozone-destroying chlorine tops out. *Science, 271,* 32.
Kerr, R. A. (1997). Greenhouse forecasting still cloudy. *Science, 276,* 1040–1042.
Kerr, R. A. (1998). Acid rain control: Success on the cheap. *Science, 282,* 1024–1027.
Kerr, R. A. (2000). Draft report affirms human influence. *Science, 288,* 589–590.
Kerr, R. A. (2001a). Rising global temperature, rising uncertainty. *Science, 292,* 192–194.
Kerr, R. A. (2001b). World stars taming the greenhouse. *Science, 293,* 583.
Keyfitz, N. (1989). The growing human population. *Scientific American, 261*(3), 118–126.
Khabibullov, M. (1991). Crisis in environmental management of the Soviet Union. *Environmental Management, 15,* 749–763.
Kiefer, I. (1974). *Incentives for tire recycling and reuse.* Washington, DC: Environmental Protection Agency.
Kiessling, K. L., & Landberg, H. (1994). *Population, economic development, and the environment.* London: Oxford University Press.
King, D. M., & Herring, D. D. (2000). Monitoring earth's vital signs. *Scientific American, 282*(4), 92–97.
King, R. T. (1947). The future of wildlife in forest use. *Transactions of the North American Wildlife Conference, 12,* 454–466.
Kitchin, R. M. (1994). Cognitive maps: What are they and why study them? *Journal of Environmental Psychology, 14,* 1–19.
Klemm, F. (1964). *A history of western technology.* (D. W. Singer, Trans.). Cambridge, MA: MIT Press. (Original publication in 1954)
Kneese, A. V. (1977). *Economics and the environment.* New York: Penguin.
Kneese, A. V. (1984). *Measuring the benefits of clean air and water.* Washington, DC: Resources for the future.
Kneese, A. V., & Schulze, W. D. (1985). Ethics and environmental economics. In A. V. Kneese & J. L. Sweeney (Eds.), *Handbook of natural resources and energy economics* (pp. 191–220). New York: North Holland.
Knopf, R. C. (1983). Recreational needs and behavior in natural settings. In I. Altman & J. F. Wohlwill (Eds.), *Behavior and the natural environment* (pp. 205–240). New York: Plenum.
Knopf, R. C., Driver, B. L., & Basset, J. R. (1973). Motivations for fishing. In *Transactions of the 28th North American wildlife and natural resources conference* (pp. 191–204). Washington, DC: Wildlife Management Institute.
Koenig, D. J. (1975). Additional research on environmental activism. *Environment and Behavior, 7,* 472–485.
Koenig, R. (1995). Rio signatories to negotiate new goals. *Science, 268,* 197.
Kohlenberg, R., & Phillips, T. (1973). Reinforcement and rate of litter depositing. *Journal of Applied Behavior Analysis, 6,* 391–396.

Kohlenberg, R., Phillips, T., & Proctor, W. (1976). A behavioral analysis of peaking in residential electrical energy consumers. *Journal of Applied Behavior Analysis, 9,* 13–18.
Kohm, K. A. (Ed.). (1991). *Balancing on the brink of extinction.* Washington, DC: Island Press.
Kohut, A., & Shriver, J. (1989, June). *The environment* (Report No. 285). Princeton, NJ: The Gallup Report.
Koltnow, P. G. (1988). Advanced technology: Vehicle and automobile guidance. In *A look ahead: Year 2020* (Special Report 220). Washington, DC: Transportation Research Board, National Research Council.
Komorita, S. S., & Parks, C. D. (1996). *Social dilemmas.* Boulder, CO: Westview
Kraft, M. E., & Clary, B. B. (1993). Citizen participation and the NIMBY syndrome: Public responses to radioactive waste disposal. *Western Political Quarterly, 44,* 299–328.
Krajick, K. (2001). Long-term data show lingering effects from acid rain. *Science, 292,* 195–196.
Krause, D. (1993). Environmental consciousness: An empirical study. *Environment and Behavior, 25,* 126–142.
Krauss, R., Freedman, J., & Whitcup, M. (1978). Field and laboratory studies of littering. *Journal of Experimental Social Psychology, 14,* 109–122.
Kremen, C., Niles, J. O., Dalton, M. G., Daily, G. C., Ehrlich, P. R., Fay, J. P., Grewal, D., & Guillery, R. P. (2000). Economic incentives for rain forest conservation across scales. *Science, 288,* 1828–1832.
Krimsky, S., & Golding, D. (1991). Factoring risk into environmental decision making. In R. A. Chechile & S. Carlisle (Eds.), *Environmental decision making: A multidisciplinary perspective* (pp. 92–119). New York: Van Nostrand Reinhold.
Krimsky, S., & Plough, A. (1988). *Environmental hazards: Communicating risks as a social process.* Dover, MA: Auburn House.
Kromm, D. E., Probald, F., & Wall, G. (1973). An international comparison of response to air pollution. *Journal of Environmental Management, 1,* 363–375.
Krumenaker, L. (1993). Virtual libraries, complete with journals, get real. *Science, 260,* 1066–1067.
Krupnick, A. J., & Portney, P. R. (1991). Controlling urban air pollution: A benefit-cost assessment. *Science, 252,* 522–528.
Krutilla, J. V., & Fisher, A. C. (1985). *The economics of natural environments: Studies in the valuation of commodity and amenity resources.* Washington, DC: Resources for the Future.
Kuipers, B. (1982). The "map in the head" metaphor. *Environment and Behavior, 14,* 202–220.
Kumar, A., Leetmaa, A., & Ji, M. (1994). Simulations of atmospheric variability induced by sea surface temperatures and implications for global warming. *Science, 266,* 632–634.
Kunda, Z. (1987). Motivation and inference: Self-serving generation and evaluation of evidence. *Journal of Personality and Social Psychology, 53,* 636–647.
Kwok, K. (1979). Semantic evaluation of perceived environment: A cross-cultural replication. *Man-Environment Systems, 9,* 243–249.
La Brecque, M. (1989). Detecting climate change: I. Taking the world's shifting temperature. *Mosiac, 20*(4), 2–9.
Lal, R., & Stewart, B. A. (1990). *Soil degradation.* New York: Springer-Verlag.
Langer, E. J., & Rodin, J. (1976). The effects of choice and enhanced personal responsibility for the aged: A field experiment in an institutional setting. *Journal of Personality and Social Psychology, 34,* 191–198.
Lanier, J. (2001). Virtually there. *Scientific American, 285*(1), 66–75.
Lansana, F. (1992). Distinguishing recyclers from nonrecyclers: A basis for developing recycling strategies. *Journal of Experimental Education, 23,* 16–23.

LaPage, W. F., & Ragain, D. P. (1974). Family camping trends: An eight-year panel study. *Journal of Leisure Research, 6,* 101–112.

La Piere, R. (1934). Attitudes versus actions. *Social Forces, 13,* 230–237.

La Rivière, J. W. M. (1989). Threats to the world's water. *Scientific American, 261*(3), 80–94.

Larsen, K. S. (1995). Environmental waste: Recycling attitudes and correlates. *Journal of Social Psychology, 135,* 83–88.

Latimer, D. A., Daniel, T. C., & Hogo, H. (1980). *Relationship between air quality and human perception of scenic areas*. San Rafael, CA: Systems Applications.

Latimer, D. A., Hogo, H., & Daniel, T. C. (1981). The effects of optical conditions on perceived scenic beauty. *Atmospheric Environment, 15,* 1865–1874.

Lauridsen, P. K. (1977). *Decreasing gasoline consumption in fleet-owned automobiles through feedback and feedback-plus-lottery*. Unpublished thesis, Drake University.

Lave, L. B., Hendrickson, C. T., & McMichael, F. C. (1995). Environmental implications of electric cars. *Science, 268,* 993–995.

Lave, L. B., & Seskin, E. P. (1977). *Air pollution and human health: Resources for the future*. Baltimore, MD: Johns Hopkins University Press.

Lave, L. B., & Upton, A. C. (1987). *Toxic chemicals, health, and the environment*. Baltimore, MD: The Johns Hopkins University Press.

Lawton, J. H., & May, R. M. (Eds.). (1995). *Extinction rates*. Oxford, UK: Oxford University Press.

Lawton, M. P. (1985a). Housing and living environments of older people. In R. Binstock & E. Shanas (Eds.), *Handbook of aging and the social sciences* (pp. 450–478). New York: Van Nostrand Reinhold.

Lawton, M. P. (1985b). The elderly in context: Perspectives from environmental psychology and gerontology. *Environment and Behavior, 17,* 501–519.

Lazo, J. K., Schulze, W. D., McClelland, G. H., & Doyle, J. K. (1992). Can contingent valuation measure nonuse values? *American Journal of Agricultural Economics, 74,* 1126–1132.

Leaf, A. (1989). Potential health effects of global climatic and environmental changes. *New England Journal of Medicine, 321,* 1577–1583.

Leavitt, J., & Saegert, S. (1989). *From abandonment to hope: Community households in harlem*. New York: Columbia University Press.

Lederberg, J. (1978). Digital communications and the conduct of science: The new literacy. *Proceedings of the IEEE, 66,* 1314–1319.

Lehman, R. L., & Warren, H. E. (1978). Residential natural gas consumption: Evidence that conservation efforts to date have failed. *Science, 199,* 879–882.

Lents, J. M. (1991). Letter to the editor (Air pollution benefit-cost assessment). *Science, 253,* 607–608.

Leonard-Barton, D. (1981). The diffusion of active-residential solar energy equipment in California. In A. Shama (Ed.), *Marketing solar energy innovations* (pp. 243–257). New York: Praeger.

Leutwyler, K. (1995). The price of prevention. *Scientific American, 272*(4), 124–129.

Levenson, H. (1974). Activism and powerful others: Distinctions within the concept of internal-external control. *Journal of Personality Assessment, 38,* 377–383.

Leventhal, H. (1970). Findings and theory in the study of fear communications. In L. Berkowitz (Ed.), *Advances in experimental social psychology* (Vol. 5, pp. 119–186). New York: Academic Press.

Levi, D. J., & Holder, E. E. (1986). Nuclear power: The dynamics of acceptability. *Environment and Behavior, 18,* 385–395.

Levi, D., & Kocher, S. (1999). Virtual nature: The effects of information technology on our relationship to nature. *Environment and Behavior, 31,* 203–226.

Levi, D., Kocher, S., & Aboud, R. (2001). Technological disasters in natural and built environments. *Environment and Behavior, 33,* 78–92.

Levine, S. H. (1991). Ecosystem perspectives in environmental decision making. In R. A. Chechile & S. Carlisle (Eds.), *Environmental decision making: A multidisciplinary perspective* (pp. 38–63). New York: Van Nostrand Reinhold.

Levitt, L., & Leventhal, G. (1986). Litter reduction: How effective is the New York State bottle bill? *Environment and Behavior, 18,* 467–479.

Levitus, S., Antonov, J. I., Boyer, T. P., & Stephens, C. (2000). Warming of the world ocean. *Science, 287,* 2225–2229.

Levitus, S., Antonov, J. I., Wang, J., Delworth, T. L., Dixon, K. W., & Broccoli, A. J. (2001). Anthropogenic warming of earth's climate system. *Science, 292,* 267–270.

Levy, S. B. (1998). The challenge of antibiotic resistance. *Scientific American, 278*(3), 46–53.

Levy, S. B., & Miller, R. V. (Eds.). (1989). *Gene transfer in the environment.* New York: McGraw-Hill.

Lewis, C. A. (1979). Healing in the urban environment: A person/plant viewpoint. *Journal of the American Planning Association, 45,* 330–338.

Lewis, H. (1980). The safety of fission reactors. *Scientific American, 242,* 53–65.

Lewis, H. (1990). *Technological risk.* New York: Norton.

Lichtenstein, S., Fischhoff, B., & Phillips, L. D. (1977). Calibration of probabilities: The state of the art. In H. Jungermann & G. de Zeeuw (Eds.), *Decision making and change in human affairs* (pp. 275–324). Dordrecht: Reidel.

Lichtenstein, S., Fischhoff, B., & Phillips, L. D. (1982). Calibration of probabilities: The state of the art to 1980. In D. Kahneman, P. Slovic, & A. Tversky (Eds.), *Judgment under uncertainty: Heuristics and biases* (pp. 306–334). Cambridge: Cambridge University Press.

Lichtenstein, S., Slovic, P., Fischhoff, B., Layman, M., & Combs, B. (1978). Judged frequency of lethal events. *Journal of Experimental Psychology: Human Learning and Memory, 4,* 551–578.

Lichtenstein, S., & Slovic, P. (1971). Reversals of preference between bids and choices in gambling decisions. *Journal of Experimental Psychology, 89,* 46–55.

Licklider, J. C. R. (1965). *Libraries of the future.* Cambridge, MA: MIT Press.

Lieber, C. M. (2001). The incredible shrinking circuit. *Scientific American, 285*(3), 58–64.

Lifset, R. J. (2000). Full accounting. *The Sciences, 40*(3), 32–37.

Likens, G. E., Bormann, F. H., & Johnson, N. M. (1972). Acid rain. *Environment, 14,* 33–40.

Likens, G. E., Wright, R. F., Galloway, J. N., & Butler, T. J. (1979). Acid rain. *Scientific American, 241*(4), 43–51.

Lime, D. W. (1971). *Factors influencing campground use in the Superior National Forest* (USDA Forest Service Research Paper NC–60). St. Paul, MN: North Central Forest Experiment Station.

Lime, D. W., & Stankey, G. H. (1971). Carrying capacity: Maintaining outdoor recreation quality. *Recreation Symposium Proceedings* (pp. 174–184). Upper Darby, PA: USDA Forest Service.

Lindskold, S. (1978). Trust development, the GRIT proposal, and the effects of conciliatory acts on conflict and cooperation. *Psychological Bulletin, 85,* 772–793.

Lindzen, R. S. (1990). Global warming report (Letter to the Editor). *Science, 247,* 14.

Linn, N., Vining, J., & Feeley, P. A. (1994). Toward a sustainable society: Waste minimization through environmentally conscious consuming. *Journal of Applied Social Psychology, 24,* 1550–1572.

Lippert, F. W., & Morris, S. C. (1991). Letter to the editor (Air pollution benefit-cost assessment). *Science, 253,* 606.

Lipsey, M. W. (1977). The personal antecedents and consequences of ecologically responsible behavior: A review. *JSAS Catalog of Selected Documents in Psychology, 7,* 70–71.

Lipske, M. (1990). How much is enough? *National Wildlife, 28*(4), 18–22.

Litai, D., Lanning, D. D., & Rasmussen, N. C. (1983). The public perception of risk. In V. T. Covello, W. G. Flamm, J. V. Rodricks, & R. G. Tardiff (Eds.), *The analysis of actual versus perceived risks* (pp. 213–224). New York: Plenum.

Livingston, J. (1981). *The fallacy of wildlife conservation.* Toronto, Ontario: McClelland & Stewart.

Locke, E. A., & Latham, G. P. (1990). *A theory of goal setting and task performance.* Englewood Cliffs, NJ: Prentice-Hall.

Longstreth, M., Turner, J., Topliff, M. L., & Iams, D. R. (1989). Support for soft and hard American energy policies: Does gender play a role? *Women's Studies International Forum, 12,* 213–226.

Loomes, C., & Sugden, R. (1983). A rationale for preference reversal. *American Economic Review, 73,* 428–432.

Lovering, D. (2001). Taming the killing fields. *Scientific American, 285*(2), 66–71.

Loucks, D. P., Stedinger, J. R., & Haith, D. A. (1981). *Water resource systems planning and analysis.* Englewood Cliffs, NJ: Prentice-Hall.

Lubchenco, J. (1998). Entering the century of the environment: A new social contract for science. *Science, 279,* 491–497.

Lubin, D. (1994). The role of the tropical super greenhouse effect in heating the ocean surface. *Science, 265,* 224–227.

Lucas, R. C. (1964). Wilderness perception and use: The example of the Boundary Waters Canoe Area. *Natural Resources Journal, 3,* 394–411.

Lucky, R. W. (1989). *Silicon dreams.* New York: St. Martin's Press.

Lutz, A. R., Simpson-Housley, P., & de Man, A. F. (1999). Wilderness: Rural and urban attitudes and perceptions. *Environment and Behavior, 31,* 259–266.

Luyben, P. D. (1980). Effects of informational prompts on energy conservation in college classrooms. *Journal of Applied Behavior Analysis, 13,* 611–617.

Luyben, P. D. (1982). Prompting thermostat setting behavior: Public response to a presidential appeal for conservation. *Environment and Behavior, 14,* 113–128.

Luyben, P. D. (1982–1983). A parametric analysis of prompting procedures to encourage electrical energy conservation. *Journal of Environmental Systems, 12,* 329–339.

Luyben, P. D. (1984). Drop and tilt: A comparison of two procedures to increase the use of venetian blinds to conserve energy. *Journal of Community Psychology, 12,* 149–154.

Luyben, P. D., & Bailey, J. S. (1979). Newspaper recycling: The effects of rewards and proximity of containers. *Environment and Behavior, 11,* 539–557.

Luyben, P. D., & Cummings, S. (1981–82). Motivating beverage container recycling on a college campus. *Journal of Environmental Systems, 11,* 235–245.

Luyben, P. D., Warren, S. B., & Tallman, T. A. (1979–1980). Recycling beverage containers on a college campus. *Journal of Environmental Systems, 9,* 189–202.

MacCalden, M., & Davis, C. (1972). *Report on priority lane experiment on the San Francisco-Oakland Bay bridge.* San Francisco, CA: Department of Public Works.

MacDonald, G. J. (1989). Scientific bases for the greenhouse effect. *Mitre Journal,* 205–222.

Machina, M. J. (1990). Choice under uncertainty: Problems solved and unsolved. In P. B. Hammond & R. Coppock (Eds.), *Valuing health risks, costs, and benefits for environmental decision making* (pp. 134–188). Washington, DC: National Academy Press.

Mackie, D. M. (1987). Systematic and nonsystematic processing of majority and minority persuasive communications. *Journal of Personality and Social Psychology, 53,* 41–52.

MacLean, D. E. (1990) Comparing values in environmental policies: Moral issues and moral arguments. In P. B. Hammond & R. Coppock (Eds.), *Valuing health risks, costs, and benefits for environmental decision making* (pp. 83–106). Washington, DC: National Academy Press.

MacNeill, J. (1989). Strategies for sustainable economic development. *Scientific American, 261*(3), 154–165.

Mahlman, J. D. (1997). Uncertainties in projections of human-caused climate warming. *Science, 278,* 1416–1417.

Mainieri, T., Barnett, E. G., Valdero, T. R., Unipan, J. B., & Oskamp, S. (1997). Green buying: The influence of environmental concern on consumer behavior. *Journal of Social Psychology, 137,* 189–204.

Makar, H. V. (1993, June). *Mineralogy Today.*

Malakoff, D. (1998). Restored wetlands flunk real-world test. *Science, 280,* 371–372.

Malm, W., Kelley, K., Molenar, J., & Daniel, T. (1981). Human perception of visual air quality (uniform haze). *Atmospheric Environment, 15,* 1875–1890.

Manabe, S., & Wetherald, R. T. (1980). On the distribution of climate change resulting from an increase in $CO_2$ content of the atmosphere. *Journal of the Atmospheric Sciences, 37,* 99–118.

Mandell, L., & Marans, R. (1972). *Participation in outdoor recreation: A national perspective.* Ann Arbor, MI: Institute for Social Research.

Mann, C. C. (1991). Extinction: Are ecologists crying wolf? *Science, 253,* 736–738.

Mann, M. E., Bradley, R. S., & Hughes, M. K. (1998). Global-scale temperature patterns and climate forcing over the past six centuries. *Nature, 392,* 779–787.

Marans, R. W., & Spreckelmeyer, K. F. (1982). Evaluating open and conventional office design. *Environment and Behavior, 14,* 333–351.

Marans, R. W., & Stokols, D. (Eds.). (1993). *Environmental simulation: Research and policy issues.* New York: Plenum.

Mares, M. A. (1992). Neotropical mammals and the myth of Amazonian biodiversity. *Science, 255,* 976–979.

Margolin, J. B., & Misch, M. R. (1978). *Incentives and disincentives for ridesharing: A behavioral study.* Washington, DC: U.S. Government Printing Office.

Marshall, E. (1993a). Fitting planet earth into a user-friendly database. *Science, 261,* 846–848.

Marshall, E. (1993b). Is environmental technology a key to a healthy economy? *Science, 260,* 1886–1888.

Marshall Institute. (1991). *Two environmental issues: 1. Ozone, 2. The greenhouse problem.* Washington, DC: The George C. Marshall Institute.

Martichuski, D. K., & Bell, P. A. (1991). Reward, punishment, privatization, and moral suasion in a commons dilemma. *Journal of Applied Social Psychology, 21,* 1356–1369.

Martindale, D. (2001a). Leaking away. *Scientific American, 284*(2), 54–55.

Martindale, D. (2001b). Waste not, want not. *Scientific American, 284*(2), 55.

Matson, P. A., Parton, W. J., Power, A. G., & Swift, M. J. (1997). Agricultural intensification and ecosystem properties. *Science, 277,* 504–509.

Matthies, E., Höger, R., & Guski, R. (2000). Living on polluted soil: Determinants of stress symptoms. *Environment and Behavior, 32,* 270–286.

Mayo, E. J., & Jarvis, L. R. (1981). *The psychology of leisure travel: Effective marketing and selling of travel services.* Boston: CBI Publishing.

McCaul, K. D., & Kopp, J. T. (1982). Effects of goal setting and commitment on increasing metal recycling. *Journal of Applied Psychology, 67,* 377–379.

McClelland, L. (1980). *Encouraging energy conservation in multifamily housing: RUBS and other methods of allocating energy costs to residents* (Report to the U.S. Department of Energy). Boulder CO: Institute of Behavioral Science, University of Colorado.

McClelland, L., & Belsten, L. (1979–1980). Promoting energy conservation in university dormitories by physical, policy, and resident behavior changes. *Journal of Environmental Systems, 9,* 13–18.

McClelland, L., & Canter, R. J. (1981). Psychological research on energy conservation: Context, approaches, methods. In A. Baum & J. E. Singer (Eds.), *Advances in environmental psychology: Vol. 3. Energy conservation: Psychological perspectives* (pp. 1–25). Hillsdale, NJ: Lawrence Erlbaum Associates.

McClelland, L., & Cook, S. W. (1979–1980). Energy conservation effects of continuous in-home feedback in all-electric homes. *Journal of Environmental Systems, 9,* 169–173.

McClelland, L., & Cook, S. W. (1980). Promoting energy conservation in master-metered apartments through financial incentives. *Journal of Applied Social Psychology, 10,* 19–31.

McGinn, A. P. (1998). Promoting sustainable fisheries. In L. R. Brown, C. Flavin, H. Frenck, J. Abramovitz, C. Bright, S. Dunn, G. Gardner, A. McGinn, J. Mitchell, M. Renner, D. Roodman, L. Starke, & J. Tuxill (Eds.), *State of the world 1998* (pp. 59–78). New York: Norton.

McKechnie, G. E. (1974). *Environmental response inventory manual.* Palo Alto, CA: Consulting Psychologists Press.

McKenna, F. P. (1993). It won't happen to me: Unrealistic optimism or illusion of control? *British Journal of Psychology, 84,* 39–50.

McKenna, F. P., Stanier, R. A., & Lewis, C. (1991). Factors underlying illusory self-assessment of driving skill in males and females. *Accident Analysis and Prevention, 23,* 45–52.

McKenzie-Mohr, D. (2000). Fostering sustainable behavior through community-based social marketing. *American Psychologist, 55,* 531–537.

McKibben, B. (1990). *The end of nature.* New York: Anchor Books.

McKibben, B. (1996. December 2). Out there in the middle of the buzz. *Forbes,* pp. 107–129.

Meadows, D. H., Meadows, D. L., & Randers, J. (1992). *Beyond the limits.* Post Mills, VT: Chelsea Green.

Meier, M. F. (1984). Contribution of small glaciers to global sea level. *Science, 226,* 1418–1421.

Meier, M. F. (1990). Reduced rise in sea level. *Nature, 343,* 115.

Mekjavik, I. B., Banister, E. W., & Morrison, J. B. (1988). *Environmental ergonomics: Sustaining human performance in harsh environments.* London: Taylor & Francis.

Melnick, R. S. (1990). The politics of benefit-cost analysis. In P. B. Hammond & R. Coppock (Eds.), *Valuing health risks, costs, and benefits for environmental decision making* (pp. 23–54). Washington, DC: National Academy Press.

Mellers, B. A., Ordóñez, L. D., & Birnbaum, M. H. (1992). Preferences, prices, and ratings in risky decision making. *Journal of Experimental Psychology: Human Perception and Performance, 18,* 347–361.

Melosi, M. V. (1981). *Garbage in the cities: Refuse, reform, and the environment, 1980–1990.* College Station, TX: Texas A & M University Press.

Mendell, M. J., & Smith, A. H. (1990). Consistent pattern of elevated symptoms in air-conditioned office buildings: A reanalysis of epidemiologic studies. *American Journal of Public Health, 80,* 1193–1199.

Merkhofer, M. W. (1987). *Decision science and social risk management: A comparative evaluation of cost-benefit analysis, decision analysis, and other formal decision-aiding approaches.* Norwell, MA: D. Reidel.

Messick, D. M., & Brewer, M. B. (1983). Solving social dilemmas. In L. Wheeler & P. Shaver (Eds.), *Review of personality and social psychology (Vol. 4),* Beverly Hills, CA: Sage.

Meux, E. P. (1973). Concern for the common good in an N-person game. *Journal of Personality and Social Psychology, 28,* 414–418.

Michaels, P. J. (1992). *The sound and the fury: The science and politics of global warming.* Washington, DC: CATO Institute.

Michelson, W. (1976). *Man and his urban environment: A sociological approach* (2nd ed.). Reading, MA: Addison-Wesley.

Midden, C. J., Meter, J. E., Weening, M. H., & Zieverink, H. J. (1983). Using feedback, reinforcement and information to reduce energy consumption in households: A field experiment. *Journal of Economic Psychology, 3,* 65–86.

Midden, C. J., & Verplanken, B. (1990). The stability of nuclear attitudes after Chernobyl. *Journal of Environmental Psychology, 10,* 111–119.

Milbrath, L. W. (1985). Environmental beliefs and values. In M. G. Herman (Ed.), *Political psychology.* San Francisco: Jossey-Bass.

Miller, B. (1991). Letter to the editor (Air pollution benefit-cost assessment). *Science, 253,* 608.

Miller, R. D., & Ford, J. M. (1985). *Shared savings in the residential market: A public/private partnership for energy conservation.* Baltimore, MD: Urban Consortium for Technology Initiatives, Energy Task Force.

Miller, R. V. (1998). Bacterial gene swapping in nature. *Scientific American, 278*(1), 66–71.

Milner, A. (1989). Building participation. *Biocycle, 30,* 88–89.

Milstein, J. S. (1977). *How consumers feel about energy: Attitudes and behavior during the winter and spring of 1976–77.* Washington, DC: Federal Energy Administration.

Minnis, P., Harrison, E. F., Stowe, L. L., Gibson, G. G., Denn, F. M., Doelling, D. R., & Smith, W. L., Jr. (1993). Radiative climate forcing by the Mount Pinatubo eruption. *Science, 259,* 1411–1415.

Mitchell, G. (1987). Clean air: Congress must get tough. *National Parks, 61*(7–8), 12–13.

Mitchell, J. F. B. (1989). The greenhouse effect and climate change. *Reviews of Geophysics, 27,* 115–129.

Mitchell, R. (1990). Public opinion and the Green lobby: Poised for the 1990s? In N. Vig & M. Craft (Eds.), *Environmental policy in the 1990s: Towards a new agenda.* Washington, DC: CQ Press.

Mitchell, W. J. (1997). Do we still need skyscrapers? *Scientific American, 277*(6), 112–113.

Moffat, A. S. (1992). Does global change threaten the world food supply? *Science, 256,* 1140–1141.

Mohai, P. (1985). Public concern and elite involvement in environmental conservation issues. *Social Science Quarterly, 66,* 820–838.

Mohnen, V. A. (1988). The challenge of acid rain. *Scientific American, 259*(2), 30–38.

Mokhtarian, P. L. (1997). Now that travel can be virtual, will congestion virtually disappear? *Scientific American, 277*(4), 93.

Molina, M. J., & Rowland, F. S. (1974). Stratospheric sink for chlorofluoromethanes: Chlorine atom catalyzed destruction of ozone. *Nature, 249,* 810–812.

Monat, A., & Lazarus, R. A. (Eds.). (1977). *Stress and coping.* New York: Columbia University Press.

Monty, R. A., Geller, E. S., Savage, R. E., & Perlmutter, L. C. (1979). The freedom to choose is not always so choice. *Journal of Experimental Psychology: Human Learning and Memory, 5,* 170–178.

Montzka, S. A., Butler, J. H., Myers, R. S., Thompson, T. M., Swanson, T. H., Clarke, A. D., Lock, L. T., & Elkins, J. W. (1996). Decline in the tropospheric abundance of halogen from halocarbons: Implications for stratospheric ozone depletion. *Science, 272,* 1318–1322.

Moomaw, W. R., & Kildow, J. T. (1991). International environmental decision making: Challenges and changes for the old order. In R. A. Chechile & S. Carlisle (Eds.), *Environmental decision making: A multidisciplinary perspective* (pp. 269–288). New York: Van Nostrand Reinhold.

Moore, D. W. (1992). *The super pollsters.* New York: Four Walls Eight Windows.

Moore, G. T. (1979). Knowing about environmental knowing: The current state of theory and research on environmental cognition. *Environment and Behavior, 11,* 33–70.

Moray, N. P. (1993). Technosophy and humane factors. *Ergonomics in Design, 1*(4), 33–39.

Moray, N. P. (1994). *Ergonomics and the global problems of the 21st century.* Keynote address at the 12th Triennial Congress of the International Ergonomics Association, Toronto, Canada.

Moray, N. P., & Huey, B. M. (Eds.). (1988). *Human factors research and nuclear safety.* Washington, DC: National Academy Press.

Morell, D., & Magorian, C. (1980). *Siting hazardous waste facilities: Local opposition and the myth of preemption.* Cambridge, MA: Ballinger.

Morgan, M. G., & Henrion, M. (1990). *Uncertainty: A guide to dealing with uncertainty in quantitative risk and policy analysis.* New York: Cambridge University Press.

Morowitz, H. J. (1991). Balancing species preservation and economic considerations. *Science, 253,* 752–754.

Morse, C. (1991). California—How can we get 50 percent? *Public Management, 10,* 4–10.

Mosler, H. J. (1993). Self dissemination of environmentally-responsible behavior: The influence of trust in a commons dilemma game. *Journal of Environmental Psychology, 13,* 111–123.

Musser, G. (2001). Climate of uncertainty. *Scientific American, 285*(4), 14–15.

Myers, F. S. (1992). Japan bids for global leadership in clean industry. *Science, 256,* 1144–1145.

Myers, N. (1980). *Conversion of tropical moist forests.* Washington, DC: National Academy Press.

Myers, N. (1989). *Deforestation rates in tropical forests and their climatic implications.* London: Friends of the Earth.

Myers, N. (1995). The world's forests: Need for a policy appraisal. *Science, 268,* 823–824.

Myers, N. (1997). Consumption: Challenge to sustainable development. *Science, 276,* 53–55.

Myrick, F. A., III. (1982). *Air and water pollution control: A benefit-cost assessment.* New York: Wiley.

Nader, R. (1991). The management of environmental violence: Regulation or reluctance? In A. B. Wolbrast (Ed.), *Environment in peril* (pp. 2–25). Washington, DC: Smithsonian Institution Press.

Nadis, S. (1990). Hydrogen dreams. *Technology Review, 93*(6), 20, 21.

Nasar, J. L. (1983). Adult viewers' preferences in residential scenes: A study of the relationship of environmental attributes for preference. *Environment and Behavior, 15,* 589–614.

Nasar, J. L. (1984). Visual preferences in urban street scenes: A cross-cultural comparison between Japan and the United States. *Journal of Cross-Cultural Psychology, 15,* 79–93.

Nash, R. (1973). *Wilderness and the American mind.* New Haven, CT: Yale University Press.

National Academy of Sciences. (1983). *Changing climate: Report of the carbon dioxide assessment committee.* Washington, DC: National Academy Press.

National Academy of Sciences. (1989). *The nuclear weapons complex: Management for health, safety, and the environment.* Washington, DC: National Academy Press.

National Research Council (Safe Drinking Water Committee). (1977a). *Drinking water and health.* Washington, DC: National Academy of Sciences.

National Research Council (Panel on Energy and Climate). (1977b). *Energy and climate.* Washington, DC: National Academy Press.

National Research Council (Committee on Medical and Biological Effects of Environmental Pollutants). (1977c). *Nitrogen oxides.* Washington, DC: National Academy Press.

National Research Council (Committee on Sulfur Oxides). (1978a). *Sulfur oxides.* Washington, DC: National Academy Press.

National Research Council (Panel on Nitrates of the Coordinating Committee for Scientific and Technical Assessments of Environmental Pollutants). (1978b). *Nitrates: An environmental assessment.* Washington, DC: National Academy Press.

National Research Council (Committee on Nuclear and Alternative Energy Systems). (1979). *Energy in transition 1985–2010.* Washington, DC: National Academy Press.

National Research Council (Committee on Lead in the Human Environment). (1980). *Lead in the human environment.* Washington, DC: National Academy Press.

National Research Council (Committee on Atmosphere and the Biosphere). (1981). *Atmosphere-biosphere interactions: Toward a better understanding of the ecological consequences of fossil fuel combustion.* Washington, DC: National Academy Press.

National Research Council. (1987). *Current issues in atmospheric change.* Washington, DC: National Academy Press.

National Research Council. (1989a). *Alternative agriculture.* Washington, DC: National Academy Press.

National Research Council. (1989b). *Improving risk communication.* Committee on Risk Perception and Communication, National Research Council. Washington, DC: National Academy Press.

National Research Council (Panel on the Improvement of Tropical and Subtropical Rangelands). (1990). *The improvement of tropical and subtropical rangelands.* Washington, DC: National Academy Press.

National Research Council. (1991). *Rethinking the ozone problem in urban and regional air pollution.* Washington DC: National Academy Press.

National Research Council. (1994). *Alternatives for ground water cleanup.* Washington DC: National Academy Press.

National Research Council. (2001). *Under the weather: Climate, ecosystems, and infectious disease.* Washington, DC: National Academy Press.

National Science Board. (1989, September). *Loss of biological diversity: A global crisis requiring international solutions.* A report to the National Science Board.

Nausser, J. I. (1982). Framing the landscape in photographic simulation. *Journal of Environmental Management, 17,* 1–16.

Neftel, A., Moor, E., Oeschger, H., Stauffer, B. (1985). Evidence from polar ice cores for the increase in atmospheric $CO_2$ in the past two centuries. *Nature, 315,* 45–47.

Nelkin, D. (1989). Communicating technological risk: The social construction of risk perception. *Annual Review of Public Health, 10,* 95–113.

Neuman, K. (1986). Personal values and commitment to energy conservation. *Environment and Behavior, 18,* 53–74.

Newell, R. E., Reichle, H. G., Jr., & Seiler, W. (1989). Carbon monoxide and the burning earth. *Scientific American, 261*(4), 82–88.

Newman, P. A. (1994). Antarctic total ozone in 1958. *Science, 264,* 543–546.

Newman, S. H., & Thompson, V. D. (Eds.). (1976). *Population psychology: Research and educational issues.* Washington, DC: Government Printing Office.

Newsom, T. J., & Makranczy, U. J. (1977–1978). Reducing electricity consumption of residents living in mass metered dormitory complexes. *Journal of Environmental Systems, 7,* 215–236.

Nickerson, R. S. (1986). *Using computers: Human factors in information technology.* Cambridge, MA: MIT Press.

Nickerson, R. S. (1992). *Looking ahead: Human factors challenges in a changing world.* Hillsdale, NJ: Lawrence Erlbaum Associates.

Nickerson, R. S. (1995). Human interaction with computers and robots. *Human Factors in Manufacturing, 5,* 5–27.

Nickerson, R. S. (1998). Confirmation bias: A ubiquitous phenomenon in many guises. *Review of General Psychology, 2,* 175–220.

Nickerson, R. S. (1999). The natural environment: Dealing with the threat of detrimental change. In F. Durso (Ed.), *The handbook of applied cognition* (pp. 757–788). New York: Wiley.

Nickerson, R. S., & Moray, N. P. (1995). Environmental change. In R. S. Nickerson (Ed.), *Emerging needs and opportunities for human factors research* (pp. 158–176). Washington, DC: National Academy Press.

Nielsen, J. M., & Ellington, B. L. (1983). Social processes and resource conservation. In N. R. Feimer & E. S. Geller (Eds.), *Environmental psychology: Directions and perspectives* (pp. 288–312). New York: Praeger.

Nierenberg, W. A. (1990). Global warming report (Letter to the Editor). *Science, 247,* 14.

Nikolai, L. A., Bazley, J., & Brummet, R. L. (1976). *The measurement of corporate environmental activity.* New York: National Association of Accountants.

NIST. (1994). *Putting the information infrastructure to work: Report of the Information Infrastructure Task Force Committee on Applications and Technology.* Washington, DC: National Institute of Standards and Technology, U.S. Department of Commerce.

Nietzel, M. T., & Winett, R. A. (1977). Demographics, attitudes, and behavioral responses to important environmental events. *American Journal of Community Psychology, 5,* 195–206.

Nilles, J. M., Carlson, F. R., Gray, P., & Hanneman, G. (1976a). Telecommuting—An alternative to urban transportation congestion. *IEEE Transactions on Systems, Man, and Cybernetics, SMC–6,* 77–84.

Nilles, J. M., Carlson, F. R., Gray, P., & Hanneman, G. J. (1976b). *The telecommunications–transportation tradeoff.* New York: Wiley.

Nordhaus, W. D. (1992). An optimal transition path for controlling greenhouse gases. *Science, 258,* 1315–1319.

Normile, D. (2001). The end—not here yet, but coming soon. *Science, 293,* 787.

Novelli, P. C., Masarie, K. A., Tans, P. P., & Lang, P. M. (1994). Recent changes in atmospheric carbon monoxide. *Science, 263,* 1587–1590.

Nowak, M. A., & Sigmund, K. (1992). Tit-for-tat in heterogeneous populations. *Nature, 355,* 250–253.

Nriagu, J. O. (1978). Deteriorative effects of sulfur pollution on materials. In J. O. Nriagu (Ed.), *Sulfur in the environment (Part 2): Ecological impacts* (pp. 1–59). New York: Wiley.

Oerlemans, J. (1994). Quantifying global warming from the retreat of glaciers. *Science, 264,* 243–245.

Office of Technology Assessment, U.S. Congress. (1984). *Protecting the nation's groundwater from contamination: Volumes 1 & 2.* Washington, DC: U.S. Government Printing Office.

Office of Technology Assessment, U.S. Congress. (1987). *New developments in biotechnology: Public perceptions of biotechnology.* Washington, DC: U.S. Government Printing Office.

Office of Technology Assessment, U.S. Congress. (1988). *Urban ozone and the clear air act: Problems and proposals for change*. Washington, DC: U.S. Government Printing Office.

Office of Technology Assessment, U.S. Congress. (1991). *Changing by degrees: Steps to reduce greenhouse gases*. Washington, DC: U.S. Government Printing Office.

O'Keefe, J., & Nagel, L. (1978). *The hippocampus as a cognitive map*. Clarendon, UK: Oxford University Press.

Oliver, S. S., Roggenbuck, J. W., & Watson, A. E. (1985). Education to reduce impacts in forest campgrounds. *Journal of Forestry, 83,* 234–236.

Olshavsky, R. W., & Granbois, D. H. (1979). Consumer decision making—Fact or fiction? *Journal of Consumer Research, 6,* 93–100.

Olson, M. (1965). *The logic of collective action*. Cambridge, MA: Harvard University Press.

Olson, R. (1995). Sustainability as a social vision. *Journal of Social Issues, 51,* 139–156.

O'Neill, G. W., Blanck, L. S., & Joyner, M. A. (1980). The use of stimulus control over littering in a natural setting. *Journal of Applied Behavior Analysis, 13,* 379–381.

O'Neill, M. J. (1991). A biologically-based model of spatial cognition and wayfinding. *Journal of Environmental Psychology, 11,* 299–320.

Ophuls, W. (1977). *Ecology and the politics of scarcity*. San Francisco: Freeman.

Oppenheimer, M., & Boyle, R. H. (1990). *Heat death: The race against the greenhouse effect*. New York: Basic Books.

Orbell, J. M., van de Kragt, A. J. C., & Dawes, R. M. (1988). Explaining discussion-induced cooperation. *Journal of Personality and Social Psychology, 54,* 811–819.

Oreskes, N., Shrader-Frechette, K., & Belitz, K. (1994). Verification, validation, and confirmation of numerical models in the earth sciences. *Science, 263,* 641–646.

Organization of Economic Cooperation and Development. (1991). *State of the environment*. Paris: Organization of Economic Cooperation and Development.

O'Riordan, T. (1976). Attitudes, behavior, and environmental policy issues. In I. Altman & J. Wohlwill (Eds.), *Human behavior and the environment: Advances in theory and research* (Vol. 1, pp. 1–36). New York: Plenum.

Oskamp, S. (1995). Resource conservation and recycling: Behavior and policy. *Journal of Social Issues, 51,* 157–177.

Oskamp, S. (2000). A sustainable future for humanity: How can psychology help? *American Psychologist, 55,* 496–508.

Oskamp, S., Harrington, M. J., Edwards, T. C., Sherwook, D. L., Okuda, S. M., & Swanson, D. C. (1991). Factors influencing household recycling behavior. *Environment and Behavior, 23,* 494–519.

Oskamp, S., Williams, R., Unipan, J., Steers, N., Mainiers, T., & Kurland, G. (1994). Psychological factors affecting paper recycling by businesses. *Environment and Behavior, 26,* 477–503.

OSTP. (1994). *High performance computing and communications: Toward a national information infrastructure*. Washington, DC: Office of Science and Technology Policy (Federal Coordinating Council for Science, Engineering, and Technology).

Ostrom, E. (1990). *Governing the commons: The evolution of institutions for collective action*. Cambridge, UK: Cambridge University Press.

Ostrom, E., Burger, J., Field, C. B., Norgaard, R. B., & Policansky, D. (1999). Revisiting the commons: Local lessons, global challenges. *Science, 284,* 278–282.

Ott, W. R., & Roberts, J. W. (1998). Everyday exposure to toxic pollutants. *Scientific American, 278*(2), 86–91.

Pallak, M. S., Cook, D. A., & Sullivan, J. J. (1980). Commitment and energy conservation. In L. Bickman (Ed.), *Applied social psychology annual* (Vol. 1, pp. 235–254). Beverly Hills, CA: Sage.

Pallak, M. S., & Cummings, W. (1976). Commitment and voluntary energy conservation. *Personal and Social Psychology Bulletin, 2,* 27–30.

Palmer, J. (1981). Approaches for assessing visual quality and visual impacts. In K. Finsterbusch & C. P. Wolf (Eds.), *Methodology of social impact assessment* (pp. 284–301). Stroudsburg, PA: Dowden, Hutchinson & Ross.

Pardini, A. U., & Katzev, R. D. (1983–84). The effect of strength of commitment on newspaper recycling. *Journal of Environmental Systems, 13,* 245–254.

Parker, A. (1955). *Report of the investigation of atmospheric pollution* (Report No. 27). London: Her Majesty's Stationary Office, Department of Scientific and Industrial Research.

Parker, E. (1973). Technological change and the mass media. In I. Pool, W. Schramm, F. Frey, N. Maccoby, & E. Parker (Eds.), *Handbook of communication* (pp. 619–645). Chicago: Rand McNally.

Parks, C. D. (1994). The predictive ability of social values in resource dilemmas and public goods games. *Personality and Social Psychology Bulletin, 20,* 431–438.

Parsons, E. A., & Keith, D. W. (1998). Fossil fuels without $Co_2$ emissions. *Science, 282,* 1053–1054.

Patrick, R., Binetti, V. P., & Halterman, S. G. (1981). Acid lakes from natural and anthropogenic causes. *Science, 211,* 446–448.

Partridge, E. (1981). *Responsibilities to future generations: Environmental ethics.* Buffalo, NY: Prometheus.

Patterson, A. H. (1985). Fear of crime and other barriers to use of public transportation by the elderly. [Special Issue: Crime and the Environment: New Perspectives.] *Journal of Architectural and Planning Research, 2,* 277–288.

Pawlik, K. (1991). The psychology of global environmental change: Some basic data and an agenda for cooperative international research. *International Journal of Psychology, 26,* 547–563.

Payne, J. W. (1982). Contingent decision behavior. *Psychological Bulletin, 92,* 382–402.

Payne, S. L. (1952). *The art of asking questions.* Princeton, NJ: Princeton University Press.

Pearce, D., Adger, N., Maddison, D., & Moran, D. (1995). Debt and the environment. *Scientific American, 272*(6), 52–56.

Pearce, D. W. (1992). *Global environmental value and the tropical forests.* London: University College.

Pearce, D. W., & Turner, R. K. (1990). *Economics of natural resources and the environment.* Baltimore, MD: Johns Hopkins University Press.

Peck, S. C., & Teisberg, T. J. (1992). *Cost-benefit analysis and climate change.* Palo Alto, CA: Electric Power Research Institute.

Peltier, W. R., & Tushingham, A. M. (1989). Global sea level rise and the greenhouse effect: Might they be connected? *Science, 244,* 806–810.

Pelton, J. N. (1998). Telecommunications for the 21st century. *Scientific American, 278*(4), 80–85.

Penkett, S. A. (1989). Ultraviolet levels down not up. *Nature, 3431,* 283.

Penner, J. E., Dickinson, R. E., & O'Neill, C. A. (1992). Effects of aerosol from biomass burning on the global radiation budget. *Science, 256,* 1432–1434.

Percy, L., & Woodside, A. G. (Eds.). (1983). *Advertising and consumer psychology.* Lexington, MA: Lexington Books.

Perlmutter, L. C., Scharff, K., Karsh, R., & Monty, R. A. (1980). Perceived control: A generalized state of motivation. *Motivation and Emotion, 4,* 35–45.

Perloff, L. S., & Fetzer, B. K. (1986). Self-other judgments and perceived vulnerability to victimization. *Journal of Personality and Social Psychology, 50,* 502–510.

Perkins, D. D., Wandersman, A., Rich, R. C., & Taylor, R. B. (1993). The physical environment of street crime: Defensible space, territoriality, and incivilities. *Journal of Environmental Psychology, 13,* 21–34.

Perl, A., & Dunn, J. A. (1997). Fast trains: Why the U.S. lags. *Scientific American, 277*(4), 106–108.

Perrow, C. (1984). *Normal accidents: Living with high risk technologies*. New York: Basic Books.

Pescovitz, D. (2000). Please dispose of properly. *Scientific American, 282*(2), 33.

Peterson, C., & Stunkard, A. J. (1989). Personal control and health promotion. *Social Science of Medicine, 28,* 819–828.

Peterson, G. L. (1974). Evaluating the quality of the wilderness environment: Congruence between perceptions and aspirations. *Environment and Behavior, 6,* 169–193.

Peterson, G. L., & Neumann, E. S. (1969). Modeling and predicting human responses to the visual environment. *Journal of Leisure Research, 1,* 219–237.

Peterson, R. (1991). The end of the beginning. In A. B. Wolbrast (Ed.), *Environment in peril* (pp. 188–201). Washington, DC: Smithsonian Institution Press.

Petit, J. R., Jouzel, J., Raynaud, D., Barkov, N. I., Barnola, I., Basile, I., Benders, M., Chappellaz, J., Davis, M., Delaygue, G., Delmotte, M., Kotlyakov, V. M., Legrand, M., Lipenkov, V. Y., Loriius, C., Pépin, L., Ritz, C., Salatsman, E., & Stievenard, M. (1999). Climate and atmospheric history of the past 420,000 years from the Vostok ice core, Antarctica. *Nature, 399,* 429–436.

Petty, R. E., & Cacioppo, J. T. (1981). *Attitudes and persuasion: Classic and contemporary approaches*. Dubuque, IA: Brown.

Petty, R. E., Cacioppo, J. T., & Goldman, R. (1981). Personal involvement as a determinant of argument based persuasion. *Journal of Personality and Social Psychology, 41,* 847–855.

Petty, R. E., Cacioppo, J. T., & Heesacker, M. (1981). The use of rhetorical questions in persuasion: A cognitive response analysis. *Journal of Personality and Social Psychology, 40,* 432–440.

Phillips, O. L., & Gentry, A. H. (1994). Increasing turnover through time in tropical forests. *Science, 263,* 954–958.

Phillips, O. L., Malhi, Y., Higuchi, N., Laurance, W. F., Núñez, P. V., Vásquez, R. M., Laurance, S. G., Rerreira, L. V., Stern, M., Brown, S., & Grace, J. (1998). Changes in the carbon balance of tropical forests: Evidence from long-term plots. *Science, 282,* 439–442.

Pickett, G. M., Kangun, N., & Grove, S. J. (1993). Is there a general conserving consumer: A public policy concern. *Journal of Public Policy and Marketing, 12,* 234–243.

Pilisuk, M., & Acredolo, C. (1988). Fear of technological hazards: One concern or many? *Social Behavior, 3,* 17–24.

Pillsbury, A. F. (1981). The salinity of rivers. *Scientific American, 245*(1), 54–65.

Pimentel, D., Harvey, C., Resosudarmo, P., Sinclair, K., Kurz, D., McNair, M., Crist, S., Shpritz, L., Fitton, L., Saffouri, R., & Blair, R. (1995). Environmental and economic costs of soil erosion and conservation benefits. *Science, 267,* 1117–1123.

Pimm, S. L., Russel, G. L., Gittleman, J. L., & Brooks, T. M. (1995). The future of biodiversity. *Science, 269,* 347–350.

Pimm, S. L., & Sugden, A. M. (1994). Tropical diversity and global change. *Science, 263,* 933–934.

Pitts, S. M., & Wittenbach, J. L. (1981). Tax credits as a means of influencing consumer behavior. *Journal of Consumer Research, 8,* 335–338.

Platt, J. (1973). Social traps. *American Psychologist, 28,* 641–651.

Plous, S. (1993). Psychological mechanisms in the human use of animals. *Journal of Social Issues, 49,* 11–52.

Pollack, H. N., Huang, S., & Shen, P. Y. (1998). Climate change record in subsurface temperatures: A global perspective. *Science, 282,* 279–281.

Ponte, L. (1976). *The cooling.* Englewood Cliffs, NJ: Prentice-Hall.

Pool, R. (1992). A visit to a virtual world. *Science, 256,* 45.

Porter, B. E., Leeming, R. C., & Dwyer, W. O. (1995). Solid waste recovery: A review of behavioral programs to increase recycling. *Environment and Behavior, 27,* 122–152.

Portney, K. E. (1991a). *Hazardous waste treatment facility siting: The NIMBY syndrome.* Dover, MA: Auburn House.

Portney, K. E. (1991b). Public environmental policy decision making: Citizen roles. In R. A. Chechile & S. Carlisle (Eds.), *Environmental decision making: A multidisciplinary perspective* (pp. 195–216). New York: Van Nostrand Reinhold.

Post, W. M., Peng, T.-H., Emmanuel, W. R., King, A. W., Dale, V. H., & DeAngelis, D. L. (1990). The global carbon cycle. *American Scientist, 78,* 310–326.

Postel, S. (1985). Thirsty in a water-rich world. *International Wildlife, 15*(6), 32–37.

Postel, S. (2001). Growing more food with less water. *Scientific American, 284*(2), 46–51.

Potter, D., Hendee, J. C., & Clark, R. (1973). Hunting satisfaction: Game, guns, or nature? *Human dimensions in wildlife programs* (pp. 62–71). Washington, DC: Wildlife Management Institute.

Potts, M. (2000). The unmet need for family planning. *Scientific American, 282*(1), 88–93.

Poulton, E. C. (1970). *Environment and human efficiency.* Springfield, IL: Thomas.

Poundstone, W. (1992). *Prisoner's dilemma: John von Neumann, game theory, and the puzzle of the bomb.* New York: Anchor.

Powell, C. S. (1990). Science and business: Plastic goes green. *Scientific American, 263*(2), 101.

Powell, C. S. (1994). Cold confusion. *Scientific American, 270*(3), 22, 26, 28.

Powers, R. B., Duus, R. E., & Norton, R. S. (1979). *The commons game; Teaching students about social traps.* Paper presented at the meeting of the Rocky Mountain Psychological Association, Las Vegas.

Powers, R. B., Osborne, J. G., & Anderson, E. G. (1973). Positive reinforcement of litter removal in the natural environment. *Journal of Applied Behavior Analysis, 6,* 579–586.

Prester, G., Rohrmann, B., & Schellhammer, E. (1987). Environmental evaluation and participation activities: A social psychological field study. *Journal of Applied Social Psychology, 17,* 751–787.

Primack, J. (1975). Nuclear reactor safety: An introduction to the issues. *Bulletin of the Atomic Scientists, 31*(7), 15–17.

Proffitt, M. H., Fahey, D. W., Kelly, K. K., & Tuck, A. F. (1989). High latitude ozone loss outside the Antarctic ozone hole. *Nature, 342,* 233–237.

Proshansky, H. M., Ittelson, W. H., & Rivlin, L. G. (Eds.). (1976). *Environmental psychology: People and their physical settings* (2nd ed.). New York: Holt, Reinhart & Winston.

Prothro, J. W., & Grigg, C. W. (1960). Fundamental principles of democracy: Bases of agreement and disagreement. *Journal of Politics, 22,* 276–294.

Punj, G. N., & Staelin, R. (1983). A model of consumer information search behavior for new automobiles. *Journal of Consumer Research, 9,* 366–380.

Purcell, A. H. (1980). *The waste watchers: A citizen's handbook for conserving energy.* New York: Anchor.

Purcell, A. H. (1981, February). The world's trashiest people: Will they clean up their act or throw away their future? *The Futurist*, pp. 51–59.
Purcell, A. T., Lamb, R. J., Peron, E. M., & Falchero, S. (1994). Preference or preferences for landscape? *Journal of Environmental Psychology, 14,* 195–209.
Railton, P. (1990). Benefit-cost analysis as a source of information about welfare. In P. B. Hammond & R. Coppock (Eds.), *Valuing health risks, costs, and benefits for environmental decision making* (pp. 55–82). Washington, DC: National Academy Press.
Ramanathan, V. (1988). The greenhouse theory of climate change: A test by an inadvertent global experiment. *Science, 240,* 293–299.
Ramanathan, V., Cess, R. D., Harrison, E. F., Minnis, P., Barkstrom, B. R., Ahmad, E., & Hartmann, D. (1989). Cloud-radiative forcing and climate: Results from the earth radiation budget experiment. *Science, 243,* 57–63.
Ramanathan, V., Cicerone, R. J., Singh, H. B., & Kiehl, J. T. (1985). Trace gas trends and their potential role in climate change. *Journal of Geophysical Research, 90,* 5547–5566.
Ramanathan, V., Subasilar, B., Zhang, G. J., Conant, W., Cess, R. D., Kiehl, J. T., Grassi, H., & Shi, L. (1995). Warm pool heat budget and shortwave cloud forcing: A missing physics? *Science, 267,* 499–502.
Ramsay, W. (1976). Priorities in species preservation. *Environmental Affairs, 5,* 595–616.
Rankin, R. (1969). Air pollution control and public apathy. *Journal of the Air Pollution Control Association, 19,* 565–569.
Raoul, J.-C. (1997). How high-speed trains make tracks. *Scientific American, 277*(4), 100–105.
Rapoport, A. (1982). *The meaning of the built environment.* Beverly Hills, CA: Sage.
Rapoport, A., & Chammah, A. M. (1965). *Prisoner's dilemma.* Ann Arbor: University of Michigan Press.
Rappaport, A., & Dillon, P. (1991). Private-sector environmental decision making. In R. A. Chechile & S. Carlisle (Eds.), *Environmental decision making: A multidisciplinary perspective* (pp. 238–268). New York: Van Nostrand Reinhold.
Rasmussen, J., & Batstone, R. (1989). *Why do complex organizational systems fail?* Summary proceedings of a cross-disciplinary workshop in safety control and risk management, World Bank, Washington, DC.
Rasmussen, W. D. (1982). The mechanization of agriculture. *Scientific American, 247*(3), 76–89.
Raup, D. M. (1988). Diversity crises in the geological past. In E. O. Wilson & F. M. Peter (Eds.), *Biodiversity* (pp. 51–57). Washington, DC: National Academy Press.
Ravishankara, A. R., Turnispeed, A. A., Jensen, N. R., Barone, S., Mills, M., Howard, C., J., & Solomon, S. (1994). Do hydrofluorocarbons destroy stratospheric ozone? *Science, 263,* 71–75.
Ray, D. L., & Guzzo, L. (1994). *Environmental overkill: Whatever happened to common sense?* New York: HarperPerennial.
Ray, M. L. (1974). Consumer initial processing: Definitions, issues and applications. In G. D. Hughes & M. L. Ray (Eds.), *Buyer/comsumer information processing* (pp. 145–156). Chapel Hill, NC: University of North Carolina Press.
Raynaud, D., Jouzel, J., Varnola, J. M., Chappellaz, J., Delmas, R. J., & Lorius, C. (1993). The ice record of greenhouse gases. *Science, 259,* 926–934.
Reams, M. A., Geaghan, J. P., & Gendron, R. C. (1996). The link between recycling and litter: A field study. *Environment and Behavior, 28,* 92–110.
Reason, J. (1990). *Human error.* New York: Cambridge University Press.
Redding, M. J. (1973). *Aesthetics in environmental planning.* Washington, DC: Environmental Protection Agency.

Reddy, K. N., & Goldemberg, J. (1990). Energy for the developing world. *Scientific American, 263*(3), 110–118.

Reganold, J. P., Papendick, R. I., & Parr, J. F. (1990). Sustainable agriculture. *Scientific American, 262*(6), 112–120.

Reichel, D. A., & Geller, E. S. (1981). Applications of behavioral analysis for conserving transportation energy. In A. Baum & J. E. Singer (Eds.), *Advances in environmental psychology: Vol. 3. Energy conservation: Psychological perspectives* (pp. 53–91). Hillsdale, NJ: Lawrence Erlbaum Associates.

Reicher, S., Podpadec, P., Macnaghten, R., Brown, R., & Eiser, J. R. (1993). Taking the dread out of radiation? Consequences of and arguments over the inclusion of radiation from nuclear power production in the category of the natural. *Journal of Environmental Psychology, 13,* 93–109.

Reid, D. H., Luyben, P. D., Rawers, R. J., & Bailey, J. S. (1976). Newspaper recycling behavior: The effects of prompting and proximity of containers. *Journal of Environmental Systems, 13,* 245–254.

Reid, W. V., & Miller, K. R. (1989). *Keeping options alive: The scientific basis for conserving biodiversity.* Washington, DC: World Resources Institute.

Reisner, M. (1988–1989). The next water war: Cities versus agriculture. *Issues in Science and Technology, 5*(2), 98–102.

Reiter, S. M., & Samuel, W. (1980). Littering as a function of prior litter and the presence or absence of prohibitive signs. *Journal of Applied Social Psychology, 10,* 45–55.

Renn, O. (1990). Public response to the Chernobyl accident. *Journal of Environmental Psychology, 10,* 151–167.

Renn, O., Burns, J., Kasperson, J., Kasperson, R., & Slovic, P. (1992). The social amplification of risk: Theoretical foundations and empirical applications. *Journal of Social Issues, 48,* 137–160.

Renner, M. (1991). Assessing the military's war on the environment. In L. R. Brown, C. Flavin, & S. Postel (Eds.), *State of the world, 1991* (pp. 132–152). New York: Norton.

Repetto, R. (1990). Deforestation in the tropics. *Scientific American, 262*(4), 36–42.

Repetto, R., & Gillis, M. (Eds.). (1988). *Public policies and the misuse of forest resources.* New York: Cambridge University Press.

Reser, J. P., & Scherl, L. M. (1988). Clear and unambiguous feedback: A transactional and motivational analysis of environmental challenge and self-encounter. *Journal of Environmental Psychology, 8,* 269–287.

Revelle, R. (1982). Carbon dioxide and world climate. *Scientific American, 247*(2), 35–43.

Revelle, R., & Suess, H. (1957). Carbon dioxide exchange between atmosphere and ocean and the question of an increase of atmospheric $CO_2$ during the past decades. *Tellus, 9,* 18–27.

Richelson, J. T. (1998). Scientists in black. *Scientific American, 278*(2), 48–55.

Rigaud, P., & Leroy, B. (1990). Presumptive evidence for a low value of the total ozone content above Antarctica in September, 1958. *Annals of Geophysics, 11,* 791–794.

Rillings, J. H. (1997). Automated highways. *Scientific American, 277*(4), 80–85

Rind, D. (1999). Complexity and climate. *Science, 284,* 105–107.

Roberts, D. F., & Maccoby, N. (1985). Effects of mass communication. In G. Lindzey & E. Aronson (Eds.), *Handbook of social psychology* (3rd ed.). New York: Random House.

Roberts, L. (1989). Global warming: Blaming the sun. *Science, 246,* 992.

Roberts, L. (1991a). Academy panel split on greenhouse adaptation. *Science, 253,* 1206.

Roberts, L. (1991b). Costs of a clean environment. *Science, 251,* 1182.

Roberts, L. (1993). Wetlands trading is a loser's game, say ecologists. *Science, 260,* 1890–1892.

Robertson, L. S. (1977). Car crashes: Perceived vulnerability and willingness to pay for crash protection. *Journal of Consumer Health, 3,* 136–141.

Robinson, J. G., Redford, K. H., & Bennett, E. L. (1999). Wildlife harvest in logged tropical forests. *Science, 284,* 595–596.

Robinson, M. H. (1991). Environmental problems in the tropics. In A. B. Wolbrast (Ed.), *Environment in peril* (pp. 140–153). Washington, DC: Smithsonian Institution Press.

Robinson, N. (1990). Sustainable development: An introduction to the concept. In J. O. Saunders (Ed.), *The legal challenge of sustainable development* (pp. 15–34). Calgary, Alberta: Canadian Institute of Resources Law.

Robinson, S. (1976). Littering behavior in public places. *Environment and Behavior, 8,* 363–384.

Robinson, S. K., Thompson, F. R., III, Donovan, T. M., Whitehead, D. R., & Faaborg, J. (1995). Regional forest fragmentation and the nesting success of migratory birds. *Science, 267,* 1987–1990.

Robock, A. (1996). Stratospheric control of climate. *Science, 272,* 972–973.

Rogers, P. (1991). The economic model. In R. A. Chechile & S. Carlisle (Eds.), *Environmental decision making: A multidisciplinary perspective* (pp. 120–155). New York: Van Nostrand Reinhold.

Rogers-Warren, A., & Warren, S. F. (Eds.). (1977). *Ecological perspectives in behavior analysis.* Baltimore, MD: University Park Press.

Rohe, W. M. (1982). The response to density in residential settings: The mediating effects of social and personal variables. *Journal of Applied Social Psychology, 12,* 292–303.

Rose, H. S., & Hinds, D. H. (1976). South Dixie Highway contraflow bus and carpool lane demonstration project. *Transportation Research Record, 606,* 16–18.

Rosen H. A., & Castleman, D. R. (1997). Flywheels in hybrid vehicles. *Scientific American, 277*(4), 75–77.

Rosenberg, A. A., Fogarty, M. J., Sissenwine, M. P., Beddington, J. R., & Shepherd, J. G. (1993). Achieving sustainable use of renewable resources. *Science, 262,* 828–829.

Rosenberg, N. J., Easterling, W. E., III, Crosson, P. R., & Darmstadter, J. (Eds.). (1989). *Greenhouse warming: Abatement and adaptation.* Washington, DC: Resources for the Future.

Rosenfeld, A. H., & Hafemeister, D. (1988). Energy efficient buildings. *Scientific American, 258*(4), 78–85.

Rosenfeld, D. (2000). Suppression of rain and snow by urban and industrial air pollution. *Science, 287,* 1793–1796.

Rosenthal, D. H., Driver, B. L., & Rauhauser, D. (1980). Skiing environments preferred by Colorado ski-tourers. *Proceedings, North American Symposium on Dispersed Winter Recreation* (pp. 57–63). St. Paul, MN: College of Forestry, University of Minnesota.

Ross, M. H., & Steinmeyer, D. (1990). Energy for industry. *Scientific American, 263*(3), 88–98.

Ross, M. H., & Williams, R. H. (1981). *Our energy: Regaining control.* New York: McGraw-Hill.

Rossman, B. B., & Ulehla, Z. J. (1977). Psychological reward values associated with wilderness use: A functional-reinforcement approach. *Environment and Behavior, 9,* 41–66.

Roszak, T. (1993). *The voice of the earth.* New York: Simon & Schuster.

Roszak, T., Gomes, M. E., & Kanner, A. D. (Eds.). (1995). *Ecopsychology: Restoring the earth, healing the mind.* San Francisco: Sierra Club.

Rothman, S., & Lichter, S. R. (1987). Elite ideology and risk perception in nuclear energy policy. *American Political Science Review, 81,* 383–404.

Rothstein, R. N. (1980). Television feedback used to modify gasoline consumption. *Behavior Therapy, 11,* 683–688.

Rotter, J. B. (1971). Generalized expectancies for interpersonal trust. *American Psychologist, 26,* 443–452.

Rotter, J. B., Chance, J., & Phares, E. (1972). *Applications of social learning theory of personality.* New York: Holt, Rinehart & Winston.

Roush, W. (1995). When rigor meets reality. *Science, 269,* 313–315.

Rowe, W. D. (1977). *The anatomy of risk.* New York: Wiley.

Rowland, F. S. (1989). Chlorofluorocarbons and the depletion of stratospheric ozone. *American Scientist, 77,* 36–45.

Rowland, F. S., & Molina, M. J. (1975). Chlorofluoromethanes in the environment. *Reviews of Geophysics and Space Physics, 13,* 1–35.

Royal Society and Royal Academy of Engineering. (1999). *Nuclear energy: The future climate.* (*www.royalsoc.ac.uk/policy/index.html*)

Ruckelshaus, W. D. (1989). Toward a sustainable world. *Scientific American, 261*(3), 166–175.

Runnels, C. N. (1995). Environmental degradation in ancient Greece. *Scientific American, 272*(3), 96–99.

Runnion, A., Watson, J. D., & McWhorter, J. (1978). Energy savings in interstate transportation through feedback and reinforcement. *Journal of Organizational Behavioral Management, 1,* 180–191.

Russell, A., Milford, J., Bergin, M. S., McBride, S., McNair, L., Yang, Y., Stockwell, W. R., & Croes, B. (1995). Urban ozone control and atmospheric reactivity of organic gases. *Science, 269,* 491–495.

Russell, J. A., & Lanius, U. F. (1984). Adaptation level and the affective appraisal of environments. *Journal of Environmental Psychology, 4,* 119–135.

Russell, J. A., & Pratt, G. (1980). A description of the affective quality attributed to environments. *Journal of Personality and Social Psychology, 38,* 311–322.

Russell, J. A., & Snodgrass, J. (1987). Emotion and the environment. In D. Stokols & I. Altman (Eds.), *Handbook of environmental psychology* (Vol. I, pp. 245–280). New York: Wiley.

Russell, J. A., & Ward, L. M. (1982). Environmental psychology. *Annual Review of Psychology, 33,* 651–688.

Russell, J. A., Ward, L. M., & Pratt, G. (1981). Affective quality attributed to environments: A factor analytic study. *Environment and Behavior, 13,* 259–288.

Russell, M. (1990). The making of cruel choices. In P. B. Hammond & R. Coppock (Eds.), *Valuing health risks, costs, and benefits for environmental decision making* (pp. 15–22).

Russell, M., & Gruber, M. (1987). Risk assessment in environmental policy-making. *Science, 236,* 286–290.

Russo, J. E. (1974). More information is better: A reevaluation of Jacoby, Speller and Kohn. *Journal of Consumer Research, 1,* 68–72.

Saarinen, T. F. (1980). Reconnaissance trip to M. St. Helens, May 18–21, 1980. *The Bridge (National Academy of Engineering), 10,* 19–22.

Saegert, S. (1981). Crowding and cognitive limits. In J. Harvey (Ed.), *Cognition, social behavior, and the environment* (pp. 373–392). Hillsdale, NJ: Lawrence Erlbaum Associates.

Saegert, S., Mackintosh, E., & West, S. (1975). Two studies of crowding in urban public spaces. *Environment and Behavior, 7,* 159–184.

Saegert, S., & Winkel, G. H. (1990). Environmental psychology. *Annual Review of Psychology, 41,* 441–477.

Sailor, W. C., Bodansky, D., Braun, C., Fetter, S., & van der Zwan, B. (2000). A nuclear solution to climate change. *Science, 288,* 1177–1178.

Salt Institute. (1980). *Survey of salt, calcium chloride, and abrasive use in the United States and Canada.* Alexandria, VA: Salt Institute.

Samdahl, D. M., & Robertson, R. (1989). Social determinants of environmental concern: Specification and test of the model. *Environment and Behavior, 21,* 57–81.

Samples, K. C., Dixon, J. A., & Gowen, M. M. (1986). Information disclosure and endangered species valuation. *Land Economics, 62,* 306–312.

Sampson, R., & Groves, W. (1989). Community structure and crime: Testing social-disorganization theory. *American Journal of Sociology, 94,* 774–802.

Santee, M. L., Read, W. G., Waters, J. W., Froidevaux, L., Manney, G. L., Flower, D. A., Jarnot, R. F., Harwood, R. S., & Peckham, G. E. (1995). Interhemispheric differences in polar stratospheric $HNO_3$, $H_2O$, ClO, and $O_3$. *Science, 267,* 849–852.

Sassin, W. (1980). Energy. *Scientific American, 243*(3), 118–132.

Schindler, D. W. (1988). Effects of acid rain on freshwater ecosystems. *Science, 239,* 149–157.

Schkade, D. A., & Johnson, E. J. (1989). Cognitive processes in preference reversals. *Organizational Behavior and Human Decision Processes, 44,* 203–231.

Schlesinger, M. E., & Mitchell, J. F. B. (1987). Climate model simulations of the equilibrium climatic to increased carbon dioxide. *Review of Geophysics, 25,* 760–798.

Schlesinger, W. H., Reynolds, J. F., Cunningham, G. L., Huenneke, L. F., Gerrell, W. M., Virginia, R. A., & Whitford, W. G. (1990). Biological feedbacks in global desertification. *Science, 247,* 1043–1048.

Schmidt, F. N., & Gifford, R. (1989). A dispositional approach to hazard perception: Preliminary development of the environmental appraisal inventory. *Journal of Environmental Psychology, 9,* 57–67.

Schneider, D. (1997). The rising sea level. *Scientific American, 276*(3), 112–117.

Schneider, D. (1998). Burying the problem. *Scientific American, 278*(1), 21–22.

Schneider, S. H. (1989a). The changing climate. *Scientific American, 261*(3), 70–79.

Schneider, S. H. (1989b). The greenhouse effect: Science and policy. *Science, 243,* 771–781.

Schneider, S. H. (1990). *Global warming: Are we entering the greenhouse century?* New York: Vintage.

Schneider, S. H. (1994). Detecting climatic change signals: Are there any "fingerprints"? *Science, 263,* 341–347.

Schneider, S. H., Gleick, P. H., & Mearns, L. O. (1990). Prospects for climate change. In P. E. Waggoner (Ed.), *Climate change and U.S. water resources* (pp. 41–74). New York: Wiley.

Schnelle, J. F., McNees, M. P., Thomas, M. M., Gendrich, J. G., & Beagle, G. P. (1980). Prompting behavior change in the community: Use of mass media techniques. *Environment and Behavior, 12,* 157–166.

Schreyer, R., & Nielson, M. L. (1978). *Westwater and desolation canyons: White water river recreation study.* Logan, UT: College of Natural Resources, Utah State University.

Schroeder, H. W., & Daniel, T. C. (1980). Predicting the scenic quality of forest road corridors. *Environment and Behavior, 12,* 349–366.

Schroeder, H. W., & Daniel, T. C. (1981). Progress in predicting the scenic quality of forest landscapes. *Forest Science, 27,* 71–80.

Schultz, P. W., & Oskamp, S. (1996). Effort as a moderator of the attitude-behavior relationship: General environmental concern and recycling. *Social Psychology Quarterly, 59,* 375–383.

Schumacher, E. F. (1973). *Small is beautiful.* New York: Harper & Row.

Schuman, H., & Johnson, M. P. (1976). Attitudes and behavior. *Annual Review of Sociology, 2,* 161–297.

Schuman, H., & Scott, J. (1987). Problems in the use of survey questions to measure public opinion. *Science, 236,* 957–959.

Schwartz, S. E. (1989). Acid deposition: Unraveling a regional phenomenon. *Science, 243,* 753–763.

Schwartz, S. E., & Andreae, M. O. (1996). Uncertainty in climate change caused by aerosols. *Science, 272,* 1121–1122.

Schwartz, S. H. (1977). Normative influences on altruism. In L. Berkowitz (Ed.), *Advances in experimental social psychology* (Vol. 10, pp. 221–279). New York: Academic Press.

Schwarz, N. (1999). Self-reports. *American Psychologist, 54,* 93–105.

Schwepker, C. H., & Cornwell, T. B. (1991). An examination of ecologically concerned consumers and their intention to purchase ecologically packaged products. *Journal of Public Policy and Marketing, 10,* 77–101.

Scientific American. (1997). 50, 100 and 150 years ago. *Scientific American, 277*(3), 12.

Scott, D. (1999). Equal opportunity, unequal results: Determinants of household recycling intensity. *Environment and Behavior, 1999,* 266–290.

Scott, D., & Willits, F. K. (1994). Environmental attitudes and behavior: A Pennsylvania survey. *Environment and Behavior, 26,* 239–260.

Seinfeld, J. H. (1989). Urban air pollution: State of the science. *Science, 243,* 752–754.

Seitz, F., Jastrow, R., & Nierenberg, W. A. (1989). *Scientific perspectives on the greenhouse problem.* Washington, DC: George C. Marshall Institute.

Seligman, C. (1986). Energy consumption, attitudes, and behavior. In M. J. Saks & L. Saxe (Eds.), *Advances in of applied social psychology* (Vol. 3, pp. 153–180). Hillsdale, NJ: Lawrence Erlbaum Associates.

Seligman, C., Becker, L. J., & Darley, J. M. (1981). Encouraging residential energy conservation through feedback. In A. Baum & J. E. Singer (Eds.), *Advances in environmental psychology: Vol. 3. Energy: Psychological perspectives* (pp. 93–113). Hillsdale, NJ: Lawrence Erlbaum Associates.

Seligman, C., & Darley, J. M. (1977). Feedback as a means of decreasing residential energy consumption. *Journal of Applied Psychology, 62,* 363–368.

Seligman, C., Kriss, M., Darley, J. M., Fazio, R. H., Becker, L. J., & Pryor, J. B. (1979). Predicting residential energy consumption from homeowners' attitudes. *Journal of Applied Social Psychology, 9,* 70–90.

Senders, J., & Moray, N. (Eds.). (1991). *Human error: Cause, prediction, and reduction.* Hillsdale, NJ: Lawrence Erlbaum Associates.

Serageldin, I. (1995). *Toward sustainable management of water resources.* Washington, DC: World Bank.

Sexton, R. J., Johnson, N. B., & Konakayama, A. (1987). Consumer response to continuous-display electricity-use monitors in a time-of-use pricing experiment. *Journal of Consumer Research, 14,* 55–62.

Shafer, E. L., Hamilton, J. F., & Schmidt, E. A. (1969). Natural landscape preferences: A predictive model. *Journal of Leisure Research, 1,* 1–19.

Shafer, E. L., & Meitz, J. (1969). Aesthetic and emotional experiences rate high with northeast wilderness hikers. *Environment and Behavior, 1,* 187–197.

Shafer, E. L., & Richards, T. A. (1974). *A comparison of viewer reactions to outdoor scenes and photographs of those scenes* (USDA Forest Service Research Paper NE–302). Upper Darby, PA: Northeastern Forest Experiment Station.

Shafer, E. L., & Tooby, M. (1973). Landscape preferences: An international replication. *Journal of Leisure Research, 5,* 60–65.

Shafir, E. (1993). Choosing versus rejecting: Why some options are both better and worse than others. *Memory and Cognition, 21,* 546–556.

Sharlin, H. I. (1986). EDB: A case study in communicating risk. *Risk Analysis, 6,* 61–68.

Shaw, K. T., & Gifford, R. (1994). Residents' and burglars' assessment of burglary risk from defensible space cues. *Journal of Environmental Psychology, 14,* 177–194.

Sheer, D. P., Baeck, M. L., & Wright, J. (1989). The computer as negotiator. *Journal of the American Water Works Association, 81,* 68–73.

Sherrod, D. R., Armstrong, D., Hewitt, J., Madonia, B., Speno, S., & Teruya, D. (1977). Environmental attention, affect, and altruism. *Journal of Applied Social Psychology, 7,* 359–371.

Shine, K. P., Derwent, R. G., Wuebbles, D. J., & Morcrette, J. J. (1990). Radiative forcing of climate. In J. T. Houghton, G. J. Jenkins, & J. J. Ephraums (Eds.), *Climate change: The IPCC assessment* (pp. 41–68). Cambridge, UK: Cambridge University Press.

Short, J. F., Jr. (1984). The social fabric at risk: Toward the social transformation of risk analysis. *American Sociological Review, 49,* 711–725.

Shriner, D. S., Richmond, C. D., & Lindberg, S. E. (1980). *Atmospheric sulfur deposition: Environmental impact and health effects.* Ann Arbor, MI: Ann Arbor Science.

Shukla, J., Nobre, C., & Sellers, P. (1990). Amazon deforestation and climate change. *Science, 247,* 1322–1325.

Shulman, S. (1989). When a nuclear reactor dies, 98 million dollars is a cheap funeral. *Smithsonian, 20*(7), 56–69.

Shuttleworth, S. (1980). The use of photographs as an environmental presentation medium in landscape studies. *Journal of Environmental Management, 11,* 61–76.

Silver, C., & DeFries, R. (1990). *One earth, one future: Our changing global environment.* Washington, DC: National Academy Press.

Simmons, D. A., Talbot, J. F., & Kaplan, R. (1984–1985). Energy in daily activities: Muddling toward conservation. *Journal of Environmental Systems, 14,* 147–155.

Simpson, S. (2001). Fishy business. *Scientific American, 285*(1), 82–89.

Singer, S. F. (2001). Global warming: An insignificant trend? *Science, 292,* 1063.

Sjöberg, L. (1980). The risks of risk analysis. *Acta Psychologica, 45,* 301–321.

Sjöberg, L. (1989). Global change and human action: Psychological perspectives. *International Social Science Journal, 41,* 413–432.

Slavin, R. E., & Wodarski, J. S. (1977). *Using group contingencies to reduce natural gas consumption in master-metered apartments* (Center for Social Organization of Schools, Report No. 232). Baltimore, MD: Johns Hopkins University.

Slavin, R. E., Wodarski, J. S., & Blackburn, B. L. (1981). A group contingency for electricity conservation in master-metered apartments. *Journal of Applied Behavior Analysis, 14,* 357–363.

Slovic, P. (1987). Perception of risk. *Science, 236,* 280–285.

Slovic, P. (1993). Perceived risk, trust, and the politics of nuclear waste. *Risk Analysis, 13,* 675–682.

Slovic, P. (1995). The construction of preference. *American Psychologist, 50,* 364–371.

Slovic, P., Fischhoff, B., & Lichtenstein, S. (1979). Rating the risks. *Environment, 21*(3), 14–20, 36–39.

Slovic, P., Fischhoff, B., & Lichtenstein, S. (1980). Facts and fears: Understanding perceived risk. In R. Schwing & W. A. Albers, Jr. (Eds.), *Societal risk assessment: How safe is safe enough?* (pp. 281–214). New York: Plenum.

Slovic, P., Fischhoff, B., & Lichtenstein, S. (1981). Perception and acceptability of risk from energy systems. In A. Baum & J. E. Singer (Eds.), *Advances in environmental psychology: Vol. 3. Energy conservation: Psychological perspectives* (pp. 155–169). Hillsdale, NJ: Lawrence Erlbaum Associates.

Slovic, P., Flynn, J. H., & Layman, M. (1991). Perceived risk, trust, and the politics of nuclear waste. *Science, 254,* 1603–1607.

Slovic, P., & Lichtenstein, S. (1983). Preference reversals: A broader perspective. *American Economic Review, 73,* 596–605.

Smith, R. A. (1852). On the air and rain of Manchester. *Memoirs. Literary and Philosophical Society of Manchester, Series 2,* 10, 207–217.

Smith, R. A. (1872). *Air and rain.* London: Longmans, Green.

Smith, R. A., Alexander, R. B., & Wolman, M. G. (1987). Water-quality trends in the nations rivers. *Science, 235,* 1607.

Smith, R. C., Prézelin, B. B., Baker, K. S., Bidigare, R. R., Boucher, N. P., Coley, T., Karentz, D., MacIntyre, S., Matlick, H. A., Menzies, D., Ondrusek, M., Wan, Z., & Waters, K. J. (1992). Ozone depletion: Ultraviolet radiation and phytoplankton biology in Antarctic waters. *Science, 255,* 952–959.

Soelberg, P. O. (1967). Unprogrammed decision making. *Industrial Management Review, 8,* 19–29.

Sokolow, J. E. S. (1980). *The role of animals in children's literature.* Unpublished manuscript, School of Forestry and Environmental Studies, Yale University.

Sommer, R. (1969). *Personal space: The behavioral basis of design.* Englewood Cliffs, NJ: Prentice-Hall.

Sonnenfeld, J. (1969). Environmental perception and adaptation level in the Arctic. In D. Lowenthal (Ed.), *Environmental perception and behavior* (pp. 42–59). Chicago: University of Chicago, Department of Geography.

Soule, M. E. (1991). Conservation: Tactics for a constant crisis. *Science, 253,* 744–750.

Spaccarelli, S., Zolik, E., & Jason, L. A. (1989–1990). Effects of verbal prompting and block characteristics on participation in curbside newspaper recycling. *Journal of Environmental Systems, 19,* 45–57.

Sparrowe, R. D., & Wight, H. M. (1975). Setting priorities for the endangered species program. *Transactions of the North American Wildlife and Natural Resources Conference, 40,* 142–156.

Sperling, L., Loevinsohn, M. E., & Ntabomvura, B. (1993). Rethinking the farmer's role in plant-breeding: Local experts and on-station selection in Rwanda. *Experimental Agriculture, 29,* 509–519.

Stamps, A. (1990). Use of photographs to simulate environments: A meta-analysis. *Perception and Motor Skills, 71,* 907–913.

Stankey, G. H. (1973). *Visitor perception of wilderness carrying capacity* (USDA Forest Service Research Paper INT–142). Ogden, UT: Intermountain Forest and Range Experiment Station.

Starr, C. (1969). Social benefit versus technological risk. *Science, 165,* 1232–1238.

Starr, C., Searl, M. F., & Alpert, S. (1992). Energy sources: A realistic outlook. *Science, 256,* 981–986.

Statistics Canada. (1993). *Environmental perspectives: Local government waste management practices survey.* Ottowa, Ontario: Minister of Supply and Services.

Steg, L. & Sievers, I. (2000). Cultural theory and individual perceptions of environmental risks. *Environment and Behavior, 32,* 250–269.

Steinhart, P. (1990, July). No net loss. *Audobon,* pp. 18–21.

Sterling, T. (2001). How to build a hypercomputer. *Scientific American, 285*(1), 38–45.

Stern, P. C. (1978). When do people act to maintain common resources: A reformulated psychological question of our times. *International Journal of Psychology, 13,* 149–158.

Stern, P. C. (1986). Blind spots in policy analysis: What economics doesn't say about energy use. *Journal of Policy Analysis and Management, 5,* 200–227.

Stern, P. C. (1992a). Psychological dimensions of global environmental change. *Annual Review of Psychology, 43,* 269–302.
Stern, P. C. (1992b). What psychology knows about energy conservation. *American Psychologist, 47,* 1224–1232.
Stern, P. C. (1993). A second environmental science: Human–environment interactions. *Science, 260,* 1897–1899.
Stern, P. C. (2000). Psychology and the science of human–environment interactions. *American Psychologist, 55,* 523–530.
Stern, P. C., & Aronson, E. (Eds.). (1984). *Energy use: The human dimension.* New York: Freeman.
Stern, P. C., Aronson, E., Darley, J. M., Hill, D. H., Hirst, E., Kempton, W., & Wilbanks, T. J. (1986). The effectiveness of incentives for residential energy conservation. *Evaluation Review, 10,* 147–176.
Stern, P. C., Dietz, T., Abel, T., Guagnano, G.A., & Kalof, L. (1999). A social-psychological theory of support for social movements: The case of environmentalism. *Human Ecology Review, 6,* 81–97.
Stern, P. C., Dietz, T., & Black, J. S. (1986). Support for environmental protection: The role of moral norms. *Population and Environment, 8,* 204–222.
Stern, P. C., Dietz, T., & Kalof, L. (1993). Value orientations, gender, and environmental concern. *Environment and Behavior, 25,* 322–348.
Stern, P. C., Dietz, T., Kalof, L., & Guagnano, G. A. (1995). Values, beliefs, and emergent social objects: The social-psychological construction of support for the environmental movement. *Journal of Applied Social Psychology, 25,* 1611–1636.
Stern, P. C., & Gardner, G. T. (1981). Psychological research and energy policy. *American Psychologist, 36,* 329–342.
Stern, P. C., & Kirkpatrick, E. M. (1977). Energy behavior. *Environment, 19,* 10–15.
Stern, P. C., & Oskamp, S. (1987). Managing scarce environmental resources. In D. Stokols & I. Altman (Eds.), *Handbook of environmental psychology.* (Vol. 2, pp. 1043–1088). New York: Wiley.
Stern, P. C., Young, O. R., & Druckman, D. (Eds.). (1992). *Global environmental change: Understanding the human dimensions.* Washington, DC: National Academy Press.
Stillman, C. W. (1977). On the meanings of "nature." In *Children, nature, and the urban environment* (pp. 25–32). (USDA Forest Service General Technical Report NE–30). Upper Darby, PA: Northeastern Forest Experiment Station.
Stix, G. (1997). Maglev: Racing to oblivion? *Scientific American, 277*(4), 109.
Stix, G. (1998). Politics and PCB. *Scientific American, 278*(2), 20–22.
Stix, G. (2001). The triumph of light. *Scientific American, 284*(1), 80–86.
Stokols, D. (Ed.). (1977). *Perspectives on environment and behavior: Theory, research, and applications.* New York: Plenum.
Stokols, D. (1978). Environmental psychology. *Annual Review of Psychology, 29,* 253–295.
Stokols, D. (1979). A congruence analysis of human stress. In I. G. Sarason & C. D. Speilberger (Eds.), *Stress and anxiety* (Vol. 6, pp. 27–53). Washington, DC: Hemisphere.
Stokols, D. (1990). Instrumental and spiritual views of people–environment relations. *American Psychologist, 45,* 641–646.
Stokols, D. (1992). Establishing and maintaining healthy environments: Toward a social ecology of health promotion. *American Psychologist, 47,* 6–22.
Stokols, D. (1993). Strategies of environmental simulation: Theoretical, methodological, and policy issues. In R. W. Marans & D. Stokols (Eds.), *Environmental simulation: Research and policy issues* (pp. 3–21). New York: Plenum.

Stokols, D., & Altman, I. (Eds.). (1987). *Handbook of environmental psychology*. New York: Wiley.

Stokols, D., & Shumaker, S. A. (1981). People in places: A transactional view of settings. In J. H. Harvey (Ed.), *Cognition, social behavior, and the environment* (pp. 441–488). Hillsdale, NJ: Lawrence Erlbaum Associates.

Stolarski, R. S. (1988). The Antarctic ozone hole. *Scientific American, 258*(1), 30–36.

Stolarski, R. S., Bojkov, R., Bishop, L., Zerefos, C., Staehelin, J., & Zawodny, J. (1992). Measured trends in stratospheric ozone. *Science, 256,* 342–349.

Stone, R. (1992). NRC faults science behind ozone regs. *Science, 255,* 26.

Stone, R. (1994a). California report sets standard for comparing risks. *Science, 266,* 214.

Stone, R. (1994b). Proposed global network for ecology data stirs debate. *Science, 266,* 1155.

Stone, R. (1995). If the mercury soars, so may health hazards. *Science, 267,* 957–958.

Stouffer, S. (1955). *Communism, conformity and civil liberties*. New York: Doubleday.

Strahilevitz, M., Strahilevitz, A., & Miller, J. E. (1979). Air pollutants and the admission rate of psychiatric patients. *American Journal of Psychiatry, 136,* 205–207.

Stroebe, W., & Frey, B. S. (1982). Self-interest and collective action: The economics and psychology of public goods. *British Journal of Social Psychology, 21,* 121–137.

Suhrbier, J. H., & Deakin, E. A. (1988). Environmental considerations in a 2020 transportation plan: Constraints or opportunities. In *A look ahead: Year 2020* (Special Report 220). Washington, DC: Transportation Research Board, National Research Council.

Sundquist, E. T. (1993). The carbon dioxide budget. *Science, 259,* 934–941.

Sundstrom, E., Bell, P. A., Busby, P. L., & Asmus, C. (1996). Environmental psychology 1989–1994. *Annual Review of Psychology, 47,* 485–512.

Sundstrom, E., Herbert, R. K., & Brown, D. W. (1982). Privacy and communication in an open-plan office: A case study. *Environment and Behavior, 14,* 379–392.

Sundstrom, E., Lounsbury, J. W., DeVault, R. C., & Peele, E. (1981). Acceptance of a nuclear power plant: Applications of the expectancy-value model. In A. Baum & J. E. Singer (Eds.), *Advances in environmental psychology: Vol. 3. Energy conservation: Psychological perspectives* (pp. 171–189). Hillsdale, NJ: Lawrence Erlbaum Associates.

Sundstrom, E., Lounsbury, J. W., Schuller, C. R., Fowler, J. R., & Mattingly, T. J., Jr. (1977). Community attitudes toward a proposed nuclear power generating facility as a function of expected outcomes. *Journal of Community Psychology, 5,* 199–208.

Svenson, O. (1981). Are we all less risky and more skillful than our fellow drivers? *Acta Psychologica, 47,* 143–148.

Swann, W. B., Jr., & Giuliano, T. (1987). Confirmatory search strategies in social interaction: How, when, why, and with what consequences? *Journal of Social and Clinical Psychology, 5,* 511–524.

Swap, W. C. (1991). Psychological factors in environmental decision making: Social dilemmas. In R. A. Chechile & S. Carlisle (Eds.), *Environmental decision making: A multidisciplinary perspective* (pp. 14–37). New York: Van Nostrand Reinhold.

Syme, G. J., Seligman, C., Kantola, S. J., & MacPherson, D. K. (1987). Evaluating a television campaign to promote petrol conservation. *Environment and Behavior, 19,* 444–461.

Talbot, J. F., Bardwell, L. V., & Kaplan, R. (1987). The functions of urban nature: Uses and values of different types of urban nature settings. *Journal of Architectural Planning Research, 4,* 47–63.

Taubes, G. (1993). The ozone backlash. *Science, 260,* 1580–1583.

Taylor, D. C. (1989). Blacks and the environment: Toward an explanation of the concern and action gap between blacks and whites. *Environment and Behavior, 21,* 175–205.

Taylor, K. (1999). Rapid climate change. *American Scientist, 87,* 320–327.

Taylor, P. J., & Pocock, S. J. (1974). Commuter travel and sickness: Absence of London office workers. In P. M. Insel & R. H. Moos (Eds.), *Health and the social environment*. Lexington, MA: Heath.

Taylor, R. (1987). Toward an environmental psychology of disorder. In D. Stokols & I. Altman (Eds.), *Handbook of environmental psychology* (Vol. 2, pp. 951–986). New York: Wiley.

Taylor, R. B., Gottsfredson, S. D., & Brower, S. (1980). The defensibility of defensible space: A critical review and a synthetic framework for future research. In T. Hitschi & M. Gottfredson (Eds.), *Understanding crime* (pp. 53–71). Beverly Hills, CA: Sage.

Taylor, S. E. (1989). *Positive illusions: Creative self-deception and the healthy mind*. New York: Basic Books.

Tchobanoglous, G., Theisen, G. H., & Eliassen, R. E. (1977). *Solid wastes: Engineering principles and management issues*. New York: McGraw-Hill.

Tedeschi, J. T. (Ed.). (1981). *Impression management theory and social psychological research*. New York: Academic Press.

Tedeschi, J. T., Schlenker, B. R., & Bonoma, T. V. (1971). Cognitive dissonance: Private ratiocination or public spectacle? *American Psychologist, 26,* 685–695.

Terborgh, J. (1992). Why American songbirds are vanishing. *Scientific American, 266*(5), 98–104.

Tesser, A., & Shaffer, D. R. (1990). Attitudes and attitude change. *Annual Review of Psychology, 41,* 479–523.

Thayer, R. L., & Atwood, B. G. (1978). Plants, complexity, and pleasure in urban and suburban environments. *Environmental Psychology and Nonverbal Behavior, 3,* 67–76.

The EarthWorks Group. (1989). *Fifty simple things you can do to save the earth*. Berkeley, CA: Earthworks Press.

The EarthWorks Group. (1991a). *The next step: Fifty more things you can do to save the earth*. Kansas City, KA: Andrews & McMeel.

The EarthWorks Group. (1991b). *The student environmental action guide: Twenty five simple things we can do*. Berkeley, CA: Earthworks Press.

Thogersen, J. (1996). Recycling and morality: A critical review of the literature. *Environment and Behavior, 28,* 536–558.

Thomas, J. C., & Stuart, R. (1992). Virtual reality and human factors. *Proceedings of the Human Factors Society 36th annual meeting* (pp. 207–210). Santa Monica, CA: Human Factors Society.

Thomas, L. (1983). An epidemic of apprehension. *Discover, 4,* 78–80.

Thomas, V., & Spiro, T. (1994). Emissions and exposure to metals: Cadmium and lead. In R. Socolow, C. Andrews, F. Berkhout, & V. Thomas (Eds.), *Industrial ecology and global change* (pp. 297–318). Cambridge, England: Cambridge University Press.

Thompson, S. C., & Barton, M. A. (1994). Ecocentric and anthropocentric attitudes toward the environment. *Journal of Environmental Psychology, 14,* 149–157.

Thompson, S. C. G., & Stoutemyer, K. (1991). Water use as a commons dilemma: The effects of education that focuses on long-term consequences and individual action. *Environment and Behavior, 23,* 314–333.

Thompson, V. D., & Newman, S. H. (1976). Training and research opportunities in population psychology. In P. J. Woods (Ed.), *Career opportunities for psychologists: Expanding and emerging areas*. Washington, DC: American Psychological Association.

Thomson, D. J. (1995). The seasons, global temperature, and precession. *Science, 268,* 59–68.

Tietenberg, T. T. (1988). *Environmental and natural resource economics* (2nd ed.). New York: HarperCollins.

Tilman, D., Fargione, J., Wolff, B., D'Antonio, C., Dobson, A., Howarth, R., Schindler, D., Schlesinger, W. H., Simberloff, D., & Swackhamer, D. (2001). Forecasting agriculturally driven global environmental change. *Science, 292,* 281–284.

Titus, J. G. (1991). Greenhouse effect and coastal wetland policy: How Americans could abandon an area the size of Massachusetts at minimum cost. *Environmental Management, 15,* 39–58.

Tourangeau, R., & Rasinski, K. A. (1988). Cognitive processes underlying context effects in attitude measurement. *Psychological Bulletin, 103,* 299–314.

Tracy, A. P., & Oskamp, S. (1983–1984). Relationships among ecologically responsible behaviors. *Journal of Environmental Systems, 13,* 115–126.

Transportation Research Board. (1988). *Transportation in an aging society: Improving mobility and safety for older persons: Vol. 1* (Special Report 218). Washington, DC: Transportation Research Board, National Research Council, Committee for the Study on Improving Mobility and Safety for Older Persons.

Transportation Research Board. (1997). *Clean air and highway transportation mandates, challenges, and research opportunities.* Washington, DC: Research and Technology Coordinating Committee, Transportation Research Board, National Research Council.

Travis, C. C., Richter, S. A., Crouch, E. A. C., Wilson, R., & Klema, E. (1987). Cancer risk management by federal agencies. *Environmental Science and Technology, 21,* 415–420.

Trettin, L., & Mushman, C. (2000). Is trust a realistic goal of environmental risk communication? *Environment and Behavior, 32,* 410–426.

Trigg, L. J., Perlman, D., Perry, R. P., & Janisse, M. P. (1976). Antipollution behavior: A function of perceived outcome and locus of control. *Environment and Behavior, 8,* 307–313.

Trimble, S. W. (1999). Decreased rates of alluvial sediment storage in the Coon Creek Basin, Wisconsin, 1975–93. *Science, 285,* 1244–1246.

Trivers, R. L. (1971). The evolution of reciprocal altruism. *Quarterly Review of Biology, 46,* 35–57.

Tuan, Y. (1974). *Topophilia: A study of environmental perception, attitudes, and values.* Englewood Cliffs, NJ: Prentice-Hall.

Turner, A. L. (1976). The therapeutic value of nature. *Journal of Operational Psychiatry, 7,* 64–74.

Turner, B. L., II, Clark, W. C., Kates, R. W., Richards, J. F., Mathews, J. T., & Meyer, W. B. (Eds.). (1991). *The earth as transformed by human action: Global and regional changes in the biosphere over the past 300 years.* New York: Cambridge University Press.

Tuso, M. A., & Geller, E. S. (1976). Behavior analysis applied to environmental/ecological problems: A review (Abstract). *Journal of Applied Behavior Analysis, 9,* 526.

Tversky, A., & Kahneman, D. (1973). Availability: A heuristic for judging frequency and probability. *Cognitive Psychology, 5,* 207–232.

Tversky, A., & Kahneman, D. (1981). The framing of decisions and the psychology of choice. *Science, 211,* 453–458.

Tversky, A., & Kahneman, D. (1986). Judgment under uncertainty: Heuristics and biases. In H. R. Arkes & K. R. Hammond (Eds.), *Judgment and decision-making: An interdisciplinary reader* (pp. 38–55). New York: Cambridge University Press. (Originally publication in 1974.)

Tversky, A., Slovic, P., & Kahneman, D. (1990). The causes of preference reversal. *American Economic Review, 80,* 204–217.

Twedt, D. W. (1965). Consumer psychology. *Annual Review of Psychology, 16,* 265–294.

Tyson, R. (1992, June 1). Poll: Environment tops agenda. *USA Today*, p. 1.

Udall, J. R. (1986). Losing our liquid assets. *National Wildlife, 24*(1), 50–55.

Ulrich, R. S. (1977). Visual landscape preference: A model and application. *Man-Environment Systems, 7,* 279–293.

Ulrich, R. S. (1981). Natural versus urban scenes: Some psychophysiological effects. *Environment and Behavior, 13,* 523–556.

Ulrich, R. S. (1983). Aesthetic and affective response to natural environment. In I. Altman & J. F. Wohlwill (Eds.), *Behavior and the natural environment* (pp. 85–125). New York: Plenum.

Ulrich, R. S. (1984). Views through a window may influence recovery from surgery. *Science, 224,* 420–421.

Ulrich, R. S., & Addoms, D. L. (1981). Psychological and recreational benefits of a residential park. *Journal of Leisure Research, 13,* 43–65.

Union of Concerned Scientists. (1993). *World scientists' warning to humanity.* Cambridge, MA: Union of Concerned Scientists.

United Nations. (1991). *1989 Energy statistics yearbook.* New York: United Nations.

United Nations. (1992). *UN framework convention on climate change.* Palais des Nations, Geneva: Climate Change Secretariat.

United Nations. (1994). *World population 1994.* New York: United Nations.

United Nations. (1996). *World population prospects: The 1996 revision.* New York: United Nations.

United Nations. (1998). *World population projections to 2150.* New York: United Nations.

United Nations Environment Program. (1987). *Montreal protocol on substances that deplete the ozone layer.* Montreal: UNEP.

Upton, A., Kneip, T., & Toniolo, P. (1989). Public health: Aspects of toxic chemical disposal sites. *Annual Review of Public Health, 10,* 1–25.

Ury, H. K. (1968). Photochemical air pollution and automobile accidents in Los Angeles. *Archives of Environmental Health, 17,* 334–342.

U.S. Bureau of the Census. (1990). *Statistical abstract of the United States.* Washington, DC: Government Printing Office.

U.S. Bureau of the Census. (1997). *Statistical abstract of the United States.* Washington, DC: Government Printing Office.

U.S. Department of Energy. (1988). *Energy conservation multi-year plan: 1990–1994.* Washington, DC: National Academy of Sciences Press.

U.S. Department of Energy. (1989, September). *Energy conservation trends: Understanding the factors that affect conservation gains in the U.S. economy* (DOE/PDE–0092). Washington, DC: U.S. Department of Energy, Office of Policy, Planning and Analysis and Office of Conservation and Renewable Energy.

U.S. Environmental Protection Agency. (1989) *The toxics-release inventory: A national perspective* (EPA 560/4–89–005). Washington, DC: U.S. Government Printing Office.

U.S. Fish and Wildlife Service. (1983). Final listing and recovery priority guidelines approved. *Endangered Species Technical Bulletin, 8*(10), 6–7.

Van der Pligt, J., Eiser, J. R., & Spears, R. (1986a). Attitudes toward nuclear energy: Familiarity and salience. *Environment and Behavior, 18,* 75–94.

Van der Pligt, J., Eiser, J. R., & Spears, R. (1986b). Construction of a nuclear power station in one's locality: Attitudes and salience. *Basic and Applied Social Psychology, 7,* 1–15.

Van Houten, R., Nau, P. A., & Merrigan, M. (1981). Reducing elevator use: A comparison of posted feedback and reduced elevator convenience. *Journal of Applied Behavior Analysis, 14,* 377–387.

Van Houwelingen, J. H., & Van Raaij, W. F. (1989). The effect of goal-setting and daily electronic feedback on in-home energy use. *Journal of Consumer Research, 16,* 98–105.

Van Liere, K. D., & Dunlap, R. E. (1980). The social basis of environmental concern: A review of hypotheses, explanations and empirical evidence. *Public Opinion Quarterly, 44,* 181–197.

Van Liere, K. D., & Dunlap, R. E. (1981) Environmental concern: Does it make a difference how it is measured? *Environment and Behavior, 13,* 651–676.

Van Voorst, B. (1992, November 9). A thousand points of blight. *Time,* pp. 68–69.

Van Vugt, M. (1997). Concerns about the privatization of public goods: A social dilemma analysis. *Social Psychology Quarterly, 60,* 355–367.

Vaughn, E. (1993a). Chronic exposure to an environmental hazard: Risk perceptions and self-protective behavior. *Health Psychology, 12,* 74–85.

Vaughn, E. (1993b). Individual and cultural differences in adaptation to environmental risks. *American Psychologist, 48,* 673–680.

Vaughn, E., & Nordenstam, B. (1991). The perception of environmental risks among ethnically diverse groups. *Journal of Cross-Cultural Psychology, 22,* 29–60.

Verderer, S. (1986). Dimensions of person-window transactions in the hospital environment. *Environment and Behavior, 18,* 450–466.

Verderer, S., & Reuman, D. (1987). Windows, views, and health status in hospital therapeutic environments. *Journal of Architectural Planning Research, 4,* 120–133.

Verplanken, B. (1989). Involvement and need for cognition as moderators of beliefs-attitude-intention consistency. *British Journal of Social Psychology, 28,* 115–122.

Vicente, K. J. (1998). Human factors and global problems: A systems approach. *Systems Engineering, 1,* 57–69.

Vincent, J. R. (1992). The tropical timber trade and sustainable development. *Science, 256,* 1651–1655.

Vincent, J. R., & Panayotou, T. (1997).... or distraction? *Science, 276,* 53–57.

Vincent, T. A. (1990). A view from the hill: The human element in policymaking on Capitol Hill. *American Psychologist, 45,* 61–64.

Vining, J., & Ebreo, A. (1990). What makes a recycler? A comparison of recyclers and nonrecyclers. *Environment and Behavior, 22,* 55–73.

Vining, J., & Ebreo, A. (1992). Predicting recycling behavior from global and specific environmental attitudes and changes in recycling opportunities. *Journal of Applied Social Psychology, 22,* 1580–1607.

Vining, J., Linn, N., & Burdge, R. J. (1992). Why recycle? A comparison of recycling motivation in four communities. *Environmental Management, 16,* 785–797.

Vinnikov, K. Y., Robock, A., Stouffer, R. J., Walsh, J. E., Parkinson, C. L., Cavalieri, D. J., Mitchell, J. F. B., Darret, D., & Zakharov, V. F. (2000). Global warming and northern hemisphere sea ice extent. *Science, 286,* 1934–1937.

Vitousek, P. M., Mooney, H. A., Lubchenco, J., & Melillo, J. M. (1997). Human domination of earth's ecosystems. *Science, 277,* 494–499.

Vlek, C., & Stallen, P. (1980). Rational and personal aspects of risk. *Acta Psychologica, 45,* 273–300.

Vogel, R. M. (1991). Resource allocation. In R. A Chechile & S. Carlisle (Eds.), *Environmental decision making: A multidisciplinary perspective* (pp. 156–175). New York: Van Nostrand Reinhold.

Vörösmarty, C. J., Green, P., Salisbury, J., & Lammers, R. B. (2000). Global water resources: Vulnerability from climate change and population growth. *Science, 289,* 284–288.

Wackernagel, M., & Rees, W. (1996). *Our ecological footprint: Reducing human impact on the earth.* Philadelphia, PA: New Society.

Wahl, D., & Allison, G. (1975). *Reduce: Targets, means and impacts of source reduction.* Washington, DC: League of Women Voters Education Fund.

Waibel, A. E., Peter, T., Carslaw, K. S., Oelhaf, H., Wetzel, G., Crutzen, P. J., Pöschl, U., Tsias, A., Reimer, E., & Fischer, H. (1999). Arctic ozone loss due to dentrification. *Science, 283,* 2064–2069.

Wali, M. K. (Ed.). (1992). *Ecosystem rehabilitation*. The Hague: SPB Academic.

Walker, J. M. (1979). Energy demand behavior in a master-meter apartment complex: An experimental analysis. *Journal of Applied Psychology, 64,* 190–196.

Wallace, D. R. (1985). Wetlands in America: Labyrinth and temple. *Wilderness, 49,* 12–27.

Wallace, L. A. (1995). Human exposure to environmental pollutants: A decade of experience. *Clinical and Experimental Allergy, 25,* 4–9.

Wallack, L. M. (1981). Mass media campaigns: The odds against finding behavior change. *Health Education Quarterly, 8,* 209–260.

Wandersman, A. H., & Hallman, W. K. (1993). Are people acting irrationally? Understanding public concerns about environmental threats. *American Psychologist, 48,* 681–686.

Wang, T. H., & Katzev, R. D. (1990). Group commitment and resource conservation: Two field experiments on promoting recycling. *Journal of Applied Social Psychology, 20,* 265–275.

Ward, B., & Dubos, R. (1972). *Only one earth: The care and maintenance of a small planet.* New York: W. W. Norton.

Ward, L. M. (1977). Multidimensional scaling of the molar physical environment. *Multivariate Behavior Research, 12,* 23–42.

Ward, L. M., & Russell, J. A. (1981). The psychological representation of molar physical environments. *Journal of Experimental Psychology: General, 110,* 121–152.

Warf, J. C. (1995). Letter to editor re radioactive waste at Ward Valley. *Science, 269,* 1653.

Watson, O. M. (1972). *Symbolic and expressive uses of space: An introduction to proxemic behavior.* Reading, MA: Addison-Wesley.

Watson, R. T., Prather, M. J., & Kurylo, M. J. (1988). *Present state of knowledge of the upper atmosphere 1988: An assessment report* (NASA reference publication 1208). Washington, DC: National Aeronautics and Space Administration.

Weart, S. (1988). *Nuclear fear: A history of images.* Cambridge, MA: Harvard University Press.

Webster, F. E. (1975). Determining the characteristics of the socially conscious consumer. *Journal of Consumer Research, 2,* 188–196.

Weddle, B., & Garland, G. (1974, October). Dumps: A potential threat to our groundwater supplies. *Nation's Cities*, pp. 21–26.

Weigel, R. H., & Newman, L. S. (1976). Increasing attitude-behavior correspondence by broadening the scope of the behavioral measure. *Journal of Personality and Social Psychology, 33,* 793–802.

Weigel, R. H., & Weigel, J. (1978). Environmental concern: The development of a measure. *Environment and Behavior, 10,* 3–15.

Weinberg, A. M. (1988–1989). Energy policy in an age of uncertainty. *Issues in Science and Technology, 5*(2), 81–85.

Weinberg, C. J., & Williams, R. H. (1990). Energy from the sun. *Scientific American, 263*(3), 146–155.

Weinstein, N. D. (1976). The statistical prediction of environmental preferences: Problems of validity and application. *Environment and Behavior, 8,* 611–626.

Weinstein, N. D. (1984). Why it won't happen to me: Perceptions of risk factors and susceptibility. *Health Psychology, 3,* 431–457.

Weinstein, N. D. (1989). Optimistic biases about personal risks. *Science, 246,* 1232–1233.

Weinstein, N. D., Klotz, M. L., & Sandman, P. (1988). Optimistic biases in public perception of the risk from radon. *American Journal of Public Health, 78,* 796–800.

Weinstein, N. D., Sandman, P. M., & Roberts, N. E. (1991). Perceived susceptibility and self-protective behavior: A field experiment to encourage home radon testing. *Health Psychology, 10,* 25–33.

Welford, A. T. (1974). *Man under stress.* New York: Wiley.

Wellmer, F. W., & Kursten, M. (1992). International perspective on mineral resources. *Episodes, 15,* 182–194.

Welter, T. R. (1990, August 20). A farewell to arms. *Industry Week*, pp. 36–42.

West, J. P., Lee, S. J., & Feiock, R. C. (1992). Managing municipal waste: Attitudes and opinions of administrators and environmentalists. *Environment and Behavior, 24,* 111–133.

Westerman, R. R. (1975). Waste management through product design: The case of automobile tires. *Proceedings, 1975 conference on waste reduction* (pp. 83–94). Washington, DC: U.S. Environmental Protection Agency.

Wheeler, M. (1976). *Lies, damn lies, and statistics: The manipulation of public opinion in America*. New York: Dell.

Whipple, C. G. (1996). Can nuclear waste be stored safely at Yucca Mountain? *Scientific American, 274*(6), 72–79.

White, R. M. (1990). The great climate debate. *Scientific American, 263*(1), 36–43.

Whiteside, G. M., & Love, J. C. (2001). The art of building small. *Scientific American, 285*(3), 38–47.

Whyte, W. H. (1980). *The social life of small urban spaces*. Washington, DC: The Conservation Foundation.

Wicker, A. W. (1969). Attitudes versus action: The relationship of verbal and overt behavioral responses to attitude objects. *Journal of Social Issues, 25,* 41–78.

Wicker, A. W. (1979). *An introduction to environmental psychology.* Monterey, CA: Brooks/Cole.

Wigley, T. M. L., & Schlesinger, M. E. (1985). Analytic solution for the effect of increasing $CO_2$ on global mean temperature. *Nature, 315,* 649–652.

Wikle, T. A. (1991). Evaluating the acceptability of recreation rationing policies used on rivers. *Environmental Management, 15,* 389–394.

Wilkie, W. L. (1974). Analysis of effects of information load. *Journal of Marketing Research, 11*, 462–466.

Williams, B. L., Brown, S., & Greenberg, M. (1999). Determinants of trust perceptions among residents surrounding the Savannah River nuclear weapons site. *Environment and Behavior. 31,* 354–371.

Williams, W. (2000). Toxins on the firing range. *Scientific American, 282*(6), 18–20.

Wilshire, H. (1995). Letter to editor re radioactive waste at Ward Valley. *Science, 269,* 1654–1655.

Wilson, E. O. (1984). *Biophilia: The human bond with other species*. Cambridge, MA: Harvard University Press.

Wilson, E. O. (1989). Threats to biodiversity. *Scientific American, 261*(3), 108–116.

Wilson, E. O. (1998). Integrated science and the coming century of the environment. *Science, 279,* 2048–2049.

Wilson, E. O., & Peter, F. M. (Eds.). (1988). *Biodiversity.* Washington, DC: National Academy Press.

Wilson, H. J., MacCready, P. B., & Kyle, C. R. (1989). Lessons of *Sunraycer. Scientific American, 260*(3), 90–97.

Wilson, R., & Crouch, E. A. C. (1987). Risk assessment and comparisons: An introduction. *Science, 236,* 267–270.

Winett, R. A. (1978). Prompting turning-out lights in unoccupied rooms. *Journal of Environmental Systems, 6,* 237–241.

Winett, R. A., Hatcher. J. W., Fort, T. R., Leckliter, I. N., Love, S. Q., Riley, A. W., & Fishback, J. A. (1982). The effects of videotape modeling and daily feedback on residential electricity conservation, home temperature and humidity, perceived comfort, and clothing worn: Summer and winter. *Journal of Applied Behavior Analysis, 15,* 381–402.

Winett, R. A., Kaiser, S., & Haberkorn, G. (1977). The effects of monetary rebates and daily feedback on electricity conservation. *Journal of Environmental Systems, 6,* 327–339.

Winett, R. A., Leckliter, I. N., Chinn, D. E., & Stahl, B. (1984). Reducing energy consumption: The long-term effects of a single TV program. *Journal of Communication, 34,* 37–51.

Winett, R. A., Leckliter, I. N., Chinn, D. E., Stahl, B., & Love, S. Q. (1985). Effects of television modeling on residential energy conservation. *Journal of Applied Behavior Analysis, 18,* 33–44.

Winett, R. A., Neale, M. S., & Grier, H. C. (1979). The effects of self-monitoring and feedback on residential electricity consumption. *Journal of Applied Behavior Analysis, 12,* 173–184.

Winett, R. A., Neale, M. S., Williams, K., Yokley, J., & Kauder, H. (1978–1979). The effects of feedback on residential electricity consumption: Three replications. *Journal of Environmental Systems, 8,* 217–233.

Winett, R. A., & Nietzel, M. T. (1975). Behavioral ecology: Contingency management of residential energy use. *American Journal of Community Psychology, 3,* 123–133.

Winkel, G. H., & Holahan, C. J. (1985). The environmental psychology of the hospital: Is the cure worse than the illness? In A. Wandersman & R. Hess (Eds.), *Beyond the individual: Environmental approaches and prevention* (pp. 11–34). New York: Haworth.

Winter, D. D. N. (2000). Some big ideas for some big problems. *American Psychologist, 55,* 515–522.

Wirl, F. (1991). Restructuring of eastern Europe and its possible consequences for the atmospheric environment. *Environmental Management, 15,* 765–772.

Wise, J. A., & Savage, S. F. (1992, October 12–16). *Human factors in environmental management: New directions from the Hanford Site.* Paper presented at the 36th Human Factors Society 36th annual meeting, Atlanta, GA

Witherspoon, S., Mohler, P. P., & Harkness, J. A. (1995). *Report on research into environmental attitudes and perceptions.* Mannheim, Germany: European Consortium for Comparative Social Surveys.

Witmer, J. F., & Geller, E. S. (1976). Facilitating paper recycling: Effects of prompts, raffles and contests. *Journal of Applied Behavior Analysis, 9,* 315–322.

Wodarski, J. S. (1982). National and state appeals for energy conservation: A behavior analysis of effects. *Behavioral Engineering, 7,* 119–130.

Wofsy, S. C. (2001). Where has all the carbon gone? *Science, 293,* 2261–2263.

Wohwill, J. F. (1970). The emerging discipline of environmental psychology. *American Psychologist, 25,* 303–312.

Wohlwill, J. F. (1974). Human adaptation to levels of environmental stimulation. *Human Ecology, 2,* 127–147.

Wohlwill, J. F. (1976). Environmental aesthetics: The environment as a source of affect. In I. Altman & J. F. Wohwill (Eds.), *Human behavior and the environment: Advances in theory and research* (Vol. 1, pp. 37–86). New York: Plenum.

Wohlwill, J. F., & Kohn, I. (1973). The environment as experienced by the migrant: An adaptation level approach. *Representative Research in Social Psychology, 4,* 135–164.

Wolbrast, A. B. (Ed.). (1991). *Environment in peril.* Washington, DC: Smithsonian Institution Press.

Wong, C. Y., Sommer, R., & Cook, E. J. (1992). The soft classroom 17 years later. *Journal of Environmental Psychology, 12,* 337–343.

World Bank. (1998). *World bank atlas.* Washington, DC: Author.

World Commission on Environment and Development. (1987). *Our common future.* New York: Oxford University Press.

World Energy Council. (1994). *Energy for tomorrow's world: The realities, the real options and the agenda for achievement*. New York: Saint Martin's Press.

World Meteorological Organization. (1992). *Global ozone research and monitoring report no. 25: Scientific assessment of ozone depletion 1991.* Geneva: Author.

World Meteorological Organization. (1995). *Global ozone research and monitoring report no. 37: Scientific assessment of ozone depletion 1994.* Geneva: Author.

World Resources Institute. (1992). *World resources, 1992–93: A guide to the global environment*. New York: Oxford University Press.

World Resources Institute. (1994). *World resources, 1994–95: A guide to the global environment*. New York: Oxford University Press.

Wouk, V. (1997). Hybrid electric vehicles. *Scientific American, 277*(4), 70–74.

Wright, K. (1990). The shape of things to go. *Scientific American, 262*(5), 92–101.

Wu, C., & Shaffer, D. R. (1987). Susceptibility to persuasive appeals as a function of source credibility and prior experience with the attitude object. *Journal of Personality and Social Psychology, 52,* 677–688.

Wulf, W. A. (1993). The collaborative opportunity. *Science, 261,* 854–855.

Yamagishi, T. (1988). Seriousness of social dilemmas and the provision of a sanctioning system. *Social Psychology Quarterly, 51,* 32–42.

Yang, B. E., & Brown, T. J. (1992). A cross-cultural comparison of preferences for landscape styles and landscape elements. *Environment and Behavior, 24,* 471–507.

Yang, B. E., & Tang, T. J. (1992). A cross-cultural comparison for landscape styles and landscape elements. *Environment & Behavior, 24,* 471–507.

Yates, S., & Aronson, E. (1983). A social-psychological perspective on energy conservation in residential buildings. *American Psychologist, 38,* 435–444.

Yuhas, B., & Hyde, J. (1991). Getting multi-family residents into the act. *Solid Waste and Power, 5*(3), 54–60.

Zakay, D. (1983). The relationship between the probability assessor and the outcome of an event as a determiner of subjective probability. *Acta Psychologica, 53,* 271–280.

Zakay, D. (1984). The influence of perceived event's controllability on its subjective occurrence probability. *The Psychological Record, 34,* 233–240.

Zerega, A. (1981). Transportation energy conservation policy: Implications for social science research. *Journal of Social Issues, 37,* 31–50.

Zilberman, D., Schmitz, A., Casterline, G., Lichtenberg, E., & Siebert, J. B. (1991). The economics of pesticide use and regulation. *Science, 253,* 518–522.

Zillman, J. W. (1997). Atmospheric science and public policy. *Science, 276,* 1084–1086.

Zolik, E. S., Jason, L. A., Nair, D., & Peterson, M. (1982–1983). Conservation of electricity on a college campus. *Journal of Environmental Systems, 12,* 225–228.

Zube, E. H. (1974). Cross-disciplinary and intermode agreement on the description and evaluation of landscape resources. *Environment and Behavior, 6,* 69–89.

Zube, E. H. (1976). Perception of landscape and land use. In I. Altman & J. Wohlwill (Eds.), *Human behavior and the environment: Advances in theory and research* (Vol. 1, pp. 87–121). New York: Plenum.

Zube, E. H., Brush, R. O., & Fabos, J. G. (1975). *Landscape assessment: Values, perceptions, and resources*. Stroudsburg, PA: Dowden, Hutchinson & Ross.

Zube, E. H., & Craik, K. (Eds.). (1976). *Perceived environmental quality indices*. New York: Plenum.

Zube, E. H., & Moore, G. T. (Eds.). (1987). *Advances in environment, behavior, and design* (Vol. 1). New York: Plenum.

Zube, E. H., & Moore, G. T. (Eds.). (1989). *Advances in environment, behavior, and design* (Vol. 2). New York: Plenum.

Zube, E. H., & Pitt, D. G. (1981). Cross-cultural perceptions of scenic and heritage landscapes. *Landscape Planning, 8,* 69–87.

Zube, E. H., Pitt, D. G., & Anderson, T. W. (1975a). *Perception and measurement of scenic resources in the Southern Connecticut River Valley* (Institute of Man and His Environment Publication R–74–1). Amherst, MA: University of Massachusetts Press.

Zube, E. H., Pitt, D. G., & Anderson, T. W. (1975b). Perception and prediction of scenic resource values on the Northeast. In E. H. Zube, R. O. Brush, & J. G. Fabos (Eds.), *Landscape assessment: Values, perceptions and resources* (pp. 151–167). Stroudsburg, PA: Dowden, Hutchinson &Ross.

Zube, E. H., Pitt, D. G., & Evans, G. W. (1983). A lifespan developmental study of landscape assessment. *Journal of Environmental Psychology, 3,* 115–128.

Zube, E. H., Sell, J. L., & Taylor, J. G. (1982). Landscape perception: Research, applications and theory. *Landscape Planning, 9,* 1–33.

Zube, E. H., Simcox, D. E., & Law, C. S. (1987). Perceptual landscape simulations: History and prospect. *Landscape Journal, 6,* 62–80.

Zuckerman, M. (1977). The development of a situation-specific trait-state test for the prediction and measurement of affective responses. *Journal of Consulting and Clinical Psychology, 45,* 512–523.

Zwally, H. J. (1989). Growth of Greenland ice sheet: Interpretation. *Science, 246,* 1589–1591.

# Author Index

## C

## D

## E



## F

## G

## H

## I



## J



## K

## L

## M

## P

## Q



## R

## S

## T

## U



## V

## W

## Y



## Z

# Subject Index

## A



## B



## C

## D



## E

## F



## G



## H

## I



## L



## M



## N



## O



## P

## U



## V



## W



## Z